Video Over IP

Video Over IP
IPTV, Internet Video, H.264, P2P, Web TV, and Streaming: A Complete Guide to Understanding the Technology

Second Edition

Wes Simpson

ELSEVIER

AMSTERDAM • BOSTON • HEIDELBERG • LONDON
NEW YORK • OXFORD • PARIS • SAN DIEGO
SAN FRANCISCO • SINGAPORE • SYDNEY • TOKYO

Focal Press is an imprint of Elsevier

Focal Press is an imprint of Elsevier
30 Corporate Drive, Suite 400, Burlington, MA 01803, USA
Linacre House, Jordan Hill, Oxford OX2 8DP, UK

∞ Recognizing the importance of preserving what has been written, Elsevier prints its books on acid-free paper whenever possible.

Library of Congress Cataloging-in-Publication Data
Simpson, Wes.
  Video over IP / by Wes Simpson. – 2nd ed.
    p. cm.
  Includes index.
  ISBN 978-0-240-81084-3 (pbk. : alk. paper)   1. Image transmission.   2. Digital video.   3. Telecommunication.   I. Title.
  TK5105.2.S56 2008
  006.7–dc22

                                                                         2008020606

British Library Cataloguing-in-Publication Data
A catalogue record for this book is available from the British Library.

ISBN: 978-0-240-81084-3

For information on all Focal Press publications
visit our website at www.elsevierdirect.com

Transferred to Digital Printing, 2010

DEDICATION

This book is dedicated in loving memory of my sister Lyn and my uncle Rufus.

"Even the death of friends will inspire us as much as their lives .... Their memories will be encrusted over with sublime and pleasing thoughts, as monuments of other men are overgrown with moss; for our friends have no place in the graveyard."

–Henry David Thoreau

CONTENTS

INTRODUCTION
TO THE SECOND EDITION

The first sentence of the introduction to the first edition of this book reads: "The field of video transport is constantly evolving." This is just as true today as when I wrote it three years ago. In that short time, we have seen a dramatic number of changes in the IP video transport world, including:

- Widespread and continuing deployments of IPTV to millions of homes.
- Imminent disappearance of analog TV broadcasts in the United States and elsewhere.
- Tremendous growth in the installed base of HD televisions and the accompanying explosion of HD programming.
- Sudden appearance and enormous popularity of Internet video websites such as YouTube and the growth of legitimate peer-to-peer file sharing.

This second edition has been written specifically to address these topics and many others. The volume you hold in your hands has been completely updated since the first edition, with dozens of completely new illustrations and updates to dozens more. Chapter 15 was added specifically to focus on Internet video, something that was only a niche application three years ago. Key new technologies, such as H.264, are discussed in much more detail, and emerging technologies such as podcasting and P2P networking are introduced for the first time. All this has been done with the consistent goal of giving people with either datacom or video backgrounds the knowledge they need to understand and embrace these exciting and beneficial technologies, which are overlapping more every year.

I would like to thank Paul Atwell, who conscientiously read every word of this book to help make it understandable to his fellow video professionals. Thanks to all the folks at Elsevier, including my editors Angelina Ward and Katy Spencer, and my production manager Lianne Hong, who was able to get this book out on time in spite of an author who missed a few deadlines. I'd like to thank Ghislain Collette for his help with bandwidth calculations and Tom Butts at TV Technology, who has helped me continue to hone my writing skills. Most of all, I'd like to thank my wife, Laurie, and my children, Taylor and Cameron, for all of their moral support and encouragement over the past year; they are looking forward to seeing more of me on nights and weekends. I am particularly eager to wish my daughter, Taylor, great success as she embarks on her college career in the fall—your dad is very, very proud of you, so keep up the good work!

Wes Simpson, May 2008

wsimpson@gmail.com

INTRODUCTION

The field of video transport is constantly evolving. As new technologies emerge, they are put to work in transporting video signals. This has been true for radio, coaxial cable, microwave, satellite, and optical fiber, and will also be true for the Internet Protocol, or IP. This latest step in the path of evolution may be the most important yet, because IP allows so many different types of video, audio, and data formats to be transported economically to any corner of the globe.

Several recent technology trends have combined to make video transport over IP networks useful for a wide variety of applications today:

- *Transition to Digital Video:* Video production has almost completely migrated from analog to digital technology during the past 20 years, and today even reaches into the home with digital camcorders, digital television displays, and digital broadcasts from terrestrial, satellite, and cable television providers. One result of this change is that video signals no longer need to be transported on specialized analog networks but can now take advantage of the wide range of digital technologies that are available.

- *Advances in Video Compression:* Compression technology has rapidly evolved from the first MPEG-1 standard in 1991 to today's Advanced Video Codec for MPEG-4 and the latest Windows Media codec, both of which have been made public in the past two years. Compression means that acceptable video signals can be sent over networks with limited capacity, including those that serve many households and most businesses around the world.
- *Growth in IP Network Capacity:* The rapid growth of Internet traffic (by a factor of 10,000 in the decade up to 2003[1]) and the widespread adoption of broadband access lines (passing the 100-million line mark worldwide by the end of 2003[2]) mean that the IP network capacity needed for video transport has reached critical mass.

Together, these developments have made it technically and economically feasible to deliver high-quality video content to a huge number of viewers over IP networks.

As with any technology, users have many different choices for video transport, with a wide range of confusing acronyms, standards, and applications. This book will help you make sense of all this information, help you understand how this technology works, and, most importantly, help you choose which technology is right for your application.

Many people who have a great deal of knowledge about video technology have limited understanding of networking, and vice versa. This book spans this gap, because successful video over IP deployments require good planning in both the networking and the video technology areas. As we will see, decisions that are made in one area can have a great impact on the other. This book will help experts in both fields gain some insight in new areas, and it will serve as an ideal starting point for readers who are new to both fields.

---

1. Internet traffic growth: Sources and Implications, A. M. Odlyzko. Optical Transmission Systems and Equipment for WDM Networking II, B. B. Dingel, W. Weiershausen, A. K. Dutta, and K.-I. Sato, eds., Proc. SPIE, vol. 5247, 2003, pp. 1-15.
2. World Broadband Statistics: Q4 2003, © Point Topic Ltd., 2004.

PURPOSE OF THIS BOOK

There are two main purposes of this book. First is helping the reader to understand the wide range of technologies that are available for video transport over IP networks. Second is helping the reader to figure out which technology is right for a given application. Along the way, we'll look at a number of real-world examples that show how people have successfully used IP technology for a wide variety of purposes.

Video content can be moved across an IP network in literally dozens of ways. Although the thought of postage-stamp-size, jerky video springs to mind when many people hear the words "Internet video," in reality, broadcast-quality, high definition video can be sent over the Internet. There are many different applications for IP video, including surveillance, videoconferencing, video to the home, corporate training, and professional video production, to name a few. Video can be sent over public networks, private networks, optical networks, and pretty much any other network that can handle IP packets, and these networks have reached the maturity levels needed to allow interoperability between these networks. Much of this video is serving a solid business purpose, whether it is paid for by advertising, subscriptions, or sponsored by companies seeking to improve productivity or reduce costs. As we will see throughout this book, there are enough different ways to move video content over an IP network to satisfy virtually any application.

With all this variety, it can be hard to pick out the right solution. To help that process, we'll spend a lot of time analyzing the benefits and drawbacks of the technologies that we discuss. In particular, we'll try to look at why a technology might be suited for an application and what the alternatives are. Because there are so many variables from one network to another, we'll try to avoid specific recipes. The goal is to give each reader the information needed to make intelligent choices and to focus on the important factors for each application.

One thing that we will try to avoid in this book is the often mind-numbing description of all the different bits and bytes that make up each of the different protocols and standards. There are lots of free, public domain sources for this information, and, frankly, they don't tell a reader much about how a protocol is used or its applications. Instead, in this book we'll look at the big picture and focus on how a protocol works and why it may (or may not) be suitable for a particular purpose. In this way, we'll be able to serve the 90% or more of the reading audience who will never need to write a line of code nor diagnose a data circuit with a protocol analyzer, but who need to know how to get the results they need through the use of video-over-IP technology.

INTENDED AUDIENCE

This book was written for a variety of audiences, including:

- *End Users*, particularly those who might say: "I have video; I have an IP network; so can I use this network to transport my video?" Many times, video projects need to be driven by end users, because they will reap the benefits. However, it is important to realize that video can use a significant amount of network resources, and many system administrators are understandably cautious about adding video to a network that is already busy with other tasks. This book will have served its purpose if end users feel comfortable in talking to system administrators about the issues and trade-offs that need to be discussed prior to video deployment.
- *Video Professionals*, some of whom have had little or no exposure to the world of data networking (aside from the dubious joys of e-mail and text-based pagers). A number of the technologies that are available today for transporting high-quality video over IP networks were simply not available five years ago, or, if they were, had a prohibitive price tag. Thanks to the relentless march of technology, a great deal of data networking technology has become useful and cost effective in the broadcast video world. This book aims to provide video professionals with the information they need about IP networking to make informed decisions about how and why to deploy this powerful technology.
- *Computer and Telecom Networking Professionals*, who know that video transport has always been a capability of their network

but have not had an easy way to learn about this sometimes daunting field of video transport. With all of the new technologies that have come onto the market, video transport has become much less of a burden for data networks and the people who manage them. This book is intended to both serve as an introduction to modern video technology and to familiarize readers with many of the different tools that are available for video transport.

- *Service Provider Staff,* who are often faced with trying to understand and support customers with a wide variety of different networking needs. As video-over-IP networking becomes more affordable and popular with users, many different departments in a large service provider need to become familiar with video, including sales, marketing, and technical support staff. This book provides a solid introduction into many of the necessary concepts, and could serve as the basis for an effective training course.
- *Investors and Managers,* who want to get a good overview of the technologies in this market but want to avoid becoming overwhelmed with technical details would also find this volume helpful. As a bonus, sections of several chapters are devoted to discussions of the financial considerations that surround the decisions about whether or not to deploy video networks.

Overall, people at several different levels (entry-level technical, system administration, purchasing/sales, managerial, and executive) in a variety of organizations (manufacturing, services, government, and carriers) would benefit from this book.

HOW TO READ THIS BOOK

Not every reader will need to read every chapter of this book to benefit from it. The first seven chapters cover the basic technologies and applications for video over IP and form a good core of information for all readers. The remaining chapters focus on more specialized topics; readers should feel free to pick and choose the topics that they find of interest. The following descriptions of each chapter should help readers navigate through the book:

Chapters 1 and 2 provide an overview of video transport in terms of technology and applications. Highlights include a discussion about the usefulness of the public Internet for video transport near the end of Chapter 1 and a peek at the economics of video services in Chapter 2. Most readers should benefit from reading these chapters, because they help set the stage for many of the applications we will be talking about in the rest of the book.

Chapter 3 is intended for readers who need an introduction to video. It explains a number of terms that will be used throughout the book and in any meaningful discussion about video technology. Folks who have a good background in video technology can safely skip this chapter.

Chapter 4 focuses on the many different forms of video and audio compression, including some that many folks (even those in the video field) may not have been exposed to. Because compression is so important to video-over-IP applications, readers are urged to carefully review this chapter.

Chapter 5 covers the essential elements of IP technology. Readers with more than a basic understanding of IP networking can bypass this material with impunity.

Chapter 6 covers the fusion of video and networking technology, particularly in the area of protocols for video transport. These are some of the key underlying technologies involved in video over IP, and are significantly different in application and behavior from standard data networking protocols. Most readers will benefit from this discussion, because these protocols have a big impact on the behavior of video streams and the networks that carry them.

Chapter 7 begins with a discussion of a number of different IP packet transport technologies. It also examines the ways in which network impairments can affect video traffic, which can be quite different from the effects on data traffic.

Chapter 8 talks about streaming, which is one of the most popular technologies for delivering video over IP. In this chapter, we will discuss how true streaming is differentiated from some very clever imposters. We'll also talk about the corporate giants of video streaming technology and look at their technology.

Chapter 9 goes into multicasting and why it is so desirable for delivering video to multiple users at the same time. We'll see why it is also one of the biggest headaches for system administrators. This chapter lays out the arguments, both for and against, the use of multicasting for video signals.

Chapter 10 focuses on videoconferencing, which has a unique set of requirements and a unique set of technologies to meet those requirements. In it, we'll cover the several important aspects of videoconferencing, including the need for low delay networks and equipment. Folks who need to send video only one way can safely skip this chapter.

Chapter 11 focuses on content ownership and security. This is important both for users who own their own content and for those who obtain content from others.

Chapter 12 discusses ways that private networks and virtual private networks can be used to provide secure transport for valuable content. This information will be important to anyone who needs to send video from one location to another.

Chapter 13 looks at a very popular application for video over IP: video to the home. Some unique technologies in this area can have a powerful impact on the technical and economic success of a mass deployment. Readers who are interested only in corporate video can safely skip this chapter.

Chapter 14 looks at how video content can be transported as data files. Because many of these files are staggeringly big and difficult to manage, several service providers have gone into business specifically to support this application. We'll look at some of the tools and techniques that have been developed to manage video file transport.

Chapter 15 (new to the second edition) describes the new technologies that have been introduced for Internet video, particularly those services that host video clips for large numbers of viewers. We'll look at how these websites work, how they are paid for, and how they can be useful for corporate as well as entertainment purposes.

Chapter 16 looks at network administration and some of the unique management concerns involved in controlling video networks. We'll look at some of the key functions of a video network management system, and we'll discuss an example of a system that is used to manage a distance-learning network.

VIDEO USER CHECKLIST

Throughout this book, we will develop a video user checklist, which we will add at the end of each chapter. This list tries to capture all of the key issues that need to be considered when planning a video network deployment. By reading this list and trying to provide suitable answers to the questions, readers will be able to anticipate and think through many of the issues that will arise during a system deployment. Although the complete list may appear to be a bit daunting at first, time spent working with it could highlight issues that are much easier to deal with before a project begins. (Remember the old rule of thumb: One day of planning can save one week of implementing a network.)

The checklists from all the individual chapters are gathered into one easy-to-read location at the back of this book in Appendix B. Readers are encouraged to copy this list and use it whenever they need to plan or evaluate a video-networking project.

ACKNOWLEDGMENTS

I would like to take this opportunity to thank many of the people who have provided me with encouragement and support during the writing of this book. My editor, Angelina Ward, and my Project Manager, Jeff Freeland, have helped immeasurably in bringing this book into being. Becky Golden-Harrell, Assistant Editor, has helped me survive a number of pressing deadlines. My publisher, Joanne Tracy, has been a valuable source of insight, inspiration, and thoughtful opinions. MJ Drouin did a fantastic job as the principal reviewer; this book would not be half as good as it is without her tireless support and meaningful suggestions. Other reviewers, including Brad Medford, Lloyd Lacassagne, and Fred Huffman, have provided many useful comments and critiques. A number of companies and organizations have also graciously permitted me to include real-world examples of current technologies and applications; their contributions are included as case studies in a number of chapters. Merrill Weiss, the editor of this series, who has been a valuable reviewer, was instrumental in making it possible for me to go on this fantastic (and somewhat grueling) adventure. And finally, I would like to thank my wife Laurie, who has been incredibly supportive of this idea, and who has graciously put up with the long hours, missing weekends, and abbreviated vacations that were necessary to make this book a reality.

Wes Simpson, June 2005

wes.simpson@gmail.com

1

OVERVIEW OF VIDEO TRANSPORT

Transporting video signals is a round-the-clock business throughout the world today. Whether for entertainment, education, or personal communication, we now live in a world where we are exposed to video content in many forms. The scale of the technologies and systems that are used to gather and deliver all of this content are amazing. For example, the 2006 FIFA World Cup™ tournament had a cumulative television audience of over 26 billion viewers during the 30-day tournament. But Internet video is rapidly catching up—a January 17, 2008 press release from comScore reported that Americans watched 9.5 billion Internet videos in November 2007, with the average viewer watching 69 videos at an average length of 2.8 minutes, representing an increase of 29 percent since the beginning of 2007.

As Internet Protocol (IP) technologies for video transport continue to mature, more of the video delivery process will take place over IP networks. This change will ultimately include all phases of video content creation and delivery, beginning at the video camera and ending at a home viewer's video display. As we will see throughout this book, many different areas of the video industry will be affected by IP technology.

In this chapter, we will look at the methods used today for delivering video signals to viewers around the world. Then we'll discuss the main technologies used in telecommunications networks. We will also investigate some of the issues surrounding video transport on the Internet. Finally, we will introduce our Video User Checklist, which will be augmented throughout the book. By the end of this chapter, you should be familiar with the common forms of video transport and the common types of telecom networks.

DEFINING IPTV

Problems can occur when new terminology is created and not everyone agrees on the meanings. Case in point: the term *IPTV*. While it is true that all Internet Protocol Television (IPTV) installations send video over IP networks, it is not true that any kind of video sent over an IP network is IPTV. For the latter, the term *Internet video* is much more descriptive.

IPTV is simply a way to deliver traditional broadcast channels to consumers over an IP network in place of terrestrial broadcast, CATV, and satellite services. Even though IP is used, the public Internet actually doesn't play much of a role. In fact, IPTV services are almost exclusively delivered over private IP networks, such as those being constructed by telephone companies in the United States and elsewhere. At the viewer's home, a set-top box is installed to take the incoming IPTV feed and convert it into standard video signals that can be fed to a consumer television.

Some of the main characteristics of IPTV include:

- Continuous streams of professionally produced content (such as a TV broadcast network feed)
- Hundreds of 24 × 7 channels
- Uniform content format (all channels typically share one compression method and use roughly the same bit rate)

- Delivered over a private network, such as a telco digital subscriber line (DSL)
- Viewed on consumer televisions by way of a set-top box

INTERNET VIDEO

Internet video is used to supply video content to viewers by way of the public Internet. In a typical Internet video installation, service providers set up a website portal that can be reached by anyone with a standard browser. At this site, a list or index of the various pieces of content will be available. Once the user has selected content, it is delivered from servers to the viewer's PC, where media viewer software can be used or where it can be downloaded to another device.

Some of the main characteristics of Internet Video include:

- Discrete content elements, ranging from clips lasting a handful of seconds to full-length movies
- Millions of content offerings
- Widely varying content formats, including dozens of different types of video compression, rights management technologies, and image resolutions
- Delivered over the public Internet
- Viewed on PCs via software, on portable video players, or on televisions by means of network adapters

VIDEO TRANSPORT TECHNOLOGIES

Television was invented for a single purpose: to transport moving pictures from one location to another. The word *television* comes from the Greek word *tele*, meaning "distant," and the Latin verb *visio*, meaning "to see." (The word *video* also comes from this same Latin root.) Hence, *television* means "seeing at a distance." Modern video transport technology is all about sending moving images to a viewer who is far away.

Today, users have many options for video transport, which presents a challenge: How does a user select the best way to transport video for each application? Many factors are involved in this choice, so there is no one best answer for all users. Let's begin by looking at the many methods used for transporting video signals today.

Broadcast TV

The first IP networking applications in broadcast TV production were video file storage and retrieval, particularly for supporting digital video-editing stations. From there, it was a small step to supporting *live ingest*, which is the process of taking live video content into the digital domain for storage in files on hard disks. Then live-to-air output over IP networks became feasible. This whole process has been driven in part by the continuing spread of high-performance computer workstations that are able to handle video streams in real time. It is actually simpler to configure these workstations with a high-bandwidth networking card (such as Gigabit Ethernet) than it is to equip each station with a video card and audio input and output cards.

Many people first encountered TV in its original form—as a signal broadcast from a central tower, through the air over a dedicated channel, to a television equipped with an antenna. Let's look at some of the key components of a modern broadcast television system (see Figure 1-1).

The master control room (MCR) is the operational hub of a television station, where video content is assembled and made ready for broadcasting to viewers. Video content can come from a variety of sources—a live local source, a broadcast network,[1] a videotape, or from a video server. Table 1-1 gives a small sample of the many functions that a modern television station must perform.

---

1. Somewhat confusingly, the term *network* has two different meanings for people with broadcast television or data communications backgrounds. In this book, we will try to use the term *broadcast network* whenever we are referring to the distributor of programming that operate in many countries, such as the BBC in the UK, ARD in Germany, or CBS in the United States. When we use the term *network* by itself or with another modifier, we are referring to a data, voice, or other type of telecommunications system.

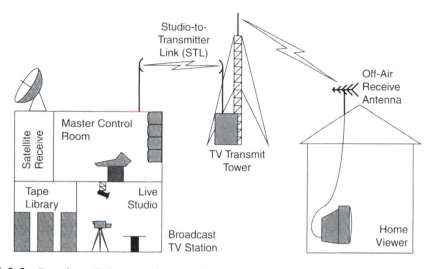

FIGURE 1-1 Broadcast Television System Diagram

A studio-to-transmitter link (STL) is used whenever the master control room is separated from the actual transmitter tower. The STL carries the television signal directly to the transmitter, normally over a dedicated facility. Microwave radio can be used where there is a direct line of sight available from the studio to the transmitter. Fiber-optic links are more reliable than microwave radio links, but they require a fiber-optic cable to be connected from the studio to the transmitter. These links can be owned by a local telephone company, some other local utility, a municipality, or even by the television station itself.

At the transmitter, the signal is received from the studio and then placed into a specific channel frequency band. For example, in the

TABLE 1-1

Television Station Functions

- Collect video content from a variety of sources, including broadcast network feeds, advertising agencies, local television studios, and syndicated program distributors.
- Prepare the video content for broadcast by editing the material to fit into time constraints and adding local programming and advertising.
- Ensure that the broadcast signal meets all of the performance standards (such as operating frequency and peak radiated power) specified in the station's broadcast license.
- Make sure there is no "dead air," i.e., times when nothing is being broadcast.

United States, Channel 30 occupies the frequencies between 566 and 572 MHz. The modulated signal is amplified to a high power level and fed into the broadcast antenna. The television signal then radiates from the antenna to viewers' locations.

At each viewer's location, a receiving antenna collects the radiated signal and generates a very tiny output signal. This signal is then demodulated and decoded to recover the video and audio signals. These signals are then amplified many times over until they are powerful enough to drive the television set's display and loudspeakers.

Satellite Television

Satellites orbiting the earth are commonly used to receive signals from one earth location and send them to another. Satellites can also be used to broadcast a collection of television signals directly to viewers' homes. Both these applications are in widespread use today.

Satellite transmission of television programs has been used since the mid-1960s to send live programming from one continent to another. Broadcast networks began using satellites to send programming to local television stations and cable TV systems in the mid-1970s. It wasn't until the late 1980s that satellite broadcasting to consumers really began, as exemplified by Sky television in the UK in 1989. This market became known as the direct-to-home (DTH) market, since satellite television service providers were transmitting their programs directly to consumers rather than to local television broadcast stations or cable television systems as in the past. This service is also commonly known as direct broadcast satellite (DBS) service. Let's look at the key components of a typical satellite DTH system (Figure 1-2).

An uplink facility transmits signals from the ground to a satellite, using a high-power signal and a large-diameter dish. The uplink facility gathers video content from a variety of sources, including local television stations in various cities, specialized programmers (such as movie and sports networks), and many others. Because a

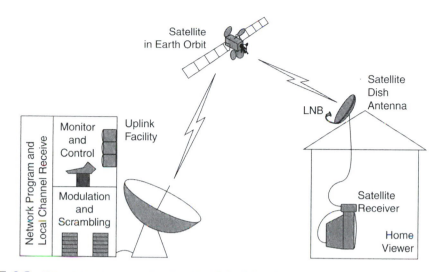

FIGURE 1-2 Direct-to-Home (DTH) Satellite Television System Diagram

single uplink facility can create multiple signals to be sent to one or more satellites (by means of a separate dish for each satellite) for rebroadcast over a large area, one facility can serve an entire continent.

Satellites are positioned above the equator at a height of 22,300 miles, which causes them to orbit the earth once every 24 hours and appear to be stationary above a fixed point on the earth's surface. Each satellite is equipped with multiple transponders, each of which receives a signal transmitted by an uplink, amplifies it, and broadcasts the signals back to earth. Current transponders don't do any processing of the uplinked signal (other than amplification and frequency conversion), so a transponder can be used for any type of content, such as voice, video, or data. This permits a DTH broadcaster to change over time the types of services offered without modifying the satellite.

One of the biggest changes in DTH satellite broadcasting was the conversion from analog to digital transmission, which allowed satellite service providers to put from 8 to 20 (or more) television channels on each transponder. Using more channels per transponder increases the number of channels that the DTH broadcaster can offer. One of the first satellite providers to offer exclusively digital satellite service was DirecTV, which began operation in 1994. All of the video signals are digitized and compressed in a digital satellite system, which helps to simplify the migration to high-definition (HD) content.

Each satellite TV customer must purchase and install a dish antenna. The antenna must normally be installed outdoors with a clear line of sight to the satellite, with no intervening buildings, branches, leaves, or other objects. The dish must be installed at the correct elevation angle (up and down tilt) and azimuth (compass direction) to point directly at the satellite. The LNB (low-noise block) converter in the dish assembly feeds an output signal to the satellite receiver, which performs the functions listed in Table 1-2.

Private satellite networks are also used heavily by television broadcasters, both for gathering content and for distributing it to local broadcasters. When content is being gathered, remote locations take turns in transmitting their content to a satellite, which retransmits the signal to the main studio. (By using only a single transponder, the broadcaster's rental costs for the satellite are minimized.) This method is commonly used for live events in remote locations, such as sports arenas. In many cases this content is scrambled to prevent unauthorized viewing of the unedited video feeds. For distribution, the main studio uplinks a signal to a satellite that rebroadcasts the signal to multiple local television stations. Much of this content is also scrambled. In many cases, content is sent to the local stations

TABLE 1-2

Satellite Receiver Functions

- Accept commands from the customer's remote control to select the desired programming.
- Ensure that the customer has authorization to watch the selected channel (sometimes by means of a special identification card).
- Receive signals from the LNB, and recover the desired channel. This step may include descrambling the incoming signal.
- In many cases, the satellite receiver must be connected to a telephone line to permit communication with the DTH service provider's central computers for billing, authorization, and other functions.

For digital programming, the following functions must also be performed:

- Demodulate and demultiplex the digital data to select the correct digital stream.
- Remove any encryption that has been performed on the signal.
- Decompress the stream to create a video output that is fed to the customer's television set.

in advance of when it is needed for broadcast and then simply stored locally and "played out" at the appropriate time. Some corporations also use IP-based networks (often called VSAT, for very small aperture terminal) for data, voice, and video transport applications.

Cable TV

Cable television (CATV) can trace its origins to broadcast television beginning in the 1950s. Originally, the acronym CATV stood for community antenna (or community access) TV, and that was exactly its purpose—to allow viewers to share a common antenna that was able to pull in signals from remote broadcast stations that would be impractical for viewers to receive on their own.

Since those days, CATV has made major strides into new areas, including subscription television (movie channels), pay-per-view, video on demand, and special-interest channels devoted exclusively to sports, weather, or other topics. The video transport mechanism is essentially the same as that used by broadcast television—each video signal is placed onto a specific carrier frequency (TV channel) and transported into each subscriber's home via a coaxial cable in place of an antenna. Let's look at a typical CATV system (see Figure 1-3).

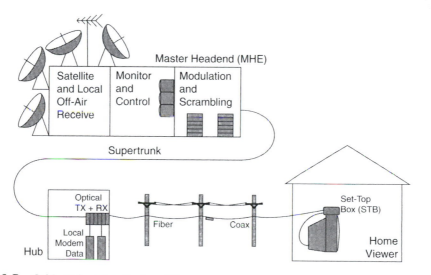

FIGURE 1-3 Cable Television System Diagram

A CATV system can serve tens or hundreds of thousands of viewers from a single master headend (MHE), where video content is gathered and made ready to transmit to viewers. Video feeds can come from local TV broadcasters (received at the MHE via an antenna or by means of a dedicated link from the TV station), from satellite feeds, from local programming sources (including educational and government institutions), and from prerecorded content, such as advertisements.

Many CATV providers have started supplying some or most of their programming in digital format, because video streams can be compressed to use network bandwidth more efficiently. This allows the transmission of multiple digital video channels in place of one analog channel and supports the delivery of HDTV. This improvement in efficiency becomes even more important as CATV providers seek to free up bandwidth that can then be used to provide other revenue-generating services, such as voice and data transport.

The techniques used to combine and organize the different digital video signals vary from one CATV provider to another. In Europe, many systems operate in accordance with standards published by the Digital Video Broadcasting (DVB) consortium. Many other techniques are used around the world, including some that are based on IP technology.

The functions of an MHE are very similar to those of a television station's master control room (MCR), with three major exceptions:

- The MHE typically handles dozens or even hundreds of channels, whereas an MCR generally handles one or possibly a handful of channels.
- A portion of the channels processed by the MHE are typically scrambled or encrypted to prevent them from being watched by subscribers who have not paid the appropriate fees. The technology required to manage this content is called a conditional access (CA) system, which controls the decryption and descrambling function for each subscriber's receiver device, commonly known as a set-top box (STB).
- In many cases (such as for pay-per-view movies or cable modem service), communications back from subscribers is permitted.

The MHE must process these return path signals to provide subscriber Internet access or to fulfill orders for pay-per-view movies.

All of the content is modulated onto radio frequency (RF) carriers and combined into a broadband RF output, typically covering a range from 50 to 860 MHz. Some systems operate up to 1 GHz in frequency, with the higher frequencies generally reserved for data and voice services. This broadband signal is then distributed to subscribers using a tree-and-branch type network that typically employs both fiber-optic and coaxial cable, creating a hybrid fiber coax (HFC) network.

From the master headend, a supertrunk is used to distribute the broadband signal to local hubs. Supertrunking may be either analog or digital, but it is almost always fiber-optic. In some CATV systems, processing is done at the hubs to add local programming or to handle cable modem data.

From the hubs, the broadband signal is sent out to the distribution network. The distribution network can be fed directly by coaxial cables, or fiber-optics can be used to cover part of the distance from the hub to the subscriber's home. Customers receive the broadband signal via coaxial cable either directly at their television sets or via STBs.

In many CATV systems, consumers are able to hook a "cable-ready" television set directly to the incoming coaxial cable. In this case, the tuner in the television set is responsible for selecting the correct channel from the incoming broadband signal. Many consumer videotape recorders and DVD recorders are also equipped with cable-ready inputs. In many other cases, customers use a set top box to receive the broadband signal, particularly when digital transmission is being used. Key functions of a typical STB are given in Table 1-3.

New Technologies

All of the technologies described in the preceding sections currently have hundreds of millions of subscribers around the world. However, some new technologies are gaining popularity. They include

TABLE 1-3
Set-Top Box (STB) Functions

- Accept commands from a user's remote control to select the desired programming.
- Verify that the user has authorization to watch the selected channel.
- Receive the broadband signal from the coaxial cable network.
- Tune to the correct RF channel.
- If the channel is scrambled or encrypted, process the signal to create an unscrambled output.
- If the channel is digital, demultiplex and decode the digital information into an output suitable for the television display.
- Generate video and audio signals for display on the customer's television.

fiber to the premises (FTTP) and digital subscriber line (DSL). Let's quickly review both of them.

Fiber to the premises (FTTP) technology involves making a direct, fiber-optic connection to each customer's home or business to replace aging, limited-capacity copper wires with new, high-capacity optical fibers. This technology also goes by the names fiber to the home (FTTH) and fiber to the business (FTTB). Recent work on passive optical networks (PONs) has created a new method for delivering video services to the subscriber.

In essence, a PON is an all-optical network with no active components between the service provider and the customer. The network is optical because the path from the service provider to the customer is entirely made up of fiber-optic and optical components. The network is passive because there are no active elements (such as electronics, lasers, optical detectors, or optical amplifiers) between the service provider and the customer.

One key feature of a PON is the use of an optical splitter near the customer premises, which greatly improves the economics of the system. In the case of one popular standard, up to 32 end customers can be served by one fiber from the service provider. A second key feature of a PON network is that the optical fibers and the optical splitter are configured to handle a wide range of laser wavelengths (colors), so new services can easily be deployed. This gives a PON a great deal of flexibility for adapting to future customer needs. Let's look at how a PON system is constructed (see Figure 1-4).

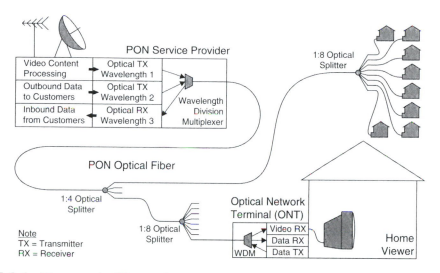

FIGURE 1-4   Diagram of a Fiber to the Premises (FTTP) System Using a Passive Optical Network (PON)

Each customer must have an optical network terminal (ONT; also known as an optical network unit, or ONU) to receive signals from the PON and convert them into electrical signals that can be used by customers' devices. The ONT also converts data being sent by the customer into optical signals that are sent back over the PON to the service provider. In general, the ONT uses normal commercial power supplied by the customer, and it must have a method to power itself (i.e., a battery) to support emergency communication.

The system shown in Figure 1-4 uses three different wavelengths (colors) of light. Two wavelengths go from the service provider to the customers. One wavelength is normally used for a multichannel video signal. A second wavelength carries data from the service provider to all the customers. A third wavelength carries data from the customers back to the service provider. At both the service provider and customer ends of the fiber, specialized filters (called wavelength-division multiplexers, or WDMs) are used to separate the three colors of light.

Video in a PON can be as simple as an optical version of a normal CATV signal that the customer's ONT feeds into a standard cable-ready television set or a set-top box. One big advantage of this system is that customers may not need a set-top box if they are not interested in scrambled, encrypted, or digital content.

Data in a PON system is multiplexed. From the provider, one stream that contains all of the data for all of the customers is created. Each customer's ONT receives and processes the incoming bit stream and selects the data for that customer. In the reverse direction, only one customer ONT can transmit at a time. For data-intensive customers such as businesses, other wavelengths of light can be used to provide dedicated, high-speed links over PON optical paths.

A major advantage of PON technology is that it can supply very high bit-rate data connections to each customer, with support for aggregate bit rates from the service provider to customers of 622 Mbps and 155 Mbps from the customers back. If all 32 users are running simultaneously at maximum speed, this works out to 19 Mbps that can be transmitted to each subscriber. This amount of bandwidth can easily handle several compressed video signals, so some PON operators simply use this bandwidth to provide IPTV, video-on-demand, and other services.

A major drawback of PON technology is that it requires the service provider to install a fiber-optic connection to each PON customer. This is not a big obstacle in new construction, but the expense of replacing a large installed base of copper cabling with optical fiber and supplying each user with an ONT can be a very large investment for existing customers.

Digital subscriber line (DSL) technology has become popular with service providers and many customers because it offers a way to use existing copper, twisted-pair telephone lines for carrying high-speed data. Many consumers are aware that they can purchase DSL service for Internet access. Some service providers also offer IPTV that is delivered using DSL service. Let's look at how a DSL system can be constructed (see Figure 1-5).

All DSL systems have to make a trade-off between speed and distance. That is, longer distances must operate at lower bit rates, because losses in the cable increase as the bit rate increases. (As technology improves, these limits change, but designers still need to

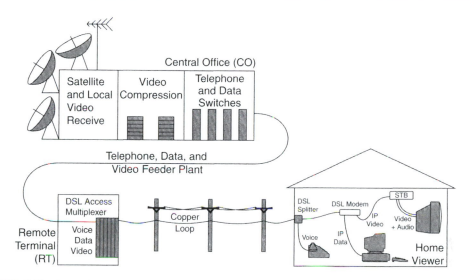

FIGURE 1-5   Digital Subscriber Line (DSL) Diagram

make compromises.) To help keep distances down, a service provider will typically install DSL equipment in remote terminals (RTs), which are located between the provider's main offices and customers.

The central office (CO) is the main hub for services. This is the location of the telephone switch that handles normal telephone traffic. The CO is also usually the place where connections are made to the Internet and where video services are processed prior to distribution.

Customers who are located close to the CO can be fed directly from copper pairs that terminate in the CO. More distant customers are typically served by an RT. Fiber-optics are commonly used to send the signals from the CO to the RT; this is called the *feeder plant*. In the feeder plant, voice, video, and data signals often travel over different transmission equipment. Feeders for video and data services are generally installed alongside existing voice feeders and typically carry much higher-rate data signals.

Each RT provides direct copper connections to each customer in the RT serving area. When DSL service is installed, a digital subscriber line access multiplexer (DSLAM) is also placed into the RT (or in a

CO for directly fed customers). The DSLAM takes video and data signals from the feeder and selects the correct ones for each customer. Then the DSLAM generates the DSL signals and places them onto the pair of copper wires (or local loop) leading to each home.

Every DSL customer must install a DSL modem. The modem receives the DSL signals from the DSLAM and converts them into the proper form for the customer's other devices, such as a PC, a data router, or an IPTV STB. The modem also takes data signals from the customer and transmits them back to the service provider. Table 1-4 lists some of the more common types of DSL services that are available.

One big advantage of a DSL system is that it uses the existing wires that already run to homes and businesses for telephone service. Another advantage is that the DSL circuits are normally designed to fail gracefully, so if a customer loses power or the DSL equipment fails, then normal telephone calls can still be made.

A disadvantage of DSL services for video is that only a few video signals at a time can be sent down a DSL line. Typically, these technologies are restricted to one video content stream per video device, each of which must be equipped with a set-top box (STB). The STB is

TABLE 1-4

Common Types of Digital Subscriber Line (DSL) Services

- Asymmetric DSL (ADSL) operates at speeds up to 8 Mbps (millions of bits per second) from the CO to the customer (downstream) and up to 800 kbps (thousands of bits per second) from the customer to the CO (upstream). Two newer technologies offer higher speeds: ADSL2 has up to 12 Mbps downstream and 1 Mbps upstream; ADSL2+ doubles the downstream speed to 24 Mbps.
- G.Lite DSL (also known as universal DSL) operates at speeds up to 1.5 Mbps downstream and up to 512 kbps upstream.
- High-speed DSL (HDSL) operates symmetrically (same speed upstream and downstream) at a rate of 1.544 or 2.048 Mbps and is mostly used to provide services to businesses.
- Very-high-speed DSL (VDSL) operates at bit rates from 4 to 52 Mbps downstream and 1.5 to 2.3 Mbps upstream, although the higher rates can be achieved only on very short links (less than 300 m). Newer standards have increased both upstream and downstream rates, but distances remain short.
- xDSL collectively refers to the preceding standards as a generic term.

Note that the actual bit rates that can be achieved on a DSL circuit are highly variable and depend on many factors, including the length of the subscriber's loop and the amount of noise or interference present on the line.

responsible for receiving the digital video signal from the DSLAM and converting it into the correct output for the user's video display. The STB is responsible for accepting channel-change commands from the viewer and sending them to the DSLAM. Each time a customer wishes to switch the program being viewed, the DSLAM must switch to send out a different video stream.

Dedicated Networks

In the world of television, movie, and video production, special-purpose links are often used to transport video. Table 1-5 lists several advantages of dedicated networks for corporate users.

Of course, all these advantages come at a price—monthly rental fees that usually run between $1,000 and $5,000 per month per dedicated TV1 video link for local service in major U.S. cities. These networks are not very flexible—installation fees normally apply, and installation lead times usually exceed a month. However, for high-end users (television stations and broadcast networks), these links are extremely valuable and widely used.

Fiber-optic links form the majority of dedicated video networks for analog and digital applications. Fiber-optic links can run over long distances (over 100 km between signal regenerators) and provide many services (including nonvideo services) on a single fiber.

TABLE 1-5

Advantages of Dedicated Video Networks

- Extremely large bandwidths as needed for uncompressed video signals (such as those described in Chapter 3).
- High-quality transport with extremely low error rates, allowing original content to be transported with essentially no degradation.
- Compatibility with video formats that are used in video production, including feeds from studio-quality cameras and professional editing systems, making it easy for video producers to use these services.
- Privacy, since many of these links operate over dedicated facilities that are extremely difficult for malicious users to access.
- Reliability, because these networks are normally isolated from traffic created by other users.

Fiber-optic links also offer much lower error rates than other technologies. Terminal devices have become very inexpensive over the past decade, which helps keep service provider costs down. Drawbacks include the need to connect fibers to both signal source and destination and the inability of some end devices to share fibers with other types of equipment. Also, most service providers offer these transport services only on a local basis; long-distance video transport is generally done over telecom networks.

TELECOM NETWORKS

Many different types of telecom networks are in use around the world today, and most of them can be used for transporting video signals. In fact, it's not at all unusual for one type of network traffic (e.g., IP) to be transported over another type of network (e.g., SONET) at some point in a long-distance circuit. So it's important to have some understanding about each of the network types and how they can affect video traffic. Let's look at some of the most commonly used networks.

Table 1-6 summarizes much of the data in the following four sections.

PDH

The original digital telecom standards were organized by means of a Plesiochronous Digital Hierarchy (PDH), which means "nearly synchronized." More technically, two circuits are considered plesiochronous if their bit rates fall within a strictly limited tolerance range. By far, the most common PDH signal in North America is a T1 (also known as a DS1), which operates at a rate of 1.544 Mbps. This is enough capacity to carry 24 voice channels, each operating at 64 kbps, plus overhead. In Europe, the corresponding signal is commonly called an E1, which operates at 2.048 Mbps and has the capacity to carry 30 voice channels (also at 64 kbps each) plus overhead. Moving up in speed in North America is a DS3 (or T3), which operates at 44.736 Mbps and carries 28 DS1's, equivalent to 672 voice channels. In Europe, the E3 rate is used, which operates at a speed

TABLE 1-6

Telecom Standards Comparison

Bit Rate	PDH USA	PDH Europe	ISDN USA	ISDN Europe	SDH	SONET	Voice Channels
64 kbps	DS0	E0					1
144 kbps			BRI	BRI			2
1.544 Mbps			PRI				23
1.544 Mbps	T1/DS1						24
2.048 Mbps		E1		PRI			30
34.368 Mbps		E3					480
44.736 Mbps	DS3/T3						672
							Payload Rate
51.840 Mbps						STS-1	50.112 Mbps
155.520 Mbps					STM-1	OC-3	150.336 Mbps
622.080 Mbps					STM-4	OC-12	601.344 Mbps
2.48832 Gbps					STM-16	OC-48	2405.376 Mbps
9.95328 Gbps					STM-64	OC-192	9621.504 Mbps

Commonly Used Video Rates
Videoconferencing: 128 kbps to 768 kbps
Compressed video: 1.5 to 15 Mbps
Uncompressed video: 270 Mbps, 1.485 Gbps

kbps: kilobits (1,000 bits) per second
Mbps: megabits (1,000,000 bits) per second
Gbps: gigabits (1,000,000,000 bits) per second

of 34.368 Mbps and carries 16 E1s, equivalent to 480 voice channels. Higher-speed PDH interfaces are no longer used; they have been replaced by SONET/SDH standards.[2]

PDH standards are still very important today, even though a lot of new technology has been developed. T1, E1, DS3, and E3 rates are still with us because of the huge installed base of networking equipment with these interfaces. Most service providers offer circuits at these bit rates to customers anywhere in their service areas. Also, these bit rates make sense for a lot of voice and data applications (and even for a few video ones) because they are relatively inexpensive.

---

2. Occasionally, you might see a reference to a circuit called a DS0 in the United States or E0 in Europe. This is simply a single voice channel, which operates at 64 kbps.

ISDN

The Integrated Services Digital Network (ISDN) provides two sub-scriber interfaces—the basic rate interface (BRI) and the primary rate interface (PRI). A BRI has two B-channels that operate at 64 kbps and one D-channel that operates at 16 kbps, for a total of 144 kbps. The PRI speed depends on its location. In North America, a PRI has 23 B-channels that operate at 64 kbps and one D-channel that operates at 64 kbps, for a total of 1.544 Mbps, including overhead. In Europe, a PRI has 30 B-channels that operate at 64 kbps and one D-channel that operates at 64 kbps, for a total of 2.048 Mbps, including overhead.

ISDN circuits can be dedicated or dial-up circuits. Dedicated circuits are similar to most other network connections—an always-on, fixed-bandwidth network link. Dial-up circuits allow temporary connections to be made from one ISDN device to another by use of special network connection procedures, which are similar to those used in placing a normal voice telephone call.

ISDN lines have some video transport applications. The H.320 video-conferencing standard (see Chapter 10) uses ISDN lines for call setup and video transport. Also, some businesses use PRI lines for data traffic and Internet access, and low-bit-rate IP video signals can flow over these links. Due to relatively high prices and low bandwidth, many ISDN services are being replaced with IP services, particularly DSL.

SONET/SDH

The Synchronous Optical Network (SONET) standard in North America and the Synchronous Digital Hierarchy (SDH) standard in Europe are based on fiber-optic technology. These networks can operate at speeds ranging up to (and beyond) 10 Gbps. What's more, SONET and SDH networks have a common set of bit rates that allow many pieces of equipment to change from one standard to the other.

Because it is easier to understand, let's look at the SDH standard first. The basic SDH building block is an STM-1, which stands for Synchronous Transport Module-1. An STM-1 operates at

155.52 Mbps and can contain a huge variety of different payloads. Mappings, or schemes for constructing payloads, are available for voice signals, data signals (including ATM and IP, see the following section), video signals, and others. STM-1 signals can be combined to form higher-speed interfaces, including STM-4 (622.08 Mbps), STM-16 (2.48832 Gbps), and STM-64 (9.95328 Gbps). Even higher speeds are possible in the future.

Now let's look at the more confusing world of SONET. The basic building block is the STS-1 (Synchronous Transport Signal), which operates at 51.84 Mbps. Because this rate is so close to DS3, it was never really offered as a stand-alone service. Instead, basically everyone agreed to use the STS-3 rate of 155.52 Mbps. (Note that this is exactly the same bit rate as an STM-1 in SDH.) Since these signals are normally provided over optical fiber, the common name for this signal is OC-3, for Optical Carrier 3.

Higher-speed links are also available. OC-12 operates at 622.08 Mbps, OC-48 at 2.48832 Gbps, and OC-192 9.95328 Gbps. Even higher speeds, such as OC-768, will become common in the future. Again, notice that there is a match between some OC signal rates and STM rates. The concept of the STS is important for only one reason—data inside an OC-x is organized into frames based on the STS-1. So an OC-12 is basically made up of 12 independent STS-1 signals, each operating at 51.84 Mbps. For higher-speed data that won't fit into a single STS-1, several of them can be concatenated to form a single, high-speed payload envelope. Concatenated signals are denoted by adding a lowercase "c" to the signal name. In order to form an envelope capable of carrying 140 Mbps of data you would need to use an OC-3c.

Most long-distance telecommunication networks operate on SONET/SDH backbones today. This has been caused by the growth of fiber-optic technology and by service providers who require their vendors to adopt these standards. So chances are pretty high that, if you are running a signal over a large geographic area or connecting to the Internet, your data will flow over a SONET/SDH network for at least part of the journey. This is true even if you are using other signal types, such as PDH, ISDN, ATM, or even IP, because there are widely used standards for inserting all of these types of signals into SONET/SDH networks.

ATM

Asynchronous Transfer Mode (ATM) was originally created to be a broadband form of ISDN. ATM was quite popular in the 1990s and beyond, but new deployments of the technology have slowed down recently due to the higher costs as compared to IP.

The core concept of ATM is a "cell," which contains 48 bytes of data and 5 bytes of control and routing information, for a total of 53 bytes in a cell. Terminal devices accept user data, break it up into 48-byte chunks, and then add the 5 bytes of header information. The way that the data is broken up depends on the application; so different ATM Adaptation Layers (AALs) have been defined for different uses, with AAL-1 and AAL-5 being the most popular for video The resulting cells can be combined with cells from other data sources to form an outgoing signal and passed into the ATM network. After each hop along the network, the header of each cell must be processed to make it ready for the next hop along the route. At the far end of the network, cell headers are removed, cell data is extracted, and the data is reassembled into the original format.

Because ATM is a connection-oriented system, before any data can flow across the network, a connection must be established between the source and the destination for the data. This connection establishes a specific route for the data called a virtual circuit (VC). Note that the process of establishing a VC requires stacks of software in the terminal devices and in each piece of network equipment along the route of the signal. Once the VC is fully established, data can flow. Software is also required to handle cell errors and to reestablish connections when failures occur or when a new VC needs to be set up.

Some service providers still use ATM within their own networks, even for non-ATM data (some IP traffic is carried over ATM facilities within carriers). The biggest benefits of ATM for a carrier are the abilities to control the amount of bandwidth used by each customer, to ensure that data from different customers are kept separate, and to ensure that adequate bandwidth exists across the entire data path from source to destination, coupled with the ability to make sure that certain types of time-sensitive traffic (such as video) have a higher priority over other types of traffic. These properties make it very easy for end devices to send and receive video smoothly and reliably.

The biggest drawback of ATM for most users is cost. First, the user must purchase an ATM multiplexer to format the data into cells. ATM devices can be quite expensive in comparison to IP devices, due, in part, to the large amounts of software required to set up and manage connections. Each user must lease an ATM access link from a carrier at each end of the data circuit. Furthermore, many carriers charge for actual network usage on the ATM links rather than the flat-rate services that are common on IP links. All these factors combine to make ATM transport typically more expensive and increasingly less popular than other services, such as IP.

IP

Since Chapter 5 is devoted to IP technology, this will be a brief introduction. IP is a standard method for formatting and addressing data packets in a large, multifunction network, such as the Internet. A packet is a variable-length unit of information (a collection of bytes) in a well-defined format that can be sent across an IP network. Typically, a message such as e-mail or a video signal will be broken up into several IP packets. Each packet must carry a destination address so that the network knows where to deliver the packet. IP can be used on many different network technologies, such as Ethernet LANs and wireless Wi-Fi links.

To help illustrate the functions of IP, an analogy might be useful. For folks who live in the United States, use of the U.S. Postal Service requires the sender to put a destination address that includes a 5-digit Zip Code on each piece of mail that is sent out. There are rules for assigning IP addresses, and their format is precisely defined. There are many excellent references on this, so we won't go into detail here. Certain IP addresses are reserved for special purposes, such as multicasting (see Chapter 9). It is the same with Zip Codes—the first two digits indicate the state (or part of a big state), the third is the region within the state, and the last two indicate the local post office.

IP is connectionless, which means that each packet can be sent from source to destination along any path that happens to be available. Each packet is handled individually; that is, the network is not required always to select the same path to send packets to the same destination. This can sometimes result with the packets being received in a different order than they were sent. In the U.S. mail, each letter is handled individually. At each sorting location, the destination Zip Code is examined on each letter. The sorter's function is to choose any available method (airplane, truck, etc.) to move the letter along toward its destination. If a particular method is full to capacity, another method will be chosen. This is why two letters mailed on the same day from the same location to the same recipient may not arrive on the same day. IP packets are variable in size. The length of each packet is included in the header information. Of course, mail messages can be of different sizes as well.

IP has some functionality for controlling which packets get priority when congestion occurs. This allows certain packets to be flagged as having high priority and others as low priority. In the U.S. mail, letters and parcels can also be assigned a priority, such as First Class, Bulk Rate, and Express Mail.

Video transport applications on IP networks range all the way from low-resolution, low-frame-rate applications like webcams to high-definition television and medical images. It is paramount that users, technologists, and service providers understand how video works on an IP network. That is a topic we will explore in great depth in the rest of this book.

THE INTERNET

The Internet is a worldwide network that provides IP-based communication services for a wide range of users and applications. One of the most familiar uses of the Internet is the World Wide Web, which can be accessed through web browsers essentially everywhere on the planet. The Internet also supports e-mail, file transfer, and many other applications. In this book, we will use Internet with a capital "I" when we are referring to this enormous, public network.

Many users would like to be able to transport high-quality video signals over the Internet. This is certainly possible and works well for prerecorded content and live content if perfect broadcast quality is not required. For the latter, private networks are typically used. Use of the Internet for video transport has both advantages and disadvantages, as detailed next.

Advantages

Ubiquitous availability—Connections to the Internet are available throughout the world (even Antarctica), and today there are hundreds of millions of regular Internet users. The Internet has many more connections than even the largest private or government network in existence.

Low cost—The cost of receiving data over the Internet is transparent to many users. A monthly fee for access through their Internet service provider (ISP) is all that most users pay. Contrast this with the cost that would be incurred to construct a private network with dedicated facilities to each customer in a worldwide video IP network.

Disadvantages

Unpredictable performance—Because the Internet's function is dependent on the interaction between so many different networks, congestion or delay can occur in many places. Also, there is no mechanism for a user to request a higher-priority level for certain types of traffic, as is often done for video traffic on private networks. These factors combine to make it very difficult to guarantee a required level of performance for any Internet connection.

No multicasting—Multicasting is a powerful tool for sending the same content to multiple destinations simultaneously, as will be described in Chapter 9. Unfortunately, the Internet is not enabled for multicasting, so each video stream needs to be sent individually from each source to each destination.

Overall, it is possible to transport video content over the Internet, and we will discuss several examples in this book. However, users must be prepared to deal with the shortcomings of the Internet and understand that many video applications will work best on specialized or private IP networks.

REVIEW AND VIDEO USER CHECKLIST

In this chapter, we began with a definition of Internet TV and IPTV, followed by descriptions of the three most popular methods for delivering broadcast television to consumers: terrestrial broadcasting, direct-to-home (DTH) satellite broadcasting, and cable television (CATV). We then examined two new technologies that can be used for consumer delivery: Passive optical networks (PONs) and digital subscriber line (DSL). We also glanced at dedicated video networks for delivering video to broadcasters. Next, we looked at some popular telecommunication networks, including PDH, SONET/SDH, and ATM. We concluded with a brief look at the basics of IP networks and discussed using the Internet for video transport.

Throughout this book, we will be covering many different aspects of video transport over IP networks. These issues affect the choices that users need to make in order to achieve success with IP video networking. To help guide the discussion, we will be creating a checklist of information that users should gather before beginning a video transport project. Following are some of the topics that will make up our checklist.

Chapter 1 Checklist Update

❑ *Source of Content:* Who will be supplying the content? Who owns the content? Are there any restrictions on use of the content? Can only certain users view the content? Will the content need to be protected against copying?

❑ *Type of Content:* What types of scenes are included in the content? How much detail is there? How much motion is present? Does the detail level of the content need to be preserved for the viewer?

❑ *Content Technical Requirements:* Does the content come from film, videotape, or a live camera? Is there a synchronized audio track? Is there more than one audio track (second language, commentary)? Is there any data that must be included with the content, such as closed captioning, V-chip data, or program descriptions? Are there any limits mandated by the content owner on the amount or type of compression that can be used?

❑ *System Funding:* How will the content be paid for? How will the network usage be paid for? Will payments be required from each viewer? Will advertising be used?

❑ *Viewer Profile:* How many users will be viewing the content? Where will they be located? What equipment will they use to view the content?

❑ *Network Capabilities:* What bit rates will the network support? Will the network support multicasting? What security features does the network offer? Who owns the network?

❑ *Performance Requirements:* How much delay will be acceptable in this application? What video and audio quality levels will users accept? Will all users get the content at the same time? Will users be allowed to pause, rewind, and fast-forward the content? What is the financial impact of a service interruption?

A more detailed list appears at the back of this book in Appendix B. In each chapter, we will be adding to this checklist as our discussion covers more topics.

2

IP VIDEO TRANSPORT APPLICATIONS

Many users have benefited from video transport technology. In this chapter, let's look at some interesting ways in which people have had success with video transport.

ENTERTAINMENT

Lots of people use television solely as a means of entertainment. This multibillion-dollar industry depends on efficient, reliable video transport for many functions. Let's look at the important distinction between contribution, distribution, and delivery networks in broadcast television (see Figure 2-1).

Contribution networks are used to gather content for creating a television program. These networks are configured as many-to-one, funneling content from a variety of sources into a central location for producing a program.

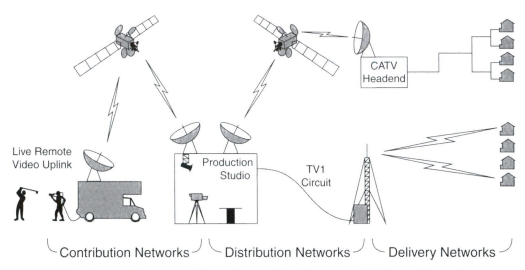

FIGURE 2-1   Broadcast Television Contribution, Distribution, and Delivery Networks

Distribution networks are used to transmit finished programming to delivery providers, including over-the-air broadcasters, cable television (CATV) providers, IPTV network operators, and direct-to-home (DTH) satellite companies. These networks are usually configured as one-to-many, spreading content from a master source to tens or hundreds of delivery service providers.

Delivery networks are used to transmit content to the final viewers by many different means, including broadcast, satellite, CATV, DSL, IP, and other types of networks.[1] Delivery networks are configured as one-to-many, and the number of viewers can range from a few hundred to many millions.

Contribution, distribution, and delivery networks have all been successfully implemented over IP networks. As we shall see in the following sections, each type of network has unique performance requirements.

---

1.   Several standards organizations have chosen to call this portion of the signal delivery chain *emission*. We will use the term *delivery* in this book, because when IP networks are employed for this function, the signal is never truly "emitted" from the network.

Contribution

For a television producer, the mission of a contribution network is clear: Deliver the highest possible quality video to the production studio while staying within budget. Quality is important because video content can go through many different processing steps before it is ready for broadcast. These steps can include editing, color correction, special effects, voice-overs, audio enhancement, logo insertion, digital compression, and others. It is not uncommon for a piece of content to undergo 100 processing steps before it is ready for broadcast. Each processing step can affect the quality of the finished video, and defects in the source material can become magnified in each successive step.

Various types of programming can emphasize different aspects of quality. News programs, for example, emphasize timeliness—the only thing worse than low-quality news video is late or missing news video. In contrast, essentially perfect video is demanded for any content that is being recorded for broadcast at a later date. If errors occur in these transmissions, the content can usually be retransmitted if necessary.

Special-purpose video circuits are usually used to form a contribution network. Whenever feasible for live broadcasts, producers like to deploy a redundant network, with both a main and a backup circuit, often from different carriers. In the United States, dedicated video circuits (commonly called "TV1" circuits) operate in one direction and are specifically designed to transport analog video and audio signals. Carriers also offer TV1-like circuits for transporting digital signals (such as the uncompressed 270-Mbps digital video signal that we will discuss in Chapter 3). Because TV1 and 270-Mbps circuits typically operate only in local service areas and require dedicated facilities, long-distance transport is frequently handled with compressed video that is transported over telecom or IP networks.

One particular challenge for a contribution network occurs when a live announcer located in a broadcast studio interviews someone in a remote location. For the interview to work well, the time delay must be strictly controlled. If the delay becomes too long, there will be an uncomfortable pause from the time one person ends speaking until the other person begins. To keep the delays reasonable, producers can choose to avoid satellite links, if possible, and to avoid using video-processing equipment that produces long delays.

Another concern for contribution networks is security, particularly for high-value content such as sporting events. Broadcasters (and certainly movie studios) don't want their raw, unedited content made available to unauthorized parties. Raw content can contain material that is unacceptable for broadcast and may also contain proprietary subject matter. Most producers want some assurance that their unedited content will not fall into the wrong hands or be viewed by the public before a finished product is produced.

IP networks perform well in contribution applications and have been deployed by carriers and broadcasters. Carriers such as Level3 in the United States and T-Systems in Germany use IP technology for high-profile sporting events. Other broadcasters use public and private IP networks for gathering live news content from locations around the globe.

Distribution

Distribution networks are used to send high-quality content to every delivery provider for the lowest cost possible. High quality is important, because the video content may need to be processed, stored, or edited to insert local advertisements. Cost is also a significant concern, because even a small recurring cost per station can mount up quickly if the signal needs to be delivered to hundreds of stations. Reliability also plays a role, since a service interruption can cause viewers to change channels or require resending programs for future broadcasts.

Satellite technology is very often used to distribute video to many delivery providers simultaneously. One feed can simultaneously serve local TV broadcasters, CATV operators, direct-to-home satellite services, IPTV carriers, and providers serving businesses, hotel rooms, college dormitories, etc. A big advantage of satellite technology is that the cost to the broadcast network for additional receivers within the satellite's coverage area is zero.

Reliability is also a concern. The loss of one frame of video (which lasts a fraction of a second) during a 30-second advertisement can mean that the broadcaster will not get paid for that advertisement. To ensure reliability, some broadcasters use two redundant distribution technologies, such as satellite and terrestrial fiber-optic IP networks.

IP-based delivery networks are economically attractive when the number of delivery providers is small and/or the geographic area to be covered is limited. Examples could be regional sports or news networks or small countries with a unique language. CATV providers also use IP networks to distribute programming and transmit customer data between delivery systems located in different cities. IP networks are also ideally suited to deliver low-bandwidth content streams to locations used in mobile TV broadcasting to handheld devices. In these cases, IP networks offer lower costs and better reliability than satellite or microwave distribution systems.

Delivery

Delivery networks are that last link in the content distribution chain. As we discussed in Chapter 1, several different technologies can be used to accomplish this task. Cost of the delivery network is the main concern; even a tiny cost per viewer can add up quickly for millions of viewers. Reliability is also important, although occasional loss of a few viewers is considered acceptable. Video quality needs only to be high enough to prevent viewers from switching to another program.

Cost concerns have a heavy impact on the decision about delivery methods. For an average prime-time program (generally between 7 p.m. and 11 p.m. each night) in the United States, a television advertiser will have to pay less than one cent per viewer for a 30-second advertisement. Other times of the day, the rates are even lower. This money needs to pay for the programming, the costs of the provider's operation, and the costs of distribution. Clearly, these costs leave a very small amount of money to pay for a delivery network.

IPTV delivery networks are generally used by service providers that want to deliver a mix of services (voice, Internet access, television programming) or that want to use existing network infrastructure (such as copper DSL circuits). Example of both types of IPTV systems are increasing in size and scope around the world and will be discussed in more detail in subsequent chapters.

Sports Programming

Live sporting events are big sources of revenue for broadcasters around the globe. Some of these events are broadcast free over the air. Others are on pay television channels, which receive a monthly fee from subscribers. Still others are available only to viewers who have paid a fee to view a single game or event (pay-per-view). Live sports place a unique set of burdens on a video network.

One of the key differences between sports and regular entertainment television is the need for timeliness. Long delays from the field of play to reception of a signal by a home viewer can cause viewer dissatisfaction.

Another difference between sports and other types of programming is the need for a flexible contribution network. Since sporting venues are typically used only a few hours per week and the location of events changes regularly, flexibility is key. Fortunately, sporting events can be planned well in advance, so specialized production vehicles can be set up on-site a few days ahead of time. Since the number of professional sports venues is fixed, some fiber-optic network service providers have installed direct links to many of these locations.

Content security may also be required in a distribution network for sports events. Content security is usually provided by some kind of scrambling and encryption that is inserted by the broadcaster. Each authorized viewer will typically have a device (such as a set-top box or a satellite receiver) that will receive authorization codes that can be used to decode the signal.

Sports fans also demand a high level of reliability, particularly for events where they have paid for viewing rights. Viewers may demand refunds of their viewing fees if the broadcast is interrupted, even for a short time. This need for reliability extends from the contribution to the delivery networks.

IP networks have been successfully used in a number of contribution networks for sporting events. For example, for the 2006 Asian Games in Qatar, video signals from all the major venues were transmitted by fiber-optic IP networks to the international broadcast center. Several of the rights-holding broadcasters also used IP networks to distribute finished programming to viewers in their home countries.

Advertising

Although advertising may or may not be considered entertainment by viewers, it is the primary source of revenue for most broadcasters. Special networking challenges abound in the creation and playback of advertising content.

First, it is important to understand that advertising video is more heavily processed than normal content. Since advertisers pay substantial sums of money to broadcast each 30-second commercial, they want to make sure that every second counts. The amount of editing time and production cost for a 30-second spot can exceed those of some 30-minute programs.

Virtually all advertising is prerecorded. This basically removes the need for live video transport during the production process. However, video transport can be involved in many other aspects of advertising.

One very important aspect of advertising production is client review and approval. Clients may wish to review the ad creation process at each step along the way. These steps can include concept review, raw film/video review, rough edit review, special effects or animation review, audio review, and final review. There are two ways that IP networks can be used to deliver ad review copies to clients. One is a simple file transfer, where a data file containing the ad content is delivered to the client, who uses media player software to view the content. The second is a video web server hosted by the advertising agency; clients are given a URL to connect to the content and view the video through a web browser. Either choice can result in saving time and expense during the ad production process.

Since most ad content is prerecorded and because quality requirements are very high, file transfer is the preferred method for transport of advertising video. IP video networks can be used to deliver advertisements to national and local broadcasters as well as to CATV, satellite, and IPTV providers. Special-purpose video servers are generally located at each facility; these can be preloaded with ads and then triggered to play back at the appropriate time in outgoing video programs.

INTERACTIVE VIDEO

Video is interactive when viewers can directly affect live content at the source. The form of the interaction can vary. Videoconferencing, whereby two or more people can view each other live on a video connection, is one of the most familiar applications of interactive video. Other interactive applications include webcams, telemedicine, distance education, and telepresence. For this discussion, note that functions like pausing, rewinding, and fast-forwarding of prerecorded content does not constitute interactivity, because the viewer cannot truly interact with the content, but can only control when it is played back. Instead, in the following sections, we will discuss applications in which the viewer actually can affect the content of the video.

Videoconferencing

Although it is loved by some and hated by many, videoconferencing is a powerful tool for business. A videoconference is simply a telephone call with video added on so that participants can see each other as well as hear each other. In its most basic form, a videoconference room can be built with a camera, a microphone, a video display, and loudspeakers for each participant, as shown in Figure 2-2. A network connects the participants and allows each participant to view and hear the others.

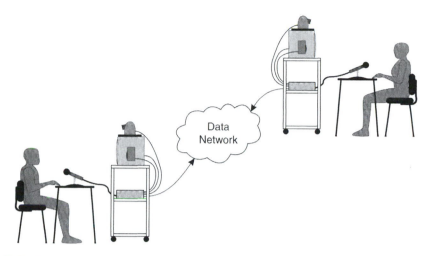

FIGURE 2-2   Typical Videoconferencing Setup

Limiting end-to-end time delay is very important in a videoconference. Long delays make it difficult to carry on a natural conversation. When people talk, they naturally pause when they anticipate that the other person might have something to say. If the other person does not begin speaking right away, then the first person might begin another thought or sentence. Long delays make this interaction difficult, because people must wait for the signal to return to see if the other person has decided to begin speaking. A widely recognized maximum delay limit for each direction in a two-way videoconference is 400 milliseconds (800 milliseconds for a complete round trip), with a preferred limit of no more than 150 milliseconds delay in each direction.

Thanks to advances in IP network technology, videoconferencing applications have expanded both in the low end and in the high end of the performance spectrum. At the low end, inexpensive web cameras and low-cost broadband links to many users' homes have made free, low-resolution video chats available. At the high end, telepresence technology uses HD video cameras and displays large enough to create life-size images of conference participants, creating a powerful illusion that all the parties are seated around a single conference table. Both of these applications would have been infeasible with prior ISDN conferencing systems, due to prohibitive costs for low-end applications and insufficient bandwidth and video quality for high-end uses.

Telemedicine

Telemedicine uses networks to enable a physician in one location to practice medicine in another location. There has been a lot of hype surrounding the idea of using remote-control robots to do surgery over the Internet, but there are many examples of using current technology for telemedicine that are benefiting patients today. Here are a few examples:

- Teleradiology, where images from X-rays, CAT scans, MRI scans, etc., are sent to a radiologist at a distant location for interpretation. While radiologists primarily use still images, motion (video) images are becoming more common.
- Telepathology, where a pathologist is able to take control of tissue sample imaging tools (such as a microscope) to make a diagnosis. Round-trip delay needs to be kept very short, to make it possible for the pathologist to operate the controls of the imaging device correctly.
- Telepsychology, where video-, audio-, and/or text-based interaction is used to provide mental health treatment for patient screening, case management, therapy, and crisis intervention. Telepsychology can be particularly helpful for patients who are geographically isolated or physically disabled.

Network reliability is essential to most telemedicine applications. Because physician and patient time is valuable, the network must be operational whenever it is needed. Private or dedicated networks often can be used to achieve this goal, which can also help ensure patient privacy.

Distance Education

Distance education includes a range of technologies for teaching students who are physically separated from their instructors. Distance education has been used successfully in applications ranging from

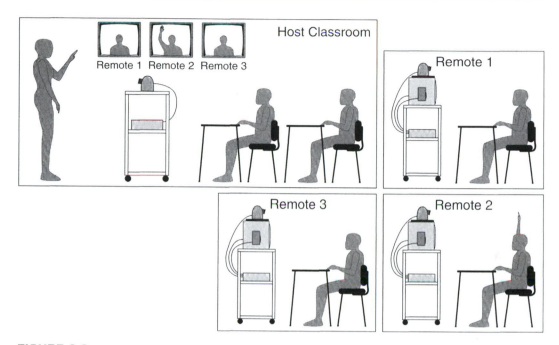

FIGURE 2-3 Distance Education Network

primary school through advanced graduate school as well as in corporate training and adult/continuing education programs.

One large segment of the distance education market is commonly called interactive distance learning (IDL). IDL takes place when students receive live instruction from a teacher and are able to respond to teacher questions and to ask questions of their own, as shown in Figure 2-3. As in any videoconferencing system, video and audio delay must be carefully managed in an IDL system.

Use of high-quality cameras and microphones is essential. Since most IDL operates using compressed digital video, performance of the compression equipment can also impact the video quality and delay. Interestingly, the need for high-quality video goes up for younger students, who tend to be more easily distracted by video artifacts and less disciplined in their classroom behavior.

IP-based IDL systems are rapidly replacing earlier systems that were based on dedicated video networks. IP technology provides two big advantages for school districts—lower equipment/networking costs and the ability to use IP networks for other applications whenever the bandwidth is not needed for teaching.

Telejustice

Telejustice provides the services of courts and lawyers to distant clients for routine court matters such as bail hearings and arraignments, as a low-cost substitute for the expense of guarding and transporting prisoners. Telejustice has also been used occasionally during actual trials in which defendants or witnesses require special safety or security precautions.

The most important feature of a telejustice network is privacy. Strict rules in the United States and elsewhere require communications between lawyers and their clients to be held strictly private. Accordingly, these systems are almost always implemented on private networks, without any connection to the Internet.

STREAMING VIDEO AND NARROWCASTING

Streaming video is a method for delivering content over an IP network that can be used for a variety of purposes. A common one is narrowcasting, which can be thought of as broadcasting to a small audience. It involves transmitting program content to only a few select people who are spread over a network. Table 2-1 lists some of the many different types of content that are applicable to narrowcasting.

TABLE 2-1

Common Uses for Narrowcasting

- Shareholder meetings
- Executive speeches
- Corporate training
- Sales presentations
- Internet radio and video entertainment
- Traffic cameras
- Security and "spy" cameras

Streaming is a process for sending video and audio content to a user that is watched immediately, just like watching a network television broadcast. This requires an active network connection to deliver the content to the viewing device, and the content is not normally stored after playback is complete.

Many different types of technology can be used for streaming. Low-quality video can be created with a low-cost webcam and a desktop PC that produces a tiny video window that updates once every few seconds. High-quality video can be achieved with a hardware-based video encoder that can send full-screen video with full motion over a high-bandwidth network. And, of course, there are a variety of solutions in between. We will discuss many of these technologies for streaming throughout this book, particularly in Chapter 8.

An important distinction needs to be made between three different methods that are used for narrowcasting: live streaming, on-demand streaming, and download and play. Table 2-2 gives a definition of each of these terms.

In contrast to streaming, when podcasting and video file–sharing technologies are used, the content is stored on the viewing device

TABLE 2-2

Methods for Video Streaming

- *Live streaming* happens when every viewer is sent a copy of the same video stream simultaneously.
- *On-demand streaming* happens when users can request that prerecorded content be streamed to them when they want to view it. In this case, each user gets to choose when to begin and end the stream (and possibly rewind or fast-forward the stream as well).
- *Download and play* (D+P) uses memory or hard disk inside a viewer's device to receive a file of audio/video content that can then be displayed (played) by the viewer's device. One big advantage of download and play is that content files can be delivered by way of HTTP, thereby improving the chances of passing through firewalls. Some content owners may not approve of download and play, because it results in a copy of the content becoming resident on every user's storage device prior to viewing.
- *Progressive download and play* is one of the most popular methods for delivering content over the Internet, and it is used by sites like YouTube. The technology is essentially identical to download and play, except the content is broken up into small files that are delivered as the content playback is occurring. Progressive D+P has the benefits of passing easily through firewalls while also delivering the speed and lower storage requirements of true streaming.

prior to viewing. In addition, these devices do not need an active network connection during playback, and these files can also be copied from one device to another, stored permanently, and sent to other users. Accordingly, podcasting and video file sharing are not really video-streaming systems at all—they are simply a method for delivering prerecorded content files to viewing device. Hence, they will be discussed in other sections of this book.

Now let's look at some of the applications of video streaming.

Shareholder Conferences

Narrowcasting is an effective way for small shareholders to listen to yearly or quarterly results conferences, because it allows participation without travel to the meeting location. With narrowcasting technology implemented over the public Internet, servers need to be set up to generate streams for each listener, as shown in Figure 2-4. Some of these servers can also simultaneously record the content that is being sent out so that the content can be made available for on-demand streaming after the end of the meeting.

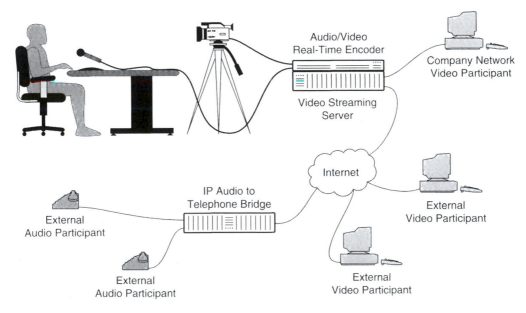

FIGURE 2-4 Internet-Enabled Shareholder Conference

Audio quality is one of the most important features of a shareholder meeting. Most of the new information being presented is in audible form. In particular, during meetings to discuss quarterly results, company management often takes questions from Wall Street analysts who follow the company's stock. Good IP audio quality ensures that all discussions will be audible to the shareholders.

Executive Speeches

Executive speeches (or what could be called "ego-casting") are commonly used by senior company executives to communicate with employees. Live streaming is a popular method for delivering these speeches to a number of employees at the same time. Multicasting uses private corporate networks and equipment such as routers to make copies of the stream for each user, removing the need to have servers create an individual stream for each viewing device (see Chapter 9 for details on multicasting). For employees who do not have PCs, hardware devices can be used to receive the stream from the network and display the content on a normal television.

High video quality is an important requirement for executive speeches. When private networks are used for distributing the streams, high-quality, high-bandwidth signals (such as MPEG-2 or MPEG-4; see Chapter 4) often can be used. For employees who are not attached to the corporate network, a low-resolution, low-bandwidth version of the stream can also be created and distributed over the Internet, or just the audio portion of the stream can be sent. A recording of the speech can also be made and placed on a server for on-demand viewing.

Corporate Training

Many corporations are using training to enhance the skills of their workforce, to improve quality and productivity, and to cut costs. Video training can remove the need for trainers to travel to each company location simply for the purpose of delivering the same presentation repeatedly. Instead, these trainers can focus on creating new content, and employees can view the training when and where they choose.

All three types of narrowcasting technology described previously are used for corporate training. Live streaming is used when multiple employees all need to be trained at the same time or for special events. On-demand streaming is used for classes delivered at each student's convenience. Download and play is used for remote or mobile users with low-bandwidth connections.

Sales Presentations

Narrowcasting can be used effectively to give information about a wide range of products and services to prospective customers. The presentations can be standardized for a wide range of viewers, or they can be custom-tailored for an individual customer. Any of the different types of narrowcasting technologies can be used.

An important consideration in designing video content for prospective customers is to understand the great variations in network capacities and display devices that customers may want to use. Creators must be careful to make sure they either produce content that is playable across many platforms and networks or produce several versions of the content to accommodate different viewer capabilities. Both desktop software and online services are available to create and manage various versions.

Internet Video and Audio Entertainment

Entertainment over the Internet has been an area of rapid change and innovation in the past decade. The rise and fall of Napster for audio file sharing has been well documented elsewhere. So has the rise of Apple's iTunes, podcasting, and other file-oriented content delivery systems. In parallel to these developments, content-streaming services have also increased their market presence, with YouTube and sites for many television broadcasters growing rapidly.

Content owners have a lot of impact on how audio and video content is provided over the Internet. Digital rights management (DRM) is an all-encompassing term that covers many different aspects of how content can be controlled, as listed in Table 2-3 and described in greater detail in Chapter 11.

TABLE 2-3

Functions of Digital Rights Management

- Scrambling or encrypting content
- Distributing encryption keys
- Managing user storage
- Tracking and limiting user playback
- Labeling content
- Managing licenses

Security, Traffic, and "Spy" Cameras

Security, traffic, and "spy" cameras are a common feature of modern life. They are used to provide surveillance of a large number of public spaces, including airports, streets, banks, casinos, and shopping malls. These cameras provide a number of benefits, including crime prevention, safety monitoring, and improved response times in emergencies. Small-scale installations, with a single camera and a recording device, are almost a fixture in businesses operating late at night, such as convenience stores and gasoline (petrol) stations.

In a traditional security camera installation, a television camera sends a video signal over a cable directly to a video monitor in a configuration known as closed-circuit television (CCTV). Early installations used a security guard to watch multiple video displays to monitor activity, but improvements have added devices to record the video and to automatically detect movement.

Security cameras are increasingly being connected to data networks, for a number of reasons, as shown in Table 2-4. Some additional

TABLE 2-4

Security Camera Data Network Benefits

- Multiple cameras can share a single data network cable or link.
- Several viewing stations can be set up, each of which can view video content from the same cameras.
- The need for video-switching equipment is greatly reduced or eliminated, because signal routing is controlled by IP addresses.
- The video network can be shared with other data applications, such as remote sensors or remotely controlled equipment.
- Commercial telecommunications networks can be used to form a backbone for large networks.

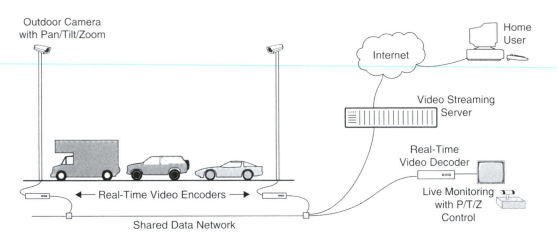

FIGURE 2-5 Network-Enabled Traffic Camera System

hardware is required to do this. First, the video signal needs to be converted into digital form and then compressed to take up less network bandwidth. Display devices must also be adapted to display the digital video signal. In many cases, this can be a desktop PC with video-viewing software. Today, many surveillance cameras have IP networking hardware built right in.

With networked digital video, it is relatively easy to make an automatic endless-loop recording of all the video flowing over a network. Also, if information such as time of day is recorded along with the video signal, users can quickly retrieve and view the content they desire. Audio transport is rarely needed; however, networks often need to transport other types of data. This can include data that comes from remote locations, such as fire alarms, smoke detectors, and intrusion sensors. The network can also be used to send out commands to the remote devices, such as rotating or zooming cameras and unlocking doors. Figure 2-5 shows a network-enabled system for gathering and distributing video images from traffic cameras.

THE TRUE MEANING OF "REAL TIME"

Real time is a common thread in discussions about video. For our discussion, we will use *real time* to refer to any activity performed

TABLE 2-5

Examples of Real-Time Video

* Radio and television broadcasting (including over-the-air, CATV, and satellite)
* Contribution networks for live events (such as sports or news)
* Videoconferencing
* Video streaming
* Highway surveillance
* Consumer video recording

with content that takes the same amount of time to complete as the duration of the content. For example, if sending a 27-minute program over a video network takes 27 minutes, then we would call that network a real-time network. Other examples of real-time activities include television broadcasts, recording of a live studio news program, and a videoconference. Table 2-5 gives a few examples of video applications that typically occur in real time.

Hard real time is an application in which success or failure depends on a low-delay video transport system. For example, a videoconference cannot take place if the video link is not up and running with minimal delay. Hard real time is required whenever live events are being broadcast (sports, awards shows, etc.) and whenever interactivity is needed. These applications place heavy demands on compression devices; dedicated, special-purpose hardware is typically used for professional video, particularly in HD applications. Hard-real-time applications that involve PC-based compression typically use reduced resolutions or reduced frame rates (or both) to simplify the compression task. IPTV networks are typically implemented using hard-real-time video.

Soft real time is any application that needs to occur in real time but that can be interrupted or delayed without creating complete failure of the application. Most Internet video is delivered in soft real time; if the video pauses to perform "buffering" during playback, most users will continue watching. Television broadcast networks also sometimes use soft real time for delivering advertisements and programming to affiliate broadcast stations—if an interruption occurs, the program can be redelivered as long as it arrives before the scheduled broadcast time.

Soft-real-time and non-real-time video is often compressed in advance of transmission. This greatly simplifies the compression task. PC-based software applications can produce high-quality compressed video when given adequate time to complete the task.

VIDEO TRANSPORT ECONOMICS

Many different benefits can be used to justify the costs of installing video transport systems. Broadly speaking, they can be sorted into two areas: revenue enhancement and cost reduction. Sometimes both can come into play. Table 2-6 lists some of the ways that companies have justified their use of video transport networks.

Video Content Costs

There are many different kinds of ownership models, but one of the most common is the ownership of entertainment content by television networks. For anyone interested in the video delivery business, it is important to understand the costs of obtaining the necessary content.

Content can generally be obtained inexpensively from local broadcast stations, partly because of the need for those stations to reach local viewers who generally don't receive their programming via over-the-air

TABLE 2-6

Video Transport Network Business Benefits

Revenue Enhancement

- Sell video content on a pay-per-view or a subscription basis
- Provide in-depth information to customers
- Increase effectiveness of sales presentations, and improve company sales
- Provide customers with interactive video help services
- Provide demonstrations of merchandise

Cost Reduction

- Improve productivity
- Develop employee skills and provide cross-training
- Increase customer and employee retention
- Reduce travel costs for customers, employees, and training staff

---

TABLE 2-7

Sample Fees for Cable TV Programming

Network Name	Fee per Subscriber per Month
ESPN	3.26
Fox Sports Net	1.94
TNT	0.91
Disney Channel	0.83
HD Net	0.81
NFL Network	0.80
ESPN HD	0.77
NHL Network	0.51
HDNet Movies	0.50
USA	0.50

Source: © 2008 SNL Kagan, a division of SNL Financial LC. All rights reserved. Used with permission.

broadcasts. For many other channels of programming, particularly those that are carried only on CATV and direct-to-home satellite systems, the delivery system operators pay monthly fees to the programmers. Table 2-7 lists some of the fees charged per subscriber per month for popular cable TV channels in the United States in 2007.

Together, these fees total $10.83 per subscriber per month. Since most of these channels are part of the basic offerings provided by CATV and DTH providers, these costs need to be paid out of the subscriber basic fees. For many delivery providers, these fees range from $20.00 to $40.00 per month, for anywhere from 20 to 50 channels. All told, it is easy to see how programming content costs can consume upwards of one-third to one-half of a delivery provider's revenues.

Consumer Video Business Modeling

Supplying video content to consumers can be a very lucrative business. After all, broadcasters and cable television operators have been doing it for years. Table 2-8 lists and explains some of the many factors that contribute to the costs of these systems.

Many new service providers explicitly go after "triple-play" services, where each consumer is offered video, voice (telephony), and data

TABLE 2-8

Consumer Video Cost Factors

- *Government permits and franchise fees*: These fees are paid to governments in exchange for the rights to construct and operate video delivery services.
- *Rights of way*: Payments may be required to gain physical access to property for installing a cable or placing a wireless transmitter or receiver.
- *Government mandates*: These can range widely, but it is very common for governments to require service providers to offer public access channels, distance learning services, and television coverage of local government meetings.
- *Network equipment and cable purchases*: These include equipment to gather programming from a variety of sources (such as satellites and local broadcasters), format video for distribution, control subscriber access, transmit and receive video signals, and support and bill customers.
- *Installation labor*: Installation labor usually comes in two phases: first, the cost to deploy the common equipment in each served area, and then the cost to connect or disconnect individual customers.
- *Cost of capital*: This can be either interest on money borrowed from a bank or the return that is promised to investors in the operation or both.
- *Consumer marketing*: Consumers need to be convinced that any services are going to be worth their expense. Marketing costs will tend to be high when a system is new and to decline somewhat over time, but this should be budgeted as a permanent, ongoing expense.
- *Programming fees*: These can easily eat up half of the consumer revenue from selling video services. Fortunately, these fees tend to be based on the number of actual subscribers, and so they will be low when the take rate is low. Staff will also be required to manage content ownership rights and to ensure that the content is being delivered as specified in the content usage contracts.
- *Program/channel guides*: Many modern video-delivery services can have hundreds of channels of programming available. For viewers to be able to find the channels they want to view, some form of program guide needs to be made available. Fortunately, there are commercial services that consolidate this information from a huge variety of program providers and then resell this information to delivery service providers.
- *Customer service and order entry*: The value of professional, efficient order entry staff should not be underestimated, and this can improve customer satisfaction and retention.
- *System maintenance*: Given human nature and Mother Nature, repairs and service changes are part of doing business. This continual expense must be budgeted, even for a brand-new installation.

---

service all from a single supplier. This strategy can work well, particularly if consumers are dissatisfied with their current suppliers. Many carriers offer package discounts to customers who purchase two or three of the triple-play services. Although the actual cost savings to the provider for offering a triple-play is debatable, there is little doubt about the marketing benefits of this approach.

REVIEW AND CHECKLIST UPDATE

In this chapter, we looked at some of the applications of video transport. We began with entertainment, by defining the difference between contribution, distribution, and delivery networks. We discussed the differences in performance and cost that are required by these three applications. We also glanced at live sports and advertising, and saw how their requirements differ from other types of programming. We discussed a number of applications of interactive television, such as videoconferencing, telemedicine, distance education, and telejustice. We covered streaming video and the use of both prerecorded and live video to serve applications such as shareholder meetings, executive speeches, training, entertainment, and security cameras. We defined hard and soft real time, and discussed their differences. Finally, we looked at some of the factors that can impact the business case for a video delivery network. One major cost, which is easy to overlook, is the cost of programming. For DTH and CATV systems, programming costs can easily consume one-third or more of the service provider's revenues.

Chapter 2 Checklist Update

❑ If the application is entertainment television, determine if the network will be used primarily for contribution, distribution, or delivery.

❑ If the network will be used for contribution, consider using lightly compressed or uncompressed video signals for feeds where lots of postproduction work will be done.

❑ If the network is to be used for distribution, make sure that all categories of delivery providers can be reached as required by the application. Also, make sure that the network is reliable enough to handle this class of traffic.

❑ If the network is to be used for delivery, determine the number of subscribers that will be served simultaneously. Make sure that the chosen delivery system can scale up to this number. Also, consider the costs that will be incurred to equip each new viewer.

❑ For interactive video, make sure that the video quality is high enough to suit the application and that the delay is low.

Generally, lower delay is more important than video quality, except for applications that require high image fidelity (e.g., telemedicine).

❏ For narrowcasting, determine if live feeds will be required, or if content can be stored and then streamed. If live feeds are required, then real-time video compression equipment will also be needed.

❏ For live narrowcasting, determine how many viewers will be served simultaneously, and select a mechanism to create an adequate number of streams for all the viewers.

❏ When creating a business plan for a video delivery system, make sure that all the key factors are analyzed. Pay close attention to costs for obtaining necessary permits and the costs of providing content security.

❏ Make sure that content/programming costs are included in any video delivery system business case.

3

VIDEO BASICS

A basic understanding of video and audio signals will make our discussions of video transport much easier to comprehend and to put in context. Readers with video experience may choose to skip this chapter, but be advised that this terminology will be used in the remainder of this book. By the end of this chapter, readers should have a good understanding of the different types of analog and digital video signals, should have gained some background about audio and other signals that can accompany video signals, and should have had a brief look at some of the different ways in which video and audio signals can be switched.

PIXELS, LUMA, SCANNING, AND CHROMA

Any discussion of video needs to start with the definition of some basic terms, and our discussion will be no different. We'll briefly introduce each term and then explain each one in more detail in the following sections.

- A *pixel* is a single picture element in a digital video image; it is the building block for all forms of digital imaging, including both still photography and video.
- *Luma* is the portion of a video signal that represents the brightness of each pixel. Maximum luma is used for an all-white pixel, and minimum luma is a black (or off) pixel.
- *Scanning* is the process used in a video signal for capturing, storing, transporting, and displaying the luma and chroma values of each pixel. Scanning puts the information for each pixel in a specific order so that video equipment can determine the information that belongs to each pixel.
- *Chroma* is the portion of a video signal that represents the color of each pixel. Colors are intended to range over the full spectrum of the human visual system, from red through green and blue, in any combination.

Each of these terms is defined in greater depth in the following sections.

Pixels

Computer displays, digital cameras, document scanners, and many other devices are specified in terms of pixels. Digital video images are also described in terms of pixels, so it is important to get a good understanding of this concept.

A pixel is the smallest possible picture element that can be represented by a digital image. Each pixel can be thought of as a single tiny dot of color that represents a portion of an image. If you magnify any digital image sufficiently, you will see that it is made up of thousands or millions of these tiny dots, each of which is a single pixel. This is true whether the image has been photographed by a digital camera (still or video), captured by a digital scanner (or facsimile machine), displayed on a digital monitor (television or computer), printed on a digital printer, or created by graphics software inside a computer or a video game console.

A pixel is similar in concept to a single character on a page of text or a single byte of data on a computer's hard drive. Taken by itself, a pixel doesn't carry very much information. However, when a pixel is combined with thousands or millions of other pixels, a very realistic image can be created. Also, as the number of pixels in an image increases, so does the amount of detail that can be represented in the image.

Like a character of text or a byte of data, each pixel has a value. This value represents the pixel's color (or hue) and the pixel's intensity (or saturation). For a still image, the value for each pixel is fixed. For television systems in North America and Japan, the information for each pixel is updated just about 30 times per second; in much of the rest of the world, each pixel on a television screen is updated 25 times per second.

In addition to its value, each pixel has a location. This location is defined in both the vertical dimension (up and down the image) and the horizontal dimension (across the image from left to right). All of the pixels for an image must be sent in the correct order to a display device so that each one ends up at its assigned location on the video display. This order proceeds from left to right across the display and from the top to the bottom of the screen. We will discuss this process (called *scanning*) in more detail shortly.

Pixel displays can be formed in many different ways. In a cathode ray tube (CRT) display, each pixel is a small group of dots of phosphor. The phosphor dots give off light when hit by an electron beam (or cathode ray). For color television, the smallest possible pixel is made up of three different colored dots, one red, one blue, and one green, as shown in Figure 3-1.[1]

Liquid crystal displays (LCDs) use liquid crystals (chemicals that can be used to block or pass light based on an electrical signal) and a light source to create a viewable image, either directly on a glass sheet or by projecting the light onto a screen. Plasma displays use electron beams and phosphors just like a CRT, except each pixel

---

1. It is possible for a pixel in an image to cover several pixels in a display. This commonly happens, for example, when a high-resolution display (such as an HD display) is used to show a low-resolution image (such as a standard-definition image). But we are getting ahead of ourselves here.

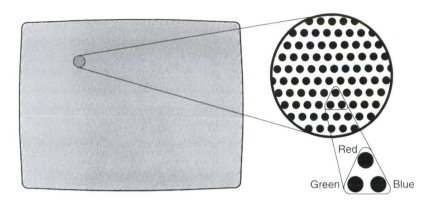

FIGURE 3-1   Typical Phosphor Dot Pattern on a Television Display

has its own microscopic beam source. Large outdoor displays can use thousands upon thousands of light-emitting diodes (LEDs, just like the ones used as power indicators on electronic devices) in three different colors to create an image. And finally, Digital Light Processing® (DLP) projectors use devices from Texas Instruments containing millions of movable microscopic mirrors to reflect light from three different color light sources onto a display screen.

Luma

The luma (or luminance) portion of a video signal contains information about the brightness (or intensity) of a video signal as perceived by the human eye. Pixels with a high luma value appear brighter to a viewer than pixels with a low luma value.

The luma signal carries a significant portion of the information contained in a video signal. The human visual system is very sensitive to changes in brightness of an image, and much of the information carried in the fine details of the image is due to changes in brightness, not color. One example of this would be an image of a person's hair: All of the strands of hair are essentially the same color, but the fine detail of the image is contained in the patterns of light and dark. If the luma portion of the signal becomes degraded, then the overall quality of the video image suffers.

An easy way actually to observe just the luma portion of a video image is to modify the settings of a television set to remove all the color from the signal (usually by way of an on-screen menu or a knob). The resulting image, which appears to be black and white, is a good approximation of the luma portion of a video signal.

The luma signal is a legacy of the original black-and-white television transmission systems. (Technically, old televisions should be called grayscale or monochrome.) When color television broadcasts began, virtually the entire installed base of televisions was monochrome, so the luma signal was retained in the video signal for use by these sets. However, the luma signal still has important uses to this day, which we will discuss in later sections.

Scanning

Scanning is the technique whereby the luma and chroma values for a video image are captured, stored, delivered, and/or displayed in sequential order. Scanning always works from left to right, so for each horizontal line the leftmost pixel of the image is scanned first and the rightmost pixel is scanned last (see Figure 3-2). At the end of each line, a short horizontal *blanking interval* is inserted to indicate when one horizontal line stops and the next begins.

A video signal is sent as a sequence of horizontal scan lines, one after the other. Each scan line contains the picture data for one row of pixels. If we were to look at the waveform of one scan line and see how it

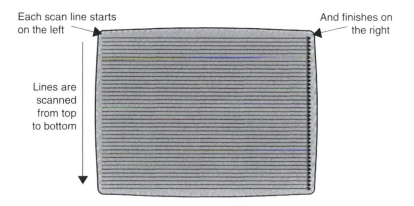

FIGURE 3-2 Video Display Scanning

changes over time, we would get something that looks like Figure 3-3. In this diagram, brighter pixels are represented by higher-level signals and darker pixels are lower-level signals.

To make scanning work properly, accurate synchronization is required. A little before the picture data in each horizontal scan line is a horizontal synchronization pulse, as shown in Figure 3-3. This pulse occurs at exactly the same time interval before the start of the first pixel signal on every horizontal line. The display detects these pulses and makes sure that each line on the display is aligned so that vertical objects in the image (which are made up from pixels on many different horizontal lines) appear vertical on the display.

The video signal also contains specially formatted horizontal lines called *vertical synchronization* that indicate which horizontal line is the first one to be drawn across the display. The display recognizes

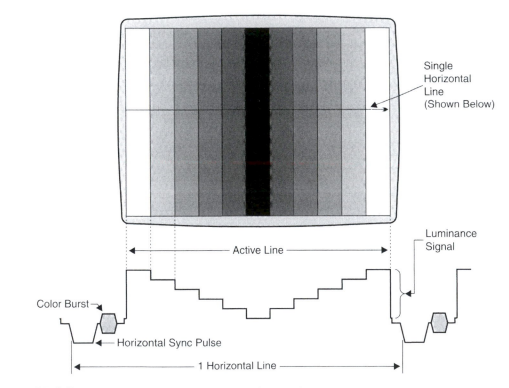

FIGURE 3-3 Horizontal Scan Line, Showing Sync Pulse

this pattern and is then able to place the first horizontal scan line of the actual image on the top row of pixels on the display.

Chroma

The chroma portion of a video signal carries the information that is needed to create a color image. This signal works in conjunction with the luma signal described earlier; neither one alone is adequate to produce a normal full-color, full-resolution video image.

Color displays differ from monochrome displays in that each pixel has three colored phosphor dots in place of one white phosphor dot. The colors are red, green, and blue, because basically all the colors that the eye can see can be represented by a combination of these three colors. In LCD displays, each pixel is made up of three individual liquid crystals, each having a different-colored light output (created with colored filters). In a plasma display, each colored dot gets its own electron gun. In a large-format LED display, each pixel is made up of three different-colored LEDs.

For short distances, sending the video color components as three different signals is easy—three distinct signal paths are needed. This is why a VGA video connector has multiple pairs of pins to connect between a computer and a display. These systems of cables and connectors are sometimes called "RGB" because they carry red, green, and blue video signals on separate wires.

The luma signal can be created from the RGB signal by combining the red, green, and blue signals in different proportions. Since the eye is most sensitive to green, the green component makes up the largest amount of the luma signal, with smaller weightings of red and blue. This new signal is called Y, to distinguish it from R, G, and B. Two other chroma signals can also be created based on the human visual system to carry the remaining color information; these are called B-Y or P_B and R-Y or P_R. Each of these chroma signals is used in both analog and digital video compression, because each of them contains less information than raw blue and red signals. This is also why three cables are still needed for analog component video (both SD and HD).

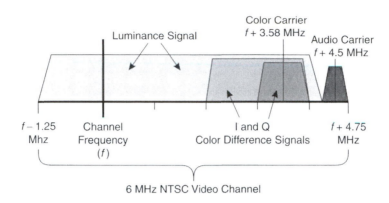

FIGURE 3-4   RF Spectrum of NTSC Color Video Signal

For analog video (including rapidly disappearing analog broadcast television) in the National Television System Committee (NTSC) color system, two other color-difference signals are used: the I and Q signals. These are modulated onto an RF carrier operating at 3.58 MHz, also known as the color carrier, and combined with the luminance signal to form a composite signal, as shown in Figure 3-4. A similar scheme is used in the Phase Alternating Line (PAL) system, except a different set of color-difference signals, called U and V, are used, and the color carrier is at 4.43 MHz.

TYPES OF VIDEO

Video signals come in many different flavors. This has occurred for three main reasons:

- *Different functional requirements:* For some applications, maximum possible quality is important, such as for computer workstations used to create special effects for cinematic movies. In other cases, quality can be compromised to make video signals affordable for mass distribution.
- *Changing limits of technology:* Techniques that are feasible today were not possible even 5 years ago. Amazingly, some standards developed 50 years ago are still being used.

- *Different development locations:* North America and Europe have long had different video standards, and the differences continue to this day. In the past few decades Japan has also emerged as a major center of video technology development, particularly for videotape and camera signal formats.

These factors have combined to create many different types of video signals, each of which has benefits and drawbacks. Numerous companies derive revenue from supplying products to change video signals from one standard to another. Let's look at the most common varieties of video.

Composite Video

A composite video signal contains all of the information required to form a full-motion, full-color image on a television screen. A composite signal is normally sent on a single coaxial cable between devices such as a videotape player and a television set. (Many consumer systems use a yellow connector, labeled "video" on the device.) Composite video signals are also used for normal analog television broadcasts, and in this case they also contain audio information.

Several different composite color video standards are used around the world:

- *NTSC* video is used in North and Central America, Japan, South Korea, Taiwan, most portions of South America, the Caribbean, and several other countries, including the Philippines. NTSC signals contain 525 interlaced horizontal lines and use a 3.58-MHz color carrier and a refresh rate of 29.97 frames per second.
- *PAL* video is used in most countries in Europe and many in Africa, the Middle East, Asia, and part of South America. Germany, China, India, and the UK all use the PAL system. PAL signals contain 625 interlaced horizontal lines and use a 4.43-MHz color carrier and a refresh rate of 25 frames per second.[2]

2. In Brazil, television broadcasts use the standard of 525 lines/29.97 frames per second but the PAL color system. Other exceptions can exist but are relatively rare.

- *SECAM* video is used in France, countries of the former Soviet Union, North Africa, and a number of other countries. Like PAL, SECAM video signals contain 625 horizontal lines that are each transmitted 25 times per second. The main difference between SECAM and PAL is the method for transmitting the chroma signals.
- **Note**: Most NTSC signals operate at 29.97 frames per second, and most PAL and SECAM signals operate at 25 frames per second. For readers who work with the exceptions (and for those who work with SECAM), please excuse the occasional lapse into using NTSC and PAL as shorthand for the two different frame rates.

Composite video has been used since the dawn of the television era. Analog over-the-air broadcasts contain a composite video signal and an audio signal (more on audio later in this chapter). Many consumer television sets have composite video inputs, which can receive signals from other consumer devices, such as VCRs, camcorders, cable TV set-top boxes, and game consoles. As with any video format, composite video has a number of benefits and drawbacks, which are discussed in Table 3-1.

S-Video

S-video signals are similar to composite video signals, with one crucial difference. In S-video, luma information and chroma information are

TABLE 3-1

Advantages and Disadvantages of Composite Video

Advantages

- Huge number of display devices available throughout the world.
- Low-cost signal sources and recorders, such as VCRs.
- All the required video signals are on a single conductor, so cables and switches can be simple and inexpensive.

Disadvantages

- The chroma and luma signals can interfere with each other, causing some degradation in the displayed image.
- The wide variety of composite standards (PAL, NTSC, SECAM, etc.) drives up complexity for video producers.
- Television displays need sophisticated signal-processing devices, called *comb filters*, to separate the luma and chroma signals in order to produce a high-quality image.

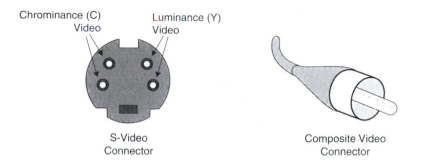

FIGURE 3-5   S-Video and Composite Video Connectors

carried on different wires. This is why an S-video cable has four pins: one pair for the chroma signal (I+Q for NTSC, U+V for PAL) and another pair for the luma (Y) (plus an outer shield, for those quibblers in the audience). See Figure 3-5 for an illustration of these connectors.

S-video can be found on a number of consumer video devices, including video displays, DVD players, digital camcorders, set-top boxes for CATV, and video game consoles, among other devices.

In general, for point-to-point consumer and semiprofessional applications, S-video should be used whenever feasible in place of composite video. S-video avoids combining and then separating the chrominance and luminance signals in the signal source. Table 3-2 shows some of the advantages and disadvantages of S-video.

TABLE 3-2

Advantages and Disadvantages of S-Video

Advantages

- Many modern consumer devices have S-video inputs and/or outputs.
- Separated chrominance and luminance signals can give better picture quality.

Disadvantages

- Cabling and connectors are slightly more complicated than for composite video; video switches require two signal paths for each video signal.
- S-video format is still closely related to composite, so a wide variety of video standards still needs to be accommodated.

Component Analog Video

Component analog video offers benefits over composite and S-video. Because different color signals are carried on different sets of conductors, processing of the signals is kept to a minimum. The two main flavors of component video are as follows:

- *RGB* component video uses one conductor for each of the three main video component signals: red, green, and blue. Each signal carries a full-resolution image, with data for every pixel. RGB component video requires the least amount of processing inside a display because the signals are directly compatible with the signals inside analog displays.
- *YUV* or *YP$_B$P$_R$* (also known as Y R-Y B-Y) component video signals use three signal paths: one for a luminance signal (Y) and one for each of two color-difference signals (U and V or P$_B$ and P$_R$). These three signals are manipulated inside the display to form the fundamental R, G, and B signals for display.

Both RGB and YUV/YP$_B$P$_R$ signals require three or more signal paths, depending on the method chosen for sending the synchronization signals. Three main standards exist:

- *Sync on green* (or on Y) requires three signal paths. This method uses one of the three signals (typically the green signal or the Y signal) to carry the horizontal and vertical synchronization information.
- *Separate composite sync* uses a fourth signal path to carry the synchronization data, including both the horizontal and the vertical synchronization.
- *Separate horizontal and vertical sync* uses a total of five signal paths: one for each color signal, one for horizontal sync, and one for vertical sync. This system is used by virtually all computer monitors and was part of the original Video Graphics Adapter (VGA) de facto standard.

Table 3-3 shows some of the advantages and disadvantages of component analog video.

TABLE 3-3

Advantages and Disadvantages of Component Analog Video

Advantages

- Highest-possible-quality analog video.
- Suitable for editing and postproduction use in professional applications.

Disadvantages

- Requires more cables (up to five for separate vertical and horizontal sync), thereby making cables and switches more complex and expensive.
- Delay through each one of the signal paths must be identical to all the others—if one cable is longer or shorter than the others, then objects can display ghosts or color fringes on the screen.

High-Definition Video

High-definition video (also known as high-definition television, HDTV, or simply HD) offers much more detail in video images because it uses many more pixels than standard video. These added pixels allow much larger video displays to be used without the loss of sharpness that can come from simply enlarging a standard-definition video signal.

HD signals use a different aspect ratio for the video image. For SD television signals (and many common computer displays), the aspect ratio is 4:3, meaning that the video image is 4 units wide by 3 units high. For most HDTV signals, the aspect ratio is 16:9, which is one-third wider than 4:3. The wider aspect ratio of HDTV was chosen in part to make it closer to the aspect ratios used in most films. Figure 3-6 gives a comparison of the different image sizes and aspect ratios for popular SD and HD video formats.

Two main HD formats are used around the world today, 720p and 1080i, and each of these is available at two different frame rates. NTSC countries use 1080-line interlaced video at a frame rate of 29.97 and 720-line progressively scanned video at a frame rate of 59.94. PAL/ SECAM countries operate 1080i at 25 frames per second and 720p at 50 frames per second. In some countries, broadcasters are free to choose either 1080i or 720p; in other countries a single format is used, such as Japan, where all the major broadcasters use 1080i.

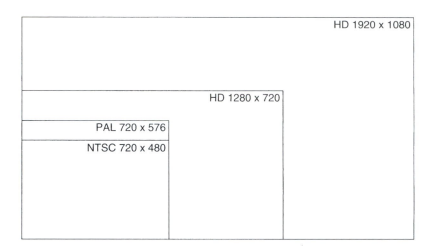

FIGURE 3-6   Comparison of SD and HD formats

The benefits of HD come at a price, both in terms of money and technology (see Table 3-4). HD signals don't really offer any benefit to viewers at small screen sizes, so HD displays tend to be large. HD broadcast signals are always digital and always delivered to consumers in compressed form. HD signals are decompressed either in a digital TV tuner, in a set-top box, or inside the display itself.

Serial Digital Video

Within the world of professional video production, virtually all new equipment installed today is digital. Video cameras produce digital

TABLE 3-4

Advantages and Disadvantages of High-Definition Video

Advantages

- Much more image detail, with many more pixels on display.
- Some versions are suitable for use in creating cinema feature films.

Disadvantages

- Requires HDTV-compatible equipment throughout the production chain, including video cameras, videotape or video disk recorders, broadcast equipment, and video displays.
- Uses compression to permit broadcasting within existing television broadcast channels, which can add considerable expense for both broadcaster and end customer.

outputs that go to digital tape recorders or digital video. Video-editing suites have also gone all digital—video content is converted into digital form and manipulated using software.

The format used in production for standard-definition digital video goes by a variety of names, including SDI, SMPTE 259 M, 270 Mbit, CCIR 601, ITU-R BT.601, and sometimes D1. This signal, which we will call SDI (Serial Digital Interface) in this book, operates at 270 Mbps and contains a single, component, serial, digital video signal. This format can accommodate both 625-line (PAL) and 525-line (NTSC) signals. SDI is a component video format, so the signal is carried in three data streams: a luminance signal (Y) and two color-difference signals (called C_B and C_R in digital form, but similar to the color-difference signals P_B and P_R discussed earlier in this chapter).

The SDI data stream is created by sampling the luma signal at a rate of 13.5 million times per second, and each color-difference signal at half that rate. At these rates, for every four luma samples, there are two C_R samples and two C_B samples, which gives this pattern the name 4:2:2. At 10 bits per sample, the luma signal generates 135 Mbps, and the two color-difference signals generate 67.5 Mbps each, for a total of 270 Mbps. Some of the samples are converted into special codes to control vertical and horizontal synchronization.

There is also a high-definition serial digital signal, commonly called SMPTE 292M, or HD-SDI (High-Definition Serial Digital Interface) that operates at 1485 Mbps, which is more than five times the data rate of the SDI signal. Just like SDI, HD-SDI uses 10-bit samples with a 4:2:2 sampling pattern.

Some other digital video formats are used, such as DV, DVC, and DVCAM, among others, often based on consumer videotape formats. Many of these formats are compressed signals and are used primarily by video camera and videotape recorder manufacturers. Also, a number of editing systems can work with these video formats. Because of the variety of these signals and because these formats can be converted easily into SDI signals to work with other equipment and for MPEG and other types of compression, we won't discuss them in detail in this book.

TABLE 3-5
Advantages and Disadvantages of Serial Digital Interface (SDI) Video

Advantages

- Very robust signal; small variations in signal amplitude or noise can be ignored by the digital format.
- Easy to transport and switch inside a production facility.
- A wide variety of equipment is available for use in all applications, including cameras, recorders, switchers, editors, displays, special effects units, and many other types of gear.
- Many converters are available for handling the changes to and from SDI and composite, component, or other analog video formats.
- Related signals, such as digital audio or program-related data, can be embedded into the SDI signal for ease of transport and switching.

Disadvantages

- Requires SDI-compatible equipment on both ends of each connection.
- Much of the equipment that handles SDI is considered professional level and can be expensive.
- High-bit-rate signals (270 Mbps for standard definition, 1485 Mbps for high definition) can be difficult and expensive to transport over wide area networks.

SDI and HD-SDI signals are used as a standardized video format for MPEG and other compression devices. Most other types of analog and digital signals are converted to SDI or HD-SDI prior to compression. Table 3-5 shows some of the advantages and disadvantages of digital video.

Consumer Digital Video

SDI and HD-SDI signals are not used in a typical consumer's home. Instead, Digital Visual Interface (DVI) and High-Definition Multimedia Interface (HDMI) connectors are used, as shown in Figure 3-7. A big advantage of these connections is that they are bidirectional, which allows a video source to determine the capabilities of the display device and also to encrypt the signal. Both these capabilities are crucial to the success of digital television, because scaling of 720p and 1080i signals is required to display correctly on the many different pixel counts used in consumer screens, and content security is required by the providers of HD content.

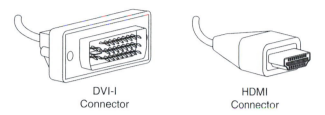

DVI-I
Connector

HDMI
Connector

FIGURE 3-7 DVI and HDMI Video Connectors

DVI carries digital or analog video signals; audio is carried separately. DVI connectors are found on many computer monitors and video graphics cards, and for a while they were used on some brands of televisions. Now this connector tends to be found more often in computer displays, not home video applications.

HDMI carries both digital video and audio signals. It builds upon the DVI spec by adding digital audio capability to the same cable, but it retains electrical compatibility to the DVI-Digital specification. HDMI appears to be the HD connection of choice for new consumer televisions.

Content security is ensured by a technology called HDCP, for High-bandwidth Digital Content Protection. Before an HDCP source can send signals to an HDCP display, a handshaking process must first take place to ensure that the connection is only to a display and that unauthorized copies of the content will not be made by a recording device. If the handshake process fails, then only limited-resolution video or no signal will be sent over the interface.

Internet Video

So far in this chapter we have been talking about traditional video signals, ones that can be delivered directly to a video display over a simple cable. In contrast, video signals delivered over the Internet require a device such as a computer or a set-top box to decode the signals properly prior to display.

All video sent over the Internet to consumers is compressed using one of the many types of compression techniques available today. Both audio and video signals must be decompressed via hardware or software before they can be delivered to the viewer. Helper applications (called *plug-ins*) are used by standard web browser software to perform the decoding; popular brands include Adobe Flash, Apple QuickTime, and Windows Media, to name a few. Internet video signals can be essentially any number of horizontal and vertical pixels, and there is a wide selection of content protection and packet delivery techniques. With all the different permutations available, Internet video providers are able to develop their own standard formats, so video produced for one site may not be directly compatible with other hosting sites.

Flexibility is also a key element of Internet video players. Viewers are free to stop, start, rewind, and pause playback at any time. Viewers can also control how large the images appear on their displays and can select from a variety of player screen formats.

Video signals are not easy to identify as they transit over the Internet or a private network. The compressed video and audio content is contained in standard IP packets, just like all other kinds of data. These packets flow over the same networks and are switched by the same routing equipment as any other data. About the only distinguishing feature is the higher sustained flow rate of video streams—a one-minute YouTube video could require a thousand packets to be delivered to the viewer.

Internet video is quite different from broadcast television in the user experience. Not only do viewers have more control over the video playback, but they are also required to seek out and select the content that they want to watch. This is quite a contrast to the continuous 7×24 streams of broadcast TV that are delivered to millions of viewers simultaneously. Two downsides to this freedom are a lack of quality control for the technical aspects of the video and audio signals as well as huge inconsistencies in the esthetics of the video pieces; many Internet viewers have become accustomed to viewing a mixed bag of worthwhile and worthless content.

VIDEO FIELDS AND FRAMES

Image frames are the fundamental units of motion imaging. Very simply, a frame is a single still image out of the sequence of images that make up a motion image. A field is a portion of a frame; in inter-laced video, two fields, each with half the horizontal lines of the total image, form one frame.

Frame Rate

Anyone who has ever looked at the film used in a movie projector knows that the film contains a series of still pictures. Each picture is slightly different from its predecessors, and when the pictures are shown to a viewer in rapid succession, the viewer perceives the image to be moving (hence the familiar term *motion pictures*). The images in a movie camera are captured at the rate of 24 photographic images each second, or 24 fps (frames per second).

A television camera operates in a similar way. Instead of film, an electronic image sensor is used. Each pixel on the image sensor captures a signal that depends on the intensity of the light that hits it. Each time a complete image (every pixel on the image sensor) is captured and read out, a complete video frame is said to have occurred. In television, two main frame rates are used: 25 and 29.97 fps.

Frame Height

A video frame is made up of a number of horizontal lines of video, stacked vertically to form the video image. The frame height is just the count of the number of lines in the visible portion of the video signal. Four different frame heights are commonly used around the world; these are listed in Table 3-6. Confusingly, the smaller-line-height images are commonly known by their total line count, whereas the HD ones are known by their image size. Also note that "i" means interlaced scanning and "p" means progressive; we will discuss these topics shortly.

Each video format includes a number of lines called the vertical blanking interval (VBI) because they are turned off, or "blanked," so that they don't appear as part of the visible image. A special ver-tical sync pattern is inserted into some of these "unused" lines that

TABLE 3-6

Common Video Frame Heights

Total Lines	Viewable Image	VBI	Common Name
525	480–486	39–45	525i/NTSC
625	574–576	49–51	625i/PAL
750	720	30	720p
1125	1080	45	1080i

identifies the first horizontal line of the video image so that the display can correctly position it. The VBI can also be used for lots of other interesting stuff, like closed captioning data and teletext, which we will discuss later in this chapter.

In video, we define *resolution* as the number of lines of alternating black and white that can be seen on the display. A pattern for testing vertical image resolution is shown in Figure 3-8A. The number of lines that can normally be resolved is about 30 percent less than the number of horizontal scan lines used by the camera. So, for example, an image with 576 visible horizontal lines has a useful vertical resolution of about 400 lines.

Horizontal Resolution

Simply put, horizontal resolution is a count of the number of alternating black and white lines that can be distinguished going across

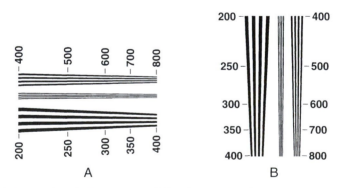

FIGURE 3-8   (A) Vertical and (B) Horizontal Resolution Test Patterns

a display horizontally. See Figure 3-8B for an illustration of a test image for horizontal resolution, which is measured in terms of lines per picture height (or LPH). This measurement relates the horizontal resolution of an image to the height of the image, in lines.

All sorts of factors affect the amount of horizontal resolution in an image. For example, the most common digital format for television production and compression uses 720 pixels for the active video image in each horizontal line for both 625-line and 525-line systems. This is not the actual resolution because it is further constrained by the circuits that are used to process the signal. These factors bring the actual horizontal resolution of the digital signal down to about 455 LPH.[3] In comparison, Super-VHS has a horizontal resolution of 300 LPH, and standard VHS has horizontal resolution of about 190 LPH.

Several other frame heights and widths are used in video compression, as shown in Table 3-7. Many videoconferencing systems use CIF, the Common Intermediate Format, which has 352 pixels on each of 288 lines. 4CIF (or 4 times CIF) has 704 pixels on each of 576 lines. QCIF (or Quarter CIF) has 176 pixels on each of 144 lines. Some video compression systems use a format that is called half-D1, with 352 pixels on each line of either 525- or 625-line systems. Note that any of these can be displayed on a standard NTSC or PAL monitor with appropriate scaling in the decoder.

Computer Image Resolution

The computer industry has adopted a significantly different meaning for the term *resolution*. If a computer image is said to have a resolution of 640 × 480 (standard Video Graphics Adapter, or VGA), it will have an active picture size that is 640 pixels wide by 480 pixels high. Table 3-8 shows the image height and width for a number of popular computer graphics formats.

---

3.   Michael Robin, *Television in Transition* (Saint-Laurent, Quebec: Miranda Technologies, 2001), p. 67.

TABLE 3-7

Image Sizes Commonly Used in Video Compression[1] (width in pixels × height in lines)

1920 × 1080 high definition
1280 × 720 high definition
 720 × 576 PAL (625-line) full resolution
 720 × 480 NTSC (525-line) full resolution
 704 × 576 4CIF[2]
 352 × 576 PAL (625-line) half-D1 resolution
 352 × 480 NTSC (525-line) half-D1 resolution
 352 × 288 CIF[3]
 176 × 144 QCIF[4]

[1]The HD image sizes in this list have an aspect ratio of 16:9. All of the other image sizes have a 4:3 aspect ratio.
[2]Resolution equal to four times that of CIF (see following footnote).
[3]CIF stands for Common Intermediate Format, often used in both PAL and NTSC videoconferencing systems.
[4]Resolution equal to one Quarter CIF Resolution.

TABLE 3-8

Popular Computer Graphics Image Sizes (width in pixels × height in pixels)

 640 × 480 VGA
 800 × 600 SVGA
1024 × 768 XGA
1280 × 1024 SXGA
1600 × 1200 UXGA

Progressive and Interlaced Scanning

Two different methods of horizontal scanning are commonly used for video: progressive and interlaced. In progressive scanning (the "p" from Table 3-6), every horizontal line in the image is scanned sequentially from the top of the image to the bottom. In other words, in each frame line 1 is scanned first, followed by line 2, then line 3, and so on. The left-hand image in Figure 3-9 illustrates a progressively scanned image.

Interlaced scanning (the "i" from Table 3-6) is different. In interlaced scanning, first only the odd-numbered lines of the frame are scanned in order from the top to the bottom of the image. Then the even-numbered lines are scanned from top to bottom. In other words, in

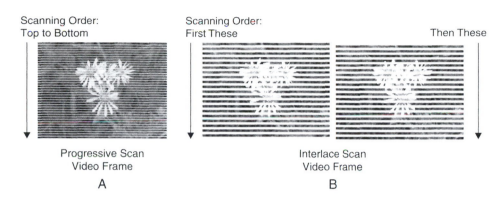

FIGURE 3-9 (A) Progressive and (B) Interlaced Scanning

each frame line 1 of the image is scanned first, followed by line 3, then line 5, etc., all the way to the bottom of the frame. Then scanning starts over again at the top of the frame with line 2, then line 4, line 6, etc. The first set of scan lines is called the *odd field*, and the second set is called the *even field*. So, for a video image that is running at 25 fps, interlaced scanning actually provides 50 fields per second: 25 odd ones and 25 even ones. The right-hand image in Figure 3-9 illustrates the concept of interlaced scanning.

Progressive scanning is used pretty much universally for computer graphics displays, primarily because it is easier to calculate shapes and create moving images with software. However, for broadcast television, interlaced scanning is often employed, because it permits a lower frame rate to be used without causing flicker for viewers.

Flicker is the perception of small, rapid changes in image brightness. Most people will perceive flicker if the image is updated less than 50 times per second. Movies, which are filmed at 24 fps, get around this problem by projecting each frame of the film on the screen two (or sometimes three) times. Television signals use interlacing to update the screen twice for each frame; first the odd field is displayed (the odd-numbered horizontal lines), and then the even field is displayed. Since half of the screen is updated with each field and the field rate (50 or 59.94 per second) is high enough, the images appear to be free of flicker to most viewers.

Unfortunately, interlaced signals can have visual artifacts, and these signals can be more difficult to create with computer software. If an object is rapidly moving horizontally in the image, the even field of lines will show the object in a different position from the odd field, causing the object to appear to have a jagged edge. This is particularly noticeable when the image sequence is paused (freeze frame).

Interlacing is used in three of the common video formats: 525i, 625i, and 1080i. The 720p format uses either 50 or 59.94 progressively scanned frames per second.

From Movie Film to Video Signal

A great deal of video content has been created using movie film over the years. Audiences can still enjoy television programs like *I Love Lucy* because the shows were originally filmed. Lots of other content is created using film, including motion pictures, numerous documentaries, and many shows destined for syndication in multiple countries. Only live shows can't be produced using film, because the delay to shoot the film, develop it, and convert it to video would simply be too long.

The process of converting film content into video content is called *telecine*. Unfortunately, film runs at 24 fps, PAL and SECAM video run at 25 fps, and NTSC video runs at 29.97 fps. This problem is solved very simply for 25-fps PAL and SECAM broadcasts: The movie is merely played at a rate of 25 fps. This has the side effect of reducing the time span of a movie by 4 percent, so a 100-minute movie takes only 96 minutes to broadcast. Note that the playback time of the audio signals also needs to be reduced so that synchronization can be maintained.

For 29.97-fps broadcasts, a method called *3:2 pulldown* was created. In 3:2 pulldown, 2½ frames of video are created from every two frames of movie. This is easier to understand when you remember that 2½ frames of interlaced video are five fields. So 3:2 pulldown operates by converting the first movie frame to three fields of video and the second movie frame to two fields of video. Then the process repeats, with the next movie frame being converted to three video

Frame Sequence of a Movie Film

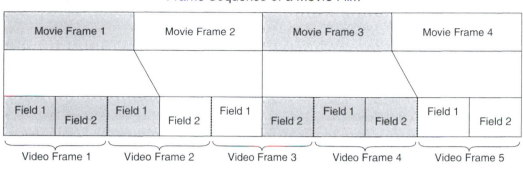

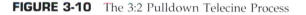

Video Frame Sequence after 3:2 Pulldown

FIGURE 3-10 The 3:2 Pulldown Telecine Process

fields, and so on. Figure 3-10 illustrates how this process works. Some video-editing software can reverse this process, and some high-end displays can also undo the 3:2 pulldown process.

TYPES OF AUDIO

Everyone in the video business understands that audio signals are required to accompany video images. Since these signals are typically handled much differently than video signals, it makes sense to devote a separate section of this chapter to audio.

Analog Audio

Analog audio is the electrical signal that can be fed directly to loudspeakers or a set of headphones to produce a sound. This covers a huge range of applications, from the tiny signals generated by a phonograph (turntable) or a microphone up to the powerful signals needed to drive the loudspeakers at an outdoor concert. Analog audio outputs can be found on devices such as DVD players, CD players, videotape players, CATV set-top boxes, and satellite receivers. Analog audio inputs can be found on stereo receivers, televisions, and audiotape or videotape recorders. Connectors on equipment for home installation often consist of a pair of round jacks, one red and one white (for stereo audio). Portable audio players (such as Apple's iPod and MP3 players) use a 3.5-mm stereo headphone jack, and many laptop computers have analog audio inputs and outputs of various styles.

The structure of an analog audio signal is very simple; it is just an electrical representation of the position of the cone (or diaphragm) of a standard speaker. When the signal goes up, the speaker's cone moves out; when the signal goes down, it moves back in. High-pitched sounds are created by rapid changes in the signal level that make the speaker cone vibrate rapidly; low-pitched sounds are represented by slower changes in the signal and slower movements of the cone. Sound volume increases with the amplitude of the signal: When the signal changes from a higher high to a lower low, the speaker cone moves over a greater distance, causing more sound pressure, and thus a louder volume, to be created.

Audio engineering has a number of challenges. Here are just a few:

- Sound levels won't sound proper if the source device and the destination device aren't correctly matched in terms of their electrical characteristics.
- There are many different ways to set up and calibrate a specific sound level, so material recorded by one organization may need adjustment when it is transferred to another organization. In particular, different organizations use different limits for peak sound level.
- Each room, each set of speakers, and each collection of listeners can change the acoustics and the sound patterns for an audience. This is why audio professionals are on hand at many live music, theatre, and lecture events.
- Most important to video people, audio signals do not have their own built-in synchronization mechanism. This contrasts with video, which has lots of embedded vertical and horizontal synchronization information. One of the most difficult challenges of video transport is ensuring that audio and video signals remain in sync.

Digital Audio

Analog audio signals will always be with us, because ultimately in every sound system there has to be some method for creating air vibrations in a listener's ears. However, more and more audio signals are being converted to digital signals, and for good reason. Digital signals have the big advantage of being much more immune to noise than analog signals.

Digital audio signals are becoming more common, particularly through the introduction of the compact disc (CD) for audio. Other now-common digital audio devices include digital telephones and mobile telephones, MP3 recorders and players, and a wide variety of digital video devices.

Digital audio signals come in two main forms: compressed and uncompressed. For the time being we are going to discuss uncompressed signals. (We will cover compressed digital audio in Chapter 4.) In particular, we will discuss the Audio Engineering Society/ European Broadcasting Union (AES/EBU) digital audio format, which is used throughout the professional video industry.

An AES/EBU digital audio signal is created by taking samples of an analog audio signal. If each sample is measured with 16 bits of accuracy, the level can be determined to an accuracy of 1 part in 65,000. If each sample is measured with 24 bits of accuracy, the level can be determined to an accuracy of 1 part in 16 million.

The rate at which the samples in AES/EBU signals are taken can also vary, from 32,000 times per second to 48,000 times per second. (Some newer professional systems offer sampling at 96,000 times per second.) Higher sampling rates are used to capture the higher-pitched (high-frequency) sounds. As a rule of thumb, the sampling rate needs to be at least twice the frequency of the highest-pitched sound to be captured and preferably slightly higher. The three main sampling rates in use today are as follows:

- 32,000 samples per second, which is used for FM radio and other broadcast audio applications that have an upper frequency response limit of 15,000 Hz
- 44,100 samples per second, which is used for compact disc (CD) mastering
- 48,000 samples per second, which is used for professional applications, including sound mastering for television and other applications

It is important to remember that the bit rate of the resulting audio stream can be quite large. For stereo, two samples are taken at each sampling instant: one for the left audio channel and one for the right. Each sample is placed in a 32-bit *subframe* for transport. Thus, an AES/EBU signal that is running at 48,000 samples per second will result in a 3.072-Mbps digital audio signal (48,000 $\times$ 32 bits per subframe $\times$ 2 audio channels for stereo). As we shall see in the upcoming chapters on video compression, 3 megabits per second is enough capacity to carry a fairly decent compressed video signal and its associated compressed audio signal.

Digital audio signals can also be embedded into digital video signals, such as SDI and HD-SDI. Audio is embedded into an SDI stream in the portions of the stream that are reserved for ancillary data. At the receiver, these bits can be copied out of the video stream and supplied as a digital audio signal. Audio embedding and extraction can be done without any degradation of either the audio or the video signal, because all of the processing is done digitally.

Audio Formats on DVDs

All DVD videodisks that use the 525-line/29.97-fps format (the North American standard) must use at least one of two audio coding formats: either linear PCM audio or AC-3 compressed audio. Linear PCM audio is a form of digital audio with the following parameters:

- Sampling is done at 48,000 or 96,000 samples per second.
- Sample resolution can be 16, 20, or 24 bits.
- A maximum of 8 audio channels is allowed (normal stereo occupies two audio channels).
- A maximum total bit rate of 6.144 Mbit/sec for an audio stream (multiple audio streams can be used, but the total cannot exceed the maximum DVD play out rate of 9.8 Mbit/sec).

Since a DVD is limited to 9.8 Mbit/sec total, and we generally want to have some video on a DVD, most disks use the AC-3 compressed audio format. This format, which has the trademarked name Dolby

Digital®, is widely used. This format can contain 5.1 audio tracks, allocated as follows:

- Left and right channels (similar to traditional stereo speakers)
- Center channel (speaker typically located with the video display)
- Left and right surround channels (speakers meant to be located alongside or behind the viewer)
- Low-frequency effects (LFE) channel, also called the ".1" channel, because it contains only a small fraction of the total sound spectrum. The LFE channel is typically fed into a subwoofer.

We'll talk about how AC-3 compression works in Chapter 4.

OTHER VIDEO SERVICES

In addition to standard audio and video content, television broadcasters and governments added features and functions to television programming for a variety of purposes. In the following sections, we'll look at some of these broadcast services, including secondary audio program (SAP), teletext, closed captioning, and the V-chip.

SAP Audio

The secondary audio program (SAP) channel was originally created in the United States to allow broadcasts to have a second language included with them. Recent changes, including a mandate by the Federal Communications Commission (FCC), have started moving the SAP channel toward being used for video description.

Video description is a process whereby a trained speaker adds comments to a video program to assist visually impaired people in understanding the content of a video program. Comments could include descriptions of scenes, actions, actors' gestures or facial expressions, or any other material that would assist a viewer in understanding what is happening on the video screen. These comments are inserted during natural pauses in the audio content of the program. This video description will be combined with the normal audio of the program and transmitted using the SAP channel.

For storage and transmission, the SAP video descriptions are simply treated as a third audio channel. When video compression is used for digital TV or other applications, SAP audio is included as another audio channel and multiplexed into the overall video stream for storage, playback, or distribution.

Teletext

Teletext was developed in the 1980s as a mechanism to broadcast text within standard television broadcasts and CATV systems by using data embedded in the VBI of the video signal. Today, most of the bold experiments with teletext have been shut down, due in no small part to the costs of creating content for a medium with a small audience.

Closed Captioning

Closed captioning provides a stream of text that can be shown on a display to assist viewers in understanding what is being said on-screen. Originally developed to help people with hearing impairments, closed captioning is also used frequently in loud environments, including noisy pubs and lounges. A great deal of broadcast video content contains closed captioning, due in part to governmental requirements.

Text for the captions is actually carried as a data stream in the VBI (vertical blanking interval; see the description earlier) portion of the video signal. In an analog video signal, closed captions are carried in line 21 of the VBI. In a digital signal, closed captions are carried as data packets within the overall digital video stream. Special decoder chips in the television tuner receive this data and generate characters that cover a small portion of the video display, as shown in Figure 3-11. This function is controlled by the viewer, who can select whether or not the captions are to be displayed.

Be careful not to confuse closed captioning with the text that crawls across the bottom of some broadcast news and finance programs. This text is inserted into the actual video image by the broadcaster and cannot be turned on or off by the viewer.

Closed
Captions

FIGURE 3-11   Closed Captioning on a Video Display

Also be careful not to confuse closed captioning with subtitles that are featured on some DVDs. Subtitles are designed for viewers with normal hearing who are watching a movie with dialog in a different language. As such, they do not include hints ("phone ringing," "footsteps") about the sounds in the content that could normally be heard through the soundtrack.

V-Chip

V-chip data provides ratings that indicate the intended audience for broadcast programming, and it is required by the U.S. and Canadian governments. Analog video signals carry V-chip data on line 21 in North America; digital TV signals use embedded data packets. V-chips can also selectively block programs based on their rating. Line 21 also has a date feature that will automatically set the time and date on home customers' videocassette recorders (VCRs).

VBI Issues

Other services can also use the VBI in analog television systems:

- For example, some electronic program guide information is sent to televisions via data carried in the VBI.

- A popular system for programming home VCRs also broadcasts program schedule data in the VBI.
- Studio production equipment (video recorders, cameras, etc.) often use the VBI for carrying a time code used to register precisely when each frame of video is shot. This signal is known as the Vertical Interval Time Code, or VITC.
- Signals that are used for system testing and video quality assurance can also be inserted into the VBI.

Many popular compression technologies, including MPEG, H.263, and others, will only process selected portions of the VBI. The reason is that most of the VBI is blank most of the time, and compressing a signal that doesn't contain any useful information would be a waste of processing power and bandwidth.

VIDEO AND AUDIO SWITCHING

Video signals are constantly being switched. Large broadcast production studios have video and audio switches that can accommodate hundreds of inputs and outputs. Broadcast and cable television signals are constantly being switched to perform functions such as changing from, say, a satellite feed to a file server or to insert a commercial into a program. Home and desktop viewers switch from video stream to video stream as they "channel surf" from program to program. IP technology can offer some radically different switching architectures.

A variety of technologies can be used for video switching:

- Baseband analog video and audio switches are used to connect analog video and audio signals.
- Digital switches handle digital video and digital audio signals.
- IP switches and routers can be used to handle video and audio signals that have been converted into Internet Protocol signals.

A note on terminology: Sometimes, baseband and digital video/audio switches are called *video/audio routers*. In this context, the two words *switch* and *router* have the same meaning. In IP hardware, these two terms have different meanings (even though they have some overlapping functions). Switches are lower-cost devices that perform a limited set of functions, primarily for local area networks. Routers are more software intensive, can include wide area network connections, and are programmed to do more sophisticated processing of IP packets. We'll discuss these functions more in later chapters.

Baseband Analog Switches

Once a staple of television production facilities, baseband audio and video switches are becoming obsolete as more programming migrates to digital formats. However, there is still a significant installed base of these switches. Analog video and audio signals are switched separately so that video outputs always get sent to video inputs, left audio outputs get sent to left audio inputs, etc. The industry term for a device that switches multiple signals at the same time is a *multilayer* switch; each signal counts as a layer. For example, a switch that handles baseband video plus left and right audio would be a three-layer switch.

One drawback to baseband switches is the number of internal connections goes up exponentially as the number of ports goes up. A 256-port switch has four times as many internal connection points as a 128-port switch. As the number of ports goes up, the physical size of the switch also goes up. It is not unusual for large switches to occupy multiple equipment racks.

Digital Switches

Digital switches operate on digital signals, such as SDI and HD-SDI. These signals can be routed using a single connection per signal, because they operate in a serial format. Some of these switches can route both SD and HD signals, so it is up to the user to make sure that the signal types don't get mixed. As with baseband switches, digital switches can grow quite large—1,000-port switches are available on the market.

Digital audio signals can be handled in two different ways in a digital switching architecture. One method is to use separate layers for the audio signals, similar to what is done on baseband systems. Another method is to embed the audio signals into digital video signals.

When separate layers are used, a greater amount of switching equipment is required, since the number of signals increases. But the system provides more flexibility, because the audio signals can be routed to a different destination than the video signals.

When audio signals are embedded in video signals, only a one-layer switch is required. Also, because the signals are tied together, the chance of mistakenly routing the video and audio signals that correspond to the same program to different destinations is greatly reduced. On the downside, it is necessary to embed all of the audio signals into the digital video signals. This can be done either using stand-alone embedding devices or through the use of products such as tape decks that support embedded audio.

IP Switching

A new concept is appearing on the horizon for live video production environments: the use of an IP network for switching video and audio signals. In this type of a system, each digital video or audio signal is converted into a stream of IP packets and sent onto a local area network. Switching is performed using standard IP networking equipment. At each destination device, the incoming stream of IP packets needs to be processed to recover the video and audio signals. Generally, the receiving devices have to buffer and process the incoming signal to make sure that all of the video timing parameters conform to the proper specifications.

One big advantage of using IP switching technology is that many different types of signals can be carried over IP, including digital video, digital audio, meta-data (data describing the video and audio signals), video files, system control data, intercom signals, and pretty much any other kind of signal used in a video production facility. When all of these functions are placed onto a single network, connections can be consolidated, network management can be simplified, and flexibility can be increased. Another advantage is the easy connection to wide area networks, many of which support IP traffic.

Of course, there are some downsides to the use of an IP network in place of more traditional video and audio switching systems.

The main issue is the significant difference in timing between packet-based and circuit-based systems. In circuit-based systems, data is sent in a continuous flow, with a steady bit rate. In contrast, IP networks require all signals to be broken into packets, which are then sent over the network. At congestion points in the network, packets can become delayed as they wait for other packets to move through. These delay variations impose a burden on destination devices, making it more difficult to reconstruct the timing of the original signals.

New generations of video and audio production equipment are beginning to include direct IP interfaces. Initially, these were for system control and monitoring, but signal inputs and outputs are increasingly migrating to IP. This is particularly true for compression and networking equipment.

Overall, the trends are in place, and progress will be made toward more and more transport of production video over IP networks. Much of the work that is done in preparing video and audio content for broadcast will end up being done on workstations that are interconnected only with IP services. In the long run, as systems become even more reliable, it is possible that all video switching will move into the IP domain. Although this goal has not yet been reached, significant progress is being made.

REVIEW AND CHECKLIST UPDATE

In this chapter, we looked at video, audio, and related signals. We covered the concepts of video fields, frames, and interlacing. Then we looked at different video signal types, including composite, S-video, component, SDI, HD-SDI, DVI, HDMI and Internet video. Next, we spent some time defining a variety of different audio signals, including analog, digital, and multichannel sound schemes. Then we examined some of the signals that are carried in the vertical blanking interval (VBI). Finally, we looked at baseband and digital switching technology and saw how IP switching technology can be used in a video production environment.

Chapter 3 Checklist Update

❏ Determine the type of video signal that will be used: NTSC, PAL, or SECAM; composite, S-video, component, SDI, or HD.

❏ Determine the audio signal type: analog, digital stereo, digital multichannel.

❏ Make sure that video and audio sources and destinations are configured for the correct signal types and that appropriate cables are used.

❏ If 270-Mbps SDI signals are used, check to see if the signals are 625/50 (PAL) or 525/60 (NTSC), since they are not compatible, even at the SDI level.

❏ If 1,485 Mbps HD-SDI signals are used, determine which of the four popular formats will be used:

  ❏ 720p with 50 frames per second
  ❏ 720p with 59.94 frames per second
  ❏ 1080i with 25 frames per second
  ❏ 1080i with 29.97 frames per second

  Note that these are not interchangeable.

❏ If SDI or HD-SDI signals are used, determine whether audio signals will be embedded.

❏ Find out about any required or optional services that are being carried in the VBI, particularly closed captioning, V-chip, or other government mandates.

❏ If compression equipment is to be used, make sure that any required VBI signals are processed.

❏ Make sure that any video or audio switches include enough conductors to handle all the required signals, such as multiple channels of audio.

4

VIDEO AND AUDIO COMPRESSION

When video signals are transported over an IP network, they are most often compressed. In this context, compression means to reduce the number of bits that are required to represent the video image. Video technology users are free to choose whether or not to employ compression for their video signals. However, it is important to understand that the choice of a compression method can sometimes mean the difference between success and failure of a video networking project.

Many communication systems that have become commonplace in the past few years depend on compression technology. For example, digital mobile telephones use compression to increase the number of users who can be served and to increase the battery life of mobile handsets. Digital TV and HDTV delivery to homes would be impossible without compression to fit content into consumer delivery systems. Digital cameras use data compression to fit more pictures into a fixed amount of storage. MP3 players and Apple iPods use compression to take files from audio CDs and make them small

Video Over IP: IPTV, Internet Video, H.264, P2P, Web TV, and Streaming: A Complete Guide to Understanding the Technology
Copyright © 2008, Wes Simpson. All rights reserved.

enough to fit into the memory of a portable player. Compression allows a 2-hour movie to fit onto a 4-inch DVD in place of an 812-foot long (248-m) VHS tape. Satellite television uses compression to allow hundreds of video channels to be distributed economically to viewers. An understanding of video and audio compression is essential to understanding and using modern video transport systems, including video over IP networks.

In this chapter we will begin by examining the reasons why compression is used and look at some of the factors that determine what form of compression is suitable for an application. Then we will examine MPEG video compression, since it is one of the most popular technologies for video and audio compression. After that, we'll discuss some of the other compression systems available for use with video and audio signals. We'll conclude with a look at some of the applications of video compression and discuss the licenses needed to use some forms of compression technology.

COMPRESSION OVERVIEW

Compression technology is a continuing field of research. As better mechanisms are developed, more information can be carried in fewer and fewer bits. Plus, as processing power increases, these techniques can be implemented on ever-faster, ever-cheaper processors. So compression is constantly being used in more and more applications. In this section, we'll look at the reasons for using compression as well as its benefits and drawbacks.

Figure 4-1 shows a simplified block diagram of a compression system. The input can be a computer file, such as a document, an image, and/or a video/audio recording. Or the input can be a continuous stream of data, such as a digital video or audio signal. Either way, this information is fed into the compression engine. The output of the compression engine is a second data file or data stream that contains fewer bits than the input file or stream. This output can be stored or transmitted over a network. Before the data file can be used, it must be restored to its original size, via a decompression engine. Note that a compression engine is often called an *encoder*, and the decompression engine is commonly called a *decoder*.

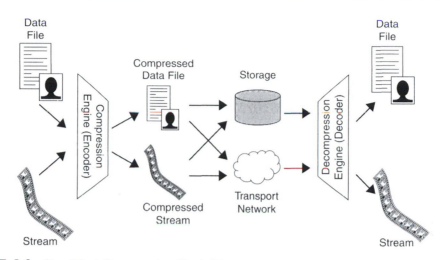

FIGURE 4-1 Simplified Compression Block Diagram

The goal of compression is to reduce the size of the incoming data file without removing useful information. In most real-world data files, some data patterns will repeat. For example, consider the following sentence: "The job of compression is to remove redundant or unnecessary information." In a typical computer file, each character in this sentence would be represented by an 8-bit code. There is a total of 73 characters, including spaces and punctuation, in the sample sentence, which would occupy 584 bits.

To make a compressed version of this sentence, we need to analyze the data. Figure 4-2 shows the result of this analysis. The first two columns list all of the characters in the sample sentence and show the count for each character. Note that space is the most common character, with 10 occurrences. There are 9 occurrences of "o," 7 of both "e" and "n," and so on down to the final period, which has one occurrence. Also note that capital "T" is counted separately from lowercase "t."

Since there are only 22 different characters in this sample sentence, we can easily encode this data using 5 bits. The results are shown in the middle two columns of Figure 4-2. By doing this, we can compress the file from 584 bits down to 365 bits, a 37 percent reduction.

Can we do even better? Yes, by using variable-length coding (VLC). In VLC, we use shorter bit patterns for more common characters

Sample Sentence Data File:

"The job of compression is to remove redundant or unnecessary information."

Standard ASCII

Char.	Count
Space	10
o	9
e	7
n	7
r	6
s	5
l	4
a	3
m	3
t	3
f	2
c	2
d	2
u	2
T	1
h	1
j	1
b	1
p	1
v	1
y	1
.	1

Fixed Length Code

Char.	5-bit
Space	00000
o	00001
e	00010
n	00011
r	00100
s	00101
l	00110
a	00111
m	01000
t	01001
f	01010
c	01011
d	01100
u	01101
T	01110
h	01111
j	10000
b	10001
p	10010
v	10011
y	10100
.	10101

Variable Length Code

Char.	3/7-bit
Space	000
o	001
e	010
n	011
r	100
s	101
l	110
a	1110000
m	1110001
t	1110010
f	1110011
c	1110100
d	1110101
u	1110110
T	1110111
h	1111000
j	1111001
b	1111010
p	1111011
v	1111100
y	1111101
.	1111110

73 characters at 8 bits per character (ASCII) gives a total file size of 584 bits

73 characters at 5 bits per character gives a total file size of 365 bits

48 characters at 3 bits per character and 25 characters at 7 bits per character give a total file size of 323 bits

FIGURE 4-2 Data Compression Analysis for Sample Sentence Data File

and longer bit patterns for less common characters (readers who are familiar with Morse code will recognize this concept). We can use a 3-bit code to represent the most common characters. We'll save one of the combinations (111) to indicate a longer code is needed; we'll form those by adding another 4 bits. The results of this are shown in the right two columns of Figure 4-2. The 7 most common characters (space through "l") are each encoded with 3 bits. The less common characters are coded with 7 bits each—3 bits of "111" and then 15 other combinations. There is a total of 48 occurrences of the most common characters (10 spaces, 9 "o," 7 "e," etc.) and 25 occurrences of the less common characters (3 "a," 3 "m," etc.). The result is $(48 \times 3) + (25 \times 7) = 144 + 175 = 319$ bits, which is a reduction of 45 percent from the original. (Plus, this reduction is lossless; see the discussion in the following section.) An even more efficient VLC scheme, called *Huffman coding*, would result in a reduction of over 50 percent; this is why Huffman coding is used in MPEG.

Many real-world signals have a large amount of redundancy and unused bandwidth. Consider the audio signals resulting from a normal conversation. If both parties are each talking half of the time, then the signal from each party's mouthpiece will be meaningful only half of the time. Similarly, in a video image, many times a large portion of the image is identical to the image immediately preceding it or immediately following it or both. As we shall see, a compression engine can use this redundancy to greatly reduce the amount of data that needs to be stored or transmitted across a network.

Compression techniques can be broken into two broad categories: lossy and lossless. *Lossless* compression is used when it is important to preserve every bit of the original material. *Lossy* compression is used when it is important to maintain the meaning of a signal but not every bit. Most of the commonly used video and audio compression systems are lossy.

Lossless Compression

Lossless compression does not remove any information from the source data. This is important in some applications, such as compressing a computer program to make it easier to download. If even one bit of the original is lost, then the program will probably not be usable. The lossless compression engine is designed to remove any redundancy in the source signal but to do so in a manner such that the decompression engine can completely re-create the original signal.

The biggest drawback to lossless compression is that it is not guaranteed to produce an output that is significantly smaller than the input. In fact, it is entirely possible to take a file and pass it through a lossless compression engine and end up saving only a small percentage of the original file size. This is not any fault of the compression engine; it simply means that the source file had very little redundancy that could be removed.

Lossy Compression and Perceptual Coding

Lossy compression, on the other hand, is designed to permanently remove less important information. In the sample sentence from Figure 4-2 we could, for example, replace the word *remove* with the word *remov* and most folks would still be able to understand the sentence. Similarly, we could replace the word *information* with the word *info*. Some folks wouldn't even notice the difference if we substituted *unecesary* for the word *unnecessary*. By making these three simple changes, we have removed 10 characters from the original file and "compressed" it by 13 percent. Since this form of compression would normally drive spell-checking software crazy, lossy compression is not typically used with text.

Perceptual coding means taking advantage of the limitation of the human senses to make the perception of an image or a sound similar (or identical) to another. For example, in human hearing a loud sound at one pitch will hide (or "mask") any quieter sounds at nearby pitches. The human vision system is better able to resolve differences in brightness than in color; this is one of several perceptual aspects that are exploited in modern video compression systems.

For video and audio compression, lossy compression with perceptual coding is normally used. As the file becomes more heavily compressed, the amount of distortion increases, and more and more fine detail from the source is lost, but this is often deemed to be an acceptable trade-off. Figure 4-3F shows the result of excessive compression, which includes loss of detail and loss of the finer gradations in image brightness.

Design of lossy, perceptual-compression algorithms is not a cut-and-dried process; work is constantly under way to create more pleasing results with fewer and fewer bits. To test these designs, it is necessary to have humans evaluate the results. In fact, one common measure of a compression system is a mean opinion score (MOS), where nonexpert viewers are asked to rate a series of video clips on a scale from 1 to 5. Scores between 4 and 5 are considered "very good"; systems scoring below 2 are rarely used.

Analog Impairments

Digital Impairments

A Original Image

D With Macroblocking

B With Random Noise

E With Lost Data

C With Ghosting

F Excessive Compression

FIGURE 4-3   Typical Image Impairments

Benefits and Drawbacks of Compression

Compression provides a number of benefits and drawbacks for video signals. Table 4-1 provides a list of some of the key factors that can influence this decision.

TABLE 4-1

Benefits and Drawbacks of Compression

Benefits

- A compressed file will occupy less space on a disk drive or other storage medium than an equivalent uncompressed file. This enables users either to put more information in a given space or to use less space for a given file.
- Compressed streams can be transmitted at lower bit rates than uncompressed streams. This can often mean the difference between getting the stream to a user or not.
- More compressed streams can fit into a given bandwidth than uncompressed streams. This is particularly true for networks that have a fixed upper limit on bandwidth. For example, satellite transponders typically cannot exceed a fixed amount of bandwidth. As compression technology has advanced, more and more signals can be squeezed into the same amount of bandwidth.
- More users can be simultaneously sent compressed streams than uncompressed streams. This is particularly true of servers that are used for video-on-demand services.

Drawbacks

- Since most compression engines used for video and audio are lossy, the overall quality of compressed signals will be lower than the original uncompressed signal. While these losses are intended to be unnoticeable to a human, the changes can be measured with the right equipment.
- Compression can introduce delay into a video or audio signal, at both the compression and decompression stages.
- Compressed signals are more difficult to edit in their compressed form. In order for editing to take place, the signals typically need to be decompressed.
- Compression can be difficult on signals that have a lot of noise in them, such as static and other interference. When there is a lot of noise in a video signal (such as in the image in Figure 4-3B) that is being fed into a compression engine, the compression system has difficulty in identifying redundant information between adjacent video frames.
- As a general rule, compression systems should not be concatenated; that is, signals should not be fed out of one compression/decompression system into another. Doing so will degrade the signal, because the losses introduced by the first compression will appear to be noise to the second compression (making the signal difficult to compress).
- Video compression requires many calculations to be done on the incoming digital video signal. If these calculations need to be done in real time, the burden on a processor can be very heavy. Even decoding compressed video streams can tax general-purpose PCs.
- Both the compression and the decompression engines for a given signal need to match in order for the overall system to work properly.

Here are some of the key parameters that need to be compatible between the encoding and the decoding engines:

- Exact frame rate (e.g., 30 fps, 29.97, 25, etc.)
- Interlaced or progressive scanning
- Vertical image size (number of lines of resolution)
- Horizontal image size (number of pixels in each horizontal

MPEG COMPRESSION TECHNOLOGIES

The Moving Pictures Experts Group has developed some of the most common compression systems for video around the world and given these standards the common name of MPEG. Not only did this group develop video compression standards, including MPEG-1, MPEG-2, and MPEG-4, but it also developed audio compression standards, which we will discuss later in this chapter. This group continues to meet and to set new standards for new applications and using new technologies.

MPEG standards have enabled a number of advanced video services. For example, MPEG-based DVDs are the preferred medium for viewing Hollywood movies in the home. Digital television, digital satellite television, and digital cable television are all based on the MPEG video compression standards. High-definition (HD) television, including Blu-ray discs, also use MPEG technology. Also, much of the content for streaming media on the Internet is compressed using MPEG or closely related technologies.

Because there are so many different flavors of MPEG, it is important for users to know which ones are suitable for their applications. Also, knowledge of MPEG terminology can help users understand how to set up their equipment to best suit their applications.

In this section we will look at some of the basic technology that makes up the MPEG standards. Then we'll look at some of the common terminology that is used throughout MPEG video standards. We'll follow this with a look at what makes up the different compression standards, including the different profiles and levels. Finally, we'll summarize with a comparison of different MPEG technologies.

4:2:0 and 4:2:2

Let's look at what these two labels mean when we are talking about MPEG compression. Building on our discussion in Chapter 3, remember that chroma data can be sent at half the resolution of luma data. This applies to MPEG as well as uncompressed video signals. MPEG groups the pixels in each input image into a whole series of

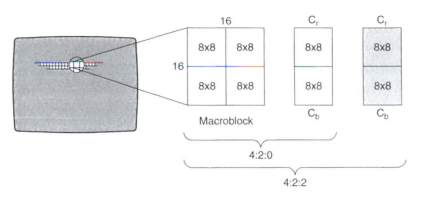

FIGURE 4-4   Macroblocks and Blocks in MPEG

blocks, called *macroblocks*. Each macroblock in MPEG is 16 pixels wide and 16 pixels high (for a total of 256 picture elements), as shown in Figure 4-4. Inside each macroblock are four luma blocks (each 8 × 8 pixels) and either two or four chroma blocks.

In 4:2:0 systems, two chroma blocks are used in each macroblock: one for the red color-difference signal (Cr) and one for the blue color-difference signal (Cb). Each chroma block has 64 elements, with each element representing the color information from four of the original pixels.

In 4:2:2 systems, four chroma blocks are used in each macroblock: two for the red color-difference signal (Cr) and two for the blue color-difference signal (Cb). Each chroma signal has 128 elements, with each element representing the color information from two of the original pixels.

Generally, 4:2:0 devices are lower cost and will operate better on low-bandwidth networks. (Also note that DVDs are encoded with 4:2:0 color resolution.) Devices using 4:2:2 are generally preferred for higher-quality-contribution networks, because they are believed to represent image colors more accurately. Because 4:2:2 signals transmit more information for each picture, they do not perform as well on low bandwidths. Furthermore, 4:2:2 compression will show a benefit only if the source signal is of very high quality, such as a signal coming from a professional-quality video camera.

I, P, B Frames and Groups of Pictures

Users of any MPEG system will quickly encounter a variety of frame types, including "I frames," "P frames," and "B frames," as well as the term *group of pictures* or *GOP*. These terms all describe the way that picture data is structured in an MPEG stream or file. Since most compression devices will support a variety of frame types, it is important for MPEG system users to understand what these terms represent and how the use of the different frame types will affect overall system performance.

To begin, Table 4-2 gives some brief definitions of these terms; we will go into more detail shortly.

To understand why MPEG uses these different frames, it is illuminating to look at the amount of data required to represent each frame type. With a video image of normal complexity, a P frame will take two to four times less data than an I frame of the same image. A B frame will take even less data than a P frame, a further reduction by a factor of 2–5. Figure 4-5 shows the relative amounts of data for each frame type in a typical MPEG-2 GOP.

To see how these different frame types work in practice, let's look at a sample GOP that could be used for a broadcast television signal, as illustrated in Figure 4-6. In our example, the GOP consists of 12 frames of video, which would last for four-tenths of a second in an NTSC system. The sequence of the frames is IBBPBBPBBPBB, which is read as an I frame, followed by two B frames, followed by a P frame, then two more B's, another P, two more B's, and a final P followed by two final B's. In a real television broadcast, this GOP would be followed by another GOP consisting of 12 more frames, and so on ad infinitum. This is an open GOP, meaning that the final two B frames are referenced to the I frame in the following GOP. This GOP has a length of 12 and what is sometimes referred to as a GOP pattern of IBBP. We will explain these concepts in more detail later.

Let's look at the frames that make up this GOP. The first frame of the GOP is always an I frame. This is by definition, but it's also because an I frame is the only kind of frame that can be decoded by itself

TABLE 4-2

Definitions of Common MPEG Terms

- A *frame* is single image from a video sequence. In NTSC countries, one frame occurs every 33 milliseconds; in PAL countries, one frame occurs every 40 milliseconds. In interlaced systems, one frame is made up of two fields—an odd field and an even field.
- An *encoder* is an MPEG compression device that takes raw video and/or audio signals and produces a compressed output stream.
- A *decoder* receives compressed MPEG streams and produces video and/or audio output signals.
- An *I frame* is a frame that is compressed solely based on the information contained in the frame; no reference is made to any of the other video frames before or after it. The "I" stands for "intra" coded.
- A *P frame* is a frame that has been compressed using the data contained in the frame itself and data from the closest preceding I or P frame. The "P" stands for "predicted."
- A *B frame* is a frame that has been compressed using data from the closest preceding I or P frame and the closest following I or P frame. Note that in MPEG-2 a B frame cannot be predicted from another B frame; in MPEG-4 there are several types of B frames that have different prediction properties. The "B" stands for "bidirectional," meaning that the frame data can depend on frames that occur before and after it in the video sequence.
- A *group of pictures,* or *GOP,* is a series of frames consisting of a single I frame and zero or more P and B frames. A GOP always begins with an I frame and ends with the last frame before the next subsequent I frame. All of the frames in the GOP depend (directly or indirectly) on the data in the initial I frame.
- *Open GOP* and *closed GOP* are terms that refer to the relationship between one GOP and another. A closed GOP is self-contained; that is, none of the frames in the GOP refer to or are based on any of the frames outside the GOP. An open GOP uses data from the I frame of the following GOP for calculating some of the B frames in the GOP.

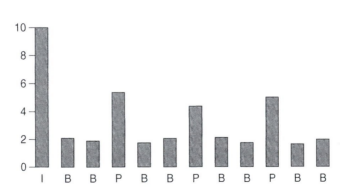

FIGURE 4-5   Relative Amounts of Data in Each MPEG Frame Type

*Note: The second I frame (shown in gray above) is the first frame of the next GOP.
B Frames 11 and 12 are based on this I frame because this is an Open GOP structure.

FIGURE 4-6 MPEG GOP Frame Viewing vs. Transmission Order

without referring to any other frames. This allows all of the other frames in the GOP to use it as a reference. At the decoder, the video frame can be completely re-created from this data. Both the encoder and the decoder store a copy of the decoded I frame in local memory, because they will need this data for upcoming calculations.

The next frame to be encoded is the first P frame after the I frame, which is frame 4 in our example. (The encoder skips over the two B frames, numbers 2 and 3 in our example, because it doesn't yet have enough data to work on them. But don't worry; we'll get back to them very soon.) The encoder first subtracts the pixel values of frame 4 from the stored pixel values from frame 1. The resulting differences show the changes that have occurred in the image between frame 1 and frame 4, which are what the encoder will now go to work on. The encoder also looks to see if any portions of frame 4 are similar to any portions of frame 1, even if they have been relocated to a different place in the frame. If so, then the encoder measures the amount of movement. These measurements (called *motion vectors*) are sent to the decoder to help reduce the amount of picture data that must be sent. The encoder then proceeds to compress the remaining pixel differences. Note that this normally results in a much smaller data file than for an I frame. This happens because many locations in the frame may have very few differences between frame 1 and frame 4, and these areas will compress virtually to nothing. The encoder then sends the compressed difference data for frame 4 to the decoder. Again, both the encoder and the decoder store a copy of the decoded P frame in local memory, because they will need this data for the next calculation.

Figure 4-7 illustrates the timing of the video data through the encoder and decoder. The first line of the diagram shows when the

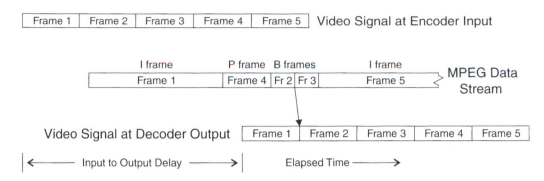

FIGURE 4-7   Timing Relationships for Encoder and Decoder

uncompressed video frames coming from the video source arrive at the encoder. The second line of the diagram shows when the data moves from the encoder to the decoder. The third line of the diagram shows when the video signal is sent out of the decoder.

The next frame to be encoded is the first B frame, or frame 2 in our example. This frame is to be encoded using bidirectional compression, which means that the encoder can look at an I or P frame that precedes this one as well as an I or P frame that follows this one. Conveniently, the encoder has stored a decoded copy of frame 1 and a decoded copy of frame 4. Now the encoder can go to work by first subtracting the pixel data of frame 2 from the stored pixel values of frames 1 and 4. These difference signals can then be encoded using motion vectors and compression and then formed into the encoder output. As in the case of a P frame, the smaller the differences, the smaller the amount of data that has to be sent. This time, after the encoder has sent the data, any reference to frame 2 is deleted, because the encoder will not need this data again. However, the encoder and decoder still keep the data from frame 1 and frame 4 in memory, because it will be needed one more time.

The next step is to encode the second B frame, which is frame 3 in our example. As before, the differences between this frame and the data from frames 1 and 4 are calculated, and the encoder output is created. This time, only the data from frame 4 need be kept by the encoder and the decoder.

Let's pause for a moment and think about what has been happening in the decoder so far. First, the decoder received the data for frame 1, the I frame, which it was able to decode and send to the video display while retaining a copy in memory for use in decoding the next three frames. Then the decoder received the data from frame 4, the P frame, which needed to be decoded but could not be sent to the video display yet because frames 2 and 3 hadn't been decoded yet. So the decoder places the decoded pixel information for frame 4 into storage. Then the decoder receives the data for frame 2, the first B frame. As soon as this data is decoded (using the data stored locally in the decoder from frames 1 and 4), it can be sent to the video display—similarly with the data for frame 3, the second B frame. As soon as this data is decoded, it can be sent to the video display. After this step is completed, the decoder can finally send the decoded data for frame 4 to the video display.

The next frame to be compressed by the encoder is frame 7, the next P frame after frame 4. Since this is a predicted frame, the encoder will start by calculating the difference between pixel data of frame 7 and the stored pixel data of frame 4. Just like before, the difference signal is encoded using motion vectors and compression, and the results are sent to the decoder. Now both the encoder and the decoder store copies of the decoded P frames 4 and 7 in local memory, because both devices will need this data for calculating the next frame.

As you might expect, the next step is to calculate and compress the difference data for the next two B frames, which are 5 and 6 in our example. At the decoder, these frames can be decoded and sent to the video display.

Next, the encoder needs to process frame 10, which is the last P frame in the GOP. As before, the differences between frames 10 and 7 are calculated, and the compressed difference data for frame 10 is sent to the decoder. Then the encoder reconfigures its local storage, keeping only the data for frames 7 and 10. The encoder needs to calculate and send the compressed bidirectional difference data for the B frames 8 and 9 where it can be decoded and sent to the display.

Because this is an open GOP, the encoder needs to look ahead and get the first frame of the next GOP. This frame (which would be frame 1 of the following GOP) must be compressed as an I frame. When the compression is complete, the data can start being sent to the decoder, and it can be stored in the local memory of the encoder, along with the decoded data from frame 10 of the current GOP. We are finally ready to compress the data for frames 11 and 12 of the current GOP, which are both B frames. The values of the B frames are calculated from the differences between frame 10 of the current GOP and frame 1 of the following GOP, and the values are sent to the decoder. Once these calculations are complete, the encoder can start fresh with frames 4, 2, and 3 from the new GOP.

GOP Length Selection

Selecting a suitable GOP length and GOP pattern can have a big impact on a video network. If the GOP is too short, then the encoded bit stream will occupy excessive bandwidth because of the increased number of I frames, or video quality will be decreased because I frames are less efficient at encoding information than P frames or B frames. If the GOP is too long, then the video stream will be hard to work with and less tolerant to transmission errors. Since most MPEG encoders allow users to select the GOP that they want to use, it is important to make an informed choice. In this section, we'll look at the relative benefits of short and long GOPs.

GOP length selection also has a big impact on channel-change time in IPTV and other compressed video delivery systems. When a decoder in an IPTV set-top box, satellite receiver, or Internet video client device is presented with a new video stream, it must wait for an I frame to be delivered, because I frames are the only frames that can be decoded without prior knowledge of the video signal. Both P frames and B frames depend on data stored in local memory from prior frames; since this data will not be present after a channel change, neither P frames nor B frames can be used for decoding the video stream. So, short GOPs help shorten channel-change times by reducing the amount of time that a decoder needs to wait to receive an I frame.

Before going any further, let's make sure we all have the same understanding of the terms *short GOP* and *long GOP*. A GOP is short when a small number of frames occur between successive I frames in an MPEG stream. In the shortest possible GOP, the stream is made up entirely of I frames, and thus the GOP is one frame. In a long GOP, many frames occur between successive I frames. There are no strict limits in some MPEG profiles for a maximum-length GOP, but certain applications do have limits. For example, the DVD standards limit GOP length to 15 frames.

Unfortunately, there is no single answer as to which GOP length is the best; the choice depends on the user's application. Table 4-3 highlights these differences.

No doubt some readers will be asking "Why not use mostly B frames and get the smallest amount of data possible"? The answer to this question is fourfold, as follows:

- A B frame can be predicted only from either I or P frames, according to the MPEG-2 standard. Therefore, every sequence of video frames must include some I or P frames on occasion.

TABLE 4-3

Comparison of Long and Short GOPs

Long GOP Benefits

- As we have seen, I frames take more bits to encode accurately than P or B frames. When a long GOP is used, fewer I frames are in the stream, so the overall bit rate is reduced.
- For a network with a fixed bandwidth, more video signals can be carried when each uses a long GOP to reduce overall bandwidth demands. This can benefit both terrestrial and satellite-based networks.

Short GOP Benefits

- When video images have lots of rapid scene changes (such as in action movies and music videos), a short GOP structure may create a better video image.
- In compressed video delivery systems (such as DSL and digital cable), short GOPs allow quicker channel-change times, since it is easier for the decoder to find an I frame to begin the decoding process for a new channel.
- With a short GOP, I frames occur more often, so any accumulated errors are cleared out more rapidly.
- When streams are edited, it is easier to make the cuts only at an I frame. With short GOP signals, I frames occur more often, so editing is easier and more precise.
- With noisy video sources, prediction errors can rapidly accumulate. Shorter GOP signals are less sensitive to noise, because few consecutive frames are based on predicted values

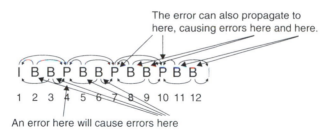

FIGURE 4-8   Effects of an Error in Frame 4 of the Sample GOP

- Whenever one frame is predicted from another, some small errors will occur. When a second frame is predicted based on another frame that has already been predicted, these errors can build on each other. As the number of generations increases, these errors will accumulate and make the resulting images unacceptable. The only way to clear out these accumulated errors is to transmit an occasional I frame.

- The process of editing a video or changing channels involves stopping one sequence of video frames and starting another. When this happens in the middle of a GOP, B frames no longer make any sense, because one of the I or P frames that they were referenced to was replaced by the new stream. Traditionally, when editing is done, any new video scenes must begin with an I frame, so the encoder and decoder can clean out their buffers and start fresh. Newer technology is coming into the market that relaxes this requirement.

- In the event of an error in a MPEG video stream, the data that is needed to predict subsequent frames can become corrupted. Using the previous 12-frame GOP example, if frame 4 of the GOP is corrupted and the image in frame 7 was predicted based on the data in frame 4, then frame 7 will also be corrupted. An error in frame 4 will also directly affect the B frames 2, 3, 5, and 6. This error can also be propagated throughout the rest of the GOP, as shown in Figure 4-8.

MPEG-1

MPEG-1 was developed in the early 1990s and was the first standard created for video compression by the Moving Pictures Experts Group. It was intended for use in creating video compact discs

(CDs), which operated at around 1 Mbps; these had some popularity in computer multimedia but never completely caught on as a consumer movie rental or purchase format. MPEG-1 is still in use today occasionally for some applications, including low-cost surveillance cameras and some web video applications, although these are becoming increasingly rare. MPEG-1 is a subset of MPEG-2, so any compliant MPEG-2 decoder should be able to decode an MPEG-1 signal. It is also interesting to note that MPEG-1 is allowed as a video compression method for DVDs, and many DVD players will play video CDs. Stand-alone and software-based MPEG-1 encoders are available for very reasonable prices from several sources.

MPEG-1 does not support interlacing or high-definition video, so it cannot be used for PAL, NTSC, 720p, or 1080i video. Also, MPEG-1 lacks some of the advanced coding techniques developed for MPEG-2 and MPEG-4 systems. These limitations helped make it easy to develop software-based MPEG-1 encoders and decoders that could operate on PC hardware that was available a number of years ago. With today's more powerful machines, MPEG-2 and MPEG-4 encoders and decoders are easier to implement, and both technologies can produce higher-quality images at lower bandwidths. As a result, MPEG-1 systems today should be considered as legacy devices and should not generally be considered for new implementations today.

MPEG-2

MPEG-2 is one of the predominant standards for MPEG video today, having been approved in 1996. It is used in a wide variety of applications, including digital TV production and broadcasting, high-definition television, satellite television, and cable television. Each day, thousands of hours of MPEG-2 video are recorded, processed, and played back by television broadcasters around the world. Millions of hours of MPEG-2 recordings are sold to the general public each day in the form of (standard-definition) DVDs. Thousands of PCs with MPEG-2 playback capability are sold each week, and the installed base of devices continues to grow. MPEG-2 is also the standard video compression system selected for use by the Advanced Television Systems Committee for digital television (DTV) broadcast in the United States.

All televisions now sold in the United States are required by law to include a DTV tuner and an MPEG-2 video decoder.

MPEG-2 offers some significant advances over MPEG-1. MPEG-2 supports interlacing, so standard NTSC and PAL signals can be supported at full resolution. It supports a variety of different resolutions and performance profiles, so a wide variety of applications, including HD television (both 720p and 1080i), can be accommodated. MPEG-2 supports multiplexing of a number of video and audio streams, so applications like multichannel satellite television become possible. MPEG-2 also supports five-channel audio (surround sound) and the Advanced Audio Coding (AAC) standard, neither of which is available in MPEG-1.

One of the key concepts that needs to be understood in MPEG-2 involves the various profiles and levels available for encoding. Selecting the correct profile and level for a particular application can have a great impact on system cost. Higher profiles and levels add to the complexity of encoders and decoders, can require more bandwidth, and can significantly increase overall system cost.

The term *level*, when used in the context of an MPEG-2 performance specification, refers to the maximum picture size that can be supported. Four levels are defined (in order from lowest to highest resolution): Low, main, high 1440, and high. Here are brief definitions of each level:

- Low level refers to picture sizes up to a maximum of 352 pixels by 288 lines, just like MPEG-1.
- Main level refers to the main picture sizes used in standard-definition television, i.e., a maximum of 720 pixels on each of 576 horizontal lines as used on PAL signals. NTSC resolutions will typically be 720 pixels on 480 lines.
- High 1440 level doubles the vertical and horizontal resolution of the main profile and so offers 1440 pixels on each of 1152 lines.
- High level expands the high 1440 level to widescreen high definition, by supporting a 16:9 aspect ratio (in place of 4:3 for normal main profile signals). This increases the maximum number of pixels per line to 1920 but leaves the line count maximum at 1152 lines, which is enough to support a 1080-line HD signal.

MPEG-2 also supports a variety of different performance profiles, which specify the types of techniques that the encoder can use in compressing the video. As the profile increases, the cost and complexity of both the video encoder and decoder increase. However, the video quality normally also increases, so trade-offs need to be considered. The six MPEG-2 profiles, in order from least complex to most complex, are simple, main, 4:2:2, SNR, spatial, and high. Here are brief definitions of each profile:

- Simple profile does not allow B frames, so only I and P frames can be used by the encoder. This reduces the complexity of the encoder and decoder. This profile may also be useful for low-delay applications, since the delays required for calculating B frames are eliminated.
- Main profile is intended to be useful in a wide variety of applications. It supports all the different resolution levels and is the most commonly used profile for most applications. Note that the color space for this profile is 4:2:0. DVDs are authored following the main profile at main level specifications.
- 4:2:2 profile was developed to support 4:2:2 color handling without all of the other features and functions required by the high profile. It is now used in video production, postproduction, and network transmission for contribution signals.
- SNR (signal-to-noise ratio) profile introduced the concept of having scalable video streams for one video signal: a basic stream that carried most of the picture data and a helper stream that could be used for enhanced video performance (lower noise, fewer compression artifacts). This capability has not been widely applied in MPEG-2 for television broadcast applications, but it has found use with MPEG-4 applications for Internet video delivery.
- Spatial profile uses the same concept of a scalable stream, but in this case the basic stream is an SD signal, and the enhanced stream is an HD signal. This profile is not commonly used in MPEG-2, but the concept of multiple-resolution streams is used widely for Internet video.
- High profile, which offers the capabilities of both the SNR and the spatial profile, is the most complex MPEG-2 profile defined. High profile was also the only profile that supported the 4:2:2 color resolution before the 4:2:2 profile was defined. Encoders and decoders that support all of the functions required by the

high profile are significantly more complex (and more expensive) than main profile encoders and decoders. High profile has found uses in high-definition video.

When profiles and levels are being specified, it is customary to abbreviate the names of the profiles and levels and to join them with an "at" (@) sign. For example, main profile at main level would be abbreviated "MP@ML" and read "main profile at main level." High profile at main level would be abbreviated "HP@ML." Also note that *not* every combination of profile and level is permitted; for example, high profile at low level is not permitted. Figure 4-9 shows the allowed profiles and levels, along with information about the permitted color resolution options (4:2:0 or 4:2:2) and the maximum supported bit rate of the compressed video elementary stream for each combination.

MPEG-2 is widely used throughout the professional video recording and broadcast market, for good reasons. It is a stable standard, and many devices, including specialized semiconductors, are in their

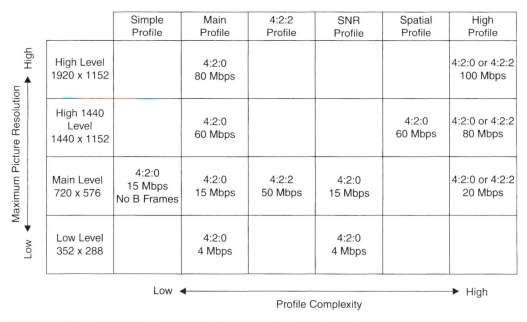

FIGURE 4-9 Summary of Supported MPEG-2 Profiles and Levels

fourth and fifth generations. Also, MPEG-2 is the only video compression format allowed for DTV broadcast in the United States and some other countries. Table 4-4 lists some of the key advantages and disadvantages of MPEG-2 technology.

TABLE 4-4

Advantages and Disadvantages of MPEG-2

Advantages

- *Flexible*: MPEG-2 has a variety of profiles and levels to support many different applications.
- *Widespread*: There are literally hundreds of millions of set-top boxes, digital satellite receivers, and DVD players installed in consumers' homes that can decode MPEG-2 signals.
- *Highly integrated*: A number of highly sophisticated MPEG-2 encoder and decoder devices are available as low-cost custom semiconductors.
- *Stand-alone encoders*: Inexpensive, stand-alone MPEG-2 encoder units are available from a number of suppliers that can be used to create compressed video streams in real time. Some of these include built-in 10/100BaseT Ethernet links.
- *Software*: Moderate-performance PCs can be used to edit and create MPEG-2 files; additional hardware may be required to process streams in real time.
- *Infrastructure*: A wide variety of equipment is available on the market for handling multiplexing, bit-rate conversion, telecom and IP network adaptation, and other functions with MPEG-2 streams
- *Test equipment*: Diagnostic tools and equipment for analyzing MPEG-2 encoder and decoder designs and for diagnosing system failures are also readily available.

Disadvantages

- *Complexity*: Because MPEG-2 has so many different profiles and levels, it is very common to find that specific hardware and software implementations support only a few of the possible combinations.
- *High bandwidth*: MPEG-2 streams for full-resolution, full-motion SD video typically operate at speeds above 2 Mbps, making it difficult to use E1 links, T1 links, or the uplink portion of many popular DSL systems. MPEG-2 streams for HD video can also easily exceed the speed of a normal 10BaseT Ethernet link.
- *Processing power*: Software-only decoders for MPEG-2 exist, but, depending on the profile/level used and the incoming bit rates, they can be difficult to run without the addition of a hardware accelerator to a desktop PC.
- *Performance limitations*: MPEG-2 standards have been in existence for over a decade, so dramatic improvements in performance are not likely in the future.
- *Video only*: All of the encoding and data representation standards for MPEG-2 are based on video images. Mechanisms to support advanced video concepts such as overlaid text and animation are not present.

Overall, MPEG-2 is a well-defined, stable compression system that is used throughout the world for professional-quality video. Because of its flexibility and power, not to mention the huge installed base of equipment, it will continue to be a popular standard for quite a while into the future.

MPEG-4

MPEG-4 is a more recent product of the standards process, the first version having become formally approved in 2000. A very important upgrade known variously as H.264, MPEG-4 Part 10, and MPEG-4 AVC (all synonyms) became a released standard in 2003. MPEG-4 incorporates a wide range of new technologies for video compression that have been developed in the past decade. All of the necessary support technology for the MPEG-4 system (such as custom semiconductors) has recently been developed, allowing MPEG-4 to become widely deployed.[1] Both MPEG-4 and H.264 are having a major impact on video compression in general, and IP video transport in particular. Each of these important innovations will be examined in this section.

Both MPEG-4 and H.264 take advantage of increases in processing power that have become available from the semiconductor industry over the past decade. Both developments require significantly more calculations to be made in both the encoder and the decoder. Together, these innovations have allowed a 50 percent reduction in bandwidth for equivalent video quality as compared to MPEG-2 and have enabled new applications such as HD video delivery over the Internet and by way of Blu-ray discs and IPTV networks.

MPEG-4 achieves many of its advances in compression efficiency through the introduction of new video objects. These objects can be created by the encoder from natural sources, such as video cameras and audio microphones, that capture input from the natural world,

---

1. Many readers may be curious about the lack of an MPEG-3 video standard. In fact, there was originally a working group set up to develop a standard for multiresolution encoding. This group's work was completed before the work on MPEG-2 was completed, so it was simply incorporated into the MPEG-2 standard. Readers should be careful not to confuse the MPEG audio coding standard called Layer III, often abbreviated as MP3, with the nonexistent MPEG-3 standard.

or they can be created as completely new objects created from synthetic sources that are generated through computer graphics or other means. The decoder must then assemble an image from multiple types of source material to form a composite image that combines elements from both natural and synthetic sources.

Take, for example, a sports broadcast. The broadcaster might want to supply an on-screen scoreboard, add some graphics to comment on the current match, and insert the local station identifier. In MPEG-2, all of these separate elements would be combined together at the broadcaster's facility and then compressed and transmitted to the viewers, who would all watch the same composite image. In MPEG-4, by contrast, each element could be generated separately and then transmitted as separate data units inside the MPEG-4 stream. The decoder at each viewer's location would process each of the different signal elements and then combine them to form a video signal that is sent to the viewer's display. In our example, once the format of the scoreboard was established, the score could be transmitted as a single number for each team, as shown in Figure 4-10. This is much more efficient from the perspective of data transport: It is far more bandwidth efficient to send simple score numbers than to send brightness and color data of dozens or hundreds of pixels that make up the scoreboard image. Synthetic-image technology provides two main benefits:

- Each user can be given control over the items being displayed. If, for example, the user doesn't want the score to be displayed, then the decoder can be instructed simply not to display the scoreboard. Or, if the user wants and the broadcaster permits, the user can move the scoreboard to another part of the screen or change its appearance.
- Much less bandwidth is consumed when synthetic signals are sent as compared to natural signals. This is due primarily to the innate complexity of natural signals and the need to reproduce accurately the pixels that make up a natural image.

Several other technological advances have been incorporated into MPEG-4. The size of each macroblock is no longer fixed, so small blocks can be used in areas of the image that are finely detailed. This also permits larger blocks to be used and encoded with fewer bits if

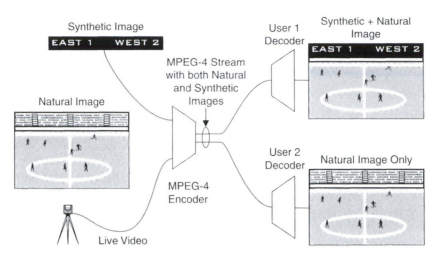

FIGURE 4-10 Natural and Synthetic Picture Elements

the pixels in portions of the image are very similar. Another innovation is the use of fractal compression, which is useful for certain types of images. Finally, MPEG-4 allows B frames to be based on other B frames, reducing the need for P frames and lowering the overall bandwidth requirement.

H.264 Advanced Video Codec

MPEG4 Part 10, also known as MPEG-4 AVC or H.264, is a powerful set of compression techniques for natural images. More efficient compression (i.e., lower encoded bit rate at same quality level) results from a number of new techniques, including:

- Multiple reference frames for each compressed frame, allowing different macroblocks to be encoded based on differences from a variety of source images. This can be useful when a foreground object conceals and later reveals a portion of the background that was encoded in a previous frame.
- Spatial prediction of a macroblock based on adjacent blocks for more efficient coding of large, repetitive areas.
- Deblocking filter, which helps to remove the sharp edges that sometimes appear at boundaries between adjacent macroblocks;

by smoothing out these sharp transitions, a more pleasing picture can be produced at a lower bit rate.

- Weighted prediction, which allows a scaling coefficient to be applied to a number of macroblocks, greatly simplifying the encoding process for scenes that involve a widespread change of brightness, such as a fade-to-black.
- Support for logarithmic (instead of just linear) step sizes for quantization, to simplify bit-rate management in the encoder for scenes with wide brightness ranges.
- Improved techniques for arithmetic compression, including CAVLC (context-adaptive variable-length coding) and CABAC (context-adaptive binary arithmetic coding). Both these techniques require significantly more calculation effort than the simple coding techniques introduced at the beginning of this chapter; however, both techniques result in a significantly more compressed bit stream.

Many other techniques and technologies are used in H.264, and they are too numerous (and too arcane) to list here. Taken as a whole, the bit-rate gains are impressive as compared to MPEG-2, and the encoders and decoders are significantly more complex. Since it would not be feasible to implement every feature for every application, different profiles have been defined for H.264 that serve a variety of different applications. Here is a partial list of the currently defined profiles:

- *Baseline profile*: Lowest amount of processing load; does not use B frames (called *slices* in H.264) and does not use CABAC coding. Suitable for use in progressive-scan videoconferencing and mobile TV applications. Some companies have defined different flavors of the baseline profile (e.g., low complexity), but these are not part of the current standards.
- *Main profile*: Designed to be the main consumer and broadcast profile; has been supplanted by high profile in some applications. Adds B slices and CABAC coding to baseline profile, so it requires more encode and decode processing power and memory.
- *Extended profile*: Targeted for streaming applications, has extra features to support recovery from data losses and to simplify stream switching. Adds SI and SP slices to main profile; these improve the performance when switching between low-bit-rate

streams by allowing an image to be generated without having to wait for an I slice. Does not use CABAC coding.

- *High profile*: Supports high-quality video storage and broadcast for professional applications; has become one of the major consumer formats, thanks to support for HD in Blu-ray discs. High-profile versions have been defined that add additional data for each pixel (10 bits per sample, 4:2:2 color sampling; 14 bits per sample), as well as versions that use only intraframe compression for easier editing.

In November 2007, scalable profiles were also added to H.264 at the baseline, high, and high intra levels. The main feature of these streams is an internal structure that allows a decoder to process only a subset of the stream data to produce images that are scaled to lower resolution, lower frames rates, or lower quality levels than the images represented by the original stream.

As of this writing, H.264 has 16 different performance levels, comparable in concept to the various levels in MPEG-2 (low, main, high 1440, and high). The H.264 levels range from 1 (64 to 256 kbps) to 5.1 (240 to 960 Mbps). These are far too numerous to discuss in this book.

Overall, MPEG-4 is an exciting new collection of technologies that promises to greatly increase the amount of video information that can be squeezed into a given amount of network bandwidth. Through MPEG-4 AVC, much more efficient video coding is possible, and the variety of object types available makes integration with computer-generated graphics simple and extremely bandwidth efficient. Table 4-5 lists some of the key advantages and disadvantages of MPEG-4 technology. MPEG-4's complexity and relative newness have spawned a huge amount of development work aimed at reaching the level of sophistication and maturity presently enjoyed by MPEG-2 technology. As of this writing, many first-generation MPEG-4 solutions have reached the market as well as a number of second- and third-generation products. These development activities will no doubt continue for the next several years.

TABLE 4-5

Advantages and Disadvantages of MPEG-4

Advantages

- *Large toolset*: The large range of new video-coding techniques makes MPEG-4 very flexible for new applications, particularly for computer-generated video and graphic (synthetic) objects.
- *Lower bandwidth*: Advanced Video Coding (AVC)/H.264 system makes it possible to transmit high-quality natural signals in half the bandwidth of MPEG-2 signals.
- *HD support*: MPEG-4 AVC may also make it possible for high-definition signals to be encoded at bit rates below 10 Mbps, opening up a much bigger range of technologies for transporting HD video signals.
- *User control*: Because the MPEG-4 decoder can form a composite image from many different sources (such as cameras, computer-generated graphics, and text files), viewers can be given control over which parts of the image they want displayed.
- *Stream scalability*: MPEG-4 has the ability to separate highly detailed portions of an image from less detailed portions. This allows an encoder to create multiple streams, one with low resolution to run on low-speed networks and multiple "helper" streams that add detail to an image, thereby allowing one stream to support multiple resolutions, frame rates, or quality levels.

Disadvantages

- *High complexity*: MPEG-4 has a large range of application profiles and performance points, significantly more than the number available for MPEG-2. Buyers need to ensure that the devices and technologies that are being purchased are compatible and capable of supporting the features required by the video application.
- *Installed base*: Literally hundreds of millions of devices in consumers' and broadcasters' possession today implement MPEG-2 technology, as well as hundreds of satellite and other television broadcast channels. Digital TV broadcasts in the United States and some other countries are also required to be MPEG-2. However, new installations, with little or no installed base, often move to adopt MPEG-4 from the beginning.
- *Processing power*: Decoders are more complex for MPEG-4 than for MPEG-2. According to the MPEG-4 Industry Forum (www.m4if.org), an MPEG-4 decoder will be 2.5 to 4 times as complex as an MPEG-2 decoder for similar applications. This means more complicated (and therefore more expensive) hardware devices and greater demand on processor resources for software decoders.
- *License fees*: Much of the intellectual property in MPEG-4 and H.264 is covered by patents and requires licensing. Some of these fees are on a per stream/per viewer basis that accumulates with usage. See the section on licensing at the end of this chapter for more detail.

MPEG Audio Compression

Just like video compression, MPEG has a variety of audio compression options. There are three layers of MPEG audio (conveniently called Layers I, II, and III) and two versions of a newer audio compression standard called Advanced Audio Coding (AAC). In this section, we'll take a short look at each one of these. Note that all of these audio compression methods will work with any type of MPEG video compression, except that MPEG-1 streams do not handle AAC audio.

Before we get into the differences between these options, let's look at their similarities. All of the MPEG audio encoders are lossy, which means that they will lose some of the information contained in the source audio signal. Furthermore, they are all perceptual encoders, which means that compression is done based on what the human hearing system can and cannot detect. Also, all of the MPEG encoders use digital audio signals with any of three audio sampling rates: 32 kHz, 44.1 kHz, and 48 kHz. In addition, each of the decoders (except AAC) must work properly with streams that have been encoded for lower layers; that is, a Layer III decoder must accept a Layer I or II stream, and a Layer II decoder must accept a Layer I stream.

In audio, perceptual coding can provide a significant amount of compression. The human ear is actually more sensitive to small distortions introduced by compression than the human eye. However, because the human ear is not perfect, some information can be discarded from the audio signal with little or no penalty. For example, the ear cannot hear signals that last for less than a millisecond (msec). A loud signal will mask (or cover up) a quieter signal that immediately precedes it or follows it. There are also limits to the range of frequencies that the ear can hear. Furthermore, a loud signal at one pitch will mask quieter sounds at other pitches that are close by and much quieter sounds at pitches that are not as close by (this is also why you can't hear the "hiss" noise that is intrinsic to an audiotape except during quiet periods). All of these limits to human hearing were taken into account when the MPEG techniques for compressing audio were designed.

MPEG audio Layer I is the simplest compression system. It uses 384 input samples for each compression run, which corresponds to 8 milliseconds of audio material using 48-kHz sampling. Layer I can produce a constant-bit-rate output at a compression ratio of 4:1, which means that a 1.4-Mbps CD-quality audio signal can be compressed to fit into a 384-kbps stream with no noticeable loss of quality. Compression beyond this to 192 or 128 kbps results in a noticeable loss of quality.

MPEG audio Layer II uses 1152 samples for each compression run, which corresponds to 24 msec of audio at 48-kHz sampling. This allows frequencies to be resolved more accurately. Layer II also eliminates some of the redundancy in Layer I, thereby achieving better compression of up to 8:1. This means that CD-quality audio can be achieved with a stream rate of 192 kbps.

MPEG audio Layer III uses the same number of samples as Layer II, but it uses them more efficiently. Layer III has an audio mode called *joint stereo*, which capitalizes on the strong similarities between the signals that make up the left and right channels of a stereo program. It also uses variable-length coding to pack the compressed audio coefficients more efficiently into the output stream. As a result, Layer III encoders can pack CD-quality audio into streams as small as 128 kbps, achieving compression ratios as high as 12:1. Note that audio files compressed using MPEG Layer III often carry the file extension ".mp3" and are popular in many music download, file-swapping, and portable player systems.

MPEG Advanced Audio Coding (AAC) is available only with MPEG-2 or MPEG-4 video streams. It supports up to 48 audio channels, including 5.1 audio, and it includes lots of tools that can be used by a sophisticated encoder to create high-performance audio streams. One option is a lossless compression mode, for applications that don't require the absolute highest levels of compression but do require high fidelity. For MPEG-4, the stream can include various audio objects, similar to MPEG-4 video. These objects can be either natural or synthetic audio. The audio decoder is responsible for assembling all of the audio objects and producing a final combined output. AAC signals are often used for streaming audio and video applications and are supported in portable devices such as Apple's iPod.

In 2004, a new form of AAC was released, called aacPlus™ or HE AAC (for high efficiency), with some advances in sound quality at higher sound frequencies. A second version, called e AAC+, HE AACv2, or aacPlus v2™ has also been developed with special support for stereo signals, called *parametric stereo*.[2] Some of these advanced versions have been incorporated into commercial products, including Adobe Flash and a number of mobile telephones. The HE AACv2 standard has also been selected for use by broadcasters in Brazil, Korea, and Japan and by the DVB consortium for use in video-over-IP applications in Europe.

Overall, MPEG audio is flexible and does not require near the magnitude of processing power of MPEG video. As the layer number goes up, the complexity of both the encoder and the decoder goes up, but so does the compression ratio. Figure 4-11 summarizes and compares the main features of the different audio levels described in this section. Software-only Layer III decoders can run smoothly in a wide variety of personal computers, including desktop and laptop systems. AAC decoders are also becoming very popular, in part due to the support from Apple. When choosing an audio-encoding method, remember that the overall transport bandwidth must be high enough to carry the video signal, the audio signal, and some overhead to make the streams operate correctly. Audio-encoding methods with higher compression ratios will allow more bandwidth to be allocated to video signals.

Compression Method	Samples per Block	Compression Ratio	CD-Quality Bit Rate (kbps)
Layer 1	384	4:1	384
Layer 2	1152	8:1	192
Layer 3	1152	12:1	128
AAC	1152	16:1	96
HE AACv2	2048	32:1	48

FIGURE 4-11 Comparison of MPEG Audio Standards

---

2. aacPlus™ and aacPlus v2™ are trademarks of Coding Technologies.

MPEG Video Comparison

With so many different flavors of MPEG available, many readers will be asking the question: "Which version of MPEG should I use for my application?" Of course, the only truly accurate answer is "It depends," but that isn't very satisfying. So, at the risk of starting some heated arguments, here is a list of general guidelines that readers might follow. (Note: These guidelines are solely the opinion of the author and should not be interpreted as hard-and-fast rules. Furthermore, as technology evolves, some of the following statements may become less accurate). With all that in mind, here is a comparison:

MPEG-1 has been in existence for a long time and requires less processing power than either MPEG-2 or MPEG-4. However, since most PCs sold in the past 5 years have more than enough processing power to handle more advanced codecs, MPEG-1 no longer has a useful role to play for new applications.

MPEG-2 is also a stable, mature technology that has widespread use in the video entertainment field. It is currently employed for most professional video applications, including broadcast, satellite, cable TV, DVD, and HD video. Hundreds of millions of devices installed around the world are capable of receiving and decoding MPEG-2 video in a wide variety of flavors. MPEG-2 is commonly used in contribution, distribution, and delivery networks, and it is the only compression format approved for digital TV broadcast in the United States and some other countries. Accordingly, MPEG-2 will be a popular format well into the future for applications that require compatibility with the installed base of STBs and DTVs. However, for new applications (particularly ones that are software based), strong consideration should be given to MPEG-4/H.264 technologies.

MPEG-4 offers a huge range of operating profiles and levels for a wide variety of applications. MPEG-4 has a number of advantages for synthetic (computer-generated) video and has already deeply penetrated IP video streaming applications. (Apple's QuickTime has fully migrated to MPEG-4.) Most desktop PCs can already decode MPEG-4 video using software that is freely available on the Internet in the form of media players. MPEG-4's scalability also enables one video source to feed multiple users at varying quality levels, allowing each to get the best possible video quality that his or her network will support.

MPEG-4 AVC/H.264 can achieve quality levels that compare favorably to MPEG-2 at half the bit rate. Of course, there is a cost to this, in terms of the greater processing power needed to encode and decode AVC signals and the license fees that need to be paid. Already, H.264 has been used in multichannel IPTV over DSL networks and Internet video applications and to support HD content on Blu-ray discs. MPEG-4 AVC/H.264 should definitely be considered a strong candidate for new video compression installations.

Table 4-6 summarizes the main differences between the various flavors of MPEG.

TABLE 4-6

MPEG Video Compression Comparison

	MPEG-1	MPEG-2	MPEG-4	MPEG-4 AVC/H.264
Standard finalized	1992	1996	2000	2003
Supports interlacing	No	Yes	Yes	Yes
Object based	No	No	Yes	Yes
Decoder complexity	Low	High	High	Very high
Decoder chipsets	MPEG-2 decoder will handle MPEG-1	Many	Available	Available
Encoder chipsets	Few	Many	Available	Available
Common stream rates	500–1500 kbps	2.5–50 Mbps	100 kbps– 10 Mbps	1–4 Mbps SD 4–10 Mbps HD
Profiles and levels	Few	12	Many	Many
Audio formats	MPEG Layers I, II, III	Adds Advanced Audio Codec (AAC)	Adds audio objects and synthetic audio	Same as MPEG-4
Stream scalability	No	Yes, but only at higher profiles (not used much)	Yes	Yes
Licensing fees	Minimal	Paid by encoder and decoder suppliers	Fees for encoders, decoders, streams, and users. Controlled by MPEG-LA	

OTHER COMPRESSION TECHNOLOGIES

Certainly, MPEG video compression technologies are very important to video networking. However, a number of other video compression technologies are used for video transport over IP networks. Fortunately, many of them use the same underlying technologies as MPEG, so our discussion can be much simpler. In the following sections, we'll look at some of these other technologies and where they are used.

H.261 and H.263

One of the most popular standards for videoconferencing on IP networks, H.323, uses the H.261 and H.263 video compression standards. Other videoconferencing formats, such as H.320 (for ISDN networks) and H.324 (for standard dial-up telephone lines, including some wireless ones), also use H.261 and H.263.[3]

H.261 compression was designed for operation on digital telephone lines that operated in multiples of 64 kbps (one DS0 or one voice connection) up to a maximum of 2048 kbps. These interfaces are collectively known by the label *px64* (read as "p times sixty-four"), where "p" can range from 1 to 30. In North America, when "p" equals 24, the system bandwidth will be equivalent to a T1 signal. This kind of compression is also available for use on other networks, including IP networks.

The basic video resolution for H.261 is based on the Common Intermediate Format (CIF), which is not directly compatible with NTSC or PAL video framing. CIF operates at 29.97 frames per second and has a picture size 352 pixels wide by 288 lines high. CIF has half the horizontal and half the vertical resolution of a PAL signal (704×576), or one-quarter the number of pixels. The other important resolution for H.261 is QCIF, which has one-quarter the resolution of CIF, or 176×144 pixels. In H.323,

3. Because of this shared use of H.261 and H.263, providing a gateway to interconnect between IP, ISDN, and dial-up videoconferencing systems is fairly simple. See Chapter 10 for more information.

any device that supports video communication must support H.261 QCIF mode. CIF mode can also be supported, but QCIF is required.

H.261 uses motion prediction and pixel compression, just like MPEG. However, H.261 uses only I frames and P frames, not B frames. It uses 4:2:0 color space, so the resolution of the color signals is cut in half in both the horizontal and the vertical directions. This works out to 88 pixels horizontally and 72 lines vertically in QCIF mode. Considering these low resolutions, it is easy to see how H.261 is able to send video images over relatively low-speed telephone lines.

H.263 and H.261 are similar in scope and application, and many devices that handle H.263 video will handle H.261 video as well (although the two compression systems are not interoperable). H.263 supports finer granularity of motion estimation, so the predicted frames can be more accurate, and thus less data needs to be sent for P frames. It has more picture-encoding options and uses a more efficient algorithm for variable-length coding of the compressed data. H.263 also supports PB frames, which are a very efficient way to code information, similar to an MPEG P frame coupled with a B frame, except they do not work as well in scenes with heavy motion.

Because H.263 was designed to work at very low bit rates, it introduces a new frame resolution, called sub-QCIF. This provides 128 pixels horizontally and 96 lines vertically, which is a bit bigger than a postage stamp on a modern computer monitor. It also supports two larger modes: 4CIF (704×576) and 16CIF (1408×1152). Any H.323 device that uses H.263 must support QCIF resolution. Also, any device that supports H.263 CIF or higher must also support the H.261 CIF format. All of these rules help promote interoperability.

H.263 version 2 provides other capabilities, including support for any number of lines between 4 and 1152 that is divisible by 4 and any number of pixels per line from 4 to 2048 that is divisible by 4. This version can be useful for specialized cameras and for displays that can show multiple images. It also supports some new encoding methods, including scalable streams (see the discussion in the MPEG section earlier in the chapter).

H.262, H.264, and Standards Cross-Reference

Curious readers might be wondering why the previous section skipped over ITU recommendation number H.262. We did this for a very good reason: We already discussed this standard when we discussed MPEG-2! Similarly, H.264 is the same as MPEG-4's AVC. Table 4-7 helps show these relationships. Note that this table is intended to be a simple guide, not an authoritative reference that covers the multiple revisions these documents have undergone.

Motion JPEG

The Joint Photographic Experts Group has developed JPEG and JPEG-2000 formats for compressing digital still photographs. JPEG is very similar to an MPEG I frame; JPEG-2000 uses a compression technique called *wavelets*. Newer versions offer lossless coding as well. When used for video signals, the formats are called Motion JPEG and Motion JPEG-2000. Each frame of the video is encoded as a separate picture, which makes the resulting stream very suitable for editing. It also makes the video stream bit rate higher than it would be with other technologies, such as MPEG-2 and MPEG-4.

TABLE 4-7

Compression Standards Cross-Reference

Common Name of Application	International Telecommunication Union (ITU)	International Organization for Standardization (ISO)
P × 64 Video ISDN Videoconferencing	H.261	N/A
MPEG 1 Video and Audio Coding	N/A	11172
MPEG-2 Video Coding Only	H.262	13818-2
MPEG-2 Advanced Audio Coding	N/A	13818-7
MPEG-2 Systems, normal audio, and other aspects	N/A	13818-1, -3 to -6, -8 to -11
Low Bit Rate Video IP, Dial-up Videoconferencing	H.263	N/A
MPEG-4 (except AVC) Audio and Visual Objects	N/A	14496
MPEG-4 Advanced Video Coding	H.264	14496-10

Wavelets perform a similar function to the MPEG compression algorithms, but they use a different mathematical operation. One advantage of wavelet encoding is that the process has built-in scalability, allowing low-speed users to receive just one low-resolution stream, whereas users with higher-speed interfaces can also receive "helper" streams that enhance the video signal.

Three main video applications have been implemented using Motion JPEG:

- Motion JPEG-2000 has been selected as the standard compression format by the Digital Cinema Initiative group. This standard applies to both 2 K (2048 × 1080) and 4 K (4096 × 2160) images for use in digital projection in cinemas.
- A number of video-editing systems have in the past used Motion JPEG as an intermediate format, because of the relative simplicity of editing these video streams. However, this format has become less popular in recent years, because more efficient coding methods have been introduced.
- A number of video transport links using Motion JPEG or JPEG-2000 have been introduced at various times in the market. Several manufacturers currently offer proprietary motion JPEG-2000 products that operate over IP networks for high-bit-rate video contribution applications.

Windows Media and Other Streaming Formats

A number of proprietary video and audio encoder/decoder (codec) systems are on the market, and many of them are suitable for use in video transport over IP networks. Because they are proprietary, the exact details of their operation are normally not provided for general publication. In addition, the different codec manufacturers are currently engaged in heated competition, so product cycles are short and performance and other specifications can change rapidly. Let's look at four of the largest codec suppliers for the video streaming market:

Microsoft has a long history of video codec development for Windows Media applications. With the introduction of the Windows

Media Video version 9 (WMV9) codec, Microsoft decided to offer their codec for standardization by SMPTE, where it became known as VC1. This became an official SMPTE standard in 2006. Tests have shown the VC1 signal quality is just about as good as H.264, with similar resolutions and bit rates.

VC1 is simply a video compression standard. In contrast, Windows Media is a complete system that includes digital rights management, file-streaming/storage formats, and a variety of other capabilities needed to form a complete video/audio storage system based on the VC1 codec. Recently, there have not been a large number of new VC1 products announced, but Microsoft has been implementing a number of large IPTV systems using their DRM and middleware product offerings.

Real Networks is another supplier of proprietary codec technology. Most of Real's products are targeted at the video streaming market, with RealVideo 10™ released in 2004. Development continues; however, Real also offers support for other video compression formats in its services and in its player products.

Apple Computer supplies QuickTime technology, which has migrated toward using standards-compliant technology, such as MPEG-4. Apple was the principal designer of the container file format that was the basis of the MPEG-4 specification. Apple relies principally on H.264 and MPEG-4 standards for its iPod and iTunes video codecs.

Adobe's Flash platform has been widely adopted for Internet video applications, including major portals such as YouTube. Traditionally, video encoding for Flash was performed by codecs supplied by Sorenson Media to create files in the .FLV (Flash Video) format. More recently, Adobe has also been offering H.264 for high-quality and HD applications. Further change is likely as the Internet video market continues to grow and evolve.

One distinguishing feature of all four of the preceding proprietary codec suppliers is their willingness to provide a free software client (or "player") for receiving their compressed video streams. Literally hundreds of millions of personal computer users have downloaded and installed these players onto their desktop and laptop computers.

In addition, most of these companies also supply a free encoder with limited functionality. More sophisticated encoders are generally available for a price; these versions often contain advanced features that can make the job of creating content files easier as well as using more efficient compression algorithms.

So far, we have discussed mainly software-based proprietary codecs, but hardware-based ones are also available for closed system applications, such as security cameras. Many of these codecs have been designed to efficiently handle specific types of video, such as security applications in which there is very little motion in the image for long periods of time. Since product cost is a big concern in many of these applications, designers will often use subsets of standard compression systems or completely proprietary algorithms that can be implemented inexpensively. As a result, most of these codecs will work only with other products from the same manufacturer.

There are no easy answers when deciding whether or not to use proprietary codecs. All four of the main software-based codec suppliers mentioned in this section have a long and distinguished track record of innovation and customer service. The same can be said for many hardware-based codec suppliers. Nevertheless, any users of a proprietary codec run the risk that their supplier will, for one reason or another, stop providing products. Prudent users will assess this risk and make sure to have a contingency plan in place in case this happens. In addition, H.264 is gaining a lot of traction across the market, so users have to give it serious consideration. Table 4-8 gives several other advantages and disadvantages of proprietary codecs.

DV, DVCAM, and DVCPRO

The popular camera and videotape formats DV, DVCAM, and DVCPRO are intended for use in a video production environment. As such, they need to meet two requirements: The video should be easy to edit, and the image quality should be very high. Since the primary applications are recording onto digital videotape or into

TABLE 4-8

Advantages and Disadvantages of Proprietary Codecs

Advantages

- *Innovation*: As compression technology advances, innovations can be incorporated into proprietary codecs very rapidly. Industry standards tend to have a slower rate of change because of the need to achieve agreement between many different parties.
- *Pricing*: Many proprietary software codec suppliers offer basic versions of their players (decoders) free and have very low-cost encoder options.
- *Backward compatibility*: Proprietary codec suppliers have a strong incentive to ensure that new versions of their codecs work with previous versions and have typically done a good job in this area.

Disadvantages

- *Portability*: Because a single vendor controls when and how proprietary codecs are implemented, versions for alternative platforms (e.g., Linux) may be late to arrive or may never be produced.
- *Change control*: Major codec suppliers determine when new features are released to market and frequently encourage end users to upgrade to the latest version. This can make it difficult for large organizations to control changes in user configurations.
- *Platform requirements*: As codecs become more powerful, the minimum requirements for other system components (operating systems, processor speeds, etc.) can also increase.
- *Archival storage*: As with any rapidly evolving technology, long-term storage of encoded video files is useful only as long as suitable decoder software is available.

memory, high-speed data is normally used. Methods have also been developed for sending these signals by means of IP networks.

The base level of these formats is a 25-Mbps compressed video signal. Video compression is performed like MPEG, with each frame of video coded separately using I frames only. When only I frames are used, subsequent editing is very simple, because edits can be made before any frame in the image. Other formats exist in this family, including DVCPRO operating at 50 and 100 Mbps. A high-definition version of the DVCAM signal also exists, called HDCAM, that operates at roughly 150 Mbps.

The Internet Engineering Task Force (IETF) has published RFC 3189, which defines a way to put DV-encoded video into IP packets. Given the high bit rates involved in this format, it is unlikely that this format will receive widespread use in general-purpose video networking applications.

Dolby AC-3 Audio

Dolby AC-3 audio coding is also commonly known as Dolby Digital. It offers a high-quality audio experience with good compression characteristics and has been approved for use in both DVDs and digital television broadcasts in the United States. Dolby AC-3 audio is included in some versions of MPEG-4 and is used on a number of satellite television systems.

Dolby AC-3 offers a sophisticated perceptual model of the human hearing systems, so extensive compression can be performed without any noticeable difference to the human ear. Dolby Digital also offers support for surround sound, including the popular 5.1 audio format (see Chapter 3).

COMPARING COMPRESSION TECHNOLOGIES

Users who deploy video transport systems often need to select equipment for compressing video and audio signals. Because of the wide variety of applications, it would be very difficult to describe one product that can fit all (or even most) needs. Plus, video compression technology is constantly evolving, and comparisons made at any one point in time can quickly go out of date. Instead of attempting to make comparisons of the various technologies, in the following sections we will discuss how the comparisons can be made and which aspects of compression are important to various applications.

Video Quality

For many users, video quality is the most important criterion for selecting a video compression system. The level of quality required for a system to support medical diagnoses is far different from that needed for simple chats between coworkers in a videoconference.

TABLE 4-9

Video Quality Comparison Guidelines

- Use several video sequences that are similar to the scenes that will be used in the real application; videoconferencing systems should not be evaluated using live sports footage.
- Use high-quality video sources and displays for the evaluation. Use digital sources if the encoder and decoder have digital inputs; and make sure to test the analog inputs and outputs as well if they will also be used.
- Examine the impact of transmission errors on the system. See what happens when bit-error or packet-loss rates climb.
- Be sure to watch the video stream for several minutes, particularly when scene changes happen, which will stress the compression system and create peaks in the compressed data rate.
- Test each system for audio/video delay matching. It is not uncommon to have synchronization problems appear only after several minutes of playing.
- Test a range of different compression configurations, such as different GOP lengths and patterns and different stream rates.
- Many multichannel transport systems multiplex video signals together, so it is important to test the system under a full load, to make sure that all necessary components are operating and that buffers are adequately sized.
- Check how different manufacturers define and control the video bit rate. Some base their specifications on the total bit stream; others simply refer to the rate of just the raw compressed video stream.
- Try to do head-to-head comparisons, where both systems are showing the same video and being displayed in the same manner, preferably on the same display (displays can be hard to match completely).
- If possible, use multiple observers to score the video performance. Since most encoding methods are perceptual, flaws that might not be noticed by one person might be very objectionable to other viewers.

However, some guidelines listed in Table 4-9 can be used when making these comparisons.

Audio Quality

Unfortunately, in the video transport business, most users end up focused on video quality and neglect audio quality. Worse yet, many audio evaluations are done with unsuitable source material and poor-quality speakers. Studies have shown that people perceive video quality to increase when audio quality is increased. The message is clear here: Make sure that audio performance is comparable

TABLE 4-10
Audio Quality Comparison Rules

- Use audio signals that match the application as closely as possible. What might be suitable for carrying normal conversations may not work well for a musical performance.
- Use high-quality audio sources and speakers for the evaluation. Use both digital and analog audio signal inputs and outputs if they are available.
- Use a similar setup for all systems, including the sampling rates and compressed signal bit rates, to allow a fair comparison.
- Evaluate the system performance at both high and low incoming sound levels. Make sure that loud sounds don't become distorted and that quiet sections of the program are not accompanied by audio noise.

to the level of video performance. Table 4-10 lists a few rules for evaluating audio compression systems.

System Delay

End-to-end delay in a video transport system is normally significant only when two-way communication is taking place for applications such as videoconferencing and distance learning.

The easiest way to measure delay is to have a camera connected to the encoder and a display connected to the decoder interconnected with a network that closely models the target application. If the delay cannot be noticed, then the system is quite suitable for any application. If the delay is noticeable but lasts less than half a second, then use on an interactive system is possible, although users may experience some discomfort.

Note that many systems can be configured to trade off bandwidth and quality for delay. In particular, MPEG systems can be configured for low delays by using very short GOP lengths, such as IP or I frame only. This reduces the delay in both the encoder and the decoder, but at a price: The amount of compression is reduced, and either the network bandwidth must be increased or the quality level will go down. It is not uncommon for different applications to require different system configurations, so a certain amount of trial and error is reasonable.

When delay is being tested, it is also a good idea to check lip synchronization. This should be tested over a significant period of time with uninterrupted source material so that low amounts of drift have a chance to accumulate and show up as a real difference in the displayed image and sound. Poor or drifting lip synchronization can be very difficult to correct in an installation, so selecting a good quality encoder and decoder is essential.

Compression Efficiency

Compression efficiency is important to evaluate when testing a video compression system. More efficient encoders can reduce use of network bandwidth, deliver higher-quality signals on fixed-bandwidth systems, and consume less storage.

Since video compression is based on human perception, the best way to compare quality is to have human observers compare the two resulting signals under controlled viewing circumstances and to score the results for different bit rates.

TECHNOLOGY LICENSING ISSUES

As we have seen in this chapter, a huge number of clever technologies have been applied to the art and science of video compression. The patent portfolio for MPEG-2 alone includes 630 patents from around the world.

MPEG LA is an organization responsible for establishing and collecting the license fees on the technology and for distributing the collected funds to the patent owners. This central clearinghouse provides big benefits to the users of this technology, because one simple payment to MPEG LA satisfies the patent obligations for the covered technology.

The license fees are assessed on a per-item basis and are officially described on www.mpegla.com. For example, the fee listed on the website for an MPEG-2 decoding device (such as a DVD player, a set-top box, or a computer with a DVD player, whether hardware or software) produced after 2002 is US $2.50. Other fees are assessed for MPEG-2 encoders, MPEG multiplexers, and recorded media such as DVDs.

For MPEG-4, there are similar fee arrangements for devices. In addition there are fees based on the number of streams created and on the number of subscribers served in cable and satellite television systems. Plus, there are fees for individual titles that are sold to viewers on a DVD or via pay-per-view, such as a video-on-demand system. These fees have created some controversy in the industry.

Fees for devices are normally collected from the device manufacturers, and publishers of media, such as DVDs, are also responsible for paying the fees required for those items. Most of the MPEG-4 license fees that are payable on a per-stream or a per-subscriber basis are targeted at companies that are charging users to view the videos. When these videos are delivered to employees within a company or are distributed free of charge for educational purposes, the intent is not to charge on a per-item basis. However, this arrangement may be subject to revision, so users of MPEG-4 should investigate the necessary license arrangements in detail before launching a large-scale system.

Disclaimer: Neither the author of this book nor the publisher claims any expertise in licensing law or in the terms of the MPEG LA license agreement. Readers should consult with MPEG LA and any other licensing bodies to confirm all details of the required licenses prior to installing a video network that relies on this technology.

REVIEW AND CHECKLIST UPDATE

In this chapter, we covered the basics of video and audio compression. We looked at the benefits and drawbacks of compression. We spent some time discussing MPEG, because it is the most widely used technology for compression today. We covered a few other types of compression that are used in videoconferencing and other applications. We talked about the ways in which compression technology and devices can be compared. We concluded with a look at the technology licensing issues.

Chapter 4 Checklist Update

❑ Decide if compression will be used on video and/or audio content. If compression isn't going to be used, will all the networks that will be used have adequate bandwidth to handle the digital video content?

❑ Examine the devices that will be responsible for transmitting and receiving the video/audio content. Will they have adequate performance to encode and/or decode the video in addition to other required tasks?

❑ If desktop PCs will be used, will hardware encoders or decoders need to be added, or will software encoders and decoders be adequate?

❑ If stand-alone hardware devices are to be used (such as set-top boxes), how will the users select programming and control other functions?

❑ Make sure that both content sources and destinations are equipped with compatible technology. Even when the chosen technology is based on the same standards, it is important to make sure that each supplier has implemented a compatible set of features. Be particularly careful to check the supported profiles and levels of MPEG-2 and MPEG-4.

❑ For MPEG systems, a fair amount of configuration of the units may be required. Make sure both encoder and decoder are configured to identical values for all parameters. Users must select a GOP length and pattern, a target video and audio bandwidth, a video resolution, a network interface bit rate, audio format, etc.

❑ Make sure to evaluate compression systems in all critical areas, including:
  ❑ video quality
  ❑ audio quality
  ❑ system delay and audio/video (lip) synchronization
  ❑ compression efficiency

❑ Make sure to use high-quality source material, displays, and speakers for evaluations. Make sure to use multiple people to evaluate the systems and score the results; different individuals will have different perceptions of compression artifacts.

❑ Make sure that the encoder and decoder correctly handle any required data contained in the VBI, such as closed captioning.

❑ Ensure that equipment and software vendors have paid the appropriate licensing fees for any technology products that are being purchased and that the proper fees are paid to all content rights holders.

❑ For applications in which viewers will be charged for video and audio content, determine whether royalties need to be paid on a per-stream or per-user basis due to the license terms for the compression technologies used, such as MPEG-4.

❑ If new networks are to be constructed, make sure that they can handle the full number of streams with each one operating at the maximum allowed bit rate.

5

IP NETWORKING BASICS

An understanding of the basic principles of Internet Protocol (IP) networking will make our discussions of video transport much easier to understand and to put into context. In this chapter, along with an overview of IP, we will look at Ethernet technology, which is the most commonly used network technology for IP transport.

Readers with significant networking experience may choose to skip this chapter, but please understand that we will cover terminology used in the remainder of this book. By the end of this chapter, readers should understand how both IP and Ethernet fit into the wide array of networking technologies and be familiar with some of the terminology associated with IP networking.

HOW IP FITS IN

IP (Internet Protocol) provides a uniform addressing scheme so that computers on one network can communicate with computers on a

Video Over IP: IPTV, Internet Video, H.264, P2P, Web TV, and Streaming: A Complete Guide to Understanding the Technology

distant network. IP also provides a set of functions that make it easy for different types of applications (such as e-mail, web browsing, and video streaming) to work in parallel on a single computer. Plus, IP allows different types of computers (mainframes, PCs, Macs, Linux machines, etc.) to communicate with each other.

IP is very flexible because it is not tied to a specific physical communication method. IP links have been successfully established over a wide variety of different physical links. One very popular technology for IP transport is Ethernet (also commonly known as 10BaseT or IEEE 802.3, although these are not strict synonyms). Many other technologies can support IP, including dial-up modems, wireless links (such as Wi-Fi), and SONET and ATM telecom circuits. IP will even work across connections where several network technologies are combined, such as a wireless home access link that connects to a CATV system offering cable modem services, which in turn sends customer data to the Internet by means of a fiber-optic backbone (which is the network setup currently employed by the author). This adaptability is one of the things that makes IP so widespread.

A Simple Analogy

A very simple, limited analogy may be appropriate here. In some respects, an IP address is like a telephone number. If you know someone's telephone number, there is a pretty good chance that you can pick up your phone and call him or her. It doesn't matter what country the person is in, as long as you dial correctly (and add the country code if needed). It doesn't matter what kind of technology that person is using—mobile phone, cordless phone, fixed rotary phone, or tone-dialed phone. Several different network voice technologies may be used to complete the circuit, including copper cable, fiber optics, microwave links, satellite links, and other wireless technologies. For data networks, an IP address provides the same function: a mechanism to uniquely identify different computers, and to allow them to contact each other and exchange data over a huge variety of different network technologies.

Stretching the analogy a bit further, just knowing someone's telephone number does not mean that you are going to be able to communicate with him or her. A call might be placed when there is nobody to answer the phone or the phone is engaged in another call. The call might go through just fine, but if both speakers don't use a common language, then communication won't occur. The same is true with IP networking—simply knowing another computer's IP address doesn't mean that it will be possible for two applications running on different machines to communicate with each other.

Of course, it is important to remember that IP networking and telephony are two very different technologies. Telephony is *connection-oriented*, meaning that a specific circuit must be established over the entire path between the sender and the receiver before any communication takes place and that all the information will flow over this same route. IP, on the other hand, is *connectionless*, meaning that the information is broken up into subunits prior to transmission and that each subunit is free to take any available path from the sender to the receiver. We'll talk more about these subunits of data, also known as *packets* or *datagrams*, shortly.

The Internet vs. Internets

The public Internet is a massive global network that interconnects billions of computers on millions of networks and supports a wide variety of applications, such as the World Wide Web. There is only one Internet in general use today, although a group of researchers has put together a newer high-speed network called *Internet2* that interconnects a number of universities and other institutions. Once you have access to the Internet, you have access to a wide variety of applications, including web browsing, e-mail, file transfer, and a variety of video services.

However, it's important to understand that many companies also run their own private "internets," commonly called *intranets*. These private networks often provide many of the services of the Internet, but in a closed environment (or one that has carefully protected links to the public Internet). Private internets are often constructed using private communication links, such as leased telecom circuits. Or they can be constructed by using virtual private network (VPN) connections that use the Internet to provide secure, private communication.

Both the Internet and internets commonly use the Internet Protocol to allow communication across a wide variety of technologies and architectures. IP addresses of individual devices can be used on an internet, on the public Internet, or on both. Also note that internets are, in many instances, more suitable for video transport than the Internet, simply because the behavior of the network can be more easily controlled.

Limitations of IP

IP doesn't do everything. IP depends on other software and hardware, and other software in turn depends on IP. Figure 5-1 illustrates how IP fits in between the actual job of data transport performed by physical networks and the software applications that use IP to communicate with applications running on other servers.

IP is neither a user application nor an application protocol. However, many user applications employ IP to accomplish their tasks, such as sending e-mail, playing a video, and browsing the web. These applications use application protocols such as the Hypertext Transfer Protocol (HTTP) and Simple Mail Transfer Protocol (SMTP). These protocols provide services to applications. For example, one of the

Functions and Examples

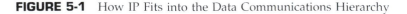

| User Applications | Functions: Act on User Commands, Provide User Interface
Examples: Netscape Navigator, Outlook Express, Windows Media Player |
| Application Protocols | Functions: Provide Services to User Applications
Examples: HTTP—HyperText Transfer Protocol, SMTP—Simple Mail Transfer Protocol |
| Transport Protocols | Functions: Format Data into Datagrams, Handle Data Transmission Errors
Examples: TCP—Transmission Control Protocol, UDP—User Datagram |
| IP: Internet Protocol | Functions: Supply Network Addresses; Move Packets Between Devices |
| Data Link Services | Functions: Send Packets Over Physical Networks
Examples: Ethernet, Token Ring, Packet over ATM/SONET |
| Physical Networks | Functions: Data Transmitters and Receivers; Wires, Optical Fibers
Examples: 10BaseT UTP, Wi-Fi, SONET, DSL |

FIGURE 5-1   How IP Fits into the Data Communications Hierarchy

services provided by HTTP is a uniform method for giving the location of resources on the Internet, called a Uniform Resource Locator, or URL. Many other protocols use IP, and we will discuss them throughout this book.

IP by itself is not even a reliable means of communications; it does not provide a mechanism to resend data that might be lost or corrupted in transmission. Other protocols that employ IP are responsible for that (see the discussion of TCP in Chapter 6). Using the telephone analogy again, IP can connect the telephone call, but it doesn't control what happens if, for example, the person being called isn't home or if the call gets interrupted before the parties are finished talking. Those occurrences are the responsibility of the protocols that use IP for communication.

IP BASICS

By understanding a few basic concepts of IP, we will be able to discuss how video traffic can successfully be sent over an IP network. In the following sections we'll talk first about one of the most common features of IP: the IP address. Then we'll cover the basic building block of any IP communication, the IP packet. We'll also take a quick look at a couple of technologies that affect how IP addresses are used in practice and how these practices affect video transport.

IP Addresses

One aspect of IP that is easy to recognize is the special format used to give an IP address. This format, called *dotted decimal*, consists of a series of four numbers separated by periods (or "dots"). For example, 129.35.76.177 is the IP address for www.elsevier.com. Most folks who have had to configure their own home network or laptop connection have probably seen information in this form. A dotted decimal number represents a 32-bit number, which is broken up into four 8-bit numbers.[1]

---

1.   IP version 4, which is what is employed in the Internet today, uses 32-bit addresses. IP version 6 has a different addressing scheme, with 128 bits for each IP address. We will limit our discussions in the rest of the book to IP version 4, also known as IPv4.

Of course, being human, we have a hard time remembering and typing all of those digits correctly (even when writing a book). Plus Elsevier might decide to change to a different Internet service provider that uses a different block of IP addresses for their web servers. To make life easy, the Domain Name System (DNS) was invented. DNS provides a translation service for web browsers and other software applications that takes easy-to-remember domain names (such as "elsevier.com") and translates them into IP addresses (such as 129.35.76.177).

Some IP addresses have special functions. For example, addresses in the range 224.0.0.0 through 239.255.255.255 are reserved for multicasting, which is discussed in Chapter 9. Other addresses are reserved for special functions, such as NAT, which is described later in this chapter.

IP Packets

Basically, IP works as a delivery service for IP packets. A packet is a single message unit that can be sent over IP, with very specific format and content rules. Since there are many excellent references available that talk about the structure of an IP packet, we'll just summarize, in Table 5-1, the key header elements that an IP packet needs to have and illustrate them in Figure 5-2.[2]

The process of sending a packet from one computer to another may involve transit through many different IP network links. At each step along the way, the IP packet must be processed. This processing involves the following procedures:

- The header of the IP packet must first have its header checksum verified. If the checksum is incorrect (due to a bit error on the data link, for example), then the packet is destroyed.

---

2. Note that IP messages are sometimes referred to as *datagrams*, particularly in standards documents such as those from the IETF (Internet Engineering Task Force). Long datagrams sometimes need to be broken up into smaller packets to traverse some networks (such as standard Ethernet, which has a maximum transmission unit [MTU] of 1500 bytes). This process is called *fragmentation*.

TABLE 5-1

Key Elements of an IP Packet

- *Destination address*: The IP address indicating where the packet is being sent.
- *Source address*: The IP address indicating where the packet came from.
- *Total length*: A count, in bytes, of the length of the entire packet, including the header.
- *Header checksum*: A basic error-checking mechanism for the header information in a packet. Any packet with an error in its header will be destroyed.
- *Type of service*: A group of bits that can be used to indicate the relative importance of one packet as compared to another. They will be discussed in Chapter 7 in more detail, but note that most Internet service providers (ISPs) and the public Internet do not routinely allow one user's packets to claim to have priority another user's.
- *Time-to-live*: A counter that is decremented each time a packet is forwarded in an IP network. When this value reaches zero, the packet is destroyed. This mechanism prevents packets from endlessly looping around in a network.
- *Fragmentation control*: These bits and bytes are used when a packet needs to be broken up into multiple packets to travel across a specific network segment.
- *Other items* include the header length field, protocol identifier, version identifier, and options that are part of the specifications for IP but would require more detail to describe than we need for the purposes of this book.

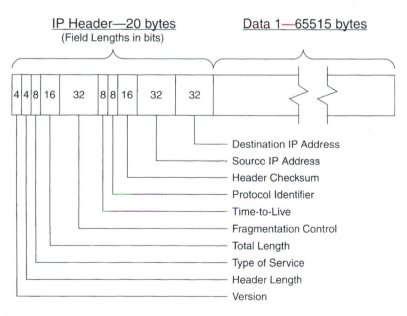

FIGURE 5-2 IP Packet Format

- The header is then examined to determine where the packet is going, by looking at the destination IP address. Based on this IP address, the network equipment (typically an IP router; see the description later in this chapter) determines what to do with the packet, such as send it out on another telecom link or transfer the packet to a local area network connected to the equipment.
- The time-to-live counter is decremented, a new checksum is calculated, and both are inserted into the packet header in place of their former values. If the time-to-live counter reaches zero, then the packet is destroyed. (This prevents packets from endlessly circulating around a network.)

We'll go into this in a little more detail when we talk about routers and switches later in this chapter.

DHCP and NAT

Just over 4 billion unique IP addresses are available, meaning there aren't always enough to go around. If this is surprising, take a moment to think about the number of IP addresses a person might use, including a work PC, a home PC, a networked printer, a file server, a mobile device, etc., and then consider the billions of people who will have access to the Internet. To solve this problem, two technologies have been invented. The first, called Dynamic Host Configuration Protocol (DHCP), assigns a temporary IP address to each computer. The second, called network address translation (NAT), allows multiple computers to share a single IP address.

DHCP is a required function in many corporate networks and with many Internet service providers (ISPs). With DHCP, a computer uses an IP address only to access the Internet or a company internet, not when it is offline or powered down. DHCP is also of benefit for mobile workers, who need a different IP address assigned each time they move to a different network. To use DHCP, a computer must find the DHCP server on the local network by broadcasting a request to all the local devices. When the DHCP server receives the request, it selects an available IP address and sends it back to the requesting computer. One big advantage of the DHCP process for corporate

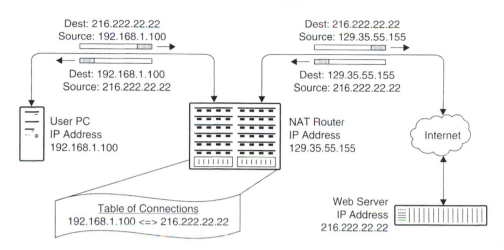

FIGURE 5-3 Example of a NAT Device in Operation

and ISP network administrators is that they don't need to configure each user's PC with a fixed IP address.

NAT operates by translating addresses between two different address spaces. A NAT device can be used to separate a stub network from the main Internet. Figure 5-3 shows a common configuration for a home gateway with NAT that was installed by a consumer to share a broadband Internet connection among several computers. To the Internet, the NAT device looks like a single (albeit very busy) device, with a single IP address. To the network stub, the NAT device looks like a connection to the Internet. Inside the stub network, all the devices are given an address from a special pool of private IP addresses.[3] When a device in the stub wants to connect to a server located outside the stub network, the NAT device accepts the packet and replaces the private IP address with its own public IP address. At the same time, it records in a table what it did. When a response comes back from the external server, the NAT device accepts the packet and finds the entry in its table where the original private IP address was recorded. Then the NAT device modifies the response packet to send it out on the stub network to the original device.

---

3. The IETF has designated several address ranges for use on stub networks, including 10.xxx.xxx.xxx, 192.168.xxx.xxx, and 172.16.0.0 through 172.31.255.255. Since these addresses can never appear on the Internet, they can be used over and over again by private network stubs.

For video transport, both DHCP and NAT can pose challenges. In many cases, video encoders and servers are configured to be data sources. In order for a user's computer to access that data, it needs to know the IP address of the data source. Both DHCP and NAT can interfere with this. If, for example, a video server was to be configured through DHCP, its IP address could change each time the server was rebooted. If a server is on a private network stub behind a NAT device, the IP address of the server would be hidden from the Internet at large. (Note that this might be desirable for companies that do not wish to have their video content made available to external users.) As a general rule, video devices supplying content need to have a fixed IP address that is accessible to any of the clients who wish to receive the video data.

ETHERNET AND IP

Ethernet and IP are not synonymous, but they are closely linked in many people's minds. This has happened because Ethernet is one of the most widely used physical networking systems for IP traffic. In the following sections we'll spend some time talking about how Ethernet addressing works and how IP and Ethernet interoperate. Then we'll spend a little bit of time discussing some of the hardware that is common in Ethernet networks and how the operation of this hardware can impact video transport.

Classic Ethernet

Ethernet was invented in the 1970s as a means to interconnect workstations on a local area network (LAN). Originally, Ethernet used a shared set of wires connected to all workstations. On this type of network, it is essential to prevent multiple workstations from trying to transmit data at the same time. Before transmitting, each workstation is supposed to check to determine if another workstation is already transmitting data. If two stations both happened to start talking at the same time, each is equipped with a mechanism to determine if such a "collision" had occurred. When a collision is detected, each station immediately stops transmitting, waits a random amount of time, and then listens and tries transmitting again.

This system, known as Carrier Sense Multiple Access with Collision Detection (CSMA/CD) has been replaced with a new system architecture. In this system, a dedicated cable connects to each Ethernet port on each workstation. The most common kind of cable used today is CAT5 UTP (which stands for category 5 unshielded twisted pair), which is capable of handling data transmission speeds up to 100 Mbps.[4] At the other end of the cable, a direct connection is made to an Ethernet hub, a switch, or a router. Each of these devices will be described in later sections of this chapter.

Ethernet Addressing

Ethernet equipment uses Media Access Control (MAC) addresses for each piece of equipment. Readers who have done home networking projects may recognize MAC addresses because they use numbers 0–9 and the letters A–F for their addresses, which are then separated into six fields of two characters each. For example, a MAC address on an Ethernet card inside a PC might be 00:01:02:6A:F3:81. These numbers are assigned to each piece of equipment, and the first six digits can be used to identify the manufacturer of the hardware. MAC addresses are uniquely assigned to each piece of hardware by the manufacturer and do not change.[5]

The difference between MAC addresses and IP addresses can be illustrated with a simple analogy. When an automobile is manufactured, it is assigned a serial number that is unchanging and stays with that car permanently. This is similar to a MAC address for a piece of hardware. When an owner goes to register the auto, he or she receives a license plate (a.k.a. number plate or marker tag). The number of the license plate is controlled by the rules of the local jurisdiction, such as a state in the United States, a province in Canada, or a country in Europe. During its lifetime, one auto may have several different license plate numbers, as it changes owners or if the owner registers the car in another jurisdiction. Similarly, one piece of

---

4. CAT6 cable is certified for operation up to 1000 Mbps (also known as gigabit Ethernet).

5. Some newer pieces of equipment, including many small routers made for sharing home broadband connections, have the ability to "clone" a MAC address of a different device. This allows a user to set up the router to match the MAC address expected by the service provider.

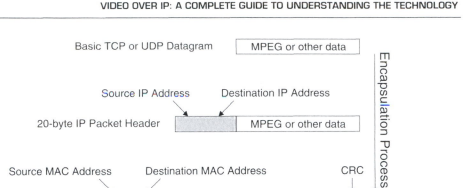
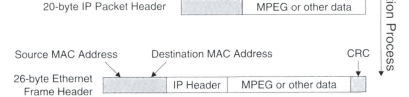

FIGURE 5-4 IP and Ethernet Framing

physical hardware may have different IP addresses assigned at different times in its life, as the hardware moves from network to network. Stretching the analogy a bit further, an auto's serial number is somewhat private information, of interest only to the owner of the car and the agency that issues the license plates. In contrast, the number of the license plate is public information and is emblazoned on the auto for all to see. Similarly, a MAC address is important only to the local Ethernet connection, commonly on a private network. The IP address is public and is used by other computers all over the Internet to communicate with a particular machine.

The MAC address is used for transport over an Ethernet network, as part of the MAC *frame* (another word for *packet*) header. Figure 5-4 shows how data is wrapped first into an IP header and then into an Ethernet frame.

Ethernet Hubs

Hubs are simple devices that provide electrical termination of Ethernet cables. They also provide retransmission of any Ethernet data that arrives from any device connected to the hub out to all of the other devices connected to the hub. An Ethernet hub provides three main functions in a network:

- First, it acts as a repeater, taking an incoming signal, amplifying it, and sending it out via all of the other ports on the hub.

- Second, the hub isolates the ports electrically so that you can add and remove connections without having to disable the rest of the network.
- Third, the hub can act as a splitter/combiner, allowing two devices to share a connection to a third device.

Hubs don't do anything to prevent collisions from occurring; they simply receive and retransmit signals. So, when multiple devices are connected to a hub, each one must follow the rules of CSMA/CD and make sure they don't overwhelm the network.

Ethernet Bridges

An Ethernet bridge can be used to connect different networks together. These networks can use the same technology, or they can use different technologies, such as wired and wireless connections. The main function of a bridge is to take packets from one network and reformat them to send out on another network. In order to do this, the bridge has to keep track of the devices that are present on each of the networks, based on their MAC addresses. Whenever a packet comes in, the bridge looks at the destination MAC address to determine if the packet needs to be sent out over a different interface. If it does, the bridge reformats the packet and sends it out using the correct protocol for the new network.

Bridges also isolate Ethernet network segments into different collision domains. This allows devices on one side of the bridge to send and receive packets without having to wait for devices on the other side of the bridge to stop transmitting. Segmenting an Ethernet network improves its performance, since the chances of collisions are reduced, allowing the network to handle more traffic from each device.

Ethernet Switches

An Ethernet switch takes the concept of segmentation to its logical conclusion: A switch provides a separate logical and physical network on every one of its connections, or *ports*. Figure 5-5 illustrates a possible switch configuration. Note that devices A and B share a common port (through the use of a hub) and therefore must avoid

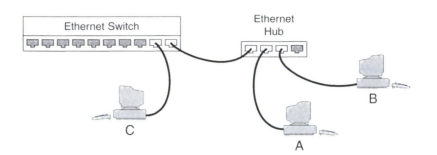

FIGURE 5-5   Ethernet Switch Setup Example

data collisions. Device C is on a dedicated port, so it does not need to worry about collisions.

Common practice is to put a single device on each connection of an Ethernet switch. This practice provides three benefits:

- Each device can transmit and receive data without worrying about collisions with other devices, so data transmission speeds can increase.
- A switch will only send out packets on a port that are addressed to devices connected to that port. This improves network security and reliability by preventing devices from viewing packets addressed to a device connected to another port on the switch.
- Certain devices can operate in full-duplex mode, which means that they can transmit and receive data at the same time. This is of particular benefit for video-streaming applications, because the large amounts of bandwidth commonly used for video transmission can overwhelm a half-duplex connection (where only one direction of transmission is permitted at a time).

Routers

Routers[6] provide a crucial function for IP networks by examining the headers and addresses of IP packets and then transmitting them onward toward their destinations. Routers come in a wide variety of configurations, from small access routers that provide a connection to an internet

---

6. Many people in the video industry are familiar with video routers, which we discussed in Chapter 3. Although IP routers and video routers provide similar functions (switchable connections between signal sources and destinations), they are completely different types of equipment and will not work interchangeably.

for a small group of users, through a range of enterprise routers that may handle the networking needs of an entire company, and on to core routers that provide IP connectivity at the heart of the Internet.

Routers are the workhorses of IP networks, and they are the subject of many excellent books of explanations and documentation. Without going into much detail, the basic functions of a router include:

- Accepting IP packets from devices and forwarding them to the recipient devices.
- Forwarding packets to another router when the recipient device is not local to the router.
- Maintaining *routing tables* for different IP destinations so that an incoming packet can be forwarded along a path toward a remote destination.
- Bridging between different network technologies, such as Ethernet LANs and telecom circuits, so that IP traffic can flow over a variety of network types.
- Monitoring the status of connected networks, to determine if they are vacant, busy, or disabled, and routing packets to avoid congested networks when possible.
- Queuing packets of different priority levels so that high-priority packets have precedence over low-priority packets. (Note: This feature is typically enabled only on private networks. Public networks normally pay little or no attention to packet priority flags.)
- Informing other connected routers of network configurations and changes to available resources and network connections.
- Performing many other administrative and security-related functions that are too numerous to discuss here.

Routers differ from switches in that routers process the IP address of data packets, whereas switches process the MAC address. This simple concept has some important implications, because MAC addresses are important only in the local segments of an Ethernet network, whereas IP addresses have global meaning throughout the Internet. This means that switches can limit their focus to devices that are connected locally, whereas routers may need to know how to forward packets toward destinations that may be on the other side of the world. As a result, routers tend to have many more decisions to make before they can properly process a packet, and they require much more complex software. Accordingly, routers tend to be more expensive to purchase and operate than switches with similar amounts of bandwidth and port capacity.

Ethernet Interfaces

Billions of RJ-45 connectors (see Figure 5-6) have been installed around the world for use with Ethernet signals, and they are standard equipment on essentially all PCs, laptops, and servers. The eight pins in the RJ-45 connect to four pairs of wire in a CAT5 or CAT6 UTP cable. Other forms of Ethernet wiring, including coaxial cable and fiber, can also be used, but we won't discuss them here.

Ethernet UTP connections are configured in a strict physical star. That is, each end device (such as a PC, a printer, or a server) must have a direct, uninterrupted connection to a port on a network device. This network device can be a hub, a bridge, a switch, or a router. The network device accepts the signals from the end device and then retransmits the data to other end devices or out over a shared network interface.

Common UTP interfaces include

- 10BaseT, which operates at a nominal bit rate of 10 Mbps
- 100BaseT, which operates at a nominal bit rate of 100 Mbps
- 1000BaseT, also known as gigabit Ethernet, which operates at a nominal bit rate of 1000 Mbps.

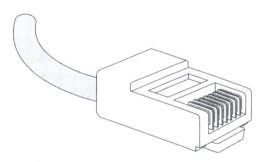

FIGURE 5-6   The RJ-45 Connector

Note that all of the preceding speeds are described as "nominal." This is a reflection of reality because, due to overhead, required dead time, and turnaround time, actual sustained throughput will be much less, depending on the application. For system implementers, it is important to realize that it isn't possible to send a 10-Mbps MPEG video stream over a 10BaseT link.

Wireless Ethernet Interfaces

Wireless Ethernet standards, such as 802.11a, 802.11b, and 802.11 g, offer unprecedented flexibility for users to move devices from one location to another within a network's coverage area. Low-cost wireless access devices are available for desktop PCs and laptops and for connecting to (and sharing) high-speed network connections, such as DSL and cable modems.

Video users need to be very careful about using wireless links for high-quality, streaming video connections. The speed and quality of a wireless link depends on a number of factors, including the distance between the wireless transmitter and receiver, the configuration of antennas, and any local sources of signal interference or attenuation. If the local environment changes (say, a laptop is moved or a metal door is closed), the error rate on the wireless link can change, and change rapidly. If the packet loss rate increases significantly, 802.11 links are designed to drop down to a lower operating speed, which helps lower the error rate. If the error rate goes down, the transmission speed can be increased. For example, in a standard 802.11b system, the bit rate can change to a different rate between 11 Mbps and 1 Mbps at any time without warning, depending on the quality of the radio channel between the two endpoints. Whenever the bit rate on a wireless connection drops, all of the services flowing over that link can be affected, including video file downloads, video streams, etc. In particular, if the wireless network bit rate drops below the bit rate required by a real-time video stream, then the content becomes unusable. Accordingly, the portability of wireless links must be balanced against the potential problems that can be created for video applications.

REVIEW AND CHECKLIST UPDATE

In this chapter, we covered the basics of IP transport. We looked at how IP fits into the overall world of data communications. We covered issues regarding IP addressing, including NAT and DHCP. We then spent some time discussing Ethernet, because it is the most popular technology for IP transport in the local-area network (LAN) environment. We also talked about some of the devices involved in Ethernet transport, including hubs, bridges, switches, and routers. We also glanced at some of the issues surrounding video on wireless Ethernet.

Chapter 5 Checklist Update

❑ What is the IP addressing scheme—private network or Internet compliant?

❑ For video sources, will NAT be used? If so, how will clients link to source?

❑ For video sources, DHCP may not be suitable.

❑ Will the Ethernet network have shared segments, or will each device have a dedicated switch port? Dedicated ports are preferred for high-bandwidth video.

❑ Will the Ethernet connections be half-duplex or full-duplex? Full duplex is better for video, if available.

❑ Ensure that the network bandwidth is greater than the combined video/audio data rate and that there is enough bandwidth for other devices using the same network.

❑ Will wireless Ethernet links be used? If so, will the video application be able to tolerate sudden bit rate changes?

6

FROM VIDEO INTO IP PACKETS

Now that we have looked at video, video compression, and the basics of IP, we are ready to look at the process of creating IP packets out of a digital video stream. This chapter will begin by covering the process of chopping up the video stream so that it will fit into IP packets, known as *encapsulation*. Then we will discuss the ways that MPEG formats data for transport. We'll examine the different protocols that run on top of IP to control the flow of packets, and we'll look at a few techniques that are used to make video transport more reliable.

By the end of this chapter, readers should have a good understanding of the different forms of MPEG video streams and have developed a solid foundation in the UDP, TCP, and RTP transport protocols. Readers should also gain some insight into the trade-offs that happen in the encapsulation and stream formation process.

ENCAPSULATION

Encapsulation is the process of taking a data stream, formatting it into IP packets, and adding the headers and other data required to comply with a specific protocol. As we shall see, this is not simply a matter of taking a well-established formula and applying it. Rather, the process of encapsulation can be varied to meet the performance requirements of different applications and networks.

Any data that is to flow over an IP network needs to be encapsulated into IP packets, whether the data is a prerecorded file or a live digital video stream. Packet encapsulation is done in real time, just before the packets are sent out over the network, because much of the data going into the packet headers (such as the destination IP address) changes for each user. Software tools to perform encapsulation are included in a wide variety of devices, including desktop PCs and file servers.

Packet Size

Performance of IP video signals will be affected by the choices that are made for the video packet size. Of course, the length of the packets must meet the minimum and maximum sizes in the specifications for IP. However, within those constraints, there are advantages and disadvantages to using long packets, just as there are advantages and drawbacks to using short packets. Figure 6-1 shows how the percentage of overhead changes with packet length. There is no simple recipe for choosing a packet length, but here are some of the advantages of choosing long packets, followed by the advantages of choosing short packets:

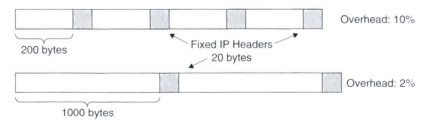

FIGURE 6-1　Short vs. Long Packet Overhead Comparison

Long Packet Benefits

- *Less overhead*: Long packets and short packets both require the same number of header bytes to comply with IP. However, a longer packet will have less header information as a percentage of the overall packet size, since the packet data is longer. In other words, the total amount of network bandwidth necessary to transport a given video stream will be lower for long packets than for short packets.
- *Reduced packet-processing load*: Each time a packet is processed by an IP client or router, the packet header must be examined, the header checksum must be verified, acknowledgments may need to be sent, and so on. Servers, routers, and client PCs must do this work for every packet, whether the packet is large or small. With larger packets, the amount of work is reduced, which can result in smoother operation of the network.[1]
- *Greater network loading*: In Ethernet and other network technologies, short gaps must be present between data packets sent by a transmitter. With longer packets, fewer gaps are required, meaning that more of the link's bandwidth can be used for user data.

Short Packet Benefits

- *Lost packets are less harmful*: In the event that a packet suffers a bit error in the header, the packet will be discarded. With short packets, each lost packet contains less of the overall video data. With some video streams (particularly ones that contain error-correction data), the video playback device may be able to recover from data loss or at least mask it from the viewer. As packet lengths go up, each lost packet means more lost data, which in turn makes it harder to recover from lost packets or other network impairments.
- *Reduced latency*: When a video stream is sent out over IP, each packet cannot be sent until it is full of data. With very low-bit-rate signals (such as a web camera with a very low frame

---

1. One of the best ways to test a router's performance is to send it large streams of minimum-size packets, which will exercise the header-processing mechanism as much as possible.

rate or an audio-only signal), the amount of time it takes to fill up a long packet can add to the end-to-end delay of the transmission system. Also, some error-correction techniques process multiple packets in one batch; these packets will be accumulated faster (and latency reduced) when short packets are used. Voice-over-IP packets typically use short packets to reduce end-to-end delay.

- *Less need for fragmentation*: Whenever a packet is too long for a particular network segment, it must be broken into smaller packets by a process known as *fragmentation*. This action can create significant overhead for routers and other devices along a network and should be avoided. The best policy is to use a packet size that is less than the maximum packet size allowed by any segment of the network between the video source and the video destination.

Clearly, there is no single answer for the question of optimum packet length. Typically, video signals tend to use the longest possible packet sizes that won't result in fragmentation on the network, to minimize the percentage of overhead. A mistake in selecting a packet size will generally not prevent video from flowing, but it can create extra work for devices all along the path of a connection. The best thing for a user to do is to start with a packet length that is reasonable, given the network conditions, and, if performance is below expectations, to test different packet lengths as needed.

MPEG STREAM TYPES

Even though MPEG is not the only kind of video that can be transported over an IP network, it is useful to look at the different stream types that have been constructed for MPEG. As you will see, each stream type has a specific purpose, and not all stream types are applicable to all situations.

Study of the MPEG stream types is useful, because the topics we will discuss in this chapter are all based on international standards. A number of non-MPEG compression systems use these same standards. In addition, because many MPEG applications involve the simultaneous delivery of multiple programs from different sources (e.g., DTH satellite systems), some very complex stream types have been developed for MPEG. So understanding MPEG stream types will allow us to understand a great deal about video transport protocols.

Before we begin our discussion of the different stream types, here is a brief overview of the different roles that each type plays, as shown in Figure 6-2. We'll go into more detail about each type in the following sections.

- Elementary streams are the raw outputs from MPEG video and audio encoders, and they are the standardized input for MPEG decoders. These streams contain only one type of content, so at least two elementary streams are required to produce an output that has both sound and an image.
- Packetized elementary streams are easier-to-handle versions of elementary streams and contain timing information that allows video and audio streams to be synchronized. A packetized elementary stream can also be made up exclusively of data such as closed captioning information. Packetized elementary streams are normally used to create program streams or transport streams, but they can also be used directly in applications like digital video recorders.
- Program streams combine several types of packetized elementary streams (video, audio, and possibly data) to support production and recording tasks, and they are used on DVDs. All

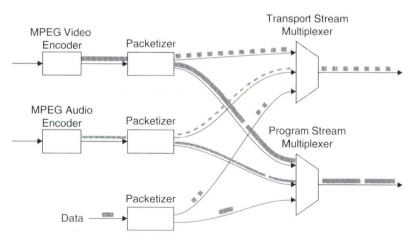

FIGURE 6-2 MPEG Stream Types Encoder Flow

of the packetized elementary streams in a program stream must be based on a common clock source so that synchronization can be maintained between the constituent video and audio signals.

- Transport streams are another way of combining several packetized elementary streams into a single entity that can be transported across a network. Transport stream packets have a fixed length, and the streams carry clock information that is needed for real-time signals. Transport streams can carry packetized elementary streams that were created from different clock sources, so they can be used for applications with multiple content sources, such as DTH satellite, IPTV, and streaming video.

Elementary Stream

The elementary stream is the most basic format for MPEG-encoded information. It is essentially the raw output of a video or an audio encoder, which is often created by separate chips within an MPEG-encoding device.

Elementary streams contain special data that is used by the decoder to determine how the data should be decoded. For example, the video frame type (I, P, or B; see Chapter 4) and the position of each data block on the video screen are indicated. In audio elementary streams, the required data is much simpler and includes information for the decoder, such as the sampling rate of the original digital audio stream and the type of audio compression used.

Elementary streams are continuous by nature: An MPEG encoder will continue to create an elementary stream as long as it is activated. This is natural for video systems but not natural for IP data networks. IP networks need to have data broken up into logical chunks or packets. So the next step is to *packetize* these streams.

Packetized Elementary Streams

A packetized elementary stream (PES) is simply an elementary stream that has been broken up into easy-to-handle "packets." We must use the word "packets" here carefully—although this is the name of this part of the MPEG standard, it should not be confused with IP packets that are a couple of layers of abstraction removed from PES packets. So we will call these chunks of an elementary stream "packets" in order to be compatible with industry documents. Note that PES packets are of variable lengths and can be a hundred kilobytes or more.

Each packet of a PES will have a header, which includes a code number that indicates the source of the elementary stream. This will become important later, when we combine video and audio data from different sources, so that we can figure out which video and audio signals belong together. Also included in at least some of the PES headers are time stamps.

For video signals, two different kinds of time stamps can be used, presentation time stamps (PTSs) and decode time stamps (DTSs). The PTS of a frame indicates the time at which it should be presented, or displayed to the viewer as a video signal. The DTS of a frame indicates the time at which it should be decoded by the MPEG decoder.

To understand the difference between a PTS and a DTS, we need to think back to our discussion of MPEG-2 I, B, and P frames from Chapter 4. Remember that I frames are coded without reference to any other frames in the video sequence. P frames are predicted from a previous I frame or P frame. B frames are bidirectionally coded from a previous and a subsequent I frame or P frame.

Let's look at an example of a GOP (group of pictures, from Chapter 4, Figure 4-6) of IBBP. In this example, frame 1, would be presented first, so it would have the earliest presentation time stamp of these four frames. Frame 2, would be presented second, followed by Frame 3. They would have PTS values that were each one frame later than the frame before them. Finally, frame 4 would be presented last, with a PTS that was three frames later than frame 1. See Figure 6-3 for an illustration of how this would work.

Using the same example, let's look at the decode time stamps. Frame 1 (an I frame) would again be first, so its decode time would be the earliest. However, the decoder needs frame 4 next, because it needs this P

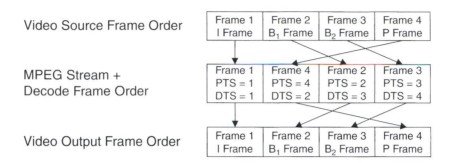

FIGURE 6-3   Presentation and Decode Time Stamps

frame data to properly decode the two B frames (frames 2 and 3, which are based on both the preceding I and the following P frames). So, in this example, the DTS of frame 4 would be set to be one frame later than frame 1. Frame 2 would have a DTS one frame later than frame 4, and frame 3 would have a DTS yet another frame later. Figure 6-3 shows how the DTS values would be calculated.

All this is important to understand for video over IP, because streams with lots of B frames use less bandwidth. Unfortunately, this comes at a cost of greater delay. In order to calculate the B frame values, the encoder needs to wait until the video signal for both the before and the after P or I frames arrive. For each added B frame in a GOP, the added wait will be 33 milliseconds on NTSC systems; this delay will be 40 milliseconds on PAL/SECAM systems.

Program Streams

In MPEG, a program is a combination of video, audio, and related data that make up a complete audiovisual experience. Typically, one video stream is combined with one or more audio streams and possibly some data streams. The first audio stream typically carries the main stereo sound track for the video; others can include surround sound, alternate language sound tracks, and commentaries. Data can include captioning information, information about the program stream (title, length, owner, content descriptions, etc.), or control information needed by recording or playback devices. Encryption systems can also require data to be included with the program stream; we will be exploring this topic in greater depth in Chapter 11.

A program stream carries a single program. It is made up of one or more packetized elementary streams and can have added data and control information. All of the elementary streams (up to 16 videos and 32 audios in some applications) in a single program use a common time base, which allows the audio and video portions of the program to provide lip-sync. Program streams are commonly used in DVD and other error-free[2] environments, such as tape and hard-disk recorders. Program streams can be variable bit rate and typically use large packets. One example of a program stream with multiple videos would be a sports video that offered multiple camera angles of the same action.

Transport Streams

Transport streams (TSs) are similar to program streams—they offer a way to combine video, audio, and related data into a logical grouping. Unlike program streams, transport streams are specifically designed to be transported across communication links that are not error free. Many applications fall into this category, including satellite, terrestrial broadcast, IPTV, and all types of wired and fiber-optic links.

Transport streams use fixed-length packets of 188 bytes each and are intended to work over satellite, telecom, and other transport links. Each packet contains data from only a single elementary stream— video, audio, data, or control information—but not a mixture. Forward error correction (FEC) codes can be added to transport stream packets through the use of standardized codes such as Reed-Solomon (RS). Digital Video Broadcasting (DVB) standards, which have widespread use in Europe and DTH satellite systems, specify 16 RS bytes (for a total TS packet of 204 bytes) that can correct up to 8 byte errors. Advanced Television Systems Committee (ATSC) applications, which are used in terrestrial digital television broadcast applications in the United States, use 20 RS bytes (for a total TS packet size of 208 bytes) that can correct for up to 10 byte errors.

---

2. The term *error free* needs to be used very carefully. In reality, no physical systems can truly be error free. When we use the term here, it simply means that any errors that are detected can easily be recovered by rereading the recording media. If the error is persistent (such as a damaged disk or tape), then the recording is faulty and should be replaced.

It is important to note that IP packets will normally contain multiple transport stream packets. IP packets containing seven transport stream packets are popular, because seven is the highest number of transport stream packets that can fit into a 1500-byte IP packet, which can be carried across an Ethernet network without fragmentation.

Interleaving can also help reduce transport stream errors. In this process, the MPEG packets are shuffled so as to make sure that no two adjacent TS packets are in the same IP packet. This can be very handy in case one of the IP packets is lost in transmission; the MPEG decoder is better at concealing the loss of several isolated transport stream packets than it is at trying to conceal the loss of a group of adjacent packets. The main drawback of interleaving is that the shuffling introduces extra delay into the system, which could be a problem for some applications.

An important concept in dealing with transport stream packets is the concept of the packet identifier, or PID. The PID uniquely identifies which elementary stream is contained in each packet. For example, the packets for a video signal within a transport stream might have a PID of 42, and the primary stereo audio signal associated with that same video might be carried in packets with a PID of 38. A second audio (with an alternate language track) for that same video could be carried with a PID of 85.

To keep track of all the PIDs, MPEG defines a series of tables that are sent as control data in the program stream. PID 0 is used to send the program association table (PAT), which gives a list of all the different programs contained in the transport stream. Each entry in the PAT points to a program map table (PMT), of which there is one for each program. (Remember that a program is a set of video, audio, and data that is from a common timing source. One program would typically represent one entertainment stream, complete with at least one video signal and one or more audio signals, and possibly closed captions or other information.) Inside the program map table is a list of all the PIDs for that program, of whatever type. When a viewer chooses a particular program to watch, the PAT and the PMT are consulted to find the correct video streams to send to the video decoder chip and the correct audio stream(s) to send to the audio decoder chip(s), as shown in Figure 6-4.

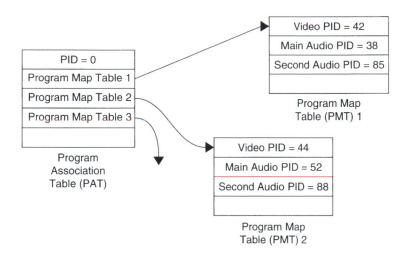

FIGURE 6-4 Program Table Usage in a Transport Stream

Program Clock References

A program clock reference (PCR) is a 33-bit number that must be inserted periodically into every transport stream to allow an MPEG decoder to synchronize with the 27-MHz clock used by the encoder when the MPEG compression was done. Synchronization must be maintained to make sure that the decoder doesn't run out of data to decode (*buffer underflow*) and that it doesn't receive more data than it can handle (*buffer overflow*). It is the responsibility of the MPEG encoder to keep a running estimate of the amount of room left in the decoder's buffer, and both ends of the network need to be synchronized to the same program clock in order for this to work.

A 33-bit counter that is linked to the encoder's 27-MHz clock represents the PCR. Periodically, the encoder copies the value of this counter and places it into a transport stream packet. At the decoder, these counter values are extracted and used to create a synchronized copy of the encoder's clock. The accuracy of the decoder's clock depends on a smooth, steady flow of data from the encoder to the decoder. Any changes in the amount of time it takes the packets to travel through the network (known as *delay variation* or *packet jitter*) need to be minimized. Nevertheless, some variation will occur, so it is important for the decoder to be designed to tolerate minor variations in the end-to-end delay.

Stream Multiplexing and DVB-ASI

Very often, it is desirable to combine several transport streams together for transport across a network. Of course, this can be done by converting each stream to IP packets and sending them over an IP network. The Digital Video Broadcasting (DVB) Project developed another method to carry multiple transport streams over links that would normally handle a 270-Mbps SDI signal. This method, called DVB-ASI (Asynchronous Serial Interface), allows multiple transport streams to be combined on a single link, even if they are operating at different bit rates.

Essentially, a DVB-ASI stream consists of a 270-Mbps bearer channel carrying one or more MPEG transport streams, each of which can be constant or variable bit rate. The total combined bit rate of the payload cannot exceed about 200 Mbps, but this is still plenty of room for a large quantity of MPEG streams that might average between 4 and 8 Mbps each.

DVB-ASI is important because it is a common interface for a whole range of video compression and processing gear, as well as a number of video servers. For example, it is very common to see satellite equipment configured for a DVB-ASI input. Many MPEG encoders have DVB-ASI outputs, and some decoders have DVB-ASI inputs. Also, DVB-ASI is easy to transport around studio facilities using SDI equipment.[3] Finally, a number of companies offer video transport services that operate at 270 Mbps across towns and across countries; essentially all of these services can also be used for DVB-ASI.

---

3. There is one practical difference between SDI and DVB-ASI signals. SDI signals are polarity insensitive, so if the signal gets inverted during transport (a surprisingly common occurrence), there is no problem. In contrast, DVB-ASI signals are polarity sensitive, so care must be taken to avoid inverting the signal during transport.

TRANSPORT PROTOCOLS

Transport protocols are used to control the transmission of data packets in conjunction with IP. We will discuss three major protocols commonly used in transporting real-time video:

- UDP, or User Datagram Protocol: This is one of the simplest and earliest of the IP protocols. UDP is often used for video and other data that is very time sensitive.
- TCP, or Transmission Control Protocol: This is a well-established Internet protocol that is widely used for data transport. The vast majority of the devices that connect to the Internet are capable of supporting TCP over IP (or simply TCP/IP).
- RTP, or Real-time Transport Protocol (or Real Time Protocol, if you prefer): This protocol has been specifically developed to support real-time data transport, such as video streaming.

In the networking hierarchy, all three protocols are considered to operate above the IP protocol, because they rely on IP's packet (datagram) transport services to actually move data to another computer (host). These protocols also provide service to other functions inside each host (such as user applications) and so are considered to sit "below" those functions in the networking protocol hierarchy. Figure 6-5 shows how

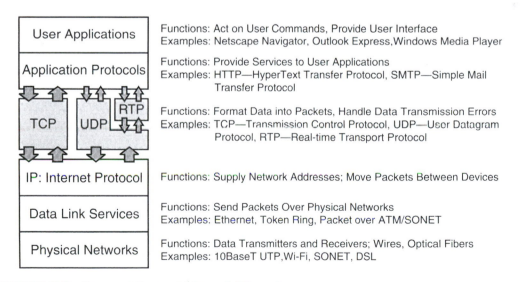

FIGURE 6-5 Transport Protocol Network Hierarchy

UDP, TCP, and RTP fit into the networking hierarchy. Note that RTP actually uses some of the functions of UDP; it operates on top of UDP.

Ports

A common feature of UDP and TCP is that they use logical ports for data communications. Ports serve as logical addresses within a device for high-level protocols and user applications.[4] Packets that are part of an ongoing file transfer will be addressed to a different port number than packets that contain network management information, even though they may be going to a single IP address on a single device. When a remote device wishes to access a specific application in another device, it must send data to the correct IP address and then indicate to UDP or TCP which port the data is intended for. A basic set of ports that support well-known services such as e-mail and web browsing is defined and numbered by the Internet Assigned Numbers Authority (IANA).

Before we get too deep into this topic, let's explore a quick analogy. One way to think of a port is that it operates like a telephone extension inside a medium-sized company. All the employees at the company share the same basic telephone number, but each employee can be given a specific extension. Each time people place a call to this company, they must dial the telephone number to reach the main switchboard and then select which extension they want to reach. Similarly, when a remote device wishes to communicate with a specific application in another device, it must send packets to the correct IP address and then indicate to UDP or TCP which port the data is intended for.

By standardizing the numbering of ports for well-known services, the IANA has done a tremendous service. For example, a web server that is supporting a Hypertext Transfer Protocol (HTTP) application always listens for remote devices to request connections on port 80. This makes it easy for a remote user with a standard browser to begin an HTTP session simply by knowing the IP address of the server and to send the

---

4. Be careful not to confuse the concept of logical ports used by protocols with the reality of physical ports on devices, such as a 10BaseT "port" on an Ethernet switch. Logical ports are used to control how datagrams are passed from the IP layer and to make sure they end up in the proper application program.

proper packet to port 80 to begin an HTTP session. Wouldn't it be nice if company telephone systems worked in the same way, by always having the accounting department, say, on extension 80? Just think how much easier it would be for people calling a company to talk to accounting—they would just need to select extension 80, and they would always be connected to the right department!

Sockets

The concept of a socket is related to the concept of a port. A socket is formed by the combination of an IP address and a port number. For example, a socket could be formed with an IP address of 23.132.176.43 and a port number of 80. The name of this socket would be written as 23.132.176.43:80 and read as "port 80 on 23.132.176.43." Different transport protocols use sockets in different ways; we will discuss these differences in each of the following sections.

UDP

User Datagram Protocol (UDP) is a connectionless transport mechanism that can support high-speed information flows, such as digital video and many other types of data transport. It is frequently used when the overhead of setting up a connection (as is done by TCP) is not needed. For example, UDP is often used for broadcasting messages from one device to all the other devices on a network segment (say, a print server alerting all the users that the printer is out of paper).

UDP is a connectionless protocol, which means there is no mechanism to set up a connection between a sending host and a receiving host. The UDP sender simply formats datagrams with the correct destination socket (IP address and port number) and passes them to IP for transport. Of course, this also means that there is no coordination between a UDP data transmitter and a UDP data receiver to ensure that the data is transferred properly.

On the face of it, this lack of coordination would seem to make UDP unsuitable for video data transfer, since missing video data can interfere with the receiver's ability to display a correct sequence of complete images. However, it is important to remember that each image in an NTSC video stream is displayed for only 33 milliseconds (40 msec for PAL video). If part of the data for an image is missing, the ideal receiver would need to

1. Recognize that the data was missing.
2. Send a message back to the sender to tell it which data needed to be retransmitted.
3. Receive and process the retransmitted data.
4. Make sure that all this happened before the image was due to be displayed.

Since completing all of these steps within a 33-msec window can be hard, it may be wise not even to try retransmitting the missing data.[5]

Many video stream formats also include a mechanism for detecting and correcting errors. For example, MPEG transport streams can include bytes for Reed-Solomon forward error correction. When these bytes are included, the MPEG decoder can correct for bit errors and can sometimes re-create lost packets, making it unnecessary to retransmit them. When these capabilities are available, UDP is a logical choice for the transport protocol, since it does not add unneeded overhead to streams that already have built-in error-correction functions.

Table 6-1 lists the advantages and disadvantages of the User Datagram Protocol.

Overall, UDP is a simple, low-overhead transport protocol that can be very useful for video traffic. UDP has a long history, and most IP-capable devices will support UDP. When video streams include their own error protection, when transmission paths are well controlled or lightly used, and particularly when end-to-end delay must be minimized, UDP can be a good choice for video transport.

---

5. Some astute readers will be thinking that more time could be gained to correct these errors if we transmitted the data before it was needed to form the image and let it sit in a buffer for a short while. If errors or missing data was detected, then the corrected data could be retransmitted while the good data simply sat in the buffer. This scheme will definitely work; however, it has one drawback: The time that the video data sits in the buffer will add to the overall end-to-end delay of the video signal. Added delay can make users less happy, particularly if they are trying to carry on a two-way videoconference.

TABLE 6-1

Advantages and Disadvantages of UDP

Advantages

- *Very low overhead*: Packet headers for UDP are among the smallest of all the protocols that use IP.
- *Simple port addressing scheme*: This scheme allows any data arriving at a particular socket to be forwarded directly to the application attached to that socket. It also removes the need for the transport protocol (in this case UDP) to keep track of multiple, different connections to a single port.
- *Very fast setup time*: In UDP, the sending host does not need to set up a connection prior to starting data transmission. This allows the sending host to begin transmission without having to wait for connection setup.
- *Low delays*: UDP does not buffer data to wait for acknowledgments, so one big source of system delay is eliminated.
- *Flexible architecture*: Because UDP does not require two-way communication, it can operate on one-way networks (such as satellite broadcasts). In addition, UDP can be used in multicasting applications where one source feeds multiple destinations (see Chapter 9 for more information on multicasting).
- *Wide availability*: UDP is available on the vast majority of equipment used in IP networking.

Disadvantages

- *Unreliable transport*: In UDP, there is no built-in mechanism to automatically retransmit data that has become corrupted or gone missing.
- *Firewall blocking*: Some firewall administrators configure their systems to block UDP traffic. This is done because it is possible for a hacker to inject malicious data packets into a UDP stream.
- *No built-in communication "back-channel" between the receiver and the sender*: This means that the sender does not have an automatic way to get feedback from the receiver.
- *No automatic rate control function*: It is the responsibility of the sending application to make sure that the outbound data stream does not exceed the capacity of the transport link.

TCP

Transmission Control Protocol (TCP) is a connection-oriented protocol that provides highly reliable data communications services. TCP is easily the most widely used protocol on the Internet and many intranets.

When we say TCP is "connection oriented," we mean that TCP requires that a connection be set up between the data sender and the data receiver before any data transmission can take place. Either the sender or the receiver of the data can initiate a connection, but acknowledgment messages must be sent between both ends of the circuit before it is ready for use. A standard handshake sequence has been defined for TCP; however, it is beyond the scope of this book.

One of the essential features of TCP is its ability to handle transmission errors, particularly lost packets. TCP counts and keeps track of each byte of data that flows across a connection, using a field in the header of each packet called the *Sequence Identifier*. In each packet, the Sequence Identifier indicates the sequence number of the first byte of that packet. If a packet is lost or arrives out of order, the Sequence Identifier in the next packet to arrive will not match the count that the receiver has made of all the previously received bytes. Through a fairly elaborate system of control flags and a field in the TCP header called the *Acknowledgment Identifier*, the receiver in a TCP circuit tells the sender that some data is missing and needs to be retransmitted. This is how TCP ensures that the receiver gets every byte that the sender wanted to transmit. This system is great for transmitting files that cannot withstand corruption, such as e-mails and executable program code.

Another feature of TCP is the ability to control the flow of data across a connection. The receiver is responsible for establishing a buffer to receive data and for informing the sender about the status of the data in this buffer after each packet is received. The sender is responsible for ensuring that the receiver's buffer does not overflow and for speeding up or slowing down the data rate as conditions change. This activity is managed through the use of data counters and acknowledgment messages that travel between the receiver and the sender.

Unfortunately, some of these very mechanisms that make TCP valuable for data transmission can interfere with video transport. Remember, the data for a video signal not only needs to arrive intact but also needs to arrive on time. So a mechanism that retransmits lost packets can be harmful in two ways:

- If a packet is retransmitted but arrives too late for display, it can tie up the receiver while the packet is examined and then discarded.
- When packets are retransmitted, they can occupy network bandwidth that is needed to send new data.

Also, the flow control mechanism that is built into TCP can interfere with video transport. If packets are lost before they are delivered to the receiver, TCP can go into a mode where the transmission speed is automatically reduced. This is a sensible policy, except when a real-time video signal needs to be sent. Reducing the transmit speed to less than the minimum needed for the video stream can prevent forming any video image at all. With lost packets on a real-time video stream, the better policy is to ignore the losses and to keep sending the data as fast as necessary to keep up with the video (and audio) content.

TCP uses ports and sockets differently from UDP. In TCP, each connection is set up as a socket pair, that is, an IP address and port number at each end of the connection. When two connections share the same socket at one end (for example, two connections to the HTTP service socket 192.163.84.67:80), TCP requires that the other end of each connection have a different socket. This is what allows a single web server to handle multiple clients simultaneously, which is different from UDP, which combines all the data going to a socket.

Table 6-2 lists the advantages and disadvantages of using the Transmission Control Protocol.

RTP

The Real-time Transport Protocol (or Real Time Protocol, if you prefer) is intended for real-time multimedia applications, such as voice and video over the Internet. RTP was specifically designed to carry signals where time is of the essence. For example, in many real-time signals, if the packet delivery rate falls below a critical threshold, it becomes impossible to form a useful output signal at the receiver. For these signals, packet loss can be tolerated better than late delivery. RTP was created for these kinds of signals, to provide a set of functions useful for real-time video and audio transport over the Internet.

One example of a nonvideo real-time signal that is well suited to RTP is a voice conversation. As most mobile telephone users can attest, an occasional noise artifact (such as an audible "click") is not enough to grossly interfere with an ongoing conversation. In contrast, if a mobile phone were designed to stop transmission and rebroadcast the voice data packets each time an error occurred, then the system would become constantly interrupted and virtually useless. Video is similar: A short, transient disruption is better than a "perfect" signal that is continuously stopped and restarted to allow missing bits to be rebroadcast. RTP is built on this same philosophy: Occasional data

TABLE 6-2

Advantages and Disadvantages of TCP

Advantages

- *Automatic data retransmission*: TCP has built-in, automatic mechanisms to ensure that every byte of data that is transmitted by the sender makes it all the way to the receiver. If data is lost or corrupted along the way, TCP will retransmit the data.
- *Data byte sequence numbers*: These numbers allow the receiving data application to determine whether data is missing or if packets arrived in a different order than they were sent.
- *Multiple connections to a single port*: TCP keeps track of messages based on socket pairs so that multiple simultaneous connections can be made from a single port on one host to several other machines. This allows multiple clients to access a server through a single common port.
- *Universal availability*: Any device used in IP networking will support TCP.

Disadvantages

- *Connection setup required*: The connection setup process must be completed before communications can flow in TCP. In networks with long end-to-end delays, the back-and-forth handshake process can take a relatively long time.
- *Flow control can harm video*: TCP's automatic flow control mechanism will slow down data transmission speeds when transmission errors occur. If this rate falls below the minimum rate needed by a video signal, then the video signal receiver will cease to operate properly.
- *Retransmission not useful*: If packets are retransmitted, they may arrive too late to be useful. This can interfere with other traffic that would have arrived in a timely fashion.
- *No multicasting*: Multicasting is not supported, meaning that a separate dedicated connection needs to be established by the sender for each receiver. One-way networks cannot be used, because TCP requires handshaking.
- *Delay reduces throughput*: On networks with long end-to-end delays, TCP can dramatically reduce network throughput, because of the time spent waiting for acknowledgment packets.

---

errors or lost packets are not automatically retransmitted. Similarly, RTP does not try to control the bit rate used by the sending application; it does not have the automatic rate reduction functions that are built into TCP to handle congested networks.

RTP is used in a variety of applications, including the popular H.323 videoconferencing standard (which we will discuss in Chapter 10). One of the nice features of RTP is that it supports multiparty conferencing by allowing different parties in the conference to keep track of the participants as they join and leave. RTP can also support multicasting.

RTP also provides a time-stamping function that allows multiple streams from the same source to be synchronized. Each form of payload (video, audio, voice) has a specific way of being mapped into RTP. Each payload type is carried in separately by RTP, which, for example, allows a receiver to receive only the audio portion of a video-conference call. (This can be very useful for a conference participant who has a low-speed network connection.) Each source inserts time stamps into the outgoing packet headers, which can be processed by the receiver to recover the stream's clock signal that is required to correctly play audio and video clips.

RTP is not a true transport protocol, like UDP or TCP, as illustrated in Figure 6-3. In fact, RTP is designed to use UDP as a packet transport mechanism. That is, RTP adds a header to each packet, which is then passed to UDP for further processing (and another header).

RTCP, or the RTP Control Protocol (a somewhat confused acronym), is used alongside RTP. Whenever an RTP connection is made, an RTCP connection also needs to be made. This connection is made using a second neighboring UDP port; if the RTP connection uses port 1380, then the RTCP connection uses port 1381.

RTCP provides the following functions:

- Allow synchronization between different media types, such as video and audio. The RTCP carries time-stamp information that is used by the receiver to align the clocks in each different RTP stream so that video and audio signals can achieve lip-sync, for example.
- Provide reception-quality status reports to the senders. This comprises data sent from each receiver giving statistics about how the sender's data is being received.
- Provide identification of the senders in the RTP session so that new receivers can join and figure out which streams they need to obtain in order to participate fully.
- Provide identification of the other participants in the RTP session. Since each receiver is required periodically to identify itself using RTCP, each participant (sender or receiver) can determine which receivers are present. This is not really a security mechanism; for that purpose, some form of encryption or other access control mechanism should be used.

Each receiver is also required to maintain a count of the number of other receivers present in the session. This count is used to calculate how often each receiver should send out a report. As more receivers join a session, each one needs to send status reports less often, so as not to overwhelm the network or the other receivers. The guideline used for calculating this is that the RTCP traffic should be no more than 5 percent of the RTP stream traffic that it is associated with.

Overall, RTP adds a lot of functionality on top of UDP, without adding a lot of the unwanted functions of TCP. For example, RTP does not automatically throttle down transmission bandwidth if packet loss occurs. Instead, RTP provides information to the sending application to let it know that congestion is happening. The application could then, for example, lower the video encoding bit rate (sacrificing some quality), or it could simply ignore the report if, say, only a few of the receivers were affected by the congestion. RTP also supports multicasting, which can be a much more efficient way to transport video over a network.

Table 6-3 lists the advantages and disadvantages of using the Real-time Transport Protocol.

TABLE 6-3

Advantages and Disadvantages of RTP

Advantages

- *Multiple formats*: Built-in support for many different types of audio and video stream types allows applications easily to share MPEG video and many different types of audio using well-defined formats.
- *Packet sequence numbers*: These numbers allow the receiving data application to determine whether packets are missing or have arrived out of sequence, alerting the receiving application that resequencing, error correction, or masking needs to be performed.
- *Multicasting support*: RTP streams can be distributed using multicasting, so a single video source can feed several (or several hundred) destinations simultaneously.
- *Embedded sync data*: Synchronization between multiple stream types allows multimedia signals (video, audio, etc.) to be transmitted separately and realigned to a common time base at the receiver.
- *Multiple stream speeds*: Receiving devices can choose to decode only portions of the overall program, so devices with low-speed network connections could choose to decode only the audio portion of a program, for instance.

Disadvantages

- *Firewall issues*: Some firewalls may block RTP traffic, because UDP packets are routinely blocked in many installations.
- *No priorities*: There is no mechanism built into RTP that ensures the timely transport of packets (such as priority queuing).
- *Limited deployment*: Not all network devices support RTP, so care must be taken to ensure that the network is properly configured before using this protocol.

CASE STUDY: UNCOMPRESSED VIDEO OVER IP

Most of the video signals transported over IP networks have been compressed using MPEG or some other technology. However, compression is not a requirement for successful IP transport. In this case study, we will discuss the MD6000 product from Media Links, Inc., of Milford, Connecticut, that allows uncompressed digital video signals to be transported over IP networks. Uncompressed standard-definition (SD) video, often called "SDI" runs at 270 Mbps. Uncompressed high-definition (HD) video runs at 1.5 Gbps and is often called "HD-SDI."

Uncompressed video is easier to work with in production applications, for a number of reasons. First, because a complete set of data is present for each frame of video, editing is very simple; a video sequence can start and stop at any frame. Second, many video compression systems introduce a delay that must be precisely duplicated in the audio signal path, or else audio/video synchronization problems will arise. Third, uncompressed signals can simplify production operations by eliminating expensive compression and decompression equipment and simplifying the connections between system components.

Of course, there is a major challenge to working with uncompressed video: System networking and storage resources can be heavily taxed. An uncompressed SDI signal will occupy over 2 gigabytes of storage for every minute of video, and HD-SDI will take up close to 12 gigabytes per minute. For networking, only high-speed network interfaces can be used, such as gigabit Ethernet for SD signals and 2.488-Gbps SONET/SDH links for HD-SDI signals. The latter network interface is the main one used on the MD6000 product.

IP encapsulation is used in this application for a number of reasons. First, when the uncompressed video data is broken into packets, Reed-Solomon codes can be added to allow most errors that occur in the telecom network to be corrected without affecting the video signal. Second, each IP packet receives a time stamp at the origin that allows the destination device to accurately re-create the timing of the original video signal. Third, use of IP standards allows other types of data to share the same transmission network as the video signal.

IP encapsulation also supports automatic protection switching between a main path and a standby path. In the event of a failure of the main path, the destination device automatically switches to use the backup path. For video signals, it is important that these two streams be perfectly synchronized. IP encapsulation aids this process because each outbound packet can be given a sequence number, which the destination device can use to realign the incoming streams by adding a small delay to one of the incoming streams. Once the main and the standby signals are aligned, a failure of the main channel can be immediately recovered by a switch to the backup channel with no loss of video data.

This technology is currently deployed in Japan to connect between broadcasters in different cities. It has also been used for broadcasting several major sporting events, including the 2006 FIFA™ World Cup, which used three STM-16 signals to deliver 2 uncompressed HD-SDI and 11 uncompressed SDI signals from each of 12 different stadiums to the International Broadcast Center in Munich, as shown in Figure 6-6. During the entire 30-day tournament, not a single frame of video was corrupted by the video transport system.

REVIEW AND CHECKLIST UPDATE

In this chapter, we looked at how IP packets are created from compressed video streams. We began by discussing the trade-offs of using long or short packets. Then we looked at the different types of MPEG streams in order to gain an understanding of the role of each stream. We glanced at the popular DVB-ASI signal format, which is used throughout the video industry for carrying MPEG transport streams. We followed this with a detailed discussion of two transport protocols that can be used (with varying degrees of success) to transport video streams: TCP and UDP. We concluded with a look at RTP, which is a valuable method for handling real-time audio and video signals.

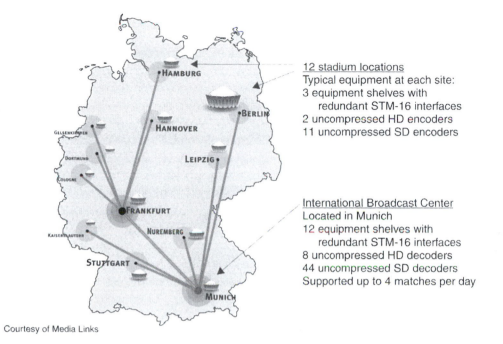

12 stadium locations
Typical equipment at each site:
3 equipment shelves with
    redundant STM-16 interfaces
2 uncompressed HD encoders
11 uncompressed SD encoders

International Broadcast Center
Located in Munich
12 equipment shelves with
    redundant STM-16 interfaces
8 uncompressed HD decoders
44 uncompressed SD decoders
Supported up to 4 matches per day

Courtesy of Media Links

FIGURE 6-6   FIFA™ World Cup 2006 Uncompressed Video Contribution Network

Chapter 6 Checklist Update

❏ Determine if long or short packets are going to be used for video
transport, keeping in mind the pros and cons of each approach.

❏ Make sure that the selected packet length will not be so long as to
cause fragmentation over the data networks that will be used.

❏ When choosing a stream format, keep in mind that transport
streams have several functions specifically designed to operate
in difficult environments, such as RS error correction, and a
robust mechanism for handling the required clocks.

❏ Elementary streams should not, as a general rule, be used for video
transport.

❏ If multiplexed DVB-ASI signals with multiple transport streams
are used, make sure that the receivers are configured to process
the correct stream, based on the PAT, PMT, and PID values.

❏ If non-MPEG streams are to be used, make sure that a mechanism
exists to identify which audio and video content belongs to a

given program and that there is a way to synchronize the streams after they have been transported across a network.

❑ Use Reed-Solomon forward error correction and packet interleaving to make video streams less sensitive to transmission errors. When doing so, keep in mind the extra bandwidth required for the RS data, and be careful not to allow packets to become so large that they cause fragmentation.

❑ If possible, choose RTP instead of TCP or plain UDP. TCP has some built-in behaviors that are great for data transfer but are not well suited for real-time video transport. UDP alone lacks some of the nice features of RTP for real-time streams. RTP with UDP is well suited for video transport, provided the network devices support RTP.

❑ Keep in mind that RTP streams, which ride inside UDP packets, may be blocked by some firewalls. This should not be a problem for users with private networks (either physical or VPNs), but it may be an issue if the streams are to be sent over the Internet.

7

IP PACKET TRANSPORT

One of the great strengths of IP networking is the huge variety of different technologies that have been successfully used to move packets over long and short distances. We begin this chapter with a discussion of some of the major systems that are used to transport packets. We will then discuss several factors that need to be considered when evaluating transport technologies. A discussion of some of the impairments that can occur on networks follows next. The chapter concludes with a discussion of the Internet as a transport medium and a brief look at service levels. By the end of this chapter, the reader should have a good appreciation of the wide variety of options available for IP packet transport and should understand some of the network conditions that can affect video signal transport.

TRANSPORT METHODS

In many cases, end users have little control over how their IP traffic is transported between locations. Packets are handed to a network provider at one location and delivered back at another. In between may be multiple networks, belonging to different service providers. In other cases, users with private networks can decide which technologies they will use for video packet transport. In either case, the following sections will help users to understand a few of the more popular available methods and some of the differences between the various choices.

One of the most popular network technologies for IP packet transport in local areas is Ethernet. It is also the common interface between different networks. Unfortunately, Ethernet itself is not intended for long-distance transport; standard applications have a distance limit of 2 km from end to end. Fortunately, there are many other technologies to transport IP packets over long distances and to provide Ethernet interfaces at both ends. Since we spent a fair amount of time discussing Ethernet in Chapter 5, we will discuss some of the other technologies used for packet transport.

Packet Over SONET/SDH

SONET, which stands for Synchronous Optical Network, and SDH, which stands for Synchronous Digital Hierarchy, comprise a significant majority of the world's long-distance telecommunications capacity. Since we covered the SONET/SDH bit rates and hierarchy in Chapter 1, we will focus on how SONET/SDH can be used for packet transport.

Packet over SONET/SDH (PoS) technology efficiently places IP packets into SONET/SDH payload envelopes for transport. Since all connections in SONET are logically point-to-point (even if they operate over a ring topology network), PoS is based on Point-to-Point Protocol (PPP). PPP offers basic framing for variable-length packets and some error-detection capability. PoS is primarily used between routers that have been equipped with internal SONET/SDH interfaces.

A key feature of SONET/SDH transport is support for redundant networks that will continue operating even if a key component of the network fails, such as when an optical fiber is cut. This process, called an *automatic protection switch (APS)* event, is great for voice and data, because the restoration times must be less than 50 milliseconds and are typically much less than that. With an interruption this short, all that a voice user might hear is an audible "click." Data users might lose some bytes during an APS event, but most times the data will be either retransmitted or recalculated using checksums. However, a video signal could lose a full frame of video during an APS event.

Losing a frame can be very hard on a video display. Often, the display will lose synchronization and may need to take a short while to regain it. To a viewer, this interruption would be comparable to one caused by changing channels on a television—not horrible, but definitely noticeable. For downstream processing equipment, particularly MPEG encoders and decoders, a lost frame can create errors that may require as much as a second for recovery.

SONET/SDH network users need to know that an APS event could be triggered if the bit-error rate goes above a preset threshold. Also, it is not uncommon for carriers, without warning users in advance, to force an APS event on a network when new equipment is being installed or major repairs are being made. So users should not be surprised if their SONET and SDH networks become unusable for 50 milliseconds every now and then. By understanding this and by being prepared for the consequences, end users will be able to set their expectations and select or configure their video equipment appropriately.

Cable and DSL

Many local service providers currently offer high-speed Internet connections based on cable modem and digital subscriber line (DSL) technologies. These systems use specially designed protocols to deliver IP packets between customers and the service provider, typically with an Ethernet connection to the end user.

One key factor to keep in mind about DSL and cable modem services is that many are asymmetrical, which means that the data flows faster in one direction than the other. A common version of asymmetrical DSL service flows at 128 kbps from the user to the provider (upstream) and 768 kbps from the provider to the user (downstream). Similar upstream limits can also apply in cable modem services. For many forms of video, 128 kbps simply won't be enough to support delivering video content from an end user location.

One major source of confusion when discussing cable modem and DSL is the concept of shared versus dedicated mediums. A *shared* medium means that multiple users share the same physical connection between the service provider and the end users. A *dedicated* medium means that only one user has access to the physical connection to his or her service provider. Figure 7-1 shows user access networks with shared (cable modem) and dedicated (DSL) access mediums.

Both shared- and dedicated-medium systems offer comparable levels of performance for video systems. In the area of security, modems compliant with DOCSIS (Data-Over-Cable Service Interface Specification) provide encryption between the customer's modem and the service provider's headend, giving cable modem users a level of security comparable to that of DSL users.

A common area of misunderstanding is the perception that DSL offers dedicated bandwidth access to the Internet, whereas a cable modem offers only shared access. In reality, both cable modem and DSL service providers will typically combine traffic from many users into a single high-speed connection from the service provider to the Internet. The amount of Internet bandwidth available to each user depends much more on the internal capacity and configuration of the service provider's network than on the connection to each customer. This point is important for video users to understand—even

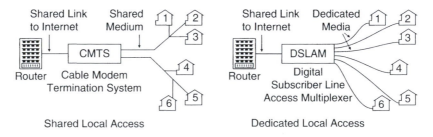

FIGURE 7-1 Comparison of Shared and Dedicated Local Access

though they might see great results when doing a speed test on their connection to their local service provider, the actual speed that can be sustained all the way through the Internet to the video source may be dramatically different.

Overall, users of cable modem and DSL services will see little or no difference as a result of the access technology chosen. There can be bottlenecks with either technology that can arise close to or far away from any user. When shopping for service, it is more important to look at the provider's reputation and quality of customer support than to look at which access technology is being deployed. As far as video is concerned, neither cable modem nor DSL service has any clear advantage over the other.

Private Optical Networks

Some companies may elect to construct their own fiber-optic networks. Generally, the biggest barriers to construction are obtaining the necessary construction permits and rights-of-way and the cost of construction, which can easily range from $20,000 to $500,000 or more per kilometer. "Dark" fibers, which allow customers to attach their own optical networking equipment, can also be leased from some local municipalities or service providers.

Providing a redundant or backup link in case of a network failure is common, since studies have shown that fiber cuts cause 70 percent of all fiber-optic network failures.

Most private optical networks transport video signals in their native format (such as HD, SDI, or DVB-ASI), avoiding the complexity and expense of converting video signals into IP packets. They may also install IP transport equipment that can be used for data and voice transport.

Leased Wavelengths

For users who need to transport high-bandwidth signals over long distances, leased wavelengths can be an attractive solution. Carriers with long-haul networks that can carry 40 or more 10-Gbps signals will sometimes lease capacity to users who are able to connect directly at the 10-Gbps rate. Companies using these services must provide their own multiplexing equipment at both ends of the circuit to interface video, data, and other signals that they wish to transport over the backbone. For carriers, these leases can generate revenues with fairly low support costs on long-haul trunks that would otherwise sit idle. For users, these leases can give them unprecedented amounts of bandwidth and control without the enormous expense of installing their own fiber-optic networks.

IP Over ATM

ATM circuits work quite well for transporting IP packets containing video content. Many service providers with installed ATM backbones and access networks are willing to sell IP services to users who wish to transport video. In fact, many users who purchase IP services from carriers are unaware that their packets are actually traveling over ATM circuits. However, for new installations and network upgrades, carriers are much less likely to select ATM equipment than they were in the past, due to the expense and complexity of ATM installations. As a result, IP signals are more likely to be transported over native IP networks than over ATM networks.

MPLS

Multiprotocol Label Switching (MPLS) was developed to improve the management of IP network resources, simplify the functions of high-speed routers, and support multiple priority levels for data traffic. MPLS works on IP, ATM, and frame relay networks. MPLS has been successfully implemented on a number of networks and supports service offerings from a number of carriers.

The basic concept of MPLS is label switching, which uses simple labels on packets, cells, or frames to send data along preestablished paths, known as Label Switched Paths (LSPs). MPLS is connection oriented, which means that a path from the sender to the receiver is established prior to data transmission, similar to ATM and TCP. LSPs run from one edge of the MPLS network to the other and can be configured via a variety of different software protocols that are used by routers. This task is not easy; a significant amount of effort has gone into creating the software that distributes the labels to all of the routers along a given LSP. Once the labels have been distributed to all the network elements, MPLS networks are very fast, because each router along the LSP needs to look only at the label, rather than processing the entire packet.

Each LSP is a unidirectional flow of data from a source to a destination. Note, however, that the protocols used to set up LSPs (such as LDP—the Label Distribution Protocol) require bidirectional communications between the routers that will carry the LSPs. For applications requiring bidirectional data flows (such as voice calls and most data applications), two LSPs must be constructed—one in each direction of communication.

A big advantage of LSPs is that they are connected before data begins to flow and thus can be used to reserve bandwidth from one end of a network to another. This function is very useful for video streams, because a properly constructed LSP can ensure that all of the packets of a video stream arrive at the destination on time and in the right order. Although this is similar to the functions provided by TCP, MPLS achieves this result without the constant back-and-forth communications and flow control provided by TCP. MPLS makes the job of the video decoder easier by smoothing out the packet delivery, and it potentially supports the delivery of higher-quality video. MPLS also provides a fast-reroute function that is similar to a SONET/SDH APS, except that outages can last 200 milliseconds in some circumstances.

Basic MPLS networks do not offer multipoint services, which allow a sender to deliver one stream to multiple receivers. Several methods have been developed to extend MPLS services to support multipoint networks.

MPLS functions are not normally available throughout the public Internet. Instead, MPLS is usually implemented on private networks or on carrier backbones that have the ability to configure their routers to offer MPLS services. Some carriers also offer MPLS services for interconnecting customer locations with virtual private networks. One big benefit of MPLS for carriers is the ability to subdivide a high-capacity backbone link and offer a large number of customers secure, private communications at whatever bandwidth they require.

VPNs and Pseudowires

Virtual private networks (VPNs) and pseudowires are both techniques for sending IP packets over other networks. In the case of VPNs, IP packets can be sent privately over a public network; i.e., the Internet can be used to provide connectivity between a remote user and a private corporate network (this configuration is sometimes known as an *extranet*). In the case of a pseudowire, an IP network can be used to transport a variety of protocols over a private connection. Both technologies can be used for video content.

A VPN is often constructed to allow private networks to share traffic without having to expose packet traffic to outsiders. For example, consider a private corporate LAN containing servers that hold confidential company data. If an employee needed to have access to this data from a home network, the company would have two basic choices. The first would be to construct a private physical network connection from the company location to the employee's home, possibly by using private leased line services from a carrier. The second choice would be to set up a VPN service, which would allow a PC to set up a private virtual connection to the corporate LAN through the public Internet. To ensure security on this connection, encryption could be used, and the employee would require a public IP address to support the handshaking necessary to set up the VPN. (This is why wireless hotspots sometimes allow users to obtain a separate, public IP address).

A pseudowire can be used to transmit a variety of protocols over a fixed IP network connection. For example, two LANs could be connected to provide transport of Ethernet frames (Layer 2 packets) over the public Internet. This could be done for a number of reasons, such as providing a simple way to connect two networks without having to perform extensive reconfiguration of an existing router setup.

IP video traffic can easily flow over a VPN or a pseudowire, provided that adequate bandwidths are made available and that packet length limits aren't exceeded. The latter issue might be of some concern, because each packet or frame that flows over a VPN or a pseudowire has additional header data added to make it flow properly. Carriers are starting to offer VPNs and pseudowires to support the private networking needs of their clients. Since multiple VPN or pseudowire connections can share a single backbone link without the possibility of having data flow from one customer's network to another, these technologies can provide substantial cost savings for carriers as compared to the expense of constructing separate private-line circuits between each pair of customer locations.

Wireless

Wireless Ethernet provides essentially all the same functions as normal Ethernet, without the need for wires to connect the data sender and receiver. Instead, high-frequency radio waves are used to carry the signals, similar to cordless telephones and other RF-based devices.

Wireless Ethernet provides users with much greater flexibility to change location at their whim. Wireless access points (also known as *hotspots*) are available in a number of public venues, including restaurants and airports. Companies provide users with desktop-quality data services as they move around the facility. See Figure 7-2 for an illustration of a typical wireless network. Note the variety of different devices that can be used to provide access, including laptops with built-in wireless modems, internal PCMCIA modems, and external USB modems as well as handheld devices and wireless webcams.

There are three principal forms of wireless Ethernet: 802.11a, 802.11b, and 802.11g. Let's discuss them in the order of their release.

- 802.11a operates in a 5-GHz frequency band and offers high speeds: 54 Mbps at the top end, although the effective rate is in the vicinity of 25 Mbps.
- 802.11b works in the 2.4-GHz frequency band and offers transmission speeds up to 11 Mbps. Note that this is the raw bit rate;

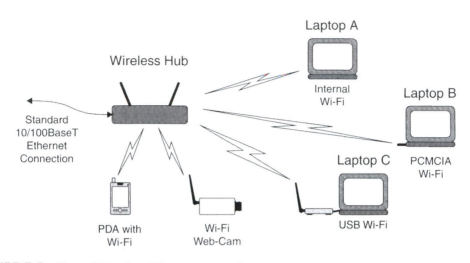

FIGURE 7-2 Typical Wireless Ethernet Network

with overhead and other factors, the effective maximum throughput is on the order of 5 Mbps.

- 802.11g offers raw transmission bandwidth up to 54 Mbps (actual throughput is much closer to 25 Mbps) and operates in the 2.5-GHz band. Note that 802.11g is backward compatible with 802.11b.

Unfortunately, wireless Ethernet is not an ideal medium for high-quality video traffic, because interference is difficult to control. Interference on a wireless system can cause bit errors and packet loss, both of which are bad for video and data signals. In addition, 802.11 operates in the 2.5-GHz band and the 5-GHz band, which are both unlicensed bands in the United States. This is both good news and bad—good because it eliminates license-filing paperwork and avoids payments of fees, but bad because users cannot be sure that others won't be using the same frequencies. Small variations in the local environment, created by, say, people walking around, can also cause significant changes in system performance.

Because of the difficult environment in which they were intended to operate, the 802.11 standards have been designed to work with significant levels of bit errors and packet loss. When bit errors occur or packets are lost, the wireless receiver notifies the wireless transmitter. The transmitter can choose from two automatic mechanisms that are used to cope: Either the bit rate is reduced, or lost packets are retransmitted, or a combination of the two.

Unfortunately video can be harmed when either of these mechanisms is used. If the bit rate of the wireless link drops below the rate of the video stream, then the video signal will essentially become useless. Similarly, if the wireless system retransmits packets, then chances are that they will arrive too late and clog up the data channels and the buffer of the video receiver. Neither situation is particularly good for video.

Overall, use of wireless Ethernet technology should be approached cautiously for video and audio streams. Since the amount of bandwidth available over the link can change rapidly in response to subtle variations in the RF environment, video users need to build flexibility into their applications. Use of large buffers and low-bandwidth signals will help ensure success.

TRANSPORT CONSIDERATIONS

When video is being transported over an IP network, users need to consider a number of factors. These factors can significantly affect the end users' viewing experience, so they should be taken into account when planning a network. The topics described in the following sections are not listed in any significant order, so most readers should review all of them.

Multiplexing

Often in a video distribution system, it is necessary to combine video streams from different sources. This procedure requires a multiplexer, which needs to process the video signals as they are combined. The output of a multiplexer can be a single data signal (for example, a gigabit Ethernet signal) or multiple signals, each of which contains multiple video streams. Multiplexing can be done for a number of reasons:

- One large stream can be easier to transport and administer than several smaller streams.

- When variable-rate streams are combined, the peaks in one stream can correspond to valleys in another, allowing the overall system bandwidth to be used more efficiently.
- Some transmission channels, including satellite and telecom links, offer fixed amounts of bandwidth per channel for a fixed monthly rate. When these systems are used, it makes good economic sense to combine as many streams as possible to completely fill up the channel.

Of course, multiplexing is not a free lunch. Adding a multiplexer, either as a stand-alone box or as part of another piece of equipment, can add cost to the transmit side of a network. Typically, a minor or possibly zero cost will be added on the receive side of the network, because many video receivers and decoders have built-in demultiplexers. Multiplexing can also add a small amount of delay to the video signals.

Two forms of multiplexing are commonly used today: time-division multiplexing and statistical multiplexing. See Figure 7-3 for a comparison.

- *Time-division multiplexing* provides a fixed amount of bandwidth to each incoming (tributary) stream. Operation is simple: Packets from each incoming stream are placed into one or more time-slots in the combined stream. In most systems, this allocation can be adjusted to accommodate streams that require more or

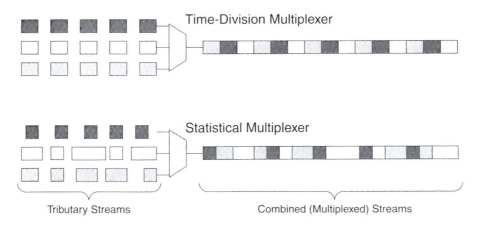

FIGURE 7-3 Comparison of Time-Division Multiplexing and Statistical Multiplexing

less bandwidth, although the allocation typically cannot be changed very rapidly or while the system is in use.

- *Statistical multiplexing* provides bandwidth to incoming channels in response to their changing rates; higher-speed tributaries are dynamically given a larger amount of the overall network capacity. Many systems can be configured with a maximum and a minimum bit rate for each tributary stream. A rate limit is also imposed on the combined stream.

Time-division multiplexing has the advantage of being fairly simple and generally has very low overhead. It is also used extensively in modern telecommunications, including SONET/SDH networks. For fixed-rate tributary streams, it can be quite efficient. However, when the tributaries are variable rate, overall efficiency drops, because each tributary needs to be allocated enough bandwidth to handle the peak rate of the tributary, or else data loss can occur. Time-division multiplexing also has the benefits of providing constant end-to-end delay through a network (which is good for video) and being easy to switch (more on switching later in this section).

Statistical multiplexing works well when the tributaries have data-rate peaks that occur at different times, as is common in compressed video, where different amounts of data are created for the different MPEG frame types (I, P, and B). Video streams typically have variable data rates, with peaks occurring when rapid movement is present in a video scene and lower data rates occurring when there is little action or movement. When these signals are combined, as shown in Figure 7-4, the peak data rate of the combined data stream is less than the sum of the peaks of the individual streams, so the network bandwidth is used more efficiently.[1]

Another key function of a video multiplexer is the correction of the presentation time stamp (PTS) and program clock reference (PCR) values contained in the MPEG streams. As we discussed in Chapter 6, these values are inserted into the MPEG stream by the MPEG

---

1. Some statistical multiplexers take this process a step further by actually controlling the amount of data produced by the tributary MPEG encoders. For this scheme to work, the multiplexer needs to be tightly coupled with (and generally co-located with) the MPEG encoders.

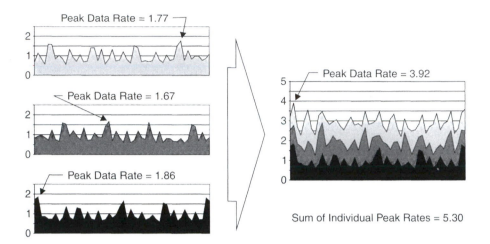

FIGURE 7-4   Effect of Multiplexing Data Streams

encoder and used to control the timing of the video decoding. When MPEG signals are sent through a multiplexer, it may need to delay slightly a packet from one stream while a packet from another stream is being transmitted. When this happens, the multiplexer recalculates the PCR and PTS values, which are then reinserted on all the streams being processed by the multiplexer.

Statistical multiplexing has the drawback that it is generally more complicated than time division and that it can require more over-head to supply the information needed to demultiplex the stream at the receiving side. Note that Ethernet networks are inherently multiplexed, because devices that send packets more often are automatically given more bandwidth.

Switching is used whenever video signals from one data stream need to be transferred into another data stream, such as when satellite signals are switched into a terrestrial network. When data is traveling on a time-division multiplex link, switching is very simple. The switch just needs to copy all the data from a timeslot within an input signal to a timeslot of the same bit rate on an output signal. With statistically multiplexed links, the case is quite different: The switch needs to look at the entire contents of the input signal to find all of the necessary packets. (Note that they may arrive sporadically or in bursts.) Then the switch needs to transmit these packets while making sure that the output link has enough capacity and that the newly added packets don't collide with other packets, possibly through the use of buffers.

When deciding whether to use multiplexing, three cost factors need to be balanced:

1. The cost of the multiplexer itself
2. The cost (if any) of adding a demultiplexer to all of the signal destinations
3. The network cost savings generated by transporting one multiplexed signal in place of multiple individual signals

Time-division multiplexing is simple, but it is not as bandwidth efficient as statistical multiplexing for signals like video that have large bit-rate peaks and valleys. Statistical multiplexing is more bandwidth efficient for video signals but can be more costly to implement than time-division multiplexing. In general, multiplexing should be considered whenever multiple video signals need to be delivered to the same set of destinations or when network costs are high.

CALCULATING NETWORK BANDWIDTH

Calculating the amount of actual bandwidth consumed by an MPEG stream is very important. It is also somewhat tricky. Let's look at how one manufacturer (HaiVision Systems of Montreal, Quebec) does this for one H.264 product (the hai200 TASMAN video encoder).

As in most MPEG devices, the hai200 user is given control over the rate of the raw MPEG stream. For this device, the video bit rate can be set anywhere from 150 kbps to 2 Mbps. The user can also set the audio stream rates over a range from 64 kbps to 256 kbps. For the purposes of our example, we will use a video bandwidth of 2 Mbps and an audio bandwidth of 128 kbps.

Since we are going to be transporting these raw streams over a network, the first thing we want to do is convert the raw MPEG streams (in MPEG-2 these are known as *elementary streams*, in H.264 these are known as NAL units) into a transport stream (TS). Since fractional TS packets aren't

Continued on next page

allowed, so each video frame will occupy 46 TS packets and each audio frame will occupy 2 TS packets. For audio, this adds 9.3 percent overhead to the raw bandwidth and for video 3.8 percent is added. So our original audio stream is now a 140-kbps TS, and our video TS now occupies 2.076 Mbps. We also need to add 46.5 kbps to these streams to provide room for the PMT and the PCR (program map table and program clock reference; see Chapter 6). Figure 7-5 illustrates this example.

The next step is to calculate the IP and Ethernet overhead. Since the hai200 TASMAN uses RTP over UDP, we must allow for a 12-byte RTP header and an 8-byte UDP header. Then we must add a 20-byte IP header and a 26-byte Ethernet header,[2] bringing the total of all the headers to 66 bytes. We can accommodate anywhere from two to seven TS packets (which are always 188 bytes long) in each Ethernet frame. For our example, let's use seven TS packets (or 1316 bytes) per Ethernet frame, because this gives us the highest ratio of data to headers. With 66 bytes of header for 1316 bytes of data, we have an overhead of approximately 5 percent. So our total bandwidth for both the audio and video streams comes out to 2.376 Mbps. This calculates to 11.6 percent overhead on the original raw streams (2 Mbps plus 128 kbps). In terms of packets, this equates to roughly 215 packets per second.

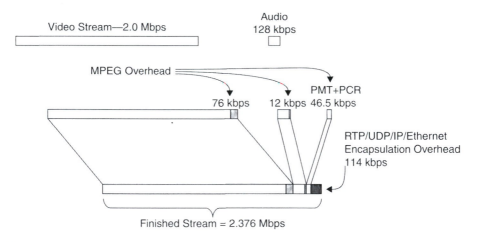

FIGURE 7-5 Sample Total Bandwidth Calculation for an MPEG-2 Stream

2. The Ethernet frame structure consists of a 7-byte preamble, a 1-byte start frame delimiter, a 6-byte destination MAC address, a 6-byte source MAC address, a 2-byte length/type identifier, and a 4-byte frame check sequence in addition to the payload.

Traffic Shaping

Video traffic shaping consists of various techniques used to make video traffic easier to handle on a network. Shaping can consist of a variety of technologies, but often the overall goal is to make a stream less prone to sudden peaks in bit rate. Traffic is considered to be well shaped if the peaks are relatively small (or nonexistent) in comparison to the average bit rate. Figure 7-6 shows the difference between a poorly shaped and a well-shaped stream.

Networks generally operate more efficiently with streams that are well shaped. Since most networks have a constant basic bit rate (e.g., an OC3 or an STM-1 runs at 155.52 Mbps), more total data can be carried if all the streams are well shaped. For example, if several video signals each have an average bit rate of 20 Mbps and a peak data rate of 50 Mbps, then an OC3 or STM-1 could carry only three of these signals using time-division multiplexing. If, on the other hand, several video signals each have an average bit rate of 20 Mbps and a peak bit rate of 30 Mbps, then the OC3/STM-1 link could carry five of these signals. In the first case, the SONET/SDH link would be 40 percent utilized on average (three streams at 20 Mbps in a 150-Mbps pipe), whereas in the second case, the SONET/SDH link would be 66 percent utilized (five streams at 20 Mbps in a 150-Mbps pipe).

Video elementary streams are prone to having a lot of peaks. For example, in MPEG-2 video streams, an I frame requires much more data than a B frame. Without any buffering, the bit rate would have a peak whenever an I frame was being created. Also, each time the video scene changes (say, from an indoor scene to an outdoor one or from program to commercial), the amount of data that needs to

Before Traffic Shaping

After Traffic Shaping

FIGURE 7-6 Comparison of a Stream Before and After Traffic Shaping

be sent also jumps because of the large number of differences between the two frames.

One version of traffic shaping operates using the "leaky bucket" approach, which is a good analogy. Think of a bucket with a small hole in the bottom where the useful data comes out. Now think about data sources, such as an MPEG-2 encoder. Each time the encoder has some data ready, it is put into the bucket. If it is an I frame or a scene change, then a lot of data is put in. If it is a B frame, then a small amount of data is added. As long as the bottom hole is big enough to handle the average rate of the data inflow, then the output stream will be constant. The temptation is to use a large bucket so that data peaks would never overflow the bucket, which would cause MPEG picture data to be lost. However, as the bucket size goes up, there is more delay in the transmitted video signal, which can be bad for some applications.

Overall, traffic shaping is a good thing for video networking. In fact, many newer MPEG encoders have a built-in traffic-shaping capability. Shaping increases the number of channels that can be carried on a data link. It also makes the streams more predictable, so equipment in the network will not have to work as hard to accommodate dramatic changes in bit rates. However, traffic shaping needs to be used carefully, because it can create additional delay in the network.

Buffering: Pros and Cons

A *buffer* is basically a collection of memory used to store information temporarily prior to taking some action. Buffers are used extensively in video processing and networking; they can have a major impact on video network performance.

In MPEG, certain buffers are required. They are used on the encoding and decoding sides to support motion estimation, which compares successive frames to see what has moved from one frame to the next (see Chapter 4). Buffers are also used to support the frame reordering function that allows B frames to work. An important function of an MPEG encoder is making sure that the buffers that are present in every MPEG decoder are never filled beyond its capacity.

Error correction also requires use of buffers. Typically, a whole packet needs to be processed to add forward error-correction (FEC) coding. Also, packet interleaving uses buffers with room for multiple packets. (Both of these topics are discussed in Chapter 6.) For low-quality networks, larger buffers are needed to support these functions because of the increased amount of FEC that is performed.

Buffering is normally also needed in a network receiver. Buffers are required to smooth out variations in data arrival times that are caused by statistical multiplexing and switching. Other buffers are needed to perform the FEC calculations and to de-interleave the incoming packets. Depending on the network, these buffers can be very small or quite large.

For one-way broadcast video, the total amount of end-to-end delay can be fairly large (as much as 5 to 10 seconds) without having any impact on the viewer. In fact, it is very common for live shows to use a device called a *profanity delay* to inject several seconds of delay into the outgoing signal. If someone on-screen uses inappropriate language, then the studio staff has time during the delay to remove the offensive language before it is broadcast. Delays amounting to handfuls of seconds are not an issue for broadcast television, and special effort is not needed to reduce the delay.

In contrast, interactive or two-way video is very sensitive to delay. As delay is increased, it becomes difficult for normal conversation to occur, because it is hard for speakers to know when the other person is beginning to talk. Table 7-1 shows what the International

TABLE 7-1

Recommendations for One-Way Delay (Based on ITU G.114)

Delay	User Impact
0–140 milliseconds	Minor or unnoticeable impairment to normal conversation; acceptable to most users.
140–400 milliseconds	Possible to notice impairment; acceptable for use; however, some user applications may be impaired.
Over 400 milliseconds	Not acceptable for general use; should be avoided in network planning; may be used in exceptional circumstances.

Telecommunications Union (ITU) specifies in Recommendation G.114 for one-way delay of a link used for a two-way conference.

Large buffers in the receiver can also make up for a lot of network transmission problems. If packets are temporarily misrouted, they can be reinserted in their proper position in the bit stream after they are received. If the packet arrival rate is jumpy instead of smooth, a receive buffer can be used to smooth them. The receive buffer is also the ideal place to perform any needed error correction or to de-interleave the packets.

Large receive buffers are almost universally used in IP streaming media applications. In fact, these buffers can hold up to 10 or 20 seconds' worth of video and audio information. To keep viewers entertained while the buffers are filling, many Internet video player applications will show a user the status of the receive buffer, either through some kind of graphic (such as a bar graph) or by means of a text status message (such as "Buffering: 87%"). The main purpose of the buffer is to ensure that adequate data is ready for the video decoder when it is needed, even if the incoming stream is disrupted for a few seconds. If the buffer ever does become empty, then the video will stop, and most player applications will display a message to the user indicating that the buffer is being replenished.

The overall benefits and drawbacks of buffers are summed up in Table 7-2.

Firewalls

A firewall is used to control the types of information flowing between two networks. In many cases, firewalls are used between user computers and the Internet, to keep unauthorized users from gaining access to private information or network resources. While it may be true that a firewall would not be needed if each user PC and server in a network followed proper security policies, it is generally more convenient for a system administrator to manage the security policies for a single firewall instead of a whole collection of user devices.

TABLE 7-2

Buffer Advantages and Disadvantages

Advantages

- Large buffers can make up for a large number of network impairments, such as uneven packet arrival rate and packets arriving in the wrong order.
- Buffers are mandatory for MPEG compression, since successive frames of video need to be compared as part of the compression process. If B frames are used, then additional buffering is needed to put the video frames back in the correct order for presentation to the viewer.
- Buffers can be an ideal place to perform functions such as traffic shaping, forward error correction, and packet interleaving.

Disadvantages

- Buffers add delay to the end-to-end video delay. Large buffers can make the delay unacceptable for applications in which interactivity is involved, such as videoconferencing.
- Even for non–real-time video, the delay that a user experiences while the buffer is filling up can become annoying if it is excessive (just ask anyone trying to watch a movie preview over a dial-up link).
- Buffers can add cost and complexity to both the video encoder and the decoder. While this is typically not an issue for rack-mount servers and desktop PCs, as more handheld devices are configured to work with video, the additional memory and power consumption of large buffers needs to be considered.

Firewalls vary greatly in their level of sophistication and in their methods for providing security. Most firewalls provide at least a packet filtering function, which examines each packet passing through the firewall on a packet-by-packet basis. More sophisticated firewalls provide stateful inspection, which not only examines the contents of each packet but also tracks the connection status of each of the TCP or UDP ports that are used by the packet, to make sure that unrequested packets are not delivered to user devices.

Packet filtering involves looking at the source and destination IP addresses of each packet as well as the source and destination TCP and UDP ports in each packet. This inspection is generally direction sensitive, where internal users are allowed to perform one set of functions and external users are allowed to perform another. For example, consider TCP port 80, which is used by Hypertext Transfer Protocol (HTTP) on the World Wide Web (www). Anytime a user types "http://www.xxx.com" on his or her web browser, a packet is sent to port 80 on the "xxx" server (see Figure 7-7). This packet

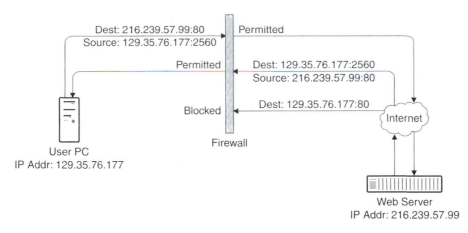

FIGURE 7-7   Web Browsing Firewall Example

will also include a port number on the user's PC for the reply from the website to come back to, in our example 2560. Once a connection is established, every packet between the user and the server will contain the user's IP address and port number (2560) as well as the server's IP address and port number (80). The firewall can block packets addressed to other ports on the user's machine, and it can also block packets from sources other than "xxx.com."

Let's assume that the user does not have an HTTP server in his network that he wants to make available on the Internet. Then it is very easy to exclude external users; all the firewall needs to do is block any incoming packets addressed to port 80. This can prevent tragedy if, for example, one of the PCs in the user's network was set up to be an HTTP server by a careless or uninformed user. The firewall can also make sure that any HTTP servers that are for internal use only (such as employee payroll records) cannot be accessed from the Internet. The firewall can also be configured to block other well-known TCP and UDP ports, such as e-mail portals.

Firewalls can interfere with video traffic in two main ways. First, the firewall can block outside users from being able to access a video source or server. Since many video servers will not send video data to a user until requested to do so, it can be impossible for a user to make a request if well-known ports (such as 80) are blocked by the firewall. Placing the video server outside the firewall, at an Internet hosting service, for example, can solve this problem. Alternatively, a special subnetwork can be created that is only partially protected by the firewall, commonly called a DMZ (after the military term *demilitarized zone*).

The second way in which firewalls can interfere with video traffic is by blocking all UDP traffic, which is a very common firewall setup. UDP traffic is harder to police than TCP traffic, because it is possible for an intruder to insert unauthorized packets into a UDP stream. (Remember, TCP packets use sequence numbers for bytes, which are not present in UDP packets.) Unfortunately, UDP has a number of benefits for streaming video, so many video sources use the UDP protocol. So if UDP is to be employed for streaming, any firewalls that are along the path from source to destination must be checked to make sure they do not block UDP traffic.

Overall, video system implementers need to be aware of the constraints that firewalls impose on video services. Firewalls create a quandary for network administrators, who must balance the need for users to have access to services against the need for administrators to ensure network security. Careful planning can avoid making a firewall a barrier to IP video transport success.

NETWORK IMPAIRMENTS

Many things can happen between a video source and a video viewer. Of course, there are gross network failures (such as large electric power blackouts or major cable cuts), but there are also subtle failures. In the following sections, we are going to look at some of these more subtle failures, also known as *impairments*. While they may not be as dramatic as a power failure that affects 50 million people, these impairments can mean the difference between success and failure on a video network.

Packet Loss

A packet is declared "lost" when it does not arrive at its intended destination. This can be caused by any number of circumstances, such as a network failure. It can also be caused by subtle errors, such as a single bit error inside a packet header. It can also be caused by faulty network configuration, which sends packets to the wrong destination. In any case, packets will occasionally get lost in transmission on essentially all IP networks.

One way that packets can be lost is when the header has become corrupted in transmission. Each time a packet is received by any device, the header checksum is recalculated. If the result of the calculation does not match the incoming checksum, then a bit error has occurred and the header has been corrupted, so the packet will be destroyed.

To get a feel for how often this can happen, let's consider some ways to measure an error rate on a network. For example, a network could be designed to deliver packets from one end to the other with a Six Sigma success rate. Six Sigma means 3.4 parts per million, or 99.9997 percent defect free, or one packet error out of every 294,000 packets, on average, which would be exemplary performance for an IP network. Using the example given earlier in this chapter for a 2.376-Mbps combined audio and video stream, we came up with 215 packets per second. At a Six Sigma packet loss rate, this would mean that a packet would be lost every 1367 seconds, or about once every 23 minutes. Since we don't know what data would be contained in that packet, it could cause anything from some minor loss of data in one video frame to a complete screen freeze for a fraction of a second or an audio noise spike or audio dropout.

Another way to get an understanding of error rates on networks is to look at the bit error ratio (BER). A BER is the number of bit errors divided by the total number of bits transmitted. Many types of fiber-optic telecom equipment specify their BER performance as 1 bit out of every billion in error, or an error rate of 1×10^{-9}, which would also be considered very good for an IP network. Going back to the example in this chapter, each packet is 1382 bytes long (66 header and 1316 data), which is 11,056 bits. At 215 packets per second, we have just over 2.37 Mbps (million bits per second). We would see a billion bits every 422 seconds, or about every 7 minutes. Again, since we don't know where the error would be, we can't really know if the error would affect a small part of one video frame or a group of video frames or one of the audio channels.

Packets can also get lost when networks become saturated with traffic. In fact, IP routers have built-in mechanisms to discard packets when more arrive than can be sent over a network segment. As traffic builds up and the router's buffers fill up, more and more packets are discarded. This is all done with good intentions: By discarding packets, the router is trying to trigger a mechanism in TCP devices that makes them automatically slow down their transmission speed when packets are lost along the way. Unfortunately, video encoders typically cannot adapt easily to bit rates below the rate they have been configured to use, so lost packets mean lost video data. Compounding this problem, many video streams use the UDP protocol, which does not have a built-in rate reduction mechanism.

Clearly, packet errors are part of life on an IP network. Even when these errors are reduced to fairly low intensity, they can still cause errors in the displayed video pictures. When configuring a network, it is very important to make sure there is enough bandwidth to carry the video from end to end in order to minimize packet loss due to congestion. It is a good idea to have some mechanism (such as FEC) to correct errors that do occur. It's also important to monitor packet loss rates on transmission links to ensure that the loss rates don't become worse over time, which could indicate a problem in the network.

COP3 Row-Column FEC

COP3 (Code of Practice 3) is a powerful mechanism for correcting packet errors that has become standardized as SMPTE 2022. COP3 is a common name originally assigned by the Pro-MPEG Forum, which has been incorporated into the Video Services Forum.

Row-Column FEC operates by arranging groups of packets in rows and columns and then adding an FEC packet to each row and each column. For example, a 10-row, 5-column FEC scheme would add 10 row FEC packets and 5 column FEC packets to every 50 data packets, as shown in Figure 7-8A. In the SMPTE 2022 standard, these FEC packets are calculated by using the XOR (exclusive-OR, a standard binary logic) function. Interestingly, if any one packet in a row is lost, then its value can be calculated by performing an XOR on all the other packets in the row, including the FEC packet; the result of

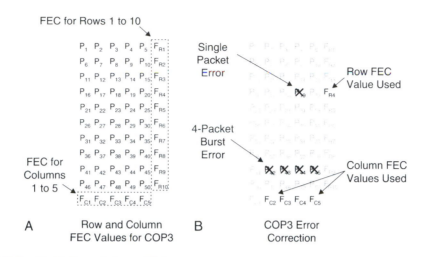

FIGURE 7-8   (A, B) Row-Column FEC

this calculation is the original packet. This same calculation also applies to columns with at most one missing packet.

By adding both the row and column FEC data, it becomes possible to correct burst errors of up to 5 packets in length and even replace packets that are completely missing. However, there are limits to what can be corrected. Figure 7-8B shows two examples of different error patterns that can be corrected.

- Packet 19 has been corrupted by a short burst of bit errors. Since none of the other packets in row 4 have been affected, the error can be corrected by relying on the FEC packet for row 4.
- Packets 42, 43, 44, and 45 have also been corrupted. These errors can't be corrected with the FEC for row 9 because there are too many errors, so instead the corrections must be based on the FEC data for columns 2, 3, 4, and 5. Columns 2, 3, and 5 can easily be corrected since there is only a single packet error in each column. For column 4, packet 19 must be corrected first using the row-4 FEC, and then packet 44 can be corrected using the FEC for column 4.

Of course, the added row and column FEC data is fairly costly in terms of bandwidth, adding 15 extra packets for every 50 transmitted, for 30 percent overhead. End-to-end delay of the system is also increased, because the receiver needs to buffer the block of

65 incoming packets (50 data packets plus 10 row FEC packets plus 5 column FEC packets) in order to check the FEC values and correct any errors in the data block.

Packet Reordering

Packet reordering occurs in a network when the packets arrive in a different order from how they were sent. For many types of data, such as e-mail and file transfer, this is not a problem, since the data is not normally used until all the packets have arrived. However, for video data streams, out-of-order packets can cause problems.

Streaming video data, particularly MPEG video packets, has a very precisely defined structure and sequence. This structure is necessary to allow the decoder to correctly determine where each pixel needs to be placed in the image. The timing of this data is important as well. If some of the data for an image is not available when it is time to display that image, then the image can have missing portions or might not be displayable at all. Out of order packets can also change the timing of packets containing MPEG PCR values, which would affect the system clock. When packets arrive out of order, they must be put back in the right sequence for the video decoder to operate.

Packets can get out of order in a network for a variety of reasons. One possible cause was discussed earlier in this chapter: automatic retransmission in a wireless link. When there are multiple paths from the source to the destination, packets can (under certain circumstances) take different paths and different times to arrive.[3] Also, as networks become congested, packets may get delayed while waiting for their turn to be sent.

Packets that arrive out of order can easily be put back in order through the use of a buffer. However, this can add delay to the signal. Plus, if the buffer isn't large enough, a severely delayed packet will have to be treated as a lost packet.

---

3. Routers are designed to forward packets in a repeatable manner based on a set of rules. Typically, all packets from a source to a single destination will take the same path. However, video packet receivers need to be able to handle any exceptions.

Hence, when evaluating a network for video traffic, make sure to examine the packet-reordering performance. There are a number of test sets that can check for reordering, and some network devices can report reordering when it happens. If reordering happens frequently, the network may not be a good choice for video.

Delay

Delay is going to happen in any network, whether from a desktop to a server or around the globe. There are two main sources of delay on an IP network: propagation delay and switching delay. We'll examine these two separately, although combined impact must be considered when looking at the end-to-end delay of a network.

Propagation delay is the amount of time it takes for information to travel from one location to another. As any physics student knows, the speed of light is an absolute limit on how fast information can travel. This limit does affect modern communications networks, since we can easily send information at the speed of light using radio waves or optical fibers. Table 7-3 gives a few examples of the propagation delays that could be encountered in real networks. (Note that a millisecond is equal to 1 million nanoseconds.)

Switching delay occurs at any point in the network where a signal needs to be switched or routed. Switching can occur when moving from one network to another or within a network any time a router

TABLE 7-3

Propagation Delays

Examples	Approximate Delay
One foot of optical fiber	1.5 nanoseconds
One meter of optical fiber	5 nanoseconds
1000 kilometers of optical fiber	5 milliseconds
1000 miles of optical fiber	8 milliseconds
Halfway around the world (12,000 miles or 20,000 km) of fiber	100 milliseconds
Earth to geosynchronous satellite and back	240 milliseconds

is used to process packets. Delays inside a router are not easy to calculate or predict, because the delay depends on so many different factors, including the total number of packets that a router is processing, the presence of other packets with higher priorities, congestion, or failures of some of router's network connections or simply the processing time of the router itself. Routers use mechanisms called *queues* to handle packets; these are very similar to the cashier lines at a large supermarket. Packets get placed in different queues depending on their priority, their size, the time of day, the phase of the moon (well, not really). The amount of time it takes a packet to travel through a router is affected by the queue in which it is placed and whether there are other packets in the queue in front of it. Just like in a supermarket, the user has essentially no control over the other packets in the same queue, so delays can mount if a number of large packets is already in the queue. As a general rule, the fewer the routers in the path, the lower the delay in the path.

Jitter

Note: This section gets a bit technical and can be safely skipped by the casual reader. For those who want to know about the seamy underside of an IP network, read on!

Jitter is a measurement of variation in the arrival time of data packets. To get an understanding of this, think about how a well-behaved video source would send data into a network: nice, even-sized packets at a regular rate. Another way of saying this is that the time between packets is always the same. Ideally, if the packets arrived at the receiver in this same way, with exactly the same time between packets, the network would be perfectly jitter free. However, that's not how the world really works. In reality, receivers must be built to tolerate jitter, and networks should be designed so as not to create a lot of jitter if they are to be successfully used to transport video streams.

Let's look at an example of jitter where the sender is transmitting 500 packets per second, or one every 2000 microseconds. (This corresponds to an MPEG-2 video rate between 3 and 4 Megabits per second, which would give a fairly high-quality SD picture.) Ideally, with zero jitter, the packets would arrive at the receiver with the same timing, i.e., one every 2000 microseconds. Jitter happens when the packets arrive with different timing, say, 20 microseconds early or 50 microseconds late.

For normal data, such as e-mail or a file download, jitter doesn't have much of an impact. However, for real-time data such as video, audio, and voice signals, timing is very important, because excessive jitter can affect the recovery of the MPEG PCR. Any jitter that is present makes receiver clock synchronization harder to achieve, because the jitter adds inaccuracy to the PCR time stamps.

In the receiver, buffers can be used to reduce the jitter, by smoothing out the packet timing and by giving late packets more time to arrive. Of course, this comes at a cost: Adding a buffer increases the amount of end-to-end delay in the network. Also, the start-up time (measured from when a user requests a video until the video actually starts playing) will increase because the buffer must have time to fill before data can be withdrawn.

Overall, in any packet video network, some form of buffering will be needed at the receiver to accommodate jitter. The best systems on the market today use adaptive buffering—making the buffer small (and the delay short) when network conditions are good (i.e., low jitter and low packet loss). Buffer size is correspondingly increased if network conditions are poor or become worse. With any video stream, clean, uncongested networks with minimal packet loss and low jitter are the best choice for transport.

INTERNET TRANSPORT

At first glance, the public Internet appears to be an attractive method for video transport. It has incredible bandwidth, reaches all corners of the globe, and has little cost to the user beyond the cost of access. Unfortunately, the Internet is far from an ideal network for video traffic. Table 7-4 lists some of the key features of an ideal video network and discusses how the public Internet measures up on each feature.

With care and the proper equipment, the Internet can be used to transport high-quality, high-bandwidth video. For example, a network has been constructed to operate over the public Internet between Moscow

TABLE 7-4

Key Features of a Video Network

Feature	How the Public Internet Measures Up
High bandwidth	The public Internet certainly has a large amount of bandwidth; however, there are also plenty of users. No single user can count on having a large amount of bandwidth available at any given time for a video application.
Low jitter	Jitter is difficult to control in private networks and almost impossible to control in the public Internet. Because there is no universal mechanism to ensure that packets from a video stream all follow the same route, some jitter and packet reordering are inevitable.
Low delay	Network delay depends on two things: the time it takes a signal to physically travel over a link and the time it takes to process packets at each step of their journey. In the public Internet, users do not have control over how their packets are routed. This means that the delay can be long or short, depending on the route used and the congestion level of the devices along the route.
Priority control	The public Internet provides essentially no priority control, because the Internet connects all users equally. There is no reliable mechanism to reserve bandwidth for a specific user or to make specific packets for one user to take priority over other traffic on the public Internet.
Lossless transmission	Overall, the public Internet is extremely robust; communications can take place even if major portions of the network are not operational. However, packet loss is a fact of life on the Internet: Some carriers promise only 99 or 99.5% packet delivery, meaning that losses of 0.5 or 1% of a user's packets are not unusual.

and New York City. Table 7-5 gives the performance levels measured between these two cities during the video transmission.

Based on the values in Table 7-5, it might appear the reliable video transmission isn't possible. However, in this situation, the customer chose to use a pair of devices from Path 1 Network Technologies of San Diego, California. These devices (CX1000) take a standard video stream, add a user-selectable amount of *Forward Error Correction* (FEC; see Chapter 6), and also interleave the packets. In this case, the units were set to apply 40 percent FEC, which means that 4 FEC packets are sent for every 10 actual data packets. (This is a large amount of FEC, needed primarily to compensate for the high number of lost packets.) Also note that the end-to-end delay in this example is near the upper limit of what would be desirable for interactive video, but it is acceptable in this case because this is a one-way video broadcast from Moscow to New York.

TABLE 7-5

Moscow–New York Network Performance

Network Feature	Results
End-to-end delay	120 msec
Maximum jitter	25 msec
Raw video rate	5 Mbps
Packet-transmission rate	1350 per second
Packet-loss rate	~1000 per hour
Packet-reorder rate	~10,000 per hour

Source: VidTrans presentation from Path 1, February 2004.

QUALITY OF SERVICE

Quality of service (QoS) is a term often used to describe the overall suitability of a network for a particular use. A number of factors can affect network QoS, including delay, delay variation (jitter), bandwidth, packet-loss rates, and network availability. We discussed all but the last of these factors earlier in this chapter, so let's first get an understanding of network availability. Then we'll look at classes of service, which are a means of giving different types of data different QoS levels. Finally, we'll take a brief look at some of the items that are commonly found in service-level agreements (SLAs) for network services.

Network Availability

Network availability is a measure of what portion of the time a network is available for use by a customer. Carriers will typically guarantee a minimum level of network availability for each month (or other service period).

A network is said to be "unavailable" whenever it cannot be used for customer traffic, either due to a complete loss of connectivity or an excessively high error rate. A complete loss of connectivity would occur, for example, when a network is physically disabled due to, say, a cut fiber-optic cable or a loss of power at a critical equipment location. An excessively high error rate is often defined as an error rate of 10^{-3}, or one bit error out of every thousand bits transmitted, which could result in an error in every packet. From the perspective of a carrier billing and service guarantee, a link might not be considered unavailable until it is out of service for 5 minutes or more, based on the carrier's SLA. Short-duration outages might not be reported to the user or even counted.

Typically, network availability is measured as a percentage of the amount of time that the network was available (or not unavailable) out of the total measurement time. For example, a provider that promises 99.99 percent network availability would guarantee that the service does not become unavailable for more than 52 minutes per year. However, considering that short outages might not be counted, the potential exists for substantially more outages per year without violating the carrier's SLA.

Classes of Service

Classes of service are used to give different types of data different levels of access to network resources. Network administrators can assign different classes of service to different applications, depending on their need for high performance. For example, messages that are needed to control or maintain the network are given a very high QoS, because if these packets get blocked, the entire network can become unstable or fail completely. Similarly, data packets containing e-mail can be assigned a low class of service, because a short delay in transmission usually does not affect the value of e-mail messages. In between are classes of service used by real-time applications, such as database queries, voice-over-IP calls, and video and audio streaming.

Within the data networking community, there are many different opinions about what class of service should be assigned to video traffic. This occurs as a natural result of different opinions on the value of video traffic. On one hand, video could be viewed as a mission-critical function for a broadcaster sending programming to a remote broadcast location. On the other hand, a college network administrator could view video as a nuisance when hundreds of students try to watch the latest video of a dog on a skateboard online. Also, priority conflicts can arise when a single network is used for both voice over IP and video over IP, because both applications are highly sensitive to network delays and packet loss. So it is important to assess the value of video to an organization before the correct class of service can be assigned.

As we have discussed in this chapter, in order for video to display properly for a user, the video data needs to arrive in a smooth, continuous stream. One way to accomplish this on a crowded network is to assign a high-performance class of service to video traffic. In effect, this instructs a router or other network device to give priority to these packets.

Figure 7-9 shows three different priority queues; we'll call one high priority, one medium priority, and one low priority. These queues operate just like a line at a market for a cashier: New packets enter the rear of the queue and wait until they reach the head of the queue before they are transmitted. In this case, all of the queues are competing for a single output resource, so we have to assign operating rules. Let's set up a simple set of sample rules and see how they affect the behavior of the system.

1. Each time the output resource becomes available, a packet is chosen from one of the three queues. If no packet is available in any queue, then a null packet is sent.
2. If a packet is available in the high-priority queue, then it is sent immediately.
3. If no packet is available in the high-priority queue and a packet is available in one but not both of the medium- and the low-priority queues, then that packet is sent.
4. If no packet is available in the high-priority queue and packets are available in both the medium- and low-priority queues, then packets are sent in a ratio of three medium-priority packets to one low-priority packet.

Using this example, we can see why it might not be prudent to send large video or other frequently occurring packets using the high-priority queue: It would be very difficult for other packets to get through. Sending video as low priority would also be unsuitable to

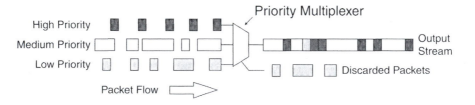

FIGURE 7-9 Example Using Three Priority Queues

the video users; their packets would be delayed while other packets were processed. Medium priority could be a choice for video, provided that most nonvideo traffic was made low priority.

Low-priority packets can get delayed, sent by a different route, or, worst case for an extremely congested network, get deleted because they were not deliverable. Deletion could also occur if the router uses "random early discard" to keep queues from overflowing. A great deal of intense science and mathematics is involved in queuing theory, so we won't spend any more time on it.

Classes of service can be useful tools to help ensure that video traffic flows smoothly across a network. However, they are not a panacea, since high-priority video service can affect the performance of other data and because their use is basically limited to private networks. Consider the dilemma if classes of service were available to everyone on the public Internet. What would prevent everyone from assigning his or her own traffic to be the highest possible class of service? Employed with discretion and with suitable policies of use, classes of service can help ensure a pleasant experience for video users on private networks.

Service-Level Agreements

Service-level agreements (SLAs) are contracts between carriers and users that specify the quality of services that a carrier will deliver. These contracts are legally binding and can sometimes be modified for large users. SLAs can cover a wide range of network features and functions and can cover any type of service, from plain voice to sophisticated private network and hosting services.

An SLA should not be confused with a tariff. A *tariff* is a document that specifies prices for specific telecommunications services that must be filed with a regulator by a licensed common telecommunications carrier in the United States. Services covered by tariffs must be offered to all customers on a nondiscriminatory basis. While tariffs sometimes include a description of the level of service that will be provided by the carrier, they are typically not as detailed and generally offer fewer specifics than SLAs.

SLAs sometimes include a unique feature: automatic compensation when the promised service level is not reached. Typically, these remedies take the form of automatic credit to the customer's bill for each instance of a problem that has occurred in a specific time period.

Table 7-6 provides a description of some items that can appear in SLAs.

TABLE 7-6

Service-Level Agreement Items

SLA Item	Description
Availability (%)	The proportion of the time that the service is available for use, i.e., not out of service. Typical SLA values are 99 percent and greater.
Packet delivery ratio (%)	The proportion of packets that are delivered to the destination out of the total number of packets sent. Note that this may be measured as a monthly average and be based on sample data, not on a count of every packet sent. Typical SLA values are 99 percent or greater.
Packet loss ratio (%)	The converse of packet delivery ratio; i.e., the number of packets lost out of the total number sent. Typical SLA values should be 1 percent or lower.
Network delay (msec)	This number specifies the average amount of time it takes data packets to flow across the network. Notice that this specification may be just between points inside the provider's network; it may not include the time needed for customer data to enter or leave the network. Also note that this measurement may be based on samples and not every packet and may be averaged over a week or a month.
Delay variation (msec)	Although it would be nice, a limit on delay variation is probably not in most current carrier SLAs. This factor is only really important for streaming applications, such as video and voice over IP. As more end users deploy streaming, expect to see this enter into new SLAs.
Service response time (hours)	This is the maximum amount of time from when a network problem is reported to the provider until the provider has to be ready to begin correcting the problem. This may vary depending on the time of day (e.g., longer times at night and on weekends) and may include travel time from the provider's site to the customer's location.
Time to repair (hours)	This is the maximum (or sometimes average) amount of time it will take the provider to correct a service problem. Note that customers may need to wait through both the service response time and then the time to repair before their service is restored.

For video services, packet loss ratios are crucial. As loss ratios approach 1 percent, video becomes very difficult to deliver smoothly, unless very robust FEC is used. Network delay may also be a consideration, but it usually comes into play only for interactive video. On the other hand, delay variation (jitter) will affect all video and should be tightly controlled. Network availability is important to all services, including video.

REVIEW AND CHECKLIST UPDATE

In this chapter, we focused on moving packets from one location to another. We covered network transport technologies, such as SONET/SDH, cable and DSL, ATM, MPLS, VPNs, pseudowires, and wireless Ethernet. We looked at an example illustrating how to calculate total network bandwidth for a video signal. We discussed a number of aspects of transport, including multiplexing, traffic shaping, buffering, and firewalls and how these technologies impact video transport. We then examined how network impairments can affect video traffic, including packet loss, packet reordering, delay, and jitter. We focused on how the public Internet can (or cannot) be used to transport video, in light of its standard behavior. And we wrapped up with a discussion of how quality of service can impact video traffic and looked at some of the factors involved in a service-level agreement.

Chapter 7 Checklist Update

❑ Verify that the wide-area network capacity and technology are suitable for the video traffic that is to be transported.
❑ Configure the video endpoint devices to handle impairments to the video stream. Consider the impact of packet loss, packet reordering, and jitter.
❑ Calculate the total bandwidth needed for the video signals, including any associated audio signals, ancillary data, MPEG overhead, and IP and Ethernet encapsulation overhead. Make sure the network can handle the expected peak bit rate.
❑ Make sure network delay is suitable for the application. For interactive video, delay in each direction should be below

150 msec and normally must be below 400 msec. For one-way applications, delay is usually not a significant factor.

❏ Consider using multiplexing to reduce the cost of bandwidth when multiple video signals are being transported.

❏ Ensure that network firewalls are configured correctly. In particular, make sure the necessary TCP or UDP ports are not blocked. Also, check whether UDP traffic is allowed to flow when RTP-over-UDP streams will be used.

❏ Decide whether the public Internet will be used. If so, ensure that video sources and destinations are configured to handle lost packets and large delay variation.

❏ If private networks will be used, determine whether different classes of service will be employed for video. Create policies for video QoS; make sure adequate bandwidth is available for nonvideo communications.

❏ Examine carrier SLAs. Will networks provide a suitable level of service for video?

8

PRIVATE VIDEO STREAMING AND MEDIA PLAYERS

Video streaming is the process of delivering video content to a viewing device for immediate display. Streaming is often the first application that springs to mind when people think about transporting video over a network. Aside from the obvious entertainment applications, streaming video can be used for a variety of business purposes, including communications, training, education, and customer support. For these applications, video providers want to control many aspects of the user experience, and they will want to control and manage their own private video streaming systems.

Business video providers have two main alternatives for hosting content for streaming delivery. The first is to use one of the major web-based services, such as YouTube, where many functions are automatic and content owners have little or no control over how their content is compressed, stored, or delivered. That subject will be covered in detail in Chapter 15. In this chapter, we will be

Video Over IP: IPTV, Internet Video, H.264, P2P, Web TV, and Streaming: A Complete Guide to Understanding the Technology

focusing on private video streaming, where the user has the ability to choose the video compression formats, the delivery methods, and how viewers will experience the video content. This chapter will explore both the concepts and the technologies available to both business users and individuals.

In this chapter, we will be limiting the discussion to one-way delivery of video content over a general-purpose data network. Two-way videoconferencing will be handled in Chapter 10. Video delivery over special-purpose video networks will be discussed in Chapter 13, on IPTV to the home. We'll begin with a discussion of some of the key concepts related to streaming, including the basic technology. Then we'll look at some of the applications of this technology. We'll conclude with a look at some of the most popular streaming formats and the media container formats that are used by all types of video files.

BASIC CONCEPTS

Video streaming is a generic term that covers a couple of different technologies. Here are the most common ones:

- *True streaming*, where the video signal arrives in real time and is displayed to the viewer immediately. With true streaming, a 2-minute video takes 2 minutes to deliver to the viewer—not more, not less.
- *Download and play*, where a file that contains the compressed video/audio data is downloaded onto the user's device before playback begins. With download and play, a 2-minute video could take 10 seconds to download on a fast network or 10 minutes to download on a slow network.
- *Progressive download and play*, which is a hybrid of the two preceding technologies that tries to capture the benefits of both. For this technique, the video program is broken up into small files, each of which is downloaded to the user's device during playback. With progressive download and play, a 2-minute video might be broken up into 20 files, each 6 seconds long, that would be successively downloaded to the viewer's device before each file is scheduled to play.

In the following sections, we'll investigate these technologies in more depth and take a brief look at how these three techniques differ.

A simplistic analogy might be useful here. Consider two of the options that are available for the supply of fuel used for home heating. One alternative is natural gas, which is piped by means of a distribution network that runs into each customer's home. Another alternative is fuel oil, which is delivered on a periodic basis to each customer's home. A true streaming system is somewhat like the natural gas system: The fuel (content) is delivered at exactly the rate in which it is consumed, and no storage is present inside the consumer's home. A download-and-play system is like the fuel oil delivery system, since each user must own and operate a large tank (disk drive) in which the fuel (content) is loaded periodically by a fuel supplier. If the natural gas supply becomes inadequate, the rate of gas delivery to each consumer can slow down, possibly causing difficulty in heating some customers' homes. With the fuel oil tank, once the delivery has taken place, customers have control over that fuel oil and can use it however they wish.

True Streaming

True streaming harkens back to the origins of television—and the way that broadcast TV, satellite TV, and CATV work today. In these systems, the video is displayed as soon as it reaches the viewer's television; there is no way of storing the video signal. This immediacy has many benefits, not the least of which is the ability to show live content. This also helps make the viewing device less expensive, since image storage is not needed.

True streaming over an IP network starts by taking a digital video signal and breaking it up into IP packets. The video signal can be uncompressed, but generally when we are discussing streaming, the video content has been compressed using some form of MPEG or one of the proprietary video encoding formats (such as RealVideo or Windows Media). These packets are then *streamed* out over the network, which means that the packets are sent at a data rate that matches the rate of the video. In other words, a video program that lasts 10 minutes, 6 seconds will take 10 minutes, 6 seconds to stream. Special software, called *player software*, accepts the incoming packets and creates an image on the viewing device.

For streaming to work properly, video content needs to arrive at the display exactly when it is needed. This is not as simple as it sounds, because many factors can affect the timely delivery of the video packet data. Servers running specialized software (and often containing specialized hardware) are used to send video content in a smooth, constant-speed stream over a network. The network needs to be capable of delivering the stream to the viewer intact without losing packets or drastically changing their timing. The player software needs to accept the incoming packets and deal with any imperfections in the data flow caused by the network. Typically, this requires a small amount of buffering in the player device.

Streaming has been used successfully on a number of different network technologies, from low-speed, dial-up connections to broadband-access networks. The only requirement is that the available network bandwidth be greater than or equal to the data rate of the stream.

Table 8-1 shows some of the advantages and disadvantages of streaming.

Download and Play

Download and play takes a video content file and delivers it to a viewing device, where it can then be decoded and displayed. This technology is very similar to the process used by websites, where user browsers are constantly requesting web pages from a server. In fact, download and play uses the same protocols as normal web surfing: HTTP and FTP over standard TCP.

Whether web pages or video clips are being requested, operation of a download-and-play network is fairly simple: Each time content is requested, it is sent to the requesting device. If the content is a 2-kilobyte web page, then the download occurs rapidly, and the page will quickly appear on the user's browser, even if a slow network

TABLE 8-1

Advantages and Disadvantages of Video Streaming

Advantages

- Content is delivered to the viewer when it is needed and is not stored inside the viewer's device. While this will not deter the determined hacker, it can make it easier to control copyrighted or other valuable content.
- True streaming can be used for live content, particularly in hard real-time applications.
- Multicasting normally uses true streaming, because the same content is delivered to all viewers simultaneously.
- Video streaming can be set up to allow users to begin watching prerecorded video and audio content at any point in the stream and can allow users to jump ahead or back in the stream (like switching chapters while playing a DVD).
- For applications where viewers will be changing frequently between content streams (as in IPTV), true streaming is normally used. This approach eliminates the delays from file downloading.

Disadvantages

- The quality of the network between the streaming source and the destination can have a major impact on the quality of the video signal that is delivered to the user. Any interruptions or congestion that occurs in this network can severely degrade the video image.
- Firewalls and network address translation (NAT; see Chapter 5) can interfere with video streaming. Some firewalls are configured to prevent RTP and UDP traffic from passing, so many types of streaming data can't get through.
- Lost video packets are not retransmitted in true streaming, so the playback device should be designed to handle any lost packets in a graceful manner.

connection is used. If, however, the content is a five-minute HD video clip, the time to download the clip to the player software can be quite long, even on a fast network connection.

Video and audio content can be hosted on standard web servers when download and play is used. The protocols and procedures needed to send the content to a viewer are the same for download-and-play content as for simple pages of HTML text. However, just as with any web server, system performance may need to be tuned to handle high volumes of requests for large content files.

One big advantage of download-and-play technology is that it can work over any speed network connection. This is because there is no requirement for individual video packets to arrive at any specific time or in any specific order, since all of the content is delivered before playback begins.

TABLE 8-2

Advantages and Disadvantages of Download and Play

Advantages

- Firewalls and NAT routers are less of a nuisance for download-and-play files, because normal HTTP and FTP transfers over TCP are used for delivering the content to subscribers.
- Download-and-play servers for video can use normal FTP or HTTP software, because content files are treated just like any other web content. This removes the need to install special video streaming software on content servers.
- Network errors that cause bit errors or lost packets while the video file is being downloaded are automatically corrected by TCP, making the job of the playback device much simpler.

Disadvantages

- As each file is being downloaded, even slight network delays or degradations can trigger TCP's flow control mechanism, which can significantly increase download time.
- Video and audio content must generally be downloaded completely, from start to finish. Some users may abandon their attempt to view the content if the download takes too long.
- Enough storage (either memory or disk space) must be available on the playback device to store the video file before it is played.
- Because of their large size, video files can be difficult to work with, both on the content server and in the network. If a major problem occurs during download, the whole process may need to be repeated from the beginning.

Table 8-2 shows some of the advantages and disadvantages of download and play.

Progressive Download and Play

Progressive download and play is a variation on download and play. It is used to simulate streaming for applications in which streaming won't work properly, such as when true streaming behavior is blocked by a firewall. Progressive download takes the video content file and breaks it up into smaller segments, each one of which can be sent in turn to the player software. As soon as a segment is completely downloaded, the player can begin to process and display it, while the next segment is being downloaded. As long as each new segment arrives before its time to play, the playback device will be able to create a smooth, unbroken video image.

Anyone who has tried to watch a movie preview online has probably experienced progressive download. A typical scenario would be for a

TABLE 8-3

Advantages and Disadvantages of Progressive Download

Advantages

- Progressive download provides a quicker start for playback than a full download and play.
- Progressive download avoids the headaches encountered by true streaming for traversing firewalls.
- The entire video file eventually arrives on the viewer's PC and is stored (temporarily) on disk. Once the file arrives, some viewers (such as QuickTime) allow the user to fast-forward and rewind inside the content.

Disadvantages

- Content has to be specially segmented into progressive download format, and not all media players support it.
- Managing the multiple files that make up a single element of content on the server and during playback can add cost and complexity.
- Progressive download works best on networks where the average available speed equals or exceeds the speed of the stream. That way, each segment can be downloaded in advance of the time when it needs to playback.
- As the available network bandwidth degrades, it becomes much more likely that the next file in a progressive download won't be completely stored in the viewing device when it is needed, forcing the stream to temporarily halt.

---

user to click a link on a website to request a video clip. The user would then see a video player displaying a message saying something along the lines of "Connecting to Media" or "Buffering" and a percentage of completion. Once the first segment was completely downloaded, playback would begin. If the next segment had completed downloading when the first segment finished playing back, then playback would continue uninterrupted. If, however, the next segment was not completely downloaded, then the video viewing window would freeze, go blank, or begin to display the "Buffering" message once again.

Progressive download can best be thought of as a compromise between streaming and download and play. Table 8-3 summarizes the advantages and disadvantages of using this technology.

STREAMING SYSTEM ARCHITECTURE

When implemented on an IP (or any other technology) network, streaming requires a fair amount of infrastructure. One of the key pieces is the streaming server, which has the responsibility to deliver streams to each user's device. Another key piece is the media player software that actually generates an image on the user's display. The final pieces in this puzzle are the content preparation station and the transport network between the server and the viewing device. Figure 8-1 shows how these key functions work together. In the following sections, we'll examine each of these pieces in more detail.

Content Preparation

Raw video content, such as a live image generated by a camera or video that has been recorded to a tape, is generally not well suited for streaming applications. Normally, the content needs to be processed, which can include format conversion, video compression, labeling and indexing, and publishing for streaming.

Capturing and preparing content for viewing can be a simple or a highly complex process, depending on the goals of the users and their budget for time and money. For some companies, capturing footage with a video camera and placing a compressed video file on their website is adequate. For others, professional production, with carefully edited images and graphics designed for web viewing, is required. Setting aside these artistic considerations, a certain amount of processing needs to be done to prepare video content for streaming. Table 8-4 shows some of the main functions performed during content preparation.

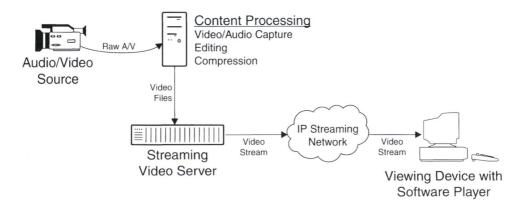

FIGURE 8-1   Architecture of a Typical Streaming System

TABLE 8-4

Streaming Content Preparation Functions

- *Capture*: This is the process of gathering video content and placing it into the preparation system in a common format.
- *Editing*: This is the process of organizing the content into the form that viewers will see, complete with synchronized audio, music, overlaid text, and other visual and audio effects.
- *Preprocessing*: This is the process of conditioning the edited video prior to compression and can include color correction, noise removal, image resizing, and other processing needed to get the best results possible from compression.
- *Compression*: This is the process of converting the video and audio streams into the formats that will actually be streamed out to viewers. If different steam rates, video resolutions, or types of player software are to be supported, then the compression process is normally repeated for each combination.
- *Labeling and indexing*: This is the process of providing descriptions of the content and organizing it so that viewers can locate the content they want.
- *Publishing*: This is the process of transferring the content to the streaming server and creating the web pages that will contain links to the media streams.

Some non-real-time software encoders use *two-pass* encoding, which means that the video is encoded once, then evaluated, and then encoded again for the final output. The benefit of a two-pass system is that the results of the first pass can be used to control how the second pass is performed. If, for example, the scene being encoded has a lot of motion, then the second-pass encoder can be set to accommodate the motion. Drawbacks of two-pass encoders are that they require more processing than a single-pass encoder, so they increase the amount of time required to encode each file, although this is not normally an issue for content being stored on a server for later playback.[1]

Content can come from a variety of different sources: video cameras, prerecorded tapes and DVDs, downloaded video clips, and others. In many editing systems, the content is all converted into a common format before processing takes place. One format that is commonly used is a 32-bit RGB, where each pixel of each frame has 8 bits of data for each of the three primary colors red, green, and blue.[2] This format is

---

1. Some professional-quality real-time encoders also use two-pass encoding by employing roughly twice the amount of encoding hardware.

2. The remaining 8 bits can be used for various purposes. One popular use is to store an indication of the transparency of the pixel, commonly called the *alpha channel*.

very easy to work with and produces very high-quality results, but it has the drawback of requiring a large amount of disk space (megabytes for each second of video). Video from a compressed format such as a DVD must be decompressed into this common format.

When the video comes from an analog format, such as from a camera or videotape, a video capture device is used to convert the video into the correct digital format. This device can be a stand-alone device or a card that is inserted into a computer workstation. Most new video cameras and camcorders are also capable of delivering digital video content directly into a workstation using FireWire or USB 2.0 connections.

Many times, content preparation is done well in advance, which allows enough time for a sophisticated compression algorithm to operate. A skilled operator can adjust compression parameters during the process so that different settings can be used for rapid action sequences versus detailed scenery shots with little movement. Less fine-tuning can typically be done on a live feed, simply due to time and processing power constraints.

Streaming Server

The streaming server is responsible for distributing media streams to viewers. It takes media content that has been stored internally and creates a stream for each viewer request. These streams can be either unicast or multicast and can be controlled by a variety of mechanisms. We'll discuss unicast in this section, since it is by far the most prevalent form of streaming. We'll discuss multicast in more detail in Chapter 9.

Content storage and retrieval is one of the main functions of a streaming server. When content is prepared, it is normally produced in a variety of compression ratios so that users with different network connection speeds can select the video rate they require. For example, on many websites the user is given a choice between playback speeds that are suitable for a dial-up connection (56 kbps, sometimes called *low speed*), a medium-speed connection (100–300 kbps), and a high-speed connection (500–1500 kbps, sometimes called *broadband* or *DSL/cable modem speed*). Each of these different playback speeds requires a different version of the content file to be created during the compression process. This means that one piece of content may be contained in three different files inside the server, one for each of the playback speed choices.

This situation can be further complicated by the fact that a server may support several different types of players, such as QuickTime or Windows Media Player. Since most content providers want to reach as wide an audience as possible, they will normally encode the video to be compatible with two or three of the most popular player software packages.

Tallying this all up, a streaming server can end up with a multitude of different copies of each piece of content. For example, if the server needs to handle three different connection speed options (dial-up, medium, and high) and three different media player formats (Flash, Windows Media, and QuickTime), then a total of nine different video file formats would need to be stored on the server.

A significant processing job of the streaming server is to create packets for each outbound stream in real-time. As we have discussed, each IP packet must have a source and a destination IP address. In order for the video packets to reach the correct destination, the server must create headers for these packets with the correct IP destination address. If the server is sending out standard RTP packets, the video and audio streams must be sent as separate packet streams, each to a different port on the receiving device (see Chapter 6 concerning ports and RTP).

Another responsibility of the server is to encrypt the packets in the outgoing stream, if required by the content owner. Since most modern encryption uses public key cryptography (see Chapter 11), each stream will need to be encrypted with a unique key for each user. Accordingly, encryption has to be done on each stream while it is being sent out of the streaming server.

Since streaming is done on a real-time basis, the server must also create well-behaved streams, meaning that the pace of the packets should be regular and should not rapidly speed up or slow down.

The rate of the packets also has to match the data rate required by the player software so that the player's buffers don't overflow or run out of data. The goal of a streaming server is to deliver to each viewer, for example, a 5-minute, 10-second stream in 5 minutes and 10 seconds.

Sometimes, streaming servers are given the responsibility to change the rate of the stream being sent to a viewer based on changing network conditions. For example, a stream could start out at 300 kbps and then drop to 100 kbps if the network became congested, based on status reports sent back to the streaming server from the player. The server will then switch to streaming a version of the content that was recorded at a lower speed. The real trick is to get this to happen smoothly so that the user doesn't notice the switchover, other than a small drop in video or audio quality. This process, also know as *scaling* a stream, is a feature of many advanced streaming systems.

One of the big benefits of streaming technology is that it allows a user to have *random access* to a variety of media streams. This means that the user is permitted to jump ahead or back within a piece of content. In order to implement this function, close cooperation is required between the streaming server and the player software. The player software must accept user commands and transmit them to the server. The server must then be capable of changing the outbound stream.

Streaming servers supplying a number of simultaneous viewers also require high-speed storage and network connections. For large servers handling broadband streams, use of gigabit Ethernet network interfaces is becoming common. Also, in order to support hundreds or thousands of users, the video content can be copied to multiple servers at different physical locations around the Internet.

Reflecting Server

A reflecting server takes one copy of a video stream and makes multiple copies for delivery to multiple users in real time. In this

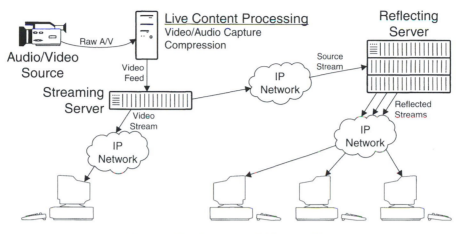

FIGURE 8-2 Streaming System with Reflecting Server

manner, it can add streams to a live event when demand peaks above the capacity of the original streaming server. Figure 8-2 shows how a reflecting server would be added to the basic streaming network from Figure 8-1.

Corporations can install their own private reflecting servers to support real-time streaming within the confines of their own corporate networks. Commercial services will also lease capacity on reflecting servers for occasional use when streams can be delivered over the Internet. When a reflecting server is involved, some users will have their connections redirected during session setup so that they will receive their stream from the nearest reflecting server that has available capacity.

IP Streaming Network

Although it would be great if any IP network could be used for streaming, in reality a streaming system will function better if some of the key network performance variables are controlled. Table 8-5 lists some of the network parameters that can affect streaming performance. (See Chapter 7 for more discussion of these parameters.)

TABLE 8-5

IP Network Parameters That Affect Streaming

- *Packet-loss ratio*: If too many packets are lost, then streaming video performance will suffer. (An occasional packet lost every now and then can generally be hidden.) Packet-loss ratios should be kept below one out of every thousand, if possible.
- *Packet-delay variation*: Because streaming is a real-time activity, if a packet arrives too late, it can't be used in the playback. Ideally, if the delay variation can be kept below 50 milliseconds, the player can accommodate the variation.
- *End-to-end delay*: This parameter is not terribly important, unless the link is being used for a two-way conversation.

Player Software

Player software that resides on the viewer's PC is responsible for accepting the incoming stream and converting it into a displayed image. A number of functions need to be performed in this software, and its performance can have a major impact on user satisfaction.

Before a streaming session can begin, the user must select the content. Typically, the list is presented to the user inside a web page that is hosted on the streaming server, and the user simply clicks on the appropriate hot link to begin content playback.

If the streaming server has encrypted the content, the player software needs to decrypt the incoming packets. This is a fairly simple process once the key is known. The keys can be obtained directly from the streaming server or by connecting to a third-party authentication service.

Since some streaming protocols, such as RTP, separate the audio and the video signals into two different streams, the player software is responsible for resynchronizing the incoming streams. This is accomplished by looking at the time-stamp data contained in each stream and comparing it to the time-stamp data contained in the associated RTCP overhead packets.

One of the most intensive jobs of the player software is to decompress the incoming signal and create an image for display. The amount of processing required varies depending on the size of the image and on the compression method. Older compression systems (such as MPEG-1) tend to be easier to decode than newer systems (such as MPEG-4) and therefore place less of a burden on the decoding device. Smaller images, with fewer pixels to process, are also easier to decode. Stand-alone devices, such as set-top boxes, usually have hardware-based decoders and are generally restricted to a limited range of compression methods (primarily in the MPEG family).

Most recent-vintage personal computers are also capable of running player software, including desktop and laptop machines, as well as Windows-, Macintosh-, and Linux-based systems. Some handheld devices also are capable of running player software. Determining whether a particular machine is capable of decoding a particular video stream is somewhat tricky; performance depends on the processor speed, the amount of memory (of all types—cache, RAM, and on the video card), and the number of other tasks the processor is performing. Generally, disk drive capacity is not a big factor, since the buffers required for video processing are generally held in memory rather than on disk. For high-quality, full-screen video decoding, a hardware decoder card can also be added to a personal computer to boost performance.

STREAMING APPLICATIONS

Video streaming is an ideal way to accomplish *narrowcasting*, the process of broadcasting to a specialized audience. There are literally hundreds of applications on the Internet today and thousands more that are hosted in private corporate settings. Some applications require live streaming; others can use previously recorded content very effectively. Let's take a brief look at some of the ways in which narrowcasting is being used today.

Corporate Video

Corporate video consists of content that is intended to improve the performance of an organization. We'll use the term *corporate* loosely here, because we want it to apply to all types of public and private organizations, including government agencies, not-for-profit organizations, and true private corporations.

Corporate video tends to focus on two areas: employee education and information sharing. Education can cover a wide range of topics, including training for new employees, instruction on new work procedures and equipment, job enrichment training, and personal skills development, to name a few. Corporate executives use information sharing to make employees aware of corporate or organizational performance, to improve communication with employees, and to deal with unusual challenges or opportunities. Sometimes the corporation produces this content strictly for internal consumption; other times content is made available to outside parties.

Live streaming is normally used for time-critical corporate video applications, such as company news distribution and executive speeches. Before IP streaming video became feasible, some companies had gone to the expense of renting satellite time and deploying portable satellite receivers for special events; a few large retail chains maintain permanent satellite systems. Today, high-quality streaming has made it possible to use corporate IP networks for this same function.

Many other forms of content are well suited to storage and subsequent on-demand streaming playback. For example, recorded training video material is very effective, because it allows students to watch at their own pace on their own schedule; they can review material or skip ahead without disturbing other students. With a centralized streaming server, content can be managed in a controlled environment, and outdated versions of content can easily be purged. Plus (particularly for content that is owned by third parties), a centralized server can be a good control point to keep track of the number of times each piece of content is viewed, which can affect the royalties paid. Contrast this with a download-and-play environment, where content gets dispatched to users around the network, thereby making accurate usage accounting difficult.

Investor Relations

Many companies have decided to give both large and small investors the ability to participate in major corporate events and shareholder meetings. An increasingly popular way of accomplishing this is by using streaming audio or video to transmit live meetings over the Internet. The content can also be recorded and played back on demand for users who were not able to participate in the original live broadcast or for those who wish to review what transpired.

During live corporate video coverage, it is not unusual for several hundred simultaneous users to be connected. Typically, this applies only to private networks, where multicasting can be enabled on the IP networking equipment. For users who are not connected to a suitable network, reflected multicasting can be used. With this technique, special servers are used to take a single incoming stream and produce multiple outgoing streams. This technology is particularly useful for investor relations, because it can scale up as more viewers connect by adding new server capacity as it is needed.

Church Service Broadcast

Many churches and other religious institutions are interested in distributing live video streams to worshippers unable to attend in person. Before the arrival of video streaming technology, one of the only ways to do this was by way of a satellite uplink, which is cost prohibitive for all but the largest congregations. Now it can be cost effective to deliver live services to local parishioners unable to attend due to illness and to send video to remote locations around the world.

A real-time video streaming encoder can be set up fairly inexpensively, alongside a simple audio and video mixer. The output of the encoder can be directed to a reflecting server with enough capacity to replicate streams for all of the intended recipients. For a fairly low cost per gigabyte, a number of streams can be delivered over the Internet.

TECHNOLOGIES FOR STREAMING

As vendors of streaming software continue to innovate, the quality of streamed video continues to go up even as bit rates drop. Today's compression algorithms are 20 to 30 percent more bandwidth efficient than those introduced three years ago. Progress continues as more efficient compression systems allow even more sophisticated techniques to be used on the encoder and more powerful PCs become available to users for running more complex player software. In addition, research continues on new algorithms that can make lower-bit-rate pictures even more appealing to the human eye.

In the following sections, we will discuss a number of different technologies used for video streaming. We'll begin with a discussion of the Real Time Streaming Protocol, or RTSP, which is used to set up and control streaming sessions. Then we'll take a quick look at the Synchronized Multimedia Integration Language, or SMIL (pronounced "smile"), which can be used to integrate video, audio, text, and still images into a web-based presentation. We'll then look at three popular streaming formats: Apple's QuickTime, Microsoft's Windows Media Player, and RealNetworks' RealPlayer.

RTSP

The Real Time Streaming Protocol (RTSP) provides a means for users to control video, audio, and multimedia sessions. RTSP does not actually provide for the transport of video signals; it allows these signals to be controlled by a user. Like a dispatcher for a delivery service, RTSP does not go out and actually deliver packages; it controls when and how packages are delivered by other protocols, such as RTP.

A good way to think about RTSP is that it is like HTTP for real-time files. A command like "rtsp://content.com/mymovie.rm" begins playback of the video file named "mymovie" on the server named "content." As you can see, this is very similar to the command that would fetch the page named "webpage" from the same site: "http://content.com/webpage.htm." In the first case, the actual video would be transported by RTP over UDP. In the second case, the web page would be transported by TCP.

An analogy might be useful here. Consider, for a moment, a VCR (normal consumer-grade videocassette recorder) with an infrared (wireless) remote control, as shown in Figure 8-3. A user enters a command by pressing buttons on the remote control, which in turn

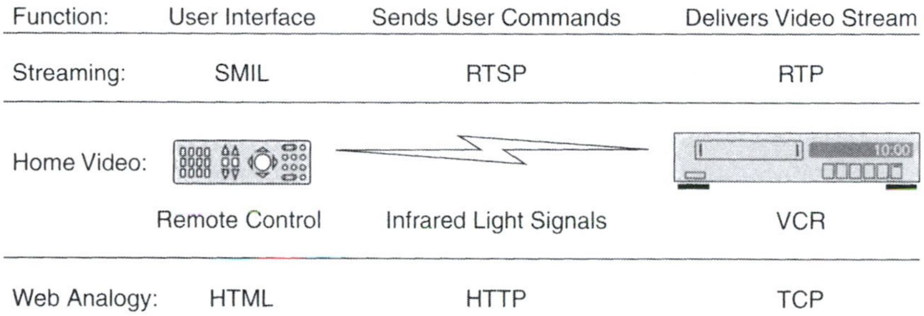

Function:	User Interface	Sends User Commands	Delivers Video Stream
Streaming:	SMIL	RTSP	RTP
Home Video:	Remote Control	Infrared Light Signals	VCR
Web Analogy:	HTML	HTTP	TCP

FIGURE 8-3 Relationship Between RTP, RTSP, and SMIL

sends the command to the player. It is useful to think of the VCR as taking the role of the video server, ready to play out content on command. The video server plays out content using RTP over UDP, because that protocol is needed to make sure that the video signals make it across an IP network. Think of the remote control as playing the role of the user's software interface. This could be implemented as a browser displaying web pages that include SMIL functions, as we will discuss in the following section. Then the infrared link between the remote control and the VCR plays the role of RTSP—a standard way for commands to be sent from user interfaces to streaming servers. The real beauty of RTSP is that it provides a standard interface so that different browsers can easily work with a variety of servers. Going back to our analogy, this would be the situation if all remote controls worked with all VCRs (wouldn't that be nice?). Of course, RTSP isn't implemented in every streaming product.

RTSP is specifically intended for use with time-oriented content, including streaming audio and video. It has the ability to move around inside content based on time stamps contained in the video, allowing a user to, say, skip ahead exactly 10 seconds in a video clip while maintaining audio synchronization. Contrast this with HTTP, which doesn't have this rich set of features for managing timed content and is further hampered by its reliance on TCP, which, as we discussed in Chapter 6, is not well suited for delivering streaming media. RTSP is also designed to work in multicast environments.

RTSP uses Uniform Resource Locators (URLs) to identify content on servers, just like HTTP. When a server receives an RTSP command, it will begin to play the stream to a specific destination, which is generally to the client that sent the RTSP command. RTSP requests can go from a client to a server or from a server to a client. Both the server and the client must keep track of the current status of the stream so that both will know when playback has begun. Table 8-6 lists some of the functions that RTSP can support.

SMIL

The Synchronized Multimedia Integration Language (SMIL) was developed to allow the design of websites that combined many different types of media, including audio, video, text, and still images. With SMIL, the web page author can control the timing of when objects appear or play and can make the behavior of objects depend on the behavior of other objects. SMIL is a recommended XML markup language approved by the World Wide Web Consortium (W3C), and it uses ".smil" as a file extension. Apple, Microsoft, Real, and several other vendors support SMIL in their media player products.

A good way to think about SMIL is that it is like HTML for multimedia. SMIL scripts can be written and embedded into standard web pages to cause actions or reactions to user inputs. For example, a SMIL script could be written as a portal into a library of multimedia content. SMIL could allow the viewer to select several pieces of content, play them back in any order, and provide a smooth video transition (such as a dissolve or a wipe) between each piece.

One example of a SMIL application would be a web-based presentation complete with graphics/animation/video that had a synchronized

TABLE 8-6

Some RTSP Functions

- Set up a stream for playing and begin client-to-server communications.
- Begin playing a stream or several related streams.
- Play a segment of a stream, beginning at a specific point in the stream.
- Record a stream that is coming from another source.
- Pause a stream during playback, without tearing down a connection.
- Tear down a stream and cease communications with the client.

---

sound track playing along with each slide. (Think of a web-based PowerPoint presentation complete with narration.) Another nice feature of SMIL is the ability to play different types of media in parallel, such as a video stream with accompanying audio. User controls can be provided to allow the content to be stopped, fast-forwarded, or rewound. Table 8-7 lists some of the capabilities of SMIL.

Container Formats

Container formats are very specific rules for constructing media files so that web browsers and media players can locate and determine how to handle various types of content that make up a file. Container formats (also called *wrapper formats*) can be used for files that are streamed as well as files that are downloaded for playing or storage. Figure 8-4 shows an excerpt of an open-source container format specification named *Matroska* that has been supported in a number of media players. A good container format would include information such as the compression method used for video and/or audio, the profile and level of the compression method, the duration of the media file (in hours, minutes, and seconds), the size of the media file (in kilobytes), the encryption method used, etc. The format could also include other data that would be useful during playback, for instance, the name of the artists, date of recording, copyright notice, a link to album cover art, and the like.

A container format is a structured list of data, where each data element is in a precisely defined location in each file. This structure makes it possible for a media player to read the data values and

TABLE 8-7

Some SMIL Capabilities

- Simple animation, such as moving objects around the screen or changing background colors of a web page
- Content control, such as starting, stopping, or rewinding
- Layout, such as positioning player windows on a web page
- Timing and synchronization, such as cuing an audio track to play when a graphic is displayed, or highlighting a graphic when it is being discussed during narration
- Video transitions, such as fades and wipes

Type specific data

Offset	Short name	Description
0x0	aspect	Aspect ratio, x:1000, where the x is stored in this field (uint16)
		• 4:3 = 1.333:1 -> **1333** • 16:9 = 1.778:1 -> **1778** • Wide = 2.350:1 -> **2350**
		Note: always make sure this is not set to zero—this would result in division by zero errors!
0x2	dimX	X-dimension, in pixels, 0 if not meaningful (uint16)
0x4	dimY	Y-dimension, in pixels, 0 if not meaningful (uint16)
0x6	rawVersion	Information about format's native uncompressed raw format; includes color spaces, sampling and bit depths (8 octets)
0xE	levelBlack	Black level, normally 0 (uint8)
0xF	levelWhite	White level, normally 255 (uint8)

FIGURE 8-4   Excerpt from Matroska Container Specification

determine how to play the media files. Each of the four major vendors in the media player business (Apple, Adobe, RealNetworks, and Microsoft) has published specifications for their container formats. Each format is associated with a unique file extension (.wmv for Microsoft, etc.). Use of stable, consistent container formats greatly simplifies the job of web browsers and media players.

COMMERCIAL PLAYERS

A number of companies have developed video and audio player software that operates on personal computer platforms. In the following sections, we will discuss three major products: those supplied by Microsoft RealNetworks, and by Apple Computer.

Third-party editing and encoding software, available from a number of sources, is capable of creating video and audio compressed files for all of these popular players. One benefit of some of these third-party packages is that they make it possible to create video files in several stream formats simultaneously. This capability can greatly simplify the amount of effort required to create streaming content in different permutations of stream rate and player software type. Many of these packages combine content capture, editing, streaming file generation, and other useful video tasks into a single, versatile package. (**Note:** It is not at all unusual for these packages to be quite expensive, particularly those that handle multiple users and have a rich feature set. On the other hand, it is good to note that all three player suppliers offer free copies of limited-capability versions of their video preparation software.)

All of the major players will play content that has been encoded using standards such as MPEG and MP3, along with a variety of other proprietary and nonproprietary formats. In these sections, we will discuss the three most popular players and see how their technology works. Most of the other software player packages available will have capabilities more or less similar to these three packages; unfortunately we don't have enough space in this book to discuss all of the other player offerings.

Microsoft

Microsoft developed Windows Media Player to allow video and audio files to be played on PCs running Microsoft operating systems. Movie Maker is a free utility that allows users to capture video from camcorders and other devices and create finished movies that can be viewed with Windows Media Player. In addition, Microsoft has developed a number of file formats specifically designed to support streaming.

Several different file formats are commonly used for Windows Media content, including:

- Windows Advanced Systems Format file (.asf): a file format designed specifically for transport and storage of content intended for streaming applications.
- Windows Media Audio file (.wma): a file that contains audio signals encoded using the Windows Media Audio compression system and is in the ASF file format.
- Windows Media Video file (.wmv): a file that contains video and audio signals encoded using the Windows Media Video and Windows Media Audio compression system and is in the ASF file format.
- Windows Active Stream Redirector file (.asx): the file that connects a web page to one or more Windows Media Video or

Windows Media Audio. The metafile contains the address of one or more clips located on a server. This type of file is also known as a *playlist*.

To understand how a metafile works, it is good to understand what happens in order to make media clips play inside a browser. First, the browser will display a page that contains a hotlink to a metafile. When a user clicks on this link, the web server delivers the metafile to the browser. The browser looks at this metafile and determines that it needs to run a plug-in (i.e., the Windows Media Player) to process the metafile. The browser then loads and starts running the plug-in and then passes data from the metafile to the plug-in. The plug-in analyzes the metafile data to determine where the actual media files are located. Then the plug-in makes a request to each of the servers listed in the metafile to start the appropriate streams flowing to the user. When the streams arrive, the plug-in takes the incoming streams and converts them into images and sounds that can be displayed to the user.

Let's also take a closer look at the ASF file format. Microsoft developed ASF and controls its destiny, due in part to patents on the fundamental stream format. ASF files can contain video, audio, text, web pages, and other types of data. Both live and prerecorded streaming signals are supported. ASF can support image streams, which are still images intended to be presented at a specific time during play. ASF provides support for industry-standard time stamps and allows streams to be played beginning at times other than the start of the media file. Non-Microsoft compression formats are supported inside ASF files; however, their data is treated as pure data and is not supported by some of the nifty features that allow skipping forward and back in a stream—this task needs to be handled by specific user applications.

RealNetworks

RealNetworks offers a number of streaming-related products, including the following:

- RealPlayer, a version of player software for content encoded in RealAudio and RealVideo formats. A second version, called

RealOne Player, also has an integrated media browser and a provision for managing premium (paid subscription) content.
- Helix servers, which come in a variety of models to handle streaming functions for servers ranging from small, private streaming sites to large, professional sites that provide massive amounts of public content.
- RealProducer and Helix Producer, which take video and audio content and convert it into RealAudio and RealVideo formats for storage and playback to streaming clients. Note that these file formats support encryption so that files can be protected when they are stored and while they are being transported over the Internet.

RealNetworks was one of the important early contributors to SMIL technology, and RTP and RTSP are used extensively. The RealPlayer also supports a variety of other media file formats, including many types of video and audio MPEG files, including MP3 audio files, Windows Media, and MPEG-4 video files.

Several different file formats and extensions are commonly used for RealNetworks content, as follows:[3]

- RealAudio clip (.ra): a clip that contains content audio encoded using the RealAudio format.
- Real Media clip (.rm): a clip that contains audio and video content that has been encoded using the RealVideo encoder. This type of clip can contain multiple streams, including both audio and video.
- RealVideo metafile (.ram or .rpm): the file that connects a web page to one or more RealVideo or RealAudio clips. The metafile contains the address of one or more clips located on a server.

The RealOne Player interacts with a Helix server using SureStream technology, which automatically switches between different stream versions based on network performance. The goal is to send the highest-speed (and therefore highest-quality) stream possible to the

---

3. Adapted from "Overview of RealVideo" located at http://service.real.com/help/videoccg/overview.html on April 12, 2004.

user for a given amount of network performance. Multiple streams are encoded at different resolutions (number of pixels), frame rates, and quality levels to balance the rate of the stream against the user experience of the video. As the stream rate decreases (which broadens the potential audience for a stream), the number of pixels, the frame rate, and the image quality can all be decreased to allow video to go through even low-speed connections.

RealNetworks' proprietary stance has a few drawbacks. Since one company has to bear all of the development costs, the resources available for innovation might be smaller than what would be available if multiple firms were all developing products. Also, users who have large libraries of content to be encoded may have some concerns about relying on a single company for all future support.

Apple

Apple Computer has been very active in developing a number of industry standards for streaming media and has made significant contributions of intellectual property. Many of these innovations center around QuickTime, which is Apple's name for its media streaming system. Apple also provides free movie-editing software (iMovie) as part of some software releases and sells a highly respected professional tool for editing movies called Final Cut Pro. Apple has also actively embraced international standards, including MPEG-4.

QuickTime was originally created to support video clips that were stored on CDs and played back on personal computers. It has become a widely used format, with hundreds of millions of copies downloaded for both Windows and Macintosh PCs. Some of the best uses of QuickTime combine video, audio, animation, and still images into a virtually seamless presentation to the viewer. A huge number of computer games and multimedia titles have been produced using QuickTime tools.

As with the other technologies described previously, several different pieces of technology are used together to support QuickTime streaming. There are components for content preparation, streaming

server management, and various versions of player software. Apple offers a free content preparation software package called QuickTime for both Mac and Windows PCs. An enhanced version, called QuickTime Pro, is available for a reasonable fee. As with some of the other systems, content can be prepared and streamed on the same computer or server, although system performance needs to be watched carefully to ensure that users will have their streams delivered smoothly.

For content owners and creators, Apple's use of standards can be a big positive. The QuickTime file format is the foundation for the MPEG-4 file format. The latest versions of QuickTime also use MPEG-4 AVC/H.264 compression technology. Apple provides players that work on both Windows and Macintosh PCs, and other companies produce player software for other operating systems. A version has even been designed for some Linux installations.

Selecting a Streaming Format

All three of the streaming solutions discussed in this chapter (Real, Windows Media, and QuickTime) are capable of delivering high-quality video and audio streams to the desktop. Because the market is competitive, these different formats are constantly being updated and upgraded to deliver more pleasing visual and audio results with fewer and fewer bits.

When selecting a streaming format to be used for content preparation, the most important consideration is to choose one that the target audience will be able to receive. This does not necessarily mean the player that came with the operating system for the PC; all the three leading players have versions that work on both Windows and Macintosh PCs. There is also a fair amount of overlap between the three players; for example, all three will play Windows Media files.

Another important consideration is the version of the player that users will be using. If the video stream is created using the latest version of an encoder but the user's player has not been upgraded, then the video stream might not play. (This is true for some upgrades but

not all.) Of course, this can be remedied by having a user download and install a new version of the player. But this may not please dial-up network users, who could face the daunting prospect of down-loading a multi-megabyte file containing a player software update.

Many third-party editing and content-preparation tools will produce output in multiple formats and at multiple stream speeds. These tools, including offerings from Adobe, Autodesk, and others, allow the creation of a group of output files from a single source stream. They allow one tool to be used to produce content for, say, Quick-Time and RealVideo at the same time or for all three formats (plus many others, such as MPEG). When you consider the number of different stream rates that might be required, it is easy to see a dozen or more different output files being created, each with a different com-bination of stream rate and player format. Many websites that offer content will list several combinations of stream format and bit rate, allowing users to select one that is compatible with their installed viewer software and network connection speed.

REVIEW AND CHECKLIST UPDATE

In this chapter, we investigated streaming. We began with the basic concepts, including a look at how streaming differs from download and play and progressive download. We analyzed the different parts of a modern streaming system, including content preparation, streaming servers, networks, and player software. We discussed a number of applications of streaming. Then we took a more detailed look at three key streaming technologies: RTSP, SMIL, and container formats. We followed this with a look at the three main vendors of streaming technology—RealNetworks, Microsoft, and Apple—and wrapped up with some thoughts about how to make a choice between the streaming formats.

Chapter 8 Checklist Update

❏ Determine the number of users who will want to view the content, and determine the maximum number of simultaneous viewers permitted.

❑ Determine if public, private, or virtual private networks will be used (or some combination thereof). If video content is going to be delivered to the general public, then ensure that there is a mechanism for users to get the necessary player software and load it onto their personal computers.

❑ Select a video streaming format—download and play, progressive download, or true streaming—based on the application and the capabilities of the viewer devices.

❑ For live content, true streaming is used.

❑ Determine the requirements for a content preparation system. Will this system be used frequently or occasionally? All three major streaming-format vendors offer free or very low-cost software encoders for their own format, but paid versions offer better performance and may be easier to use.

❑ Capacity requirements can vary greatly for streaming servers, depending on the amount of content, the number of simultaneous viewers, and the speed of each created stream.

❑ Evaluate and select authoring tools to create the necessary compressed data files.

❑ Select a wrapper format that will be compatible with the chosen viewer(s); ensure that any desired ancillary data (such as album cover art) is supported and prepared for each file.

❑ If third-party content is to be used, ensure that reliable copy protection/encryption software is available for file creation, storage, and playback.

9

MULTICASTING

Multicasting is the process of sending a single video signal simultaneously to multiple users. All viewers get the same signal at the same time, just as in traditional television broadcasting. Virtually all commercial video broadcasting operates using multicasting, including cable TV, satellite TV, over-the-air TV, and the vast majority of IPTV installations. However, for video streaming and Internet video, multicasting is the exception rather than the rule. In this chapter, we'll examine how multicasting works and then look at a few applications. We'll also investigate the technology of IP multicasting and get an understanding of the impact that multicasting has on a data network.

BASIC CONCEPTS

To understand multicasting, it is helpful to compare it to the process of unicasting. In unicasting, each video stream is sent to exactly one recipient. If multiple recipients want the same video, the source

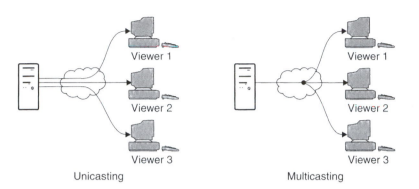

FIGURE 9-1 IP Unicasting vs. Multicasting

must create a separate unicast stream for each recipient. These streams then flow all the way from the source to each destination over the IP network.

In multicasting, a single video stream is delivered simultaneously to multiple users. Through the use of special protocols, the network is directed to make copies of the video stream for every recipient. This process of copying occurs inside the network rather than at the video source. Copies are made at each point in the network only where they are needed. Figure 9-1 shows the difference in the way data flows under unicasting and multicasting.

Note that IP networks also support a function called *broadcasting*, wherein a single packet is sent to every device on the local network. Each device that receives a broadcast packet must process the packet in case there is a message for the device. Broadcast packets should not be used for streaming media, since even a small stream could flood every device on the local network with packets that aren't of interest to the device. Plus, broadcast packets are usually not propagated by routers from one local network to another, making them undesirable for streaming applications. In true IP multicasting, the packets are sent only to the devices that specifically request to receive them, by "joining" the multicast.

To compare unicasting and multicasting, let's use an analogy. Take a moment and think about how a printed memorandum might be circulated to every employee inside a large corporation. One way this could happen is for the originator to make a copy of the memo for each employee. Each copy would get individually addressed and then sent via intracompany mail. For a large corporation, taking these steps would involve a significant amount of work for the originator and would put a lot of mail through the system. If a number of employees were located in a remote location, then enough copies of the memo would need to be delivered to that location for every employee. This is similar to the way unicasting works.

A different way to send the same memo would be analogous to multicasting. In this case, the originator would send one copy of the memo to a special person at each company location. This person would, in turn, be responsible for making copies of the memo for every employee in that location. These copies could then be addressed and delivered to each employee locally.

There are several benefits to the company that uses multicasting for printed memos:

- The burden on the sender is greatly reduced. When the memo is unicast, the sender has to make a copy of the memo for every employee and then apply individual addresses. When the memo is multicast, the sender needs to send only one copy of the memo to the special person in each company location.
- The amount of mail that is sent between locations is greatly reduced. In unicasting, a copy of the memo has to be delivered for every employee in every location. In multicasting, only one copy of the memo has to be delivered to each location.
- In unicasting, the sender has to know the address of each recipient. In a large corporation, the names and addresses of employees can change on a weekly or even daily basis. Tracking all of these addresses can be a huge burden. In contrast, when multicasting is used, the sender needs to know only the special addresses for the designated person in each location.

Of course, there is a cost for all of these benefits. The bulk of the cost falls on the special people at each location who are responsible for copying the memos and redistributing them. These people also have to recognize which messages need to be redistributed, which might be in the form of a special address or a note attached to the memo. This copying function is very similar to the packet replication functions performed by routers in an IP multicast network, as we shall see.

Unicasting

Unicasting in an IP network is the traditional way that packets are sent from a source to a single destination. The source formats each packet with the destination IP address, and the packet travels across the network. When the same data needs to be sent to multiple destinations, the source prepares separate packets for each destination.

In unicast streaming, each user who wants to view a video must make a request to the video source. The source must create a stream of packets containing the destination IP address of each user. As the number of simultaneous viewers increases, the load on the source increases, since it must continuously create streams of packets for each viewer. This can require a significant amount of processing power and also requires a network connection big enough to carry all the outbound packets. For example, a video source sending 20 different users a video stream of 2.5 megabits per second (Mbps) requires a network connection of at least 50 Mbps.

An important benefit of unicasting is that each viewer can get a custom-tailored video stream. This allows the video source to offer specialized features such as pause, rewind, and fast-forward video. This is normally practical only with prerecorded content but can be a popular feature with users.

Table 9-1 summarizes some of the major advantages and disadvantages of unicasting as compared to multicasting.

Multicasting

In multicasting, the burden of creating streams for each user shifts from the video source to the network. Inside the network, specialized

TABLE 9-1

Advantages and Disadvantages of Unicasting

___

Advantages

- Unicasting will work on standard IP networks, including the public Internet.
- Each user has an independent video stream. This allows the video source to offer each user playback controls, such as pause, fast-forward, and rewind. Users don't need to wait for regularly scheduled broadcasts.
- The source can determine precisely which unicast destinations are allowed to receive the data stream and keep records of each recipient.

Disadvantages

- The video source must have enough processing capacity and network bandwidth to create a stream for each user. When the source's bandwidth is fully consumed, no more users can be added.
- There must be enough bandwidth in every segment of the network to deliver all the streams from the source to their final destinations.
- The video source must know the correct IP address of every active viewer's device.

___

protocols allow IP routers to recognize packets that are being multicast and to send them to multiple destinations. This is accomplished by giving the packets special multicast addresses. There is also a special protocol that allows devices to join the multicast. (These special protocols will be discussed in more detail later in this chapter.)

Many existing routers can perform multicasting, but this capability is not enabled in many networks. Why not? Well, multicasting can place a tremendous burden on the processing resources of the equipment. Let's say, for example, that a router has users on 12 different ports that want to watch the same multicast stream. These ports could be connected directly to end users or could be connected to another router farther down the network. Multicasting requires the router to make 12 copies of each packet and to send one copy out on each port that is requesting the video feed. In addition, the router must be able to listen for and process requests for adding new ports to the multicast and to drop ports that are no longer requesting the multicast. These functions are often handled in the router's control software, so the processor burden can be significant.

TABLE 9-2

Advantages and Disadvantages of Multicasting

Advantages

- The amount of network bandwidth required can be greatly reduced using multicasting. Only one copy of a video stream needs to be sent along any branch in the network.
- Video sources can be much simpler; they are only required to transmit a single copy of the stream.
- Higher-quality (i.e., higher-bandwidth) video can often be used for multicasting.

Disadvantages

- All viewers of a multicast get the same video at the same time. Individual users cannot pause, rewind, or fast-forward the content.
- The network equipment must be multicast enabled along the entire route from the source to every multicast destination. This can require reconfiguration or possibly hardware/software upgrades for some legacy equipment.
- Some firewalls and NAT devices can block protocols used in multicasting.
- The burden on routers can be significant. They must process multicast control messages and perform packet replication.
- Controlling access to specific video content can be complicated on a multicast network.
- When hybrid public/private networks are used, system installation can be complicated.

Multicasts operate in one direction only, just like an over-the-air broadcast. There is no built-in mechanism to collect data from each of the endpoints and send it back to the source (other than some network performance statistics such as counts of lost packets). This means that any interactivity between the endpoints and the video source must be handled by some other mechanism.

Table 9-2 summarizes some of the major advantages and disadvantages of multicasting as compared to unicasting.

Joining and Leaving a Multicast

In a multicast, all users receive the same video stream at the same time. So, when users want to watch a multicast program, they must join in at whatever point the program happens to be in. (This is exactly analogous to broadcast television.) Similarly, if a multicast program is already flowing through a network, users have the option of joining or leaving that multicast, but they cannot start or stop it. In some implementations, multicast programs are sent in a continuous loop so that users who miss the beginning of a program can just keep watching to see what they missed.[1]

A multicast source is responsible for periodically announcing the availability of its data stream to the network user community. (This is accomplished by means of SAP packets, which we will discuss later in this chapter.) Users who are interested in receiving a multicast must listen for these announcements, which contain details on how the multicast is configured. A user device can then take these details and create a multicast join request, which it sends upstream to the nearest router.

When a router receives a request from a user to join a multicast, it must do several things. First, the router must determine whether it is already processing the multicast for another user. If it is, then the router simply needs to make a copy of the multicast stream and send it to the requesting user. If it is not, the router must request the stream from a device that is closer to the multicast source. Once this request is fulfilled, the router can send the stream to the user. Note that in this scenario, requests are made from router to router; this procedure can be repeated as many times as necessary to find a complete route from the user's location to the multicast source.

The key point to observe in this process is that each router must track all of the multicast streams it is currently processing. If it is already receiving a stream, it must make a copy for any new users that request it. Only if it is not receiving the stream is it allowed to request the stream from another router. This is the beauty of multicasting—only one copy of the multicast stream needs to be sent to the routers that have users (or other downstream routers) that are actually using the stream. This means that the bandwidth between routers is employed very efficiently: A router that may be a gateway to a complex network hosting hundreds of users needs to receive only one copy of the multicast stream. Compare this to what would happen in a unicast environment: A gateway router supporting

---

1. Some video providers offer several simultaneous multicasts of the same video content at staggered start times. This technique is used for near video-on-demand and will be discussed in more detail in Chapter 13.

hundreds of users would need to have enough capacity to handle a copy of the video stream for each user.

The process of leaving a multicast is also very important to maintain overall system efficiency. When users want to leave a multicast, their devices must send a "leave" message to the router. The router then stops delivering the stream so that the users' bandwidth can be freed up for other uses. Likewise, when a router no longer has any users (or other routers) that are requesting the stream, it must also leave the multicast. The leave process is important; without it, a multicast network could easily become choked with streams that nobody is watching.

APPLICATIONS

Multicasting is uniquely suited to transmitting live video to many viewers simultaneously. Because only one stream is created by the source, all the viewers receive the video data at the same time. Here are some of the applications for this technology.

IPTV

Multicasting is a powerful tool for IPTV because it is well suited for private networks and it solves a number of problems. Accordingly, multicasting is used in many IPTV installations for delivering the television channels that are supplied by the major television networks, which comprise the bulk of the audience for any TV delivery service. In contrast, streams that are delivered only to individual users (such as video-on-demand movies) are frequently delivered using unicast technology, so viewers can use fast-forward, rewind, and pause commands during viewing.

IPTV system architectures are well suited for multicasting because many of them are custom-built, private networks. Accordingly, it is an easy decision to select routers capable of handling the processing loads of multicasting. Also, many IPTV systems are hierarchical, with centralized program collection and processing points feeding signals to multiple delivery locations. In the extreme, one or two super-headends can be responsible for delivering programming to an entire country.

With multicasting, only one copy of each live TV stream needs to be delivered from the super-headend to each of the delivery networks, with copies made for each viewer at the local level.

Multicasting also helps IPTV systems to scale easily. The number of audience members watching any particular live video stream (television channel) is hard to predict in advance for an IPTV system. When large sports event occur, it is possible for 30 percent or more of the audience to be watching a single program. If these signals were delivered with unicast servers, the output capacity of the server would have to be enormous for even a moderate-sized community (particularly for HD video). With multicasting, the routers that feed the IP connections to each viewer are responsible for making the copies on an as-needed basis. While this places a burden on the routers, it greatly reduces the amount of networking bandwidth that would be needed to handle unicast streams from the source.

Channel change in an IPTV system that uses multicasting is a fairly simple affair. The television viewer uses his or her remote control to command an STB to switch to a different channel. The STB issues a leave command for the current channel and then issues a join command for the new channel. The leave command is very important, because that step is required to terminate delivery of the stream to the STB and to free up the bandwidth on the DSL line or other IP link that will be needed for the viewer's new selection. At the router, the processing burden increases slightly for users who change channels often, but the burden of packet replication remains fairly constant, since each viewer is almost always being fed a copy of one stream or another that is already being processed by the router.

Live Events

For many corporations and other organizations, delivering announcements to many people simultaneously can have some big benefits. Whether the news is good or bad, there is a value in having every participant get the same message at the same time. If some kind of audience participation is allowed (such as questions for the speaker), then the broadcast has to be live and with a minimal amount of delay.

In the past, a few organizations have gone to great expense to broadcast speeches or other messages to a widely dispersed audience. Temporary satellite links have been used, which involves dispatching satellite receivers to each location. The output of these receivers is then sent to display devices (video projectors, television sets) located in areas where employees can gather to watch them. Typically, these types of transmissions have to be planned well in advance to handle the complicated logistics. Equipment needs to be rented and shipped to each location, and technicians need to be dispatched to set up the equipment and make sure it operates correctly during the event. Clearly, this type of broadcast can be justified only for very valuable content. Figure 9-2A shows a typical temporary satellite broadcast.

If an IP multicast is used instead, the situation changes dramatically. Now users with desktop PCs can watch the video from the comfort of their own office. Any of a number of low-cost, stand-alone IP video decoders can be used to receive and decode the video for display on video projectors or television for employees without PCs. Although the setup time required to enable and test multicasting across an organization's network is not trivial, once the basic hardware and software components required for multicasting have been installed, they can be left in place, reducing the setup time and cost for future events. Figure 9-2B shows an example of multicasting for use in a live broadcast.

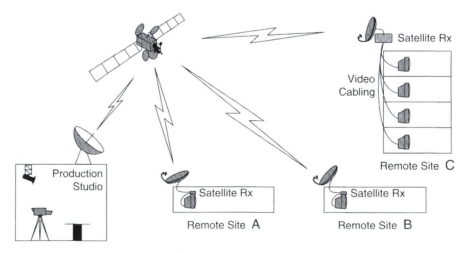

FIGURE 9-2A Live Broadcast Using Temporary Satellite

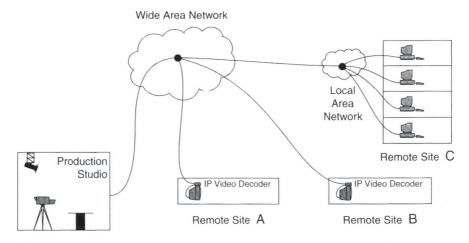

FIGURE 9-2B   Live Broadcast Using IP Multicast

Continuous Information

Another application for multicasting is to send information that is continuously changing. Live pricing data for shares and bonds is very popular, but applications also exist for weather and automobile traffic data. In these environments, live broadcasts are required, since old data are of little value.

Unfortunately, because the public Internet is not multicast enabled, these applications are limited to private networks. However, that has not stopped their deployment. IP multicasting is used by a number of brokerage firms not only to transmit share data, but also to transmit live news feeds from a variety of sources that can affect share prices. A number of installations of highway traffic monitoring systems use IP video transport; multicasting has been used when several viewing locations need to get simultaneous feeds. Similarly, weather or any other continuously changing data can be efficiently transmitted to a number of viewers on a multicast network.

Continuous-Presence Conferencing

Continuous-presence conferencing is a high-end form of videoconferencing in which the participants in each conference location can hear (and see) all the other locations during the entire conference through the use of multicasting. It is also known as *telepresence* or *virtual meeting*. Continuous presence is often used to create the illusion that all of the participants are in the same room, which is important both for executives in demanding meetings and for schoolchildren who could become distracted by video switching.

One requirement for a continuous-presence videoconference is having enough displays in each room to show the video images coming from all the other rooms. This can be accomplished, for example, in a four-location conference by having three displays (and one camera) in each location.

IP multicasting is an ideal mechanism to support this architecture. Video (and related audio/data signals) can be encoded and placed into IP packets as a stream originating at each location. Then the network is used to multicast the packets to all three destinations. At each destination, a decoder is used to receive each stream from the network and generate the video/audio/data signals for display. Since video encoders are generally more expensive than decoders, the cost of one encoder and three decoders is not exorbitant. Also, the need for a central unit to control the video switching is eliminated. One drawback to this type of system is the need to have enough incoming bandwidth at each location to handle a full video stream from all other locations; as the number of sites per conference goes up, the equipment and bandwidth costs can also climb rapidly.

CASE STUDY: MULTICAST SECURITY SYSTEM

One ingenious application of video over IP multicasting that was developed by Teracue AG of Odelzhausen, Germany, has been deployed by the City of Mannheim in Germany. In this application, a number of video cameras were set up in public spaces to allow live monitoring of any activities. The system has produced a number of benefits, which include faster response times in emergencies, providing records of reported incidents, and an overall drop in crime in the areas under surveillance due to the watchful eye of the video camera.

In this system, multicasting was a key enabling technology. It allowed two different viewing stations to observe the video simultaneously, one located in the police headquarters and one located in the local fire station. Multicasting also allowed a third location to be set up to record the video signals on a server, for later reference if needed.

Each camera location is equipped with a stand-alone video encoder. The encoder takes the live video signal from the camera, compresses it using MPEG technology, and formats the video data into IP packets. These IP packets are fed over the local access loop that is connected to each camera location. The loops have only enough bandwidth for one copy of the video stream, so multicasting technology is used inside the IP network to allow the video from the camera to flow to multiple destinations. Three destinations are shown in Figure 9-3: the video recording location, the fire department viewing location, and the video control location at police headquarters. The fire department viewing location has a PC equipped with viewing software that supports live event viewing as well as viewing of previously captured and stored video.

The video recording location is equipped with servers that take all the incoming MPEG video streams and record them onto hard disk for possible later viewing. Special software is used to file the video content so that it can be rapidly retrieved, based on the time the

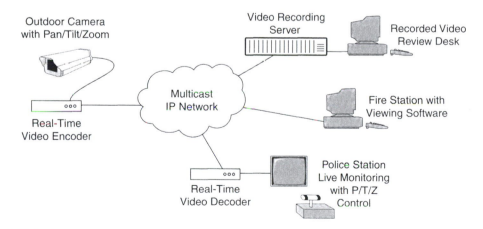

FIGURE 9-3   A Multicast-Enabled Security Network

video was recorded, for each camera. The video from different camera locations can be cross-referenced, to allow movements of key subjects to be tracked both before and after a reported incident.

The video control location has multiple monitors and MPEG decoders, although only one is shown in the figure. This location is also equipped with camera control devices that allow a user to aim the camera in different directions and to zoom in on areas of interest. The control devices operate using the same IP network as the video signals. Commands from the user are converted into IP packets, which are sent to the camera locations. At each camera location, the video encoder device receives the IP packets and generates data signals to control the camera.

It is important to remember that there is only one signal that comes out of each video camera, so every viewer of that camera will see the same image. Although it is possible to have more than one control station for the video cameras, it is good practice to ensure that each camera is controlled from only one station, or else chaos can ensue. The recording station can capture only one signal for each camera, so any decisions that have been made about aiming or zooming a camera are part of the permanent video record and can't be changed in later processing.

User stations are also set up to review the recorded video. The recorded video can be reviewed immediately or if a report is made about an incident that occurred during the most recent week. Local regulations dictate that video files cannot be stored more than seven days, unless they have been made part of an incident report.

The multicast-enabled IP network provided a number of benefits to the City of Mannheim, including the following:

- One network is used for all video and data transport, eliminating the need to install separate links for video and data signals.
- Multicasting allows the video to be observed in several locations simultaneously while also being recorded on a video server.
- Low-cost data circuits can be used at each camera location, because only one copy of the video stream needs to flow from

the camera. For most applications, a high-speed DSL link can be used, which is relatively inexpensive to lease from the local tele-com service provider.

- This same network also supports video playback from the serv-ers, allowing users to analyze video and prepare reports without tying up the live viewing stations.
- The video server provides secure, reliable video storage. The system also supports a rapid-rewind function, allowing users to look quickly back at video that was recorded as little as a few seconds or as much as a few days before.

Overall, the City of Mannheim system has benefited from installing an all-digital video networking solution. Although the initial cost was somewhat higher than competing technologies (based on analog video transport and tape-based recording), the long-term savings in operational cost and the higher quality of the resulting video have more than compensated for the cost.

MULTICASTING SYSTEM ARCHITECTURE

In the following sections, we are going to delve a little bit deeper into the technology of IP multicasting, as based on the Internet Group Management Protocol (IGMP). This protocol was first released in the 1980s and has undergone several revisions since then. One widely used version is IGMP Version 2 (V2), which has been avail-able for a number of years. A newer version, IGMP V3, is also being deployed in some networks.

The purpose of IGMP is to give information to routers about streams on a network that are being multicast. Routers have a big job in a multicast environment: They are responsible for forwarding and replicating multicast streams to all the devices that are entitled to receive the streams. Forwarding is fairly straightforward; it involves taking packets from an input and sending them to the correct output. Replication takes this a step further and is used when a single incoming stream of packets needs to be sent on more than one out-put. To replicate a packet, the router must make a copy of each packet for each destination and send each of them out via the proper interface.

In the following section, we will discuss Session Announcement Protocol (SAP) messages, which function to inform user devices about available multicast programs. Then we will talk about the processes required for a user device to join and leave a multicast session.

SAPs

Session Announcement Protocol (SAP) is used to inform multicast-enabled receivers periodically about programs (such as video or audio streams) currently being multicast on a network. In concept, SAP is similar to the TV guide service that is broadcast on many cable television systems. Each of the programs currently playing is listed, along with the channel number for that program. Similarly, SAP is used to send out information about each of the multicast streams available on a network, along with information that user devices need in order to connect to a multicast.[2]

Perhaps the most important part of a SAP message is the multicast address of the multicast stream. Once the user device has this address, it can send a request to the network to join that multicast. A single multicast source may generate multiple streams; each one of these can be announced via SAP. For example, a video encoder could provide two versions of a video stream (one for high-quality users and one for low-bandwidth users) and two different audio streams. An end user equipped with a low-speed dial-up connection to the Internet might choose to receive only the audio signal, whereas a cable modem user might want to receive high-quality video and surround-sound audio.

By default, SAP communications always take place on the multicast group address 224.2.127.254 on port 9875. Specialized software on the user device (frequently called a *multimedia player*) converts the information received from SAP into a list of choices from which the user can select. As soon as the user has made a selection, the multimedia player will send out commands to join the multicast.

---

2. Readers should be careful to distinguish SAP, the Internet protocol, from SAP, the manufacturer of enterprise management software, and from the video term *SAP*, which stands for secondary audio program. The Internet SAP is defined in IETF RFC 2974.

IGMP Join/Leave Example

Joining a multicast can be a fairly complex process. If the user device is the first one to request a particular multicast stream, then all the network devices that lie along the path between the multicast source and the user device must be configured to transport the stream. Consider the sample network shown in Figure 9-4. In this case, user device 1 (UD1) is the first to request the multicast being offered by the source. UD1 sends out a command to "join" the multicast being advertised by the source. R3, which is the closest router to UD1, determines that it is not currently receiving the multicast and requests it to be sent from R2. R2 in turn requests the multicast from R1. R1 then starts sending the multicast stream to R2, which in turn sends the stream to R3. R3 then supplies the stream to UD1.

When UD2 requests the stream, the request is processed first by R5. Since it is not currently receiving the stream, it makes a request to R4. R4 then makes a request to R2. R2 then replicates the stream and begins sending it to R4, which in turn forwards the stream to R5. As soon as R5 begins receiving the stream, it can forward the stream to UD2.

When UD3 requests the multicast stream, it sends a request to R4. Since R4 is already processing the stream, it doesn't need to obtain the stream from another router. Instead, R4 can simply begin sending a replicated copy of the stream to UD3.

Leaving a multicast can also be a fairly complex process. Let's look at what happens when UD1 decides to leave the multicast. This

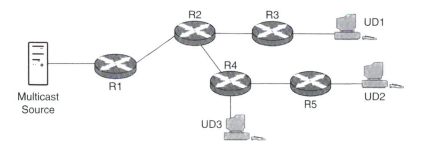

FIGURE 9-4 Multicast Join/Leave Network

request is made by sending a "leave" report to R3. R3 can then stop forwarding the stream to UD1. R3 must then check to see whether any other devices connected to it (user devices or other routers) are still using that multicast stream. Once it determines that no other device is using the stream, it can then send a "leave" report to R2. When R2 receives the "leave," it can then stop replicating the stream and sending it to R3. When R2 checks to see whether any other devices are using the stream, it determines that R4 still needs the stream, so R2 can take no further action.

As this example illustrates, the process of joining and leaving a multicast is fairly complex. This is the price paid to achieve network efficiency. Handling all of these IGMP transactions can create a significant processing load, so many routers do not have this function activated. Note that in each case in the preceding example no more than one copy of the multicast stream was sent between any pair of routers, no matter how many users downstream from the router were receiving the stream. Specifically, only one copy of the stream was sent from R1 to R2, even though three separate user devices downstream from R2 were receiving the stream. If unicasting were used in this example instead, then three copies of the stream would have been sent from R1 to R2.

SYSTEM IMPACT

Multicasting can have a range of impacts on a data network. Because many networks are installed with multicasting disabled, it is important to understand what can happen when it is enabled. Let's look at the system impact from a few perspectives, including the impact on routers, servers, and network bandwidth.

Router Reconfiguration

Because there are dozens of different networking equipment vendors and thousands of different models of routers, it is impossible to describe in detail how to reconfigure each device to handle multicasting. But it is possible to discuss the impact that multicasting can have on a router.

First and foremost, multicasting can increase the workload of a router. Here is a list of some of the functions that a router must perform to support multicasting that are beyond the support needed for standard unicasting:

- *Receive, duplicate, and forward SAP packets*, which are sent to each device that may wish to receive a multicast. Even though SAP packets do not occur very frequently, they do need to be processed and forwarded to all the ports on the router that have devices that might want to receive the multicast.
- *Process IGMP packets as required to determine when a device wants to join or leave a multicast.* Note that this requires the router to figure out when a device it serves makes a request to join a multicast that the router is not yet handling, and so needs to obtain the multicast stream from another source. This also requires the router to determine when all the devices it serves have left a multicast and can thus stop receiving the multicast.
- *Replicate multicast packets as needed to supply them to any requesting devices.* This can place a heavy load on a router. For a multicast video stream, a router might be required to duplicate several hundred packets per second.

Many times, system administrators are reluctant to enable multicasting on their networks precisely because of the impact that multicasting can have on the performance of their routers. It is not unusual for one or more key routers on a private network to require a hardware or software performance upgrade to handle multicasting. Depending on the network, this can be an expensive and time-consuming process. Therefore, users who are planning to deploy multicast services should consult with network managers.

Server Usage

For servers, multicasting can mean a significant decrease in workload as compared to unicasting. In unicasting, a server must create a separate stream for each receiving device. For servers that serve numerous clients, this can be a huge processing burden. In many cases, multiple unicast servers need to be provisioned to share the workload of sending streams to hundreds of simultaneous viewers. Specialized servers from companies such as SeaChange and Ncube are designed to handle these loads, with the added benefit of being able to provide true video-on-demand services such as pause, rewind, and fast-forward.

Multicast servers, in contrast, have a relatively light burden. Because the network makes copies of the stream, only one stream needs to be provided by the source. This can be accomplished with a low-cost, low-performance server. Because all the viewers watch the same stream at the same time, the server does not need to handle rewind or fast-forward commands from users. This does, however, limit the flexibility for users, who are only able to join a video broadcast that is already in progress. To make this more palatable to viewers, program providers will frequently offer longer content in multiple streams with staggered start times or transmit content in a continuous loop or both. Although these options increase the burden on the server, they are still much more manageable than trying to support hundreds of simultaneous unicast streams.

Bandwidth Example

With multicasting, only one copy of each stream needs to be sent between each pair of routers on the network. This can provide a tremendous savings in bandwidth usage as compared to unicasting. Let's look at a quick example.

Take a network with 100 users, of whom 16 want to view a single program. Let's say there are four routers in the network, all connected directly to each other (a *full mesh network*, for those who like technical jargon). Let's say that the video source is connected to one of the routers (let's call it Router A), and the viewers are evenly distributed among all four routers (A, B, C, D). Here is how the bandwidth would break down.

In unicasting, the source would need to provide one copy of the video stream for each active user, for a total of 16 streams leaving

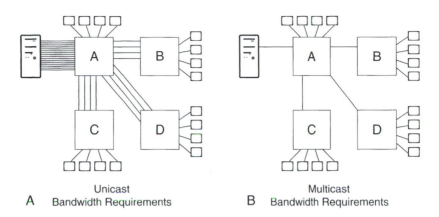

A   Unicast
     Bandwidth Requirements

B   Multicast
     Bandwidth Requirements

FIGURE 9-5   (A, B) Multicasting Bandwidth Comparison

the source and going into Router A. Router A would then take all of these streams and forward them to their destinations. Four streams would be sent from A to its local viewers, and four streams would need to be sent to each of the other three routers. This is shown in Figure 9-5A.

With multicasting, the source needs to provide only one copy of the stream to Router A. Router A would make seven copies of the stream and send four to the local viewers. The other three streams would be sent to the other routers, one each to B, C, and D. Each of these three routers would in turn make four copies of the incoming stream and send one copy to each connected local user. This is shown in Figure 9-5B.

The big difference in these two illustrations is the amount of bandwidth needed between the source and A and the amount of bandwidth needed between A and the other routers. In the first case, the bandwidth required drops by a factor of 16, and in the latter cases the bandwidth drops by a factor of 4. This can be an important savings. If the stream occupied, say, 1 Mbps of bandwidth, with multicasting the source could use a 1.5-Mbps T1 telephone link to reach Router A; without multicasting a 45-Mbps DS3 link would be required. Similarly, lower usage of the valuable backbone connection between A and the other routers would allow a great deal of other traffic to flow.

REVIEW AND CHECKLIST UPDATE

In this chapter, we looked at multicasting, which is a way to make an IP network act like a radio or television broadcasting station. We began with a discussion of unicasting and how it differs from multicasting. We discussed unicasting and multicasting in more depth, including a look at the benefits and drawbacks of each technology. We then looked at some applications of multicasting, including IPTV, live events, continuous information, continuous-presence conferencing, and a city security system that used multicasting to great benefit. In addition, we covered the technology of multicasting, including the process of controlling the users who are joining and leaving the multicast. We finished by looking at the impact of multicasting on a data network.

Overall, multicasting is a powerful technology and can be used to save a lot of network bandwidth and server load when it is deployed. The cost is mainly in the form of complexity (for managing joins and leaves, etc.) and in the extra processing power that is required from the network routers to do the packet replication. When (or if) the Internet becomes multicast enabled,[3] the possibilities for broadcasting content to many users simultaneously will create an amazing variety of content providers and choices for consumers.

Chapter 9 Checklist Update

❑ Determine whether multicasting is possible. Are all viewers going to be satisfied with receiving the same video/audio at the same time?

❑ If a private network is used, will it be technically possible to enable multicasting on all of the network routers? If so, the network should be reviewed to ensure that router performance will be adequate at each of the major nodes.

❑ If true multicasting isn't possible, it can be simulated using a unicast network or a CDN (see Chapter 15).

---

3. The semi-public Internet2 is already multicast enabled.

❏ Make sure that the viewer devices are capable of receiving and processing SAP packets and that they support IGMP Version 2 or 3.

❏ For networks that won't allow multicasting, determine the maximum number of simultaneous users that will be connected at one time. Then determine if more than one server will be required to create all of the required streams.

10

VIDEOCONFERENCING OVER IP

Videoconferencing uses synchronized audio and video signals to permit two-way communication between distant locations. As any telephone user can attest, much of the communication that takes place between people is nonverbal, involving gestures and facial expressions that simply can't be seen when using a telephone. Videoconferencing attempts to address this shortfall by allowing users both to see and to hear each other.

For many users, videoconferencing over IP networks is the ideal marriage of video technology and advanced networking. Many frequent business travelers would like to replace some of their less important business trips with a videoconference. As high-performance networking becomes more widespread in the business world and more affordable for residential connections, the demand for videoconferencing services will continue to increase. This rapidly growing market is being driven both by company cost-saving efforts and by employee demand. So it should not surprise any practitioner of video-over-IP networking to receive at least an occasional request for an IP videoconference.

Video Over IP: IPTV, Internet Video, H.264, P2P, Web TV, and Streaming: A Complete Guide to Understanding the Technology
Copyright © 2008, Wes Simpson. All rights reserved.

Videoconferencing became feasible in the early 1990s because international standards (H.320, among others) were approved and compliant equipment emerged from a variety of vendors. However, high costs limited the market for this technology. Many end-user companies created dedicated conference rooms equipped with cameras, microphones, video displays, and all of the other equipment needed to make videoconferencing feasible. H.320 systems use special digital telephone circuits (ISDN), which can have substantial installation and usage charges. Because of the expense involved for the equipment and telephone circuit usage, the number of rooms with equipment remained fairly small, and the costs per use were high.

New technology was developed and standardized in the mid-1990s to provide videoconferencing over IP networks. This new standard, called H.323, eliminated the need for special ISDN circuits from the telephone company. This also made practical the concept of desktop videoconferencing (DTVC) using either dedicated hardware or a personal computer equipped with a camera and a headset.

With the introduction of H.264 in 2004, it became possible to provide HD videoconferencing in a reasonable bandwidth (near or below 1 Mbps). Many manufacturers have implemented H.264 in their H.323 hardware and software, because it is roughly twice as bandwidth efficient as its precursor codec, H.263.

The goal of this chapter is to give readers an understanding of how videoconferencing works in general and how some specific technologies have been developed to support videoconferencing on IP networks. In this chapter, we will look at the basics of videoconferencing, such as connection setup and multipoint conferencing. We'll discuss the types of equipment that are normally used in videoconferencing, both at user locations and in the network. Then we'll cover some applications of videoconferencing and examine the technologies that make IP videoconferencing a reality. By the end of this chapter, readers should have a basic understanding of the technologies available for creating an IP videoconferencing network.

BASIC CONCEPTS

Just like telephone calls, videoconferences can be set up in several different ways. A simple point-to-point connection can be made between two locations. A conversation involving three or more parties can be supported by switching the video and audio signals in response to user action (through the use of a multipoint control unit). Or a multiparty conversation can be supported with continuous presence, where each party can see and hear all of the other parties at the same time. Also, a variety of specialized processing equipment (such as echo cancellers) is used to support videoconferencing. We will cover all of these aspects of videoconferencing in the following sections.

Session Setup

Before a videoconference can take place, a number of tasks need to be completed. This is really no different in principle than setting up a normal face-to-face meeting. Because a videoconference is inherently live and two-way (or more), special care must be taken to ensure that all of the parties are alerted and their equipment is connected before the conference can proceed. Sometimes this is done by means of a specialized communication protocol between the devices. Other times, a central reservation-and-control system is used to make all the connections. Here are some of the key tasks that must be performed in order to establish a videoconference:

- The caller needs to find the addresses of parties that are to be called. Addresses are listed in public or private directories. Note that these are not the same as IP addresses, because IP addresses can change each time a device connects to a network (see the discussion of DHCP in Chapter 5). Some videoconferencing protocols support user mobility, allowing calls to be connected to users who have changed locations or who are using different devices.
- The calling and the called devices all have to be available for the call, and enough bandwidth needs to be allocated to handle the

streams that will be generated. Most end devices support multiple video speeds, so different data rates are often negotiated for each call, depending on the network being used.

- Many conferences also employ alternative means of communication, such as document exchange or sharing a whiteboard for drawing. If these tools are to be used, then the conference setup process needs to establish connections to support these devices.
- Many videoconferencing systems gather usage and other data that can be applied to sending out bills to users and to managing system performance. Much of this data is gathered during the reservation and/or the connection processes.

Videoconferencing standards include reams of information about how the connection process takes place and how it works under a variety of network configurations. Call setup is very complex, but it is also very flexible. It would not be unfair to compare this process to the complexity of connecting a normal voice call, which requires literally millions of lines of software in complex telephone company switches.

Common channel signaling is frequently used for videoconference setup, which uses a separate, limited-bandwidth communications path to carry a specialized protocol just for conference setup and teardown. A variety of different signals flow over this path, including conference requests, acknowledgments, and device commands, such as alerting (ringing), connecting, and disconnecting. The signaling channel is used only for conference control, not for actually sending the audio and video streams that make up the videoconference.

Some IP videoconferencing systems don't use a handshaking protocol for conference setup, but instead rely on a centralized server to establish and track connections. Users make a conference reservation by selecting the devices that will be in a conversation and then indicate when the conference is to take place. Some systems can also configure equipment in the videoconferencing room as well as gateways that allow a conference to be established between one conferencing technology and another (such as bridging between H.320 and H.323).

Multipoint Conferencing

Multipoint conferencing is extremely popular in both audio and video communication. A conference is deemed to be *multipoint* whenever the number of participating locations (endpoints) is greater than two. Note that if an endpoint has multiple cameras, it will count as only one party to a conference as long as only one of the cameras is active at any time and only one outgoing audio stream is created. As soon as a conference consists of more than two video and two audio streams, it is considered to be multipoint.

In telephony, multipoint conferencing is normally known by a name like *three-way calling* or *conference calling*. It is rare indeed to find an employee of a major corporation or government agency that hasn't participated in a conference call. Special devices, called *conference bridges*, are used inside the telephone network to connect multipoint conversations. Each listener hears a combination of all the talkers on the line, with the exception of his or her own voice. A good conference bridge will amplify all the talkers on the conference to an equal level. The result is similar to what would be heard if all the talkers were in the same room.

In videoconferencing, this situation is not so simple. There is really no practical way to combine multiple video images in a single image that would make it appear that all the participants are sitting in the same room. So, for the purposes of multipoint conferences, there are two basic choices: MCU switching and continuous presence.

MCU Switching

When the MCU switching method is used, each endpoint receives a single video stream that is switched as the conference progresses. A central device, called the *multipoint control unit (MCU)*, performs the switching. Various different modes are used for switching the video; here are a few popular ones:

- *Chair or lectern control*: A single endpoint is designated as the chair of the conferences, and it controls what the other endpoints can see. This is particularly useful in distance learning environments. Procedures exist for changing which endpoint acts as the chair, so this can be a flexible but stable means to control a conference.

- *Follow the speaker*: The MCU attempts to send video from whichever endpoint is currently speaking to all of the other conference participants. Usually some delay is involved before a switch takes place, to help prevent a switch caused by a single short noise. This is one of the most popular forms of video switch control.

- *User control*: Each endpoint can select any one of the other locations to watch. This places a burden on the end user and can be hard to keep up during a long conference. Some users consider this as annoying as watching someone change channels repeatedly on a television set.

- *User-controlled broadcast*: A user can request the MCU to send his or her endpoint's video to all of the other endpoints in the conference. This might be used, for example, when one party is giving a presentation.

Figure 10-1 allows us to look at an example of a follow-the-speaker conference in action. The network consists of four endpoints, A through D, and a central MCU. Each endpoint sends a video into the MCU and receives a single video back from the MCU. When the conference begins, A is speaking. The MCU sends the video from endpoint A to endpoints B, C, and D. Endpoint A can receive video from any location, possibly the last one to join the conference. After a while, B begins speaking. The MCU switches to send the video coming from B to the endpoints A, C, and D. Endpoint B will continue to receive video from A, since it doesn't make sense to send B its own

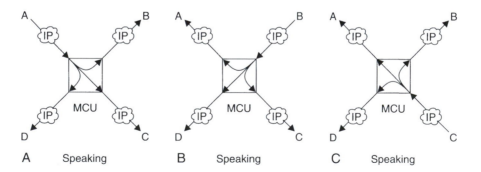

FIGURE 10-1   (A, B, C) Follow-the-Speaker Videoconferencing with an MCU

image. When C takes a turn speaking, the MCU reconfigures itself again; now A, B, and D will receive the picture from C, and C will continue to receive a picture from B. As this example shows, the conference really does "follow the speaker" as the conversation progresses.

MCUs can be built as special-purpose hardware devices, or they can be implemented as a software function on an IP-connected server. Large- and small-capacity MCUs can be purchased by companies for their own use, and MCU services are provided by a number of carriers as well as some user groups.

Continuous Presence

When the continuous-presence method of multipoint conferencing is used, each site can see all of the other sites on a continuous basis and an MCU is not required. This method requires more network resources than with MCU switching. For example, in a four-way conference, each site needs to be able to receive three incoming video signals. Continuous presence may also appear to be more natural to users because the video disruptions caused by switching are avoided.

Setting up a continuous-presence conference can be more complicated than when using MCU conferencing. When an MCU is used, each endpoint in the conference simply needs to be connected to the MCU, which handles the rest of the functions. In continuous presence, multiple copies of each signal must be created, and each copy must be sent to a different location. As we discussed in Chapter 9, one way of handling this function is multicasting, where the network is responsible for making all the necessary copies of the streams coming from each endpoint. If multicasting isn't available, then each video endpoint needs to create a separate unicast stream for each destination, thereby increasing the amount of bandwidth required to transmit from each endpoint.

Figure 10-2 shows an example of a four-way videoconference using the continuous-presence method on a multicast-enabled network. The video signal from A is sent to B, C, and D. Similarly, the video from B is sent to A, C, and D, and so on. In each location, three video

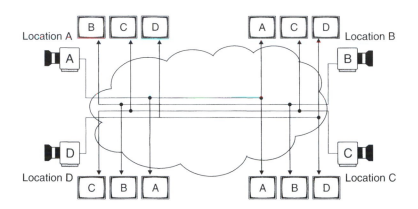

FIGURE 10-2   Continuous-Presence Videoconference

signals are displayed. Note that different switching modes (follow the speaker, lectern control, etc.) are not needed in a continuous-presence conference, because each endpoint can see all the other endpoints during the entire conference.

Telepresence

Telepresence is used to describe very high-quality videoconferencing installations, where users get the impression that they are in the same room as other participants. Telepresence is accomplished through the use of HD cameras and monitors connected in continuous-presence mode and very careful ergonomic design. Particular attention is paid to making the images on each large display appear life-size and to placing the cameras to give the illusion of eye contact between the parties. The illusion is further enhanced through the use of specially designed conference tables, controlled lighting, and the use of very low-delay codecs and networks. Several companies, including HP, have built telepresence systems for internal use and sale to customers.

Video and Audio Processing

By itself, videoconferencing requires relatively little equipment in a room. A simple setup with a camera, a microphone, a television with speakers, and an audio/video encoder/decoder (normally called a *codec*) is all that is truly required for a conference. In reality, many videoconference rooms are equipped with a much broader array of

TABLE 10-1

Optional Equipment for Videoconference Rooms

- *Document camera*, for sending video images of documents to other conference participants.
- *Camera selector*, to allow different views to be sent, possibly depending on the number of people in the room.
- *Room lighting control*, to allow the lighting to be configured properly for the camera that is in use.
- *Camera pan, tilt, and zoom (PTZ) control*, to allow the camera to point at specific locations in the room, such as different seats at a conference table. This function can also be connected to the audio system to allow the camera to point at whomever is speaking.
- *Electronic whiteboard*, which allows participants to send sketches to each other.
- *Quad-split converter*, to display four video images on a single video display.
- *Echo canceller*, which is required to produce acceptable audio in many cases.

equipment. Table 10-1 gives a short list of some of the optional equipment that can be found in a modern videoconferencing room. We'll take a closer look at the last two items in Table 10-1.

Quad-Split Converters

Quad-split converters are used to combine multiple video images into a single, composite image, primarily for use in continuous-presence conferences. There are two main reasons for doing this:

- A single, large video display may be easier to manage than four smaller video displays, particularly if the videoconferencing system is moved from one room to another.
- When four video signals are combined into one in a central location, it is possible to configure a continuous-presence system with just one video signal delivered to each site.

Figure 10-3A shows a videoconference network with a centrally located quad-split converter. Each location (A, B, C, and D) sends out a full-resolution video signal to the central location, where all of the signals are sent into a quad-split converter to be combined. The output of the converter, which is a normal video signal that combines images from all four input signals, is then sent to every location.[1]

---

1. Note that it is also possible to place a quad-split converter at each endpoint to take multiple video signals and show them on one display.

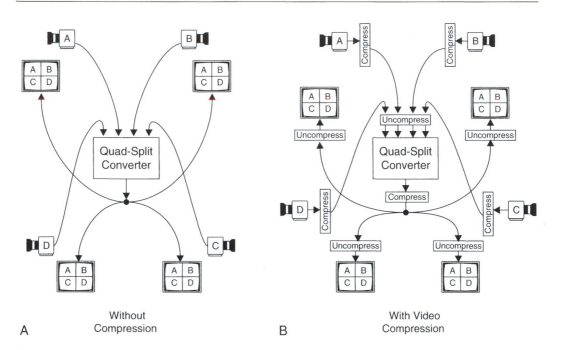

FIGURE 10-3 (A, B) Continuous-Presence Videoconferencing Network Using Quad-Split Converters

It is important to keep in mind that the video signals in this type of network may be compressed. As shown in Figure 10-3B, each location is equipped with a video encoder and a video decoder. Also, the central location is equipped with four video decoders and a video encoder (the decoders feed the inputs of quad-split converter, and the encoder processes the output). This system will operate correctly, although the compression delay will be double that of a normal compressed system, because each video signal has undergone two full compression/decompression cycles.

Echo Cancellers

Echo cancellers process audio signals to remove the echo signal that is caused by the round-trip delay of a network. They are required pieces of equipment in many videoconferencing networks. To understand the role of an echo canceller, let's trace the route of an audio signal during a videoconference (see Figure 10-4). First, a person in location 1 speaks into his or her microphone. This sound is converted into an audio signal, which travels to location 2, where

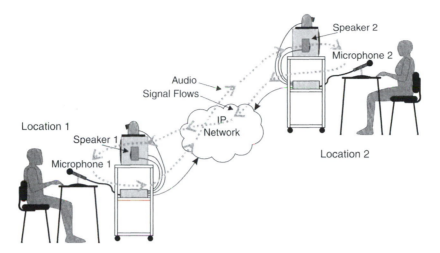

FIGURE 10-4 Two-Location Videoconferencing Room Audio Setup

loudspeakers send the sounds into the room. Because this is a two-way conference, the microphone in location 2 picks up sounds from the speakers and sends them back to location 1, thereby creating an echo in location 1. Because this signal is delayed by the total round-trip time, it can be very disconcerting to people while they are talking, becoming more noticeable as the delay increases.

An echo canceller is needed in location 2 to prevent sound that comes out of the speakers in that room from being sent back to location 1. Similarly, another echo canceller is needed at location 1 to prevent speaker sounds from being sent back to location 2. A variety of different technologies can be used for echo cancellation, but most devices need to process the incoming signal to each site as well as the outbound signal created at each site.

ITU-T G.131 specifies that echo cancellers should be used if the one-way delay for a voice circuit exceeds 25 milliseconds. Since many video encoder/decoder pairs introduce at least this much delay, this limit is quickly exceeded. So echo cancellers are a fact of life for most videoconference rooms and are incorporated into a number of commercial videoconferencing devices.

For personal video or audio conferencing using a PC, many users have chosen to use headset (headphones with an attached microphone).

These keep echoes from occurring because the speaker outputs are sent directly into the user's ears, preventing the microphone from picking up the sounds.

IP VIDEOCONFERENCING TECHNOLOGIES

A variety of technologies are used to implement videoconferencing over IP networks. In the following sections, we will look at four key technologies.

The first two technologies, H.323 and Session Initiation Protocol (SIP), support the handshaking and connection setup functions required for a videoconference. H.323 has evolved from the first generation of international standards (H.320) to become widely used in many companies for specially equipped videoconferencing rooms. SIP has been promoted as a simplified method for setting up voice-over-IP calls, but it also includes the ability to set up video and other types of conferences.

The other two technologies, H.264 and T.120, are used to format the video and data signals that are sent between endpoints during a conference. H.264 is the latest generation of video compression, which is used both for videoconferencing and broadcast television. T.120 is a technology for data conferencing that is widely used on IP networks, either on a stand-alone basis or in conjunction with video and audio conferences. Each is described in more detail in the following sections.

H.323 Multimedia Conferencing

H.323 is an international standard for packet-based multimedia communication, as defined by the International Telecommunications Union (ITU). It works on a variety of packet networking technologies, including both reliable (TCP-based) and unreliable (UDP-based) IP networks, as well as ATM networks. It is multimedia, because it supports video, audio, and data communication. H.323 does not stand alone as a standard; numerous other ITU specifications are used to support functions such as conference setup, video and audio compression, internetwork communications, etc.

Videoconferencing over IP, as implemented in H.323, requires a connection to be established between the parties in the conference before communication can take place. This is only logical, because each party's device needs to be configured to send and receive both video and audio in order for a conversation to occur. Also, because many videoconferences are used for business purposes, connection-oriented protocols help ensure that each packet is received from a single sender, not some malicious outsider. Finally, some types of networks (such as those using dial-up IP services) must be activated prior to use in order to provide the bandwidth needed to support a videoconference; the connection process can initiate allocation of the bandwidth.

A number of devices can be included in an H.323 network to support various functions. The four main device types, illustrated in Figure 10-5, are described next.

- *Terminal*: This is the endpoint of an H.323 conferencing system. It typically resides in the videoconference room and connects directly to the camera, microphone, video display, and other in-room devices. It contains the circuitry needed to compress and decompress the video and audio signals as well as the equipment needed to connect to the IP network.
- *Gateway*: Allows H.323 equipment to connect to other videoconferencing networks, such as older H.320 systems. It performs translation of the protocols that are used for call setup and teardown and converts the voice and video signals back and forth

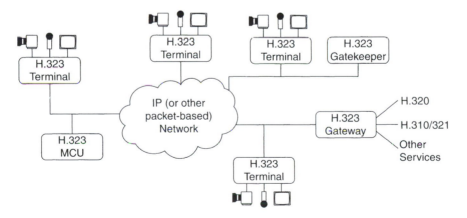

FIGURE 10-5 Main Components of an H.323 System

between the formats. A gateway is required for communication between H.323 and dissimilar networks, but it is not used for communications between pure H.323 terminals.

- *Gatekeeper*: Although it is not a required function, a gatekeeper can provide valuable database services to an H.323 network. Gatekeepers can keep directories of terminals and help remote devices contact ones on a local network. They can help route connections and allocate bandwidth. They can also gather and report network usage and billing information.
- *Multipoint control units*: These units are used whenever three or more terminals are connected in a conference. They can either be installed at a central location (such as a telephone company central office) or be colocated with one of the conference endpoints.

Although they each perform a separate function on the network, these devices do not have to be physically separate. In fact, it is common for MCUs, gatekeepers, and gateways to share hardware resources and even reside in the same processing chassis.

Overall, H.323 is a highly integrated, sophisticated videoconferencing platform. It has many features and functions and has been implemented by a number of vendors. It is a relatively mature standard, so equipment from different manufacturers will work together under most circumstances. On the downside, H.323's complexity makes software development expensive, and it is difficult to install on low-cost, low-power devices. Since it was designed for LAN or private networking applications, there are limitations on how easily it can scale up to large networks. Fortunately, groups are working to overcome these limitations and greatly expand the system's scalability.

Session Initiation Protocol (SIP)

Session Initiation Protocol (SIP)[2] is a standard for multimedia communication over IP networks. It is being developed under the auspices of the Internet Engineering Task Force (IETF) and is capable of supporting many of the connection setup and teardown functions

---

2. Note that this should not be confused with SAP, which we discussed in Chapter 9.

of H.323. Many deployments of SIP are focused on voice communication (voice over IP, or VoIP), but the standard has capabilities that can be used to support video and other types of real-time streaming.

SIP is a signaling protocol (like portions of H.323) that is used for setting up sessions but not for actual transport of multimedia data. Devices that wish to connect use SIP to communicate about how to address each other, how they are configured, and the types of streams they want to send and receive. SIP provides a number of call control functions, such as ringing, answering, and disconnecting. SIP can also support changes in call status, such as a call that starts out as a voice call and changes to a videoconference. Actual transport of voice, video, and data is handled by other well-established protocols, such as RTP (which we discussed in Chapter 6).

SIP has been designed from the ground up to be highly compatible with other protocols and services that are used on the public Internet. For example, SIP messages are text based, similar to HTTP messages. SIP works on a wide variety of devices and is easy to extend to new functions. The designers also sought to make the protocol fairly simple so that the software required to implement SIP could be installed on inexpensive and portable devices.

When you boil it all down, what SIP does, and does well, is resolve the IP addresses and port numbers that devices need to use in order to communicate. Since the actual session data (such as voice or video signals) doesn't flow over SIP, it is quite common for this data to take a different path than the SIP commands. Figure 10-6 shows how data flows in a normal session being set up with SIP.

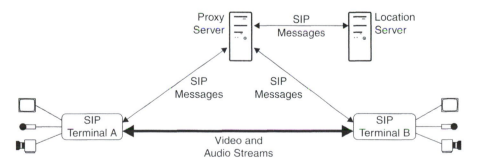

FIGURE 10-6 SIP Messages, Servers, Signaling, and Data Flows

Servers are commonly used in SIP for a variety of functions. Figure 10-6 shows how a proxy server and a location server can be used in a typical call setup. Let's say the originating party (A) wants to communicate with the called party (B). Terminal A can communicate with the proxy server to send an invite message to terminal B; it is up to the proxy server to figure out the correct address for B by using the location server. Once the proxy knows the correct address for B, the invitation from A can be sent along to B. B can then respond to A's invite by way of the proxy server. Once A has received a suitable response from B, the two terminals can bypass the proxy and communicate directly to set up multimedia connections and actually pass video and audio signals. One very useful function of the location server is called *redirection*, which can be beneficial for instances when users have moved to a new location or want to have their calls forwarded to a different location. Either A or B can redirect incoming calls simply by changing the data records stored in the location server. Other types of servers can be used to offer more advanced functions.

Inside SIP messages, a data format known as Session Description Protocol (SDP) is used by the endpoints to describe their capabilities and the types of streams that they are capable of supporting. SDP can specify things like the media type (audio, video, etc.), the encoding format (MPEG, wavelet, etc.), and the transport protocol to be used (RTP, etc.). Once both end devices agree on all the specifics, then communication can take place.

SIP does not offer some of the functions that more complex protocols (such as H.323) provide.[3] SIP does not offer multipoint conference control mechanisms (such as follow the speaker, described previously); instead, it provides a flexible set of functions (called *primitives*) that can be used to create advanced services. SIP also does not provide any capabilities to reserve end-to-end bandwidth for a given session. When multiple forms of media are used (such as those normally found on a videoconference), some mechanism outside SIP needs to be used to synchronize video and audio. On the plus side,

---

3. This simplicity is one of the key features of SIP; it helps ensure portability to a variety of platforms and eases the task of implementation. New functions may be added in the future but likely won't be if they add undue complexity.

SIP does provide a number of functions that can be used to help ensure the privacy and security of sessions.

Work is under way to extend SIP to offer two features not found in basic H.323: support for instant messaging and presence. Instant messaging (IM) supports real-time, text-based communication between two or more users and has become very popular for both desktop and mobile users. *Presence* involves informing users about the current status of other users in whom they are interested. One popular use of presence is the buddy list feature of some IM systems that lets users know whether other people with whom they want to communicate are online or off-line. This concept is being extended to let users know if, for example, one of their buddies is available for a full videoconference or just for text-based messaging. SIMPLE, the SIP Instant Messaging Presence Leveraging Extensions working group of the IETF, is responsible for this work.

Development work is continuing in SIP. Companies are building all kinds of devices that use SIP, including low-cost IP telephones. The standard is being updated to support session setup for mobile devices, such as mobile telephones that can carry videoconferencing signals. As this work continues, SIP will become a more and more important tool for IP videoconferencing.

Comparison of H.323 and SIP

When installing videoconferencing systems, users will have a variety of different choices for a system to use when making connections between participants. The three main choices are:

- H.323-based conference equipment
- SIP-based conference equipment
- Proprietary conference equipment

Proprietary systems will typically be limited to single-vendor solutions and may be hard to connect to equipment not owned by the user's organization. With respect to H.323 and SIP, there are benefits and drawbacks to each system. Table 10-2 attempts to highlight some of the major differences between the two systems.

TABLE 10-2

Differences between H.323 and SIP

Characteristic	H.323	SIP
Maturity	Mature. Has been through several iterations since 1996 and covers many advanced features, such as call waiting.	Reaching maturity. Effort continues toward enhancement of SIP standards to include more features.
Complexity	High. Has a number of sophisticated features, requiring a great deal of software.	Variable. Can be implemented very simply without a rich feature set. More features require more development.
Flexibility	Medium. Supports a variety of different audio and video compression systems; however, all implementations must have audio capability.	High. Wide variety of different types of sessions can be initiated. Similar procedures are used to initiate voice, data, video, and instant messaging sessions.
Compatibility with public switched telephone network	High. Was developed from the ground up to be compatible with public telephone networks as well as other videoconferencing standards based on ISDN and circuit-switched networks.	Not integral to the specification. Implementations can be made to be compatible with public networks, but this functionality is not an inherent part of the standard.
Compatibility with other technologies	High. Because the specification is very detailed, most systems will work together provided the standards are followed. Interoperation is common between units from different suppliers.	Variable. The inherent simplicity of SIP means that basic operations are simple and straightforward to implement by different suppliers.
Installed base	Large. There are millions of H.323 installed systems around the world, and the base continues to expand the area of voice telephony.	Widely used for Voice over IP. Growing base for videoconferencing, particularly in multifunction phones.
Backward compatibility	Rigorous enforcement. Each new generation is specified to be compatible with previous versions.	Not assured. Features can be added or removed from newer implementations, and different versions are not required to be fully compatible by the standards.

H.264 Video Compression

As we discussed in Chapter 4, H.264 is another name for the MPEG-4 Advanced Video Coding (AVC) standard. H.264 is flexible enough to be used for both low-bit-rate videoconferencing systems as well as for the relatively higher bit rates normally used with entertainment video.

Several different types of video compression technology have been used over the years for videoconferencing. The first, H.120, was developed in the early 1980s to run on 1.544- or 2.048-Mbps telephone circuits. This was followed by H.261, which was developed in the late 1980s and was designed for "p × 64" telephone circuits, or those operating on digital data circuits that function on lines running at speeds that are multiples of 64 kbps. In the 1990s, H.263 was developed to allow even better compression efficiency, particularly at low bit rates. Over time, the H.263 standard has had a number of improvements incorporated.

It is important to understand that the choice of compression technology for a videoconferencing system can be made separately from the choice of conference communication technology. In other words, H.264 video compression can be used with H.320 (for ISDN lines), with H.323 (for various packet-switched networks, including IP), or with SIP (for IP networks). Similarly, H.263 video compression can be used in H.320, H.323, and SIP applications.

H.264 implementations for videoconferencing generally use the baseline profile. This profile uses some of the key features of H.264 but not all of the more advanced ones. One unique feature that is well suited to videoconferencing applications is relaxation of the requirements in MPEG-1 and MPEG-2 that all the data for each slice of a video image arrive in order; some variability is allowed in H.264, helping to reduce the delay in the encoder and decoder. Baseline does not permit B frames, which can add significantly to round-trip delay due to reordering (see Chapter 4). Baseline profile also does not support interlaced video (as would be found in broadcast television signals), but it does work with progressive scanned images and the CIF image format, which are commonly found in videoconferencing applications.

H.264 will continue to be an important growth area for videoconferencing, particularly because of the advances in coding efficiency that support higher-quality images at lower bandwidths. In addition, most implementations of HD videoconferencing use H.264. Product development efforts should also benefit from the ability to share technology (software, custom chips, etc.) between the videoconferencing and broadcast television industries.

T.120 Data Protocols for Multimedia Conferencing

T.120 is an international standard for data conferencing. It is specified by the ITU and is used by H.323 and other software. One popular implementation of T.120 was Microsoft's NetMeeting product. Although T.120 is not strictly a videoconferencing protocol, it is commonly used in conjunction with these protocols and can provide many of the benefits of a videoconference to users who may not have access to true videoconferencing equipment. In addition, T.120 connections can normally be used on a much lower-bandwidth link as compared to real-time video transport systems.

The basic function of T.120 is to support data conferencing, similar to voice and videoconferencing. This means that multiple users can all share the same data in real time. One popular use of T.120 is to allow multiple people to share a common virtual whiteboard, where they can draw pictures and have them show up on every other user's screen. When this function is combined with an audio conference, it can be quite useful for discussing information that lends itself well to illustration (engineering drawings, architecture, etc.). T.120 also supports file sharing, so multiple users can all look at a file, such as a document or a presentation.

One application for T.120 is a videoconference in which the video and audio signals are carried by normal video and audio circuits and a presentation is transmitted over a T.120 circuit. The beauty of this arrangement is that viewers at both locations are able to see the presentation at full computer resolution. In the past, without T.120, viewers at one end might have been forced to watch the presentation through the videoconferencing circuit, with the conferencing camera pointed at a projection screen where the presentation was displayed. The resulting low-quality images can be very hard on the eyes and detrimental to the concentration level of the involved parties (based on the personal experience of the author).

T.120 actually is a suite of protocols, called the T.120 series. Here is a list of the related standards and their titles:

- T.120: Data protocols for multimedia conferencing
- T.121: Generic application template
- T.122: Multipoint communication service-Service definition
- T.123: Network-specific data protocol stacks for multimedia conferencing
- T.124: Generic conference control
- T.125: Multipoint communication service protocol specification
- T.126: Multipoint still image and annotation protocol
- T.127: Multipoint binary file transfer protocol
- T.128: Multipoint application sharing

As you can see from this list, a number of different functions can be accomplished with T.120. Let's take a quick look at some of the ways in which these technologies can be applied to users:

- *Application viewing*: Allows one user to run an application on his or her own PC and show the output (window) on other users' PCs. This is particularly useful for presentations being given by one participant.
- *Application sharing*: Allows one user running an application on his or her PC to permit other users to take control of the application. For example, a user running a word processing program on his or her PC could allow other users to edit the actual document. In this situation, only one user's PC actually needs to run the application; all of the other users can observe and control the application.
- *Whiteboarding*: Rather like a paint program for multiple users, this allows users to draw simple pictures on a shared screen. In some implementations, these pictures can be captured and copied to disk for later reference.
- *File transfer*: Much like sending attachments with e-mail, this function allows users to transfer files from one user PC to another.

- *Chat*: Permits users to exchange short text messages with each other. This function might not be used when a videoconference is in session or when only two users are connected, but it can be a handy feature for large conferences, particularly when one user is doing most of the talking.

Security can be an issue for users who wish to conduct T.120 conferences over the public Internet. Because the set of supported functions is so powerful, malicious use of T.120's capabilities can be very damaging to a computer system. For example, a malicious user could plant viruses or worms on a user's PC with the file transfer capability. Or, if application sharing was running, a user might be able to gain control of a user's PC and modify or delete files, system settings, or other items.

Because of these security concerns, many companies do not permit T.120 sessions to pass through a company firewall. Other companies use a device called a *conference server* that handles all of the connections required for a T.120 conference; it can therefore authenticate users and perform other security functions. Still other companies allow only a subset of the T.120 functions, such as whiteboarding and application viewing for sessions that go outside the company's private network domain. Overall security—requiring data encryption, user authentication, and user passwords—is also widely used in T.120 applications.

REVIEW AND CHECKLIST UPDATE

In this chapter, we discussed videoconferencing, which is one of the most common uses of video transport over IP networks. We began by looking at some of the common aspects of any type of videoconferencing, including the concept of session setup. We examined how a multipoint control unit (MCU) can be used to switch video and audio for conferences that involve more than two endpoints. Then we discussed continuous-presence conferencing and how quad-split converters can be used for this application. We covered echo cancellers, which are important for almost any type of videoconference. We closed the chapter with a discussion of some of the key technologies used in videoconferencing, including two different types of conference setup/control procedures (H.323 and SIP), a video compression system (H.264), and a standard that is widely used for data conferencing (T.120).

Chapter 10 Checklist Update

- ❏ Ensure that each videoconference location is properly equipped with cameras, microphones, and echo cancellers.
- ❏ Multipoint conferencing (with more than two parties involved in the conference) can be implemented in two different ways: switched video and continuous presence.
  - ❏ Consider using switched video for applications with limited network bandwidth and where a central video switch (MCU) can be installed.
  - ❏ Consider using continuous presence for high-bandwidth networks and for applications where users (such as schoolchildren) may be distracted by video switching.
- ❏ If multicasting is to be used for continuous-presence conferencing, make sure that all segments of the network are capable of supporting multicasts.
- ❏ Consider using H.323-based videoconferencing systems, which currently have a very large installed base of compatible systems, if videoconferences will frequently be held with parties that are outside the user's network.
- ❏ Before purchasing new systems, determine whether the supplier has the ability to support H.264.
- ❏ Many remote meeting needs can be handled with audio and data conferencing alone.
- ❏ If T.120 data conferencing is to be used, make sure that appropriate security measures and restrictions are put in place.

11

DRM, CONTENT OWNERSHIP, AND CONTENT SECURITY

DRM (digital rights management) and content security are essential features of any video delivery system, because they are required to protect the ownership rights of content providers. In most cases, the companies and individuals who want to distribute content need to purchase the rights to do so from content owners. Usually, these rights are limited in some way—to a specific number of broadcasts, to a defined period of time, to a certain number of views/downloads, or to any other restriction to which the content owners and distributors agree. These rights are usually spelled out in detail in a contract (license) between the parties.

Enforcing these contracts is the responsibility of the content distributor (such as a terrestrial/satellite broadcaster, CATV/IPTV provider, or end-user corporation). The distributor is responsible for ensuring that unauthorized copies of the content are not made and that the rights defined in the contract are protected. The penalties for poor protection can be severe—large financial penalties and often the loss of access to content in the future from that supplier. So it is quite important for any content user or distributor to ensure that the content is stored securely and viewed only in a manner permitted by the content license.

In this chapter, we are going to look at managing content, including where to get it and the responsibilities that come with it. Then we'll discuss some ways to protect the content from unauthorized copying or at least to determine who made the copy. Finally, we'll take a short look at a couple of commercial systems that are employed for controlling viewer access to content. By the end of this chapter, readers should have a basic understanding of the rights and responsibilities of content owners and users and have learned about some of the techniques used to protect those rights.

ACQUIRING CONTENT

Viewing content is easy in this day and age. A simple trip to a video store or any of a variety of retailers suffices to obtain a huge amount of high-quality, prerecorded content. Internet retailers, specialty online video suppliers, and video streaming websites can all be sources of content. Any number of video production companies also can create customized footage of almost any topic imaginable.

Unfortunately, viewing content and acquiring the rights to distribute content are two very different things. Most everyone has seen the warnings on prerecorded DVDs and videotapes that read something like: "The material contained on this videotape is licensed exclusively for private home viewing. Any other commercial or noncommercial use, rerecording, rebroadcast, or redistribution of this material is strictly prohibited." The owners of this content are sending a clear message: The consumer who owns a DVD is allowed to view the content but not to use it for a commercial purpose. The definition of "commercial purpose" can be quite broad. For example, exhibitors at a trade show are not allowed to show movies or play music unless they have obtained a license to do so from the content owner. Similarly, owners of restaurants or other public businesses are not allowed to show videos or play music they may have simply purchased on a CD; rather, these businesses need to obtain a license to play the content, since it is providing a commercial benefit to their business (i.e., improving the ambience of their building and making it more attractive to customers). Owners of telephone systems aren't even allowed to entertain callers with recorded music when they are placed on hold unless it is properly licensed.

Fortunately, obtaining a license for many routine uses of music is fairly straightforward (although not necessarily inexpensive). For example, the American Society of Composers, Authors and Publishers (ASCAP) acts as a central clearinghouse for thousands of music and video suppliers in the United States. ASCAP offers over 100 different types of licenses for various types of establishments, ranging from television stations to hotels to circuses. Similar organizations exist throughout the world to provide licensing services in other countries.

Many sources also exist for non-entertainment video and audio. There are a number of distributors of corporate or classroom training videos, television news archives, and stock footage, such as city scenes. Some of the content is distributed royalty-free, so once a license is purchased, the content can be broadcast and used to produce programming that can be put to many different uses. With a little research, it is often possible to purchase good-quality stock video content for many different purposes.

Custom-Created Content

For many users, purchasing preproduced audio and video content is not suitable. For such cases, contracting for custom-produced video or creating self-produced video is very popular. Production choices range from simple handheld video camera pieces to fully scripted and professionally videotaped works. No matter what the method, a few key rules apply for any custom-created video. These rules are listed in Table 11-1.

Custom-created video can be a powerful business tool when it is done correctly. With time, care, and a reasonable amount of money, great results can be achieved.

TABLE 11-1

Rules for Custom-Created Video

- Obtain a signed release from all people who appear in the video, whether they are paid or not. Make sure that all employees who appear have signed a release so that their images and/or performances can be used even if the employee leaves the company.
- Ensure that all necessary rights for material have been secured. This includes music, script, shooting locations, and anything else that will be in the video that is intellectual property of another person or company.
- Use high-quality cameras, media (film or videotape), lighting, and sound equipment. Small degradations in the original recording can dramatically affect the quality of the finished product, particularly if the video is to be highly compressed for streaming.
- A well-written script is always a big plus. Even if the idea is to capture "candid" comments, many people have difficulty in acting natural in front of a camera, so let them practice their lines.
- Use professionals whenever time and budget allow. This can include videographers, light and sound people, directors, performers, etc. Many talented people can be hired for reasonable prices.
- One of the cheapest elements of the production process is the recording media, so use it liberally. Take extra shots and re-takes to provide plenty of material for editors to work with.
- Keep it simple. Complicated camera angles, special effects, and fancy sets aren't needed for effective communication. Simple scenes are also easier to compress efficiently.
- Consider using a professional postproduction service, to edit, time, and color-correct the video properly. Professional-quality tools can be expensive and hard to operate for the inexperienced user.

RIGHTS MANAGEMENT

Rights management is the process of controlling the use of content. The rights for a particular piece of content are described in a license agreement that is negotiated between the content owner and the licensee. There are many different possible terms, ranging from the right to a single, immediate viewing (such as those offered by video-on-demand systems or movie theaters), all the way to the permanent, unlimited rights to the complete content. Typically, the rights for most content falls between these extremes.

Three basic tasks are required for effective content management. First and foremost, the content must be kept secure so that it does not fall into the wrong hands. Second, use of the content must be controlled and measured in some way, such as number of viewers. Third, proper payments must be made to the content owner. We'll look at each of these in the following sections.

Content Security

The need for content security must not be underestimated. Unauthorized copying of first-run movies can cause the loss of millions of dollars' worth of theater admission fees and DVD sales. Without security, it becomes difficult or impossible to restrict copying of content, thereby making proper accounting for royalty payments virtually impossible. Furthermore, content owners will be reluctant to provide their content to any application where security cannot be guaranteed.

The most common way to provide security is encryption, which will be discussed later in this chapter. Other methods include physical security (i.e., locked vaults to hold films when they aren't being shown) and copy prevention. Let's take a short look at these latter two methods.

Physical security can be very effective, although it depends on people to implement it properly. Since it is typically facilities-based (i.e., at a movie theater), physical security can interfere with a goal of maximizing the number of viewers. Due to the expense and complexity of physical security, it is normally only worthwhile for high-value content.

Copy prevention is designed to prevent viewers from making an analog recording of prerecorded video titles, such as Hollywood movies on videotape or DVDs. This system, frequently called *Macrovision*, after one of the leading technology suppliers, actively interferes with the video signals in a manner that affects recorders (videocassette, digital video recorders, etc.) but not televisions. Attempting to record a signal that is protected by Macrovision results in a recording that will have the video image slowly cycling from light to dark and, in some cases, red and blue stripes cascading down the video display.

In order for Macrovision to work, every videotape and DVD player device needs to have a special chip to detect content that is to be protected and to add the necessary distortions to the video output signal. A different type of circuit is installed in computer DVD drives, which also looks for the Macrovision signal. When it is present, the DVD drive will not allow the video content from the DVD to be copied to hard disk or another recorder.

For HD content, which is always digital from the source, there is a very real possibility that a perfect recording could be made of a signal feeding to a digital display. To prevent this, HDCP (High-bandwidth Digital Content Protection) technology was developed. This system provides for encryption of signals that flow between a digital video source (such as a Blu-ray disc player or an STB) and displays. Both the source and the display have encryption keys for setting up an encrypted link between the source and the display. Strict licensing terms for HDCP prohibit recording devices from emulating displays and receiving unprotected content, so there is no opportunity for improper copies to be made. If the display does not have DHCP capability, then only low-resolution images are generated by the source.

One drawback of these systems is that they protect video content all the time; there is no way to turn them off to make legitimate copies. (Although some content owners believe there is no such thing as a legitimate copy.) Another drawback is the requirement for the technology to be in every device, which demands good enforcement of the technology licensing rules for device manufacturers, which may be in other countries with different legal systems.

Digital Rights Management

DRM is a collective term for mechanisms that are used to control access to content through encryption or other means. DRM is virtually always a requirement for use of any recent motion picture or television content on a distribution system such as a DTH satellite system, an IPTV network, or a CATV system or on a private network. Content owners are extremely reluctant to provide content to a distributor that doesn't have an effective DRM system because of the chance that a perfect digital copy of the content could be used to create copies for illegal resale. This control needs to extend from the distributor facility all the way to devices that a viewer may use to play back the content, such as a set-top box or a PC.

DRM policies can be very loose or very tight; the content owner determines the policies for this control. Once these policies have been determined, it is the responsibility of the DRM system to

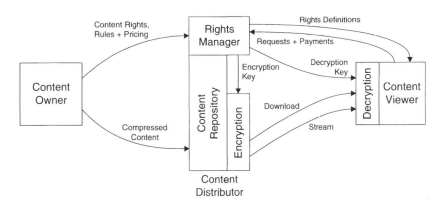

FIGURE 11-1 Simplified View of a Digital Rights Management System

enforce these policies. Let's look at how a DRM system could work. Figure 11-1 provides a simple block diagram of a DRM system.

In a typical DRM system for a video-on-demand system, the content owner has two responsibilities. First, the content must be delivered to a secure server, where it can be accessed as needed based on viewer requests. Second, the rules for viewing must be defined. For example, viewers paying one price might be able to view the content once via streaming only, whereas other viewers may be able to download the content and play it for several days.

The DRM system enforces the rules that the content owner has set up, which may need to be updated as viewers join and leave the system. The DRM system is responsible for making sure that the viewer has paid for the content, by means of either a payment per viewing, a valid subscription plan, or referral by a third party that handled the payment. (Note that rights management systems can also be used for free content, to protect it from unauthorized duplication or resale.)

Authorized viewers need to be provided with digital keys to unlock the content; a number of ways to do this will be discussed in the following sections on encryption. The DRM enforces the user rights policies by controlling access to these keys. This control can be quite literal: Many suppliers of encryption and key management systems require that their equipment be installed in a locked room with access permitted only to employees of the supplier. This high level of security is driven by the high potential value of both the content and the keys stored on the system.

The DRM system can also be responsible for tracking each time a user decides to view a piece of content and for reporting each viewing to the content owner for the purposes of paying royalties. This system has to be relatively foolproof to satisfy any contractual obligations with the content owners and to provide an audit trail so that the payments can be verified. Each of the major commercial DRM systems has a mechanism for doing this; failure of this mechanism can cause license violations and some very upset content owners.

One other function required of a DRM system is creating the data used to prepare bills for customers. In some cases, charges are billed directly to credit cards. In most cases, billing data from the DRM system needs to be fed into the distributor's billing system that prepares monthly bills for each subscriber.

ENCRYPTION

Cryptography is the science of making messages unreadable to everyone except the intended recipient. Encryption is the first step—taking the raw video and audio and encoding it in a systematic way so as to make it unreadable to anyone without the necessary key. Decryption is the reverse process—taking the key and the encrypted file and decoding it to produce an exact copy of the original signal. Proper management of the encryption keys is essential; the decoder needs exactly the same key for decryption that the encoder used for encryption. Overall, encryption can be a very complicated subject and can involve a great deal of arithmetic in different number bases (see, for example, Appendix A), which we won't go into here. Instead, we will focus on the practical aspects of encryption.

Secret vs. Public Keys

In order for an encrypted message to be decoded, the correct key must be supplied to each intended recipient. In secret key applications, the sender and the receiver have some mechanism for communicating the

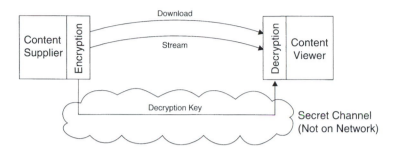

FIGURE 11-2 Secret Key Encryption System

key information between themselves and preventing it from falling into the hands of a would-be content thief. Sometimes the postal system or a fax machine is used for this purpose. The encryption process becomes worthless if the key is compromised. Figure 11-2 shows an information transfer taking place with a secret key.

Another problem with secret key cryptography is that it doesn't scale well. Sharing a single key between two people (or from one sender to many recipients) is fairly simple. However, consider the situation in which 10 parties wish to communicate securely. In this case, each user would need to manage 9 keys—one for communicating with every other person. All told, a total of 45 keys would need to be created and communicated secretly.

Public keys are quite different, although the need for secrecy is still present. Public keys are often used for encrypted e-mail or e-mail sender authentication. Public key cryptography is also used for secure Internet web browsing by means of Secure Hypertext Transfer Protocol (HTTPS) and is commonly found on websites that deal with financial transactions or online shopping.[1]

In a public key system, each user is issued one or more pairs of public and private keys. The private key of each pair must be kept secret by its owner, whereas the public key is shared with anyone who wants to send encrypted messages to the owner. This pair of keys needs to be related by a mathematical formula that allows messages

---

1. Many browsers indicate that secure communication is taking place by showing a small icon of a padlock on the user display.

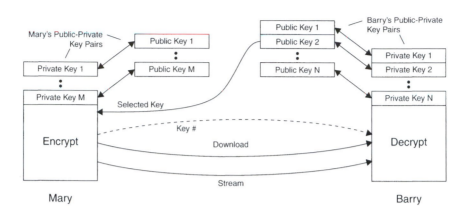

FIGURE 11-3   A Public Key Encryption System

encoded with one key to be decoded only with the other key (don't worry—these relationships exist; see Appendix A). Figure 11-3 shows how a public key encryption system would work.

In this example, Mary wishes to communicate with Barry. First, Mary must select one of Barry's public keys and use it to encrypt her message. In this case, she has selected Barry's public key number 2. Mary uses this key to encrypt her message (or video stream) and sends it to Barry. Any eavesdropper who intercepts the encrypted message at this point would see nothing but gibberish. When Barry receives the message, he is able to decrypt it using his private key number 2. Barry must keep his private keys a secret, because anyone who obtained one of his private keys would be able to read any messages sent to Barry that were encrypted with the paired public key.

Once Barry receives the message, he might wish to communicate back to Mary. In order to do this in a secure manner, he would need to select one of Mary's public keys and use it to encrypt his message. This illustrates the rule: The sender uses the public key of the recipient for encrypting messages sent to that recipient. The private portion of the key is never known by anyone but the recipient, so, even if several parties were all communicating with Mary simultaneously using the same public key, none of them would be able to decrypt the messages from the other senders. Only the holder of the private key linked to that public key would be able to decrypt the messages.

Public keys can also be used to authenticate the sender of a message. In the preceding example, Mary could encrypt a short data file using her private key and send it to Barry. Once he received the file, Barry could decrypt it using Mary's public key (this process works because of the mathematical relationship between the public key and the private key). When Barry successfully decrypts the file, he knows that nobody else but Mary could have sent the file to him. Barry has now authenticated Mary as a sender.

Watermarking

Watermarking is the process of inserting data into video or audio streams in order to track usage or prove ownership of a stream. It is similar in concept to some of the techniques used to protect currency and checks against forgery or counterfeiting. The basic idea is to insert identification without impairing the user's enjoyment of the content. Digital photographs can be watermarked to show copyright ownership and terms; these watermarks can be read by most of the major image-editing software packages. Video and audio content can also be watermarked with copyright data that can be read by some video recording and playback equipment to prevent unauthorized copying or distribution.

With digital content files, inserting a pattern into some of the less important bits in the file can be quite effective for watermarking purposes. For example, in a file with 16-bit audio samples, the least significant bit of any sample represents 1/65536 of the total output signal. When these bits are subtly manipulated, a watermark pattern can be inserted in the file with essentially no impact on the sound of the resulting piece.

Watermarking can be done differently depending on the objectives of the creator of the watermark. A watermark can be specifically designed to be fragile so that any change to the file destroys the watermark, thereby proving the file was tampered with. Alternatively, a watermark can be designed to be robust so that even if the file was significantly altered, the watermark could still be discerned. This form is useful for tracking content that has been duplicated without permission; there are even web crawlers that spend their time looking at millions of web pages to see whether they have unauthorized content.

Watermarking helps in rights enforcement when a unique watermark is created for each individual user. Individual watermarks can serve as a deterrent to unauthorized use of the content, since any misappropriations can be traced back to the specific source of the leak. If users know that any misappropriated files can be traced back to them, that can be a powerful incentive *not* to share files illegally.

Smart Cards

One of the most common ways of distributing keys used for secure video transport is the smart card. These cards are called "smart" because they incorporate a processor and memory that can be used by a variety of applications. Billions of smart cards are sold around the world each year for a variety of uses, including identification cards, prepaid telephone cards (outside the United States), debit/credit cards, and a host of other applications. Typically, a smart card contains both a processor capable of performing basic calculations and executing simple programs and memory that can hold both variable and permanent data.

Smart cards must be connected to a reading device in order to operate. In some cases, this connection is made physically, using gold-plated contacts. Figure 11-4 shows two different types of smart cards and their associated contact areas. Some cards can also connect

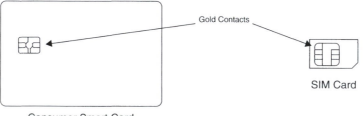

Consumer Smart Card

FIGURE 11-4 Two Common Types of Smart Cards

wirelessly to special readers by means of short-distance radio signals, eliminating the need physically to insert the card into the device.

A key feature of many smart cards is their ability to store data securely. The cards can be programmed to store secret information, such as the private part of a public/private key pair. Any unauthorized attempts to read that data would damage the card permanently and destroy the data. The smart card's internal processor can be used to decrypt data using this stored private key, and the results can be sent back out of the card without ever exposing the key to any external device.

For video applications, smart cards are one way to deliver video content descrambling/decryption keys to a user device. Each content stream (or television channel, if you prefer) has a unique descrambling key that is created when the content is prepared for broadcast. This key must be delivered to the viewer's device in order for it to be able to descramble the content properly. One way of doing this would be simply to send the key to the viewer's device; however, any other device connected to this communication path (think of a satellite link) would also receive this key and be able to decrypt the content. Instead, the descrambling keys are encrypted *before* they are sent to a viewing device.

When smart cards are used for delivering descrambling keys, each viewer device must be equipped with a smart-card reader, either built in (as in many set-top boxes, or STBs) or connected through an external port (such as a USB port on a personal computer). When an authorized viewer wants to watch scrambled content, the viewer's device needs to locate the correct descrambling key for the desired content. Instructions on how to find the appropriate decryption keys are contained in messages that are periodically sent by the server to authorized individual STBs or groups of STBs. The server then sends the encrypted descrambling key out over the communication path to the viewer's device. When the encrypted key arrives, it is fed into the smart card, and the smart card performs the decryption operation. The viewer device can then use the decrypted descrambling key to process the incoming signal and play the content for the viewer.

ENCRYPTION SYSTEMS

A great deal of work has been put into designing encryption algorithms, due to the many constraints that must be respected to create a successful design. First and foremost is the need for security so that encrypted content and the keys required to decrypt the content are hidden from third parties. Second, the system needs to be easy to use, or else users will not accept the system for regular operation. Third, there needs to be an efficient mechanism for adding new users to the system and for assigning them keys that can serve for secure communication.

In the following sections, we will look at two commercial encryption systems. The first one is for protecting content (such as Hollywood movies) on DVDs and is used in basically every DVD player in existence. The second, called *Pisys*, is a commercial product offered for use in video delivery systems, such as IPTV, CATV, and satellite systems for residential viewers.

DVD Encryption

The system used to encrypt SD DVDs is called the Content Scramble System (CSS). The information on each DVD title is encrypted using a unique 40-bit key. Any device that is going to play a DVD needs to have this key in order to descramble the content on the disk. Since other means of distributing the key were deemed unfeasible (can you imagine having to type a secret code into your DVD player each time you wanted to play a new disk?), encrypted copies of the master key are also recorded on every disk. In fact, the master key is encrypted with over 400 different player keys—one for each of the different manufacturers of DVD players (both hardware and software players). Each player has one of these 400 embedded keys; the player simply has to use its key to decode the master key for the disk in order to start the process needed to unlock the content.

CSS was defeated because one player manufacturer neglected to encrypt the player's key. Due to this lapse, certain people were able to design software to decrypt any DVD using this key. In addition, by using this key as a guide, they were able to discover over 100 other player keys. These discoveries spawned the development of a number of different software programs (called DeCSS) available today for (illegal) copying and playing of DVDs. This example illustrates the necessity to ensure that decryption keys are well secured for both the production and the playback steps of any video distribution system.

Irdeto Pisys

The Irdeto Pisys system from Irdeto Access of Hoofddorp in the Netherlands is a good example of how a conditional access system is designed to work in a real-world environment. This technology has been successfully deployed by a number of satellite, CATV, terrestrial broadcast, and IP video network providers for both video contribution and distribution applications. Secure connections can be established for unicast (one source to one destination), multicast (one source to multiple, selected destinations), and broadcast (one source serving an undefined number of destinations) operations.

As is common in many conditional access systems, one security option supplied by Irdeto Access involves a hardware-based system for managing the decryption keys used by the viewers. This takes the form of smart cards issued to each viewer and a mechanism (card reader) at each viewing location that can access the data and processing functions stored inside the cards. A second security option from Irdeto Access is a specialized module of software code located in each viewing device that offers many of the same security capabilities as smart cards without requiring management of physical smart cards and associated reader hardware.

Pisys operates as a type of middleware—connecting a variety of equipment and software from multiple vendors. At the video source location, Pisys controls the hardware and software devices that encrypt or scramble content and manages the keys required for this process. Content can be scrambled or encrypted "on the fly" (as it is being transmitted in real time), or it can be scrambled or encrypted ahead of time and stored on a server before it is sent to the viewer. Pisys also interacts with a variety of set-top box devices that are responsible for descrambling or decrypting the content when it arrivers at the viewing location, and it distributes the keys to these devices using encrypted communications.

Subscriber management and billing are handled by external software that manages a database containing subscriber contact information (address, account type, contact details, purchased services, etc.) and prepares and ships bills to customers. This software sends requests to Pisys to provision new services and change existing ones as well as to send messages of any kind to individual subscribers over the broadcast network. The subscriber management software also allows Pisys to determine the associations between the subscribers and the smart cards they possess so that descrambling/decryption keys can be sent to the proper viewer devices.

Overall, Pisys and similar systems from other manufacturers provide a variety of valuable services, allowing encryption, decryption, and subscriber management systems to be interconnected simply and securely. Any company using satellites for video contribution or distribution should strongly consider employing a high-grade encryption system such as Pisys. Similarly, terrestrial broadcasters and video service providers using IP networks that need to deliver content securely can also benefit from this type of comprehensive solution.

REVIEW AND CHECKLIST UPDATE

In this chapter, we discussed two very important aspects of content management: ownership and security. There are many sources for content, both prerecorded and custom created. Whenever content is to be used by a business, it is essential to obtain all necessary rights in advance from the content owner. Failure to do so can be extremely expensive and damaging to future business opportunities.

Content owners may insist that their content be protected from copying or unauthorized viewing as a condition for granting rights to a distributor; failure to protect the content properly can be as damaging (or worse) to the content owner as failing to obtain the proper rights. Content scrambling and encryption can also be used to protect the rights of content owners. These systems require a mechanism to scramble or encrypt the content prior to transmission, a means to descramble or decrypt the content at the viewer's location, and a way to securely transmit the necessary descrambling keys to the viewer's playback device. We reviewed several technologies for accomplishing this and looked at two examples illustrating how these technologies have been successfully implemented.

Chapter 11 Checklist Update

☐ Make sure that all video and audio content that is to be transmitted on a network is licensed for use on that network. Failure to do so can expose network owners and users to potential claims for royalties, lawsuits, and loss of access to content in the future.

☐ Consider using copy prevention circuits within video playback devices such as videotape players, DVD players, and STBs to make recording of the video content impractical or of exceedingly poor quality.

☐ When authorized to use prerecorded content from videotapes or DVDs, make sure that copy protection schemes won't interfere with the video capture or encoding process.

☐ Encryption or scrambling is normally required when transmitting valuable content over public or private networks with multiple users.

☐ Consider using automated key distribution. The biggest challenge for encryption and scrambling systems is ensuring that the proper keys are distributed to users whenever they have acquired the rights to view a piece of content.

☐ Smart-card systems, with card readers at each viewer location, are a popular means for securely distributing descrambling or decryption keys to viewers, particularly for IPTV systems that use STBs. USB-based smart-card readers are also available for personal computers.

12

PRIVATE NETWORKS SECURE AND TRANSPORT

As we discussed in the preceding chapter, a number of technologies can be used to protect content from being copied when public airwaves or public networks are involved. In this chapter, we are going to look at providing security for content through the use of secure transport technology. This is one of the best ways to provide security for high-value content, such as raw footage or first-run movies. Secure transport may also be a necessity for corporate video networks, particularly those that carry videoconferences among senior executives.

We'll begin by discussing how IP packets can be transported over some popular private network technologies, including leased lines, Frame Relay, ATM, optical technologies, and carrier IP services. We'll follow this with a look at how private IP networks can be constructed on public IP network facilities, through the use of technologies called *tunneling* and *IPSec*. By the end of this chapter, readers should have a basic understanding of some of the ways that secure transport facilities can provide content protection.

PRIVATE NETWORKS

A network is considered to be private when a single person or organization controls all the content (voice, data, and video) flowing over the network. Sometimes, the circuits that make up the network are privately owned and operated; other times, the circuits are leased from a network provider. In most cases, the network is permanently connected so that data can flow without having to wait for a network connection to be set up.

In the past, private networks were the primary method for communications within companies that had multiple locations. Many times, these networks were devoted to providing remote locations with access to central corporate computing resources, such as mainframes. Applications were typically limited to accounting, order entry, materials management, and other hard-number-oriented activities. Communications between employees were handled with printed memos, faxes, and telephone calls, instead of e-mail and instant messaging. As a result, many private networks were low speed and poorly suited for video traffic.

Modern private networks are much more sophisticated, with high-speed connections more widely deployed, to support a variety of internal communications functions. Most private networks support applications such as e-mail, file sharing, and corporate web intranets. Other services, such as voice over IP and instant messaging, are growing in popularity. As network speeds increase in order to support these applications, it also becomes feasible to transport video signals on private networks.

Leased Lines

Leased lines are telecommunication circuits that are usually provided by a telephone company or other carrier for exclusive use of a single customer on a long-term (monthly or yearly) basis. Popular speeds today include T1 (1.544 Mbps), E1 (2.048 Mbps), E3 (34 Mbps), DS3 (45 Mbps), and OC-3/STM-1 (155 Mbps). (Many local carriers offer direct IP connections as well; we'll cover those later in this chapter.) One of the biggest benefits of these services is that many of them are available anywhere in a carrier's service area, and pricing is often regulated. At the high end, some end users are able to lease OC-12/STM-4 (622 Mbps) and OC-48/STM-16 (2.488 Gbps) circuits when they have physical presence in major city centers where long-haul carriers have points of presence. A few adventuresome users are even leasing 2.5-Gbps or 10-Gbps wavelengths directly from optical service providers and then installing their own equipment to adapt multiple signals into a common backbone.

Many leased lines carry a mixture of services, including voice and data services. For example, it is not at all uncommon for a T1 private line, which has a capacity of 24 channels running at 64 kbps each, to have a dozen channels reserved for voice traffic and the other 768 kbps allocated to data traffic. At the customer location, the voice circuits might be connected to a telephone system and the data circuit connected to a local data router.

Leased lines are normally installed as point-to-point circuits that start and end at customer locations and are usually connected to customer-owned equipment, such as telephone systems or IP routers. These circuits are handled as totally private, dedicated data circuits; no data is added or removed by the carrier in transit, even if one end of the circuit is sending empty packets. In between, multiple carriers and carrier equipment locations may be involved; each is responsible for providing a full-bandwidth connection across its own network. In essence, the customer's data "tunnels" through the rest of the network, without interaction. Figure 12-1 shows an example of a private line T1 circuit, where the T1 signal is carried intact from Site A to Site B, without intermediate processing, other than being multiplexed into a high-speed DS3 circuit with other signals. Note that carriers will normally combine multiple T1s and other voice and data traffic through the process of multiplexing, and much higher data rates will normally be used to provide connectivity and transport between carrier locations.

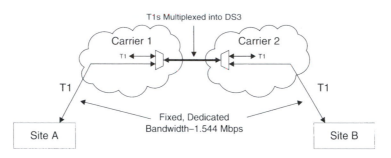

FIGURE 12-1 Leased Line Example

Leased lines can offer a great deal of security for customer traffic. In order to get access to the data on a leased line, an outsider would need to obtain physical access to the circuit, either in the local access network or inside the carrier's network. Aside from obvious legal violations, on a practical level this is a difficult task.

In small networks, with relatively few connected locations, a few leased lines can provide good connectivity. However, as the number of network locations grows, the number of leased lines needed to interconnect all of the locations grows rapidly. To solve this problem, many networks are arranged in a hub-and-spoke configuration, with one location serving as the central hub and the other locations connected via circuits that all terminate at the hub. When a location on one spoke needs to communicate with another spoke, the data must transit through the hub before it is passed along. This architecture requires large-capacity connections to the network hub and high-capacity networking equipment located at the hub.

Another drawback to leased lines is that they are inefficient for data flows that vary greatly over time. Because the capacity of a leased circuit is unable to change rapidly, a customer has two choices. One choice is to purchase a high-speed circuit that has enough capacity to handle the expected peak data load, which would leave the circuit operating below capacity most of the time. The other choice is to buy a lower-speed circuit that will create congestion whenever peak loads occur. In either scenario, the data communication resources are used less optimally than if a variable-rate service were used.

There are a number of mechanisms for sending IP packets over a standard telecom circuit, so we won't go into detail here. One of the most common protocols is the Point-to-Point Protocol (PPP) because it is very simple and easy to implement. PPP doesn't have many of the advanced features of other packet transport protocols, so it isn't suitable for use on networks other than point-to-point leased lines or on access lines from a customer to a provider's packet network.

Frame Relay

Carriers have historically offered a service called *Frame Relay*, which is a data network protocol that was designed specifically to transport IP packets in variable-length frames. This service is typically less expensive than a leased line because the backbone network is shared, allowing carriers to use their networks more efficiently. See Figure 12-2 for a simple example of a Frame Relay circuit. Today, many carriers and users are migrating away from Frame Relay technology because IP VPNs are able to provide greater bandwidths at lower costs.

At each customer site, Frame Relay Access Devices (FRADs) take IP packets and insert them into and remove them from the data frames. This function can be owned and managed by the carrier or incorporated into routers or other devices belonging to the customer.

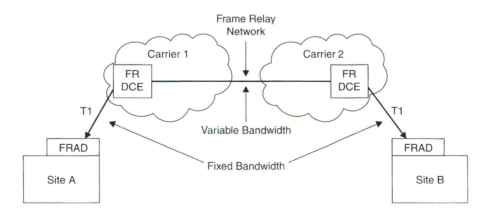

FIGURE 12-2 Frame Relay Circuit Example

Data from the FRAD is sent to a local carrier's data communications equipment (DCE) device, which is responsible for sending the data frames into the carrier's data backbone. Note that the carrier is not required to keep the data in any specific format in the internal data network; Frame Relay data can be sent over IP, ATM, or any other network, provided the data is kept private from other customers.

Frame Relay connections are priced partly on the basis of the Committed Information Rate (CIR) and partly on the basis of the access link speed. The CIR is a data rate selected by the customer that the carrier promises will be available at all times to the customer. Customers are allowed to send more data than their CIR rate; however, the network can delete any frames in excess of the CIR at any time. Higher-level protocols (such as TCP) can correct for these lost frames, so customers usually choose to keep their CIR as low as possible. For networks with heavy video usage, it might be necessary to pay for a CIR that is greater than the expected video signal rate to ensure that adequate network capacity is available.

In Frame Relay, each remote site can use a medium-speed link (a T1, for example), and the central site can use a higher-speed link (a DS3, for example). This is much more economical and efficient than using multiple leased lines between the remote sites and the central site. Figure 12-3A shows a leased line network layout, and Figure 12-3B

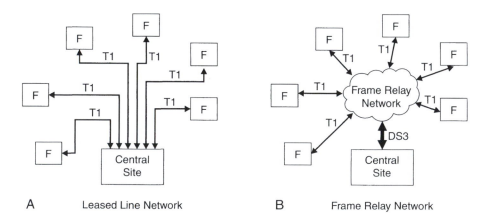

A   Leased Line Network   B   Frame Relay Network

FIGURE 12-3 Comparison of (A) Leased Line and (B) Frame Relay Networks

shows the same network implemented using a Frame Relay network. Frame Relay networks can also be configured to provide multicasting, so a single data stream from one site can be sent to multiple other sites. Alternatively, every node in the network can be designated as a multicasting site.

Asynchronous Transfer Mode (ATM)

Asynchronous Transfer Mode (ATM) is a networking technology based on the transport of fixed-length packets of data, called *cells* in ATM standards. Developed in the 1980s, ATM became popular in the 1990s for transport of many different types of services, including video. Today, carriers are increasingly migrating customers to MPLS or IP networks, so ATM is not a growth technology.

ATM services were popular partly because of the ability to control how data is routed within a network. All data in an ATM network flows over a virtual circuit (VC), of which there are two types: permanent virtual circuits (PVCs) and switched virtual circuits (SVCs). SVCs are switched connections that are set up between source and destination each time they are needed and then disconnected when the data transfer is complete. In contrast, PVCs are established on command from the system manager, and they remain connected until commanded to disconnect, which could be a period lasting days, months, or even years. (Note that PVCs can be variable bandwidth.)

Even though ATM flows are mixed within the network, the multiplexing equipment keeps data isolated at each user connection. This provides a degree of security for customer data that is more difficult to implement on an IP-based network. Another advantage of ATM circuits is that they can be configured in any size, such as 15 Mbps or 22 Mbps.[1] This gives users much more flexibility in configuring their networks.

---

1. This discussion relates to the actual data-carrying capacity of the ATM circuit for local or long-distance service. The physical local access line from a customer's facility to the local telephone company office will normally be a standard rate for the telecom hierarchy—a T1, a DS3, an STM-1, etc.

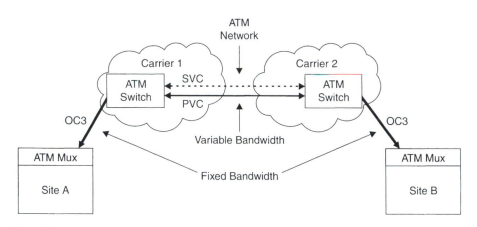

FIGURE 12-4   ATM Circuit Example

Figure 12-4 shows a simple point-to-point ATM network that crosses between two different carriers. At each customer site, an ATM multiplexer is installed; this multiplexer takes voice, data, and other services such as video and converts them into ATM cells. Inside the carrier's network, an ATM switch is used to take the incoming cells and route them toward their selected destination. These destinations can be configured either manually by the network operator (a PVC) or dynamically on request by the user (an SVC).

A VC that is set up to have a constant bit rate (CBR) will always have the same amount of data flowing through it. A VC can also be set up to use a variable bit rate (VBR) so that the end-to-end data rate varies as the customer data rate increases or decreases. The lowest class of service, called *available bit rate (ABR)*, simply uses any bandwidth that is left over in the data pipe. This service, although typically the least expensive, is normally not well suited for video traffic, because it can quickly have its bit rate reduced to zero if other, higher-priority services, such as VBR, need the bandwidth.

IP packets are frequently transported over ATM circuits. Carriers like ATM because they can use a single networking technology to serve multiple needs of a customer. Voice traffic can be transmitted using constant-bit-rate services, and data traffic can be transmitted using variable- and available-bit-rate services. Multiple customers can be served on a single communication link, because ATM has the built-in mechanisms to control the amount of bandwidth each customer is allowed to use.

One drawback to ATM networks is the complexity of establishing and tearing down VCs and also the overall management complexity of the ATM network. As a result, ATM services are more expensive than IP services operating at the same bandwidth from many carriers.

Fiber-Optic Networks

Many large users of video and data transport services would benefit by installing their own private fiber-optic network. The biggest benefit is a long-run cost reduction, because the cost of buying equipment and fiber is a one-time charge, as compared to a recurring monthly fee from a carrier. Another benefit is the flexibility of services because of the huge variety of fiber-optic equipment available to transport almost any type of signal. One more benefit is the privacy that can be achieved with fiber optics. Of course, there are downsides, including the need to hire or train staff to maintain the network. Also, geographic flexibility is nonexistent once the fiber is installed.

Figure 12-5 shows a simplified diagram of a typical fiber-optic private network. At each site, an optical transmitter (TX) and an optical receiver (RX) are installed, along with the necessary electronics to send and receive data on the local data network.

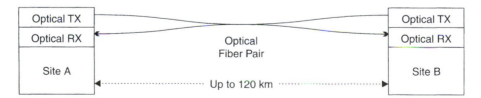

FIGURE 12-5 Optical Fiber Circuit Example

Optical fiber networks are hard to beat for quality, speed, and security. Because the signals flowing inside an optical fiber are almost perfectly isolated from the outside world, interference from other signal sources is not an issue.

Of course, there are some difficulties for users who wish to use optical networking. In order for the network to function, the data sender and receiver need to be connected by a single continuous optical fiber. While this type of networking is relatively easy to establish in a suburban college campus, it can be very difficult to achieve in a modern metropolitan area, let alone across longer distances. Since telephone companies are often reluctant simply to lease fiber, prospective users will need to lease fibers from other providers, such as power or water utilities, or even from municipalities.

Several techniques are used to send IP packets over optical fiber. Many routers can be equipped with fiber interfaces that send packets using optical Ethernet standards, which have been developed to use both short-distance and longer-distance optical technology. Longer-distance links may sometimes require the use of telecom-style interfaces, such as SONET/SDH technology. IP packets flowing over these networks can use specially developed protocols such as Packet over SONET/SDH (PoS).

Carrier IP Services

As demand for IP connectivity has continued to grow rapidly, carriers have responded by offering native IP connectivity, which can take several forms. Because IP packets can be transported over so many types of networks, carriers are free to choose a variety of technologies for their backbones, including MPLS, native IP, SONET/SDH, and even ATM networks in some legacy applications. Some carriers even offer combined private IP network access and Internet access by way of the same physical link to the customer location.

For IP services, the standard customer interface is either a 10/100BaseT Ethernet interface or a gigabit Ethernet interface. These well-established protocols can operate over wired or optical fiber interfaces. Multiple traffic streams can share a single network interface—packets for each destination receive VLAN (virtual local area network) tags and can easily be separated at the entry point to the network. In many instances, all of the services for a particular customer are routed through a single CPE (customer premises equipment) router at the customer's end of an Ethernet link to the carrier, which connects directly to a PE (provider edge) router located in the carrier's facility.

Just like Frame Relay and many other services, an IP services customer can contract for a specific amount of network bandwidth that is unrelated to the physical capacity of the connection. For example, a customer might use a gigabit Ethernet connection to the carrier, but only contract for 250 Mbps of service. Depending on the agreement, this could represent a not-to-exceed limit on the data rate, or the carrier could allow excess packets to be transported on a "best-efforts" basis with no delivery guarantees.

One drawback to carrier IP services is that they may not be available in all customer locations. Competition tends to be fiercest in major city centers, where multiple providers offer servces. Smaller cities and rural areas in particular may not have high-bandwidth services available at all. In these latter cases, telco leased lines are often used to deliver traffic from some remote locations into another site where the packets can be extracted and then delivered to a carrier IP service for transport.

VIRTUAL PRIVATE NETWORKS

Virtual private networks (VPNs) offer many of the benefits of private networks but use public networks as a transport mechanism. This technology allows users to share a single Internet connection both for private data and for access to the Internet. By accessing the Internet for transport between locations, a VPN user avoids the expense of installing or leasing a circuit between locations, although local access link charges may still apply. Some service providers also offer VPN services over shared networks that aren't part of the Internet.

VPNs are all about security. Without security, the data traveling over a VPN is subject to all types of eavesdropping or, worse, malicious data alteration. Four key security functions need to be accomplished by a packet transport system that is to be used by a VPN.[2]

- *Authentication*: The receiving device needs to know and confirm that the data came actually from the device that it claims to be coming from. This can be accomplished with digital signatures provided by a centralized authority.
- *Confidentiality*: The data that is carried in the VPN must not be understandable by other devices or users on the network, even if they are able to get copies of the packets. This can be accomplished through the use of a good encryption algorithm on all packet data.
- *Access control*: Networks that are part of the VPN should be blocked from being accessed by users who are not part of the VPN. Also, all of the user networks connected to the VPN need to be properly isolated from third parties who might attempt to gain unauthorized access to the VPN. This can be accomplished through a good combination of authentication and confidentiality for all packets, as well as good firewalls.
- *Data integrity*: Any data that passes through the VPN should be protected from tampering; if the data is tampered with, it should be obvious to the receiving device. This can be accomplished through the use of a secure encryption system and an effective mechanism to ensure that extra packets are not inserted into the data stream.

Tunneling

Tunneling involves sending data through a network without making it available to other users of that network. In order for this process to work, the data must be encrypted, to prevent it from making sense to others. When a tunnel is in place between two locations, it is generally used for all of the data communication between these two

---

2. Adapted from Web ProForum Tutorial titled "Virtual Private Networks (VPNs)" from The International Engineering Consortium, http://www.iec.org.

endpoints, requiring many different kinds of packets to be encrypted. (Contrast this with the discussions in Chapter 11, where we focused on encrypting just video streams.) Tunneling is generally used over a public wide area network for communication between two local networks in different locations. Other forms of secure transport, such as PPTP (Point-to-Point Tunneling Protocol) and L2TP (Layer 2 Tunneling Protocol), are used when a single user connects to a remote network, which we won't discuss here.

Tunneling works by encrypting normal IP packets before they are transmitted over public IP networks such as the Internet. During this process, the entire packet is encrypted, including the header information. A second, nonencrypted header is then placed onto each packet so that all of the packets can be sent through the Internet. (If this second header weren't added, then the packets would be impossible to route, because the routers wouldn't have access to the source and destination IP addresses inside the encrypted header.)

The operation of a tunneling system is shown in Figure 12-6. An IP tunnel is in use between Router A and Router B. Router A is responsible for taking packets from LAN A that are intended for LAN B and encrypting them before sending them into the Internet. Router A is also responsible for accepting packets that originated at Router B and decrypting them before placing the packets on LAN A. Router B fulfills the same

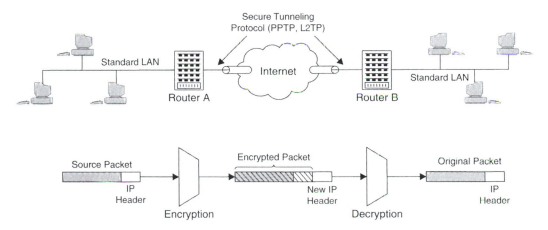

FIGURE 12-6 LAN-to-LAN Tunneling

functions for LAN B. Note that either or both routers can be configured to send all packets from their local LAN to the other LAN, or they can filter the packets and send only some through the IP tunnel.

IPSec

Internet Protocol security (IPSec) was developed to provide secure transport for IP packets over nonsecure networks. It uses a variety of tools to ensure the security of each of the packets, including encryption and authentication. IPSec is described in a number of Internet Engineering Task Force (IETF) Requests for Comments (RFCs), many of which were finalized in November 1998. Since then, IPSec has become one of the preferred methods for secure IP transport in use today.

One big advantage of IPSec is that it can be used to encrypt all packets at the IP level, so changes are not required to applications or higher-level protocols, such as TCP and UDP. Also, no special training is required for users; the security functions are taken care of by the lower layers of the protocol stack that are not normally exposed to users.

Three main aspects of IPSec are covered in the IETF standards:

- *Internet Key Exchange (IKE)*: This secure mechanism is used for exchanging keys between known entities, thereby allowing them to send encrypted messages to each other. There are several different ways to achieve this, but one of the most popular methods is to use digital certificates signed by a mutually trusted certificate authority, or CA (VeriSign is a common one). Once the two parties have verified each other's identities, they can use the Diffie–Hellman Key Exchange (see Appendix A) to create a private encryption key that is known only to them.
- *Authentication header (AH)*: This header is used to make sure that the packet senders are who they claim to be and that the contents of the packet haven't changed in transmission. In order to do this, each packet must use a checksum generated from certain portions of the packet that don't change in transmission and a secret key, known only to the sender and the receiver of the message. A software algorithm is applied to manipulate these

values and produce a *message digest* or a *hash* result, which is then appended to the message being sent. At the receiving end, the same calculation is performed, and a second result is calculated. If the two results match (both the one sent with the message and the one calculated by the receiver), then the packet is assumed to be authentically from the real sender.

- *Encapsulating Security Payload (ESP)*: ESP takes the authentication header concept one step further and actually encrypts the contents of the packets so that outsiders cannot read the data inside each packet.

Before communication can take place between a receiver and a sender using IPSec, the two parties must agree to a *security association (SA)*. The SA is established when a secure session is first set up, and it includes all of the information needed by the receiving party to understand the transmitting party. Each SA is unidirectional and unicast, meaning that the SA is valid in one direction only and only for a single recipient IP address. For a two-way IPSec connection, at least two SAs must be established, one in each direction.

One important aspect of an IPSec connection that must be specified by the SA is whether the connection will be made in transport mode or in tunnel mode, as shown in Figure 12-7. If the connection is between two gateway devices (such as firewalls or routers), then

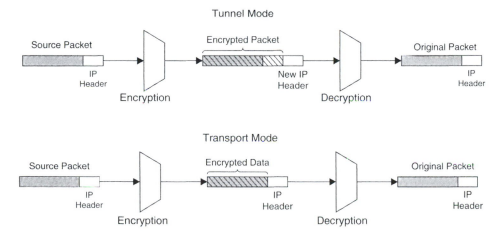

FIGURE 12-7 IPSec Connection Modes

the connection must be tunnel mode, and every packet flowing between the source and the destination must pass over the IPSec link. In tunnel mode, a new (nonencrypted) IP header is applied to each packet after it is encrypted so that they can be handled in the network by routers that aren't able to decrypt the original packet. At the receiving end of the tunnel, the extra packet headers are removed and the packet is decrypted and then sent to the correct destination. In contrast, transport mode can be used only between end devices on the network (such as user PCs or servers), and the original destination IP address remains visible on the packet. Only the contents of the IP packet are encrypted in transport mode. The choice of whether to use transport mode or tunnel mode really depends on whether the secure connection is between networks (such as from LAN to LAN) or between devices (such as one processor to another). Individual devices are also permitted to use tunnel mode, but gateway devices are not permitted to use transport mode.

Overall, a VPN is a very desirable method for implementing secure communication over a public network, such as the Internet. With a VPN, users can avoid many of the headaches involved with setting up and maintaining a private network and still receive many of the benefits. Of course, nothing is free, and charges from a local ISP may increase if significant local access bandwidth is added to support VPNs. Plus, the performance of the virtual network will be no better (in terms of error rates, etc.) than the actual network underneath it. The only real drawback to a VPN is that guaranteeing a large amount of bandwidth can be difficult, unless the network provider makes specific accommodations for the VPN.

REVIEW AND CHECKLIST UPDATE

In this chapter, we investigated secure transport from two perspectives. First, we looked at transport technologies that provided physical or other forms of data security, including leased lines, Frame Relay, ATM, optical networks, and carrier IP services. Then we examined two aspects of virtual private networks and saw how tunneling and IPSec could be used to transport confidential traffic securely over the Internet.

Chapter 12 Checklist Update

❑ Transport security is an inherent trait of private networking technology.

❑ ATM, Frame Relay, leased line, and IP services can be obtained from most public network providers (telephone companies). Local and long-distance segments may need to be purchased from different suppliers, which may require user coordination.

❑ Optical networks are typically built to customer specifications and may require the end user to purchase and maintain the necessary optical equipment. Obtaining fiber and associated rights-of-way can be expensive and difficult.

❑ Many carriers are phasing out Frame Relay and ATM services in favor of direct IP transport, so these technologies should be avoided for new applications.

❑ Virtual private networks have to be configured properly to protect video content. A secure encryption scheme such as IPSec needs to be implemented to prevent content from being copied by others sharing the same network.

❑ Private networking technology does not prevent authorized viewers from making unauthorized copies of content (such as copying video that streamed over a private network). To prevent this, some form of copy protection is needed, as discussed in Chapter 11.

13

IPTV—DELIVERING TELEVISION TO CONSUMERS

IPTV is a method for delivering traditional, linear television programming to consumers over a private IP network. It can be considered a direct substitute for broadcast, satellite, or CATV systems, because it accomplishes the same purpose: delivering hundreds of channels of continuous programming that are displayed on a television by way of an STB. Contrast this with Internet video, which consists of millions of video clips that are viewed by means of a PC display and delivered over a public network. (Internet Video will be covered in Chapter 15.)

The distinctions between IPTV and Internet video are not merely semantic; there are significant differences in the technologies used to provide these services. In particular, the delivery networks are very different, with IPTV hardware and software systems typically custom built for video delivery and Internet video simply leveraging existing infrastructure. Business models differ greatly: IPTV is almost always a paid subscription service, where many Internet

Video Over IP: IPTV, Internet Video, H.264, P2P, Web TV, and Streaming: A Complete Guide to Understanding the Technology
Copyright © 2008, Wes Simpson. All rights reserved.

video services are provided for free to the user. Viewer expectations are also divergent—it's not an issue if a few seconds of buffering are required before an Internet video clip begins to play, but no IPTV system would survive long if it introduced 5–10 seconds of "dead air" between each program or every time the channel was changed.

In this chapter, we will start out by defining more completely what IPTV is and then look at two IPTV applications. We'll explore the reasons for using IPTV. Then we will examine some of the key technologies that support IPTV. We'll conclude with an example of an actual IPTV delivery system.

Service providers who wish to deliver multiple consumer services over a single network often choose IP technology because a single platform can provide voice and high-speed data access in addition to IPTV. In a typical system, a private, high-speed IP network is used to deliver video programming continuously to hundreds or thousands of viewers simultaneously. Figure 13-1 shows a typical IPTV network.

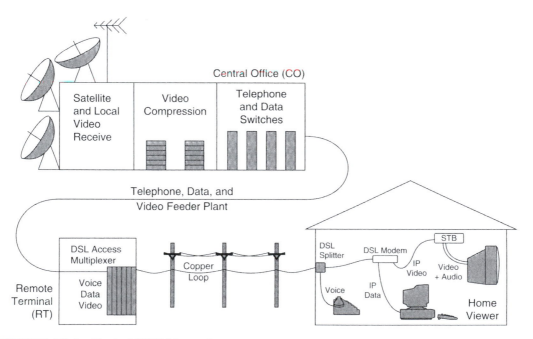

FIGURE 13-1 Typical IPTV Network

CHARACTERISTICS OF IPTV

Several key characteristics define the ways in which IPTV is different from other video applications that use IP networks:

Continuous content streams: IPTV is designed to send streams of video programming to each viewer. These streams are continuous; that is, each viewer can select the stream he or she wants to view but must join the stream in progress. This process is functionally identical to the programming delivered by local broadcasters, CATV companies, and satellite providers, where the viewer is able to select the channel to be viewed but not the content of the channels. Of course, many IPTV providers also offer video-on-demand (VOD) and interactive services using their IPTV networks, but these services can also be delivered in many other ways.

Multiple channels: The primary content delivered over an IPTV network is produced by a range of broadcast networks and delivered simultaneously to a large number of viewers. Viewers typically choose which channel they want to watch on their television by interacting with the IPTV set-top box (STB). This can be done simply by entering the desired channel number on a remote control keypad or by making a selection from an Electronic Program Guide (EPG).

Uniform content format: Most IPTV systems use only one video encoding format (or possibly two) for each type of content. The choices typically range from MPEG-2 or MPEG-4 to VC-1. IPTV providers will typically choose one compression format and one bit rate for all SD video signals and another combination for HD signals. This greatly simplifies the overall management of the IPTV system, allowing for a uniform system design and easing the burden on technicians maintaining the system. This also simplifies the STB design by eliminating the need to support multiple video decompression engines. Of course, this approach requires that any content not in the correct format be converted when it arrives at the IPTV system.

Private delivery network: In order to deliver continuous channels of content to thousands of viewers in a repeatable manner, an IPTV network must be carefully provisioned and controlled. This task is very daunting on a private network, where all of the video content and other network traffic can be controlled. This task would be impossible on the public Internet.

Viewed on consumer televisions via set-top boxes: The role of an STB is extremely important for an IPTV network. At a minimum, it must receive an incoming IP video stream, reassemble the data packets in the correct order, decode the video signal, and produce an output that can be fed to a television (or projector) for display. The STB normally serves as the terminus for the IPTV network, so it must be able to receive commands from the user's remote control and send them into the network for action. It may also need some built-in intelligence to be able to generate text or other graphics to communicate with the viewer, for functions like the EPG.

APPLICATIONS

Many readers of this book are aware of the rich variety of technologies that can be used for video delivery into the home. With this in mind, let's look at two different types of services that IP networks are currently being used to deliver: entertainment to the home and hotel/motel applications.

Entertainment

Some very large IPTV networks have been installed to provide home video services, similar to those provided by traditional CATV and DTH satellite providers. In all these systems, individual households are supplied with a variety of broadcast television channels in exchange for a monthly subscription fee. These fees pay for three basic costs of the service provider: the cost of the programming, the initial capital cost of installing the video delivery system, and the ongoing costs of performing maintenance on the delivery system and providing customer service.

Typically, entertainment systems provide service for a particular geographic area, such as a city, a town, or a neighborhood (or, in the case of satellite services, a country). In many cases a license or franchise from the local government is required to operate the system; this may require an annual fee to be paid to the government (called a *franchise fee*). Exclusive rights for a certain territory are sometimes given to the service provider in exchange for certain concessions, such as providing video services for governmental or educational use. However, just because a service provider has an exclusive franchise for an area does not mean that the provider is guaranteed to capture all of the television viewers in that area.

In any video delivery system, a number of potential subscribers will choose not to receive video programming and become actual subscribers. The ratio of actual subscribers to potential subscribers, called the *take rate,* can be influenced by a number of factors. These factors include the availability of competing video services (such as CATV and satellite), the take rates of those other services, the amount of local programming available, and the intensity of the marketing program for the service, among many other factors.

Normally, a service provider does not install all of the equipment needed to service every single residence in a given area, because the take rate will begin at a low percentage. Instead, distribution equipment is added as needed to handle new subscribers as they sign up. However, a large amount of common equipment (for content gathering and system operation, as described later in this chapter) must normally be installed to equip an area for video delivery. Because of this, the system economic breakeven point might not be reached unless the take rate reaches 20–30% or possibly even more. Overall, it is very difficult to design a profitable business plan for a new video-only network unless one out of every five households that can subscribe to the service actually does (a 20% take rate).

IP technology offers a way for these service providers to capture more than just video subscribers: the ability to offer "triple-play" services. For example, many CATV companies are adding IP capabilities to their networks to provide voice over IP and data services. On a properly designed pure IP network, video services can be offered, data services such as Internet access can easily be supported, and voice services can be provided using voice-over-IP technology. With a triple-play network, a service provider can more easily achieve the take rate needed to reach economic breakeven.

Hotel/Motel Video Services

IP video technology can also be applied to delivering in-room entertainment video to hotel guests. This technology can be used to provide all of the video services to each room or just the premium movie channels offered by many hotels. Because the video display in a hotel room is normally a television set, an IP-enabled STB is required in each room to receive the incoming signals and convert them.

Typically, hotel systems are configured to use a video server in each building. The server outputs are connected to a data transport system that delivers the IP streams to each room in the hotel. This can be accomplished via existing telephone wiring if DSL technology is used. IP traffic can also be sent over coaxial cable normally used for distributing television signals in a hotel through the use of IP cable modem technology.

One advantage of IPTV in a hotel setting is due to the growing demand for in-room Internet access. With careful provisioning, it is completely possible to use the same in-hotel DSL circuits to deliver both data and video services to each room. With many hotels upgrading their television systems to offer digital TV and HD video services, IPTV becomes an attractive option. In-room telephones can also be converted to voice over IP, but that trend is not yet strong.

BASIC CONCEPTS

Video delivery to the home has created a variety of new terminology and business models that need to be understood in order to make sense of the reams of articles and company literature that have been produced on this topic. In the following sections, we'll look at some of these new terms and how industry insiders are using them. Along the way, we'll also discuss some of the market forces that are pushing service providers to seek out and apply innovative new technologies, such as video over IP.

Why Use IP for Video to the Home?

The hardware and software systems that deliver terrestrial broadcast, DTH satellite, and CATV services are the products of hundreds of thousands of hours of development and refinement, and they provide services that are very popular with the home viewing audience. In the face of all this proven technology, the logical question becomes: Why introduce a new technology, such as IP video transport, for video delivery to the home?

The answer is not a single compelling reason but, instead, a combination of factors that can influence this decision. Briefly, these factors are local loop technology, user control, convergence, and flexibility. Let's look at how IP technology can impact each of these factors.

Local telephone technology has been evolving rapidly over the past decade. With the emergence of digital subscriber line (DSL) technology, service providers are now able to deliver thousands of kilobits per second of data to each customer's home. This capacity far exceeds what was possible even a decade ago, when speeds were typically limited to a basic-rate ISDN line operating at 144 kbps or a simple dial-up modem circuit operating at 56 kbps. With the added capacity of DSL, the logical question for providers has become: What other services besides telephony and Internet access can we provide to customers that they will be willing to pay for? The answer, in many cases, is video services. To accomplish this, IPTV has often proven to be the best choice for providing video over DSL circuits. By adding IPTV, service providers can earn additional revenue to help pay for DSL speed upgrades.

User control is another powerful trend in the video delivery business. By enabling users to choose what they want to watch at any time, service providers have been able simultaneously to increase user satisfaction and increase the fees that customers pay. For example, personal video recorders (PVRs, which have been popularized by suppliers such as TiVo) allow users to record television broadcasts automatically on a computer hard disk for later, on-demand playback (sometimes called *time shifting*). This service is not free: Users have to pay a significant sum to purchase the PVR device and then many pay an additional monthly service fee to receive the electronic program guide. Another example is a service being offered by cable television companies in the United States called HBO on Demand, which allows users to select programs from a list of shows and movies for viewing at any time, in exchange for a substantial monthly fee. This service has become popular with customers in those cable systems that offer it. Clearly, users are demanding, and willing to pay for, programming they can control to meet their viewing habits. IPTV is a great technology for providing this control capability, because every viewer can have a customized stream from the provider.

Another big market driver is convergence. Unfortunately, the term *convergence* got rather a bad reputation during the "dot-com" bubble of the late 1990s. However, the concept is still with us, and it is a powerful force in the video delivery business. By *convergence*, we mean the use of a single network to deliver multiple services to consumers. The term *triple play* has come to mean the simultaneous offering of voice, video, and data services, all billed to the subscriber in a single, convenient monthly package. By offering converged triple-play services, many providers are convinced that they can increase customer retention and reduce the costs of their customer service operations.

As the pace of technical innovation has picked up, so has the need for service providers to add flexibility to their service offerings. From a purely economic standpoint, providers strongly prefer installing technologies that will still be usable in 10–20 years. (Without that kind of life cycle, it is hard to justify the significant up-front capital costs of the network while still being able to offer services at prices that customers will pay.) By making sure that their networks are flexible, service providers can adapt to changing market demands while minimizing the cost of adding these new services. IP networks have certainly proved to be one of the most flexible technologies ever created and should remain that way due to the relentless march of technology in the computer industry. IPTV takes full advantage of this flexibility, making it easy for service providers to achieve a low-cost, multipurpose service delivery network.

Faced with the foregoing market forces, many service providers have decided to take a hard look at using IPTV as their basic technology underlying a variety of other service offerings. Not all video providers will adopt IPTV technology, but many will give it serious consideration.

Video-on-Demand

Video-on-demand (VOD) has a great deal of appeal to many consumers. The luxury of being able to sit down in front of the television and select a program or a movie and begin watching immediately is very appealing, and millions of consumers have installed PVRs for exactly this purpose. In response to these customer trends, IPTV providers need to ensure that their systems have a means to support VOD as a current or future offering.

The basic concept of VOD is based on video programming that is stored and then delivered to a viewer when it is requested. This storage can take the form of a centralized server equipped to send programming simultaneously to hundreds of viewers, or it can take the form of more distributed storage throughout the network. At the limit, individual storage devices for each viewer can be located in individual STBs.

Various forms of VOD have been tried over the years, and most of them still exist in one form or another. Table 13-1 lists the most popular types of VOD services.

One of the big controversies surrounding PVR service is the role of advertising in recorded content. Advertisers have two main concerns:

- *Ad skipping*, where viewers fast-forward through ads. This capability is often listed as the motivation for many consumer PVR purchases.
- *Ad timeliness*, where viewers watch programs at times far removed from their original broadcast date. This is a big concern for advertisers who have their ad campaigns targeted for specific time windows, such as promotional ads for a movie being released to theaters the following day.

Service providers have a limited amount of control over content that has been recorded by viewers on their own devices for later playback. They have only a slight bit more control over PVRs embedded in an STB supplied by the service provider—at least they can ensure that the DRM function is working to protect any

TABLE 13-1

Types of Video-on-Demand Service

Type	Description
True video-on-demand (VOD)	This is the purest form of VOD, where each viewer receives an individual video stream over which he or she has complete control. Viewers are allowed to start, stop, pause, rewind, and fast-forward the content. Viewers typically pay a fee for each title viewed; the charges are either debited from a prepaid account or included on a monthly bill.
Near video-on-demand (NVOD)	Similar to true VOD, but without the individual video stream control capabilities. One common form of NVOD is sometimes called *staggercasting*, in which multiple copies of a program are played starting at five-minute intervals, thereby limiting any individual viewer to no more than a five-minute wait before his or her program begins to play.
Subscription video-on-demand (SVOD)	Same delivery technology and viewer control as VOD, but with a different payment system. In SVOD, subscribers pay a fixed monthly fee for unlimited access to a library of titles. In many systems, the library is updated monthly.
Free video-on-demand (FVOD)	A variation on VOD where payment is eliminated. In most systems, this content is restricted to long-form advertisements, how-to guides and other low-cost content.
Everything on demand (EOD)	For some technology visionaries, this is the ultimate form of video delivery system, where all programming is available to all viewers at all times.
Personal video recorders (PVRs)	These devices take incoming video programming, compress it, and record it to a hard disk that is typically located either in an STB or a stand-alone device. Viewers then control the PVR to play back content, including pause, fast-forward, and rewind capabilities. With this capability, also called *timeshifting*, viewers normally program the PVRs to record specific programs at specific times. One of the pioneers of this technology is a company called TiVo.
Network personal video recorders (NPVRs)	Offers functionality similar to PVRs, but recording is performed inside the service provider's network rather than in the viewer's location. Some content owners contend that this technology is so similar in capability to true VOD that it needs to be licensed as such.
Pay per view (PPV)	This precursor technology to VOD is used primarily to deliver live paid programming, such as concerts and sporting events.

copyrighted content while it is on disk. Providers actually have the potential to influence viewers who use a networked PVR, where the video recordings are actually stored on the service providers' own video servers.

Network PVRs have exciting potential to make advertisers much happier than other PVR technologies. Why? Well, consider what happens in a normal PVR scenario with an advertisement. The machine faithfully records the commercials along with the program content and gives the user the ability to fast-forward through any parts of the program or advertisements at their whim. For example, say the viewer recorded a program on December 20 and decides to watch the program on December 29. As you might imagine, the program contained a number of ads that pertained to special last-minute shopping opportunities for Christmas. Unfortunately, when the viewer watches the program, the sales are over and the ads are completely worthless to both the viewer and the advertiser. Now consider the same scenario with a networked PVR and some advanced technology in the server. With this technology, the service provider is able to replace the commercials in the original program with ones that are timely and relevant whenever the viewer watches the content. In our example, the ads might be for something great to do on New Year's Eve, which the viewer might actually be willing to watch and for which an advertiser might be willing to pay.

All that's needed to make this a reality is some pretty serious software inside the VOD server and some kind of legal framework to govern the "bumping" of one commercial by another. The industry isn't quite there yet, but this technology is certain to be available in the not-too-distant future.

Interactivity

Interactivity is like beauty—very much in the eye of the beholder. Because of the many different meanings that can be assigned to this word, let's examine three different ways in which viewers can interact with their televisions. We'll begin with basic interactive functions, then look at "VCR-like" controls, and end with content-oriented interactivity. Each of these terms will be defined in this section.

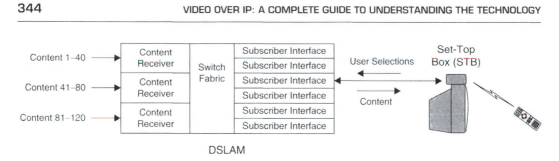

FIGURE 13-2   Example of a DSL Video Delivery System

The most basic way that viewers interact with a television (*basic interactivity*) is to turn it on and off and to select a programming channel to view. In a typical broadcast, DTH satellite, or CATV system, this is a very simple function to implement and can be completely controlled by equipment in the viewer's location, such as a TV tuner or a set-top box. With the current generation of video over DSL, there is usually only enough network bandwidth to deliver one video signal per television. This forces the channel-switching function to move out of the viewer's location and into the provider's facility. The equipment required to implement this for a DSL system is a bit more complex than for a CATV system, as shown in Figure 13-2.

In this example, the viewer interacts with his or her digital STB. Whenever he or she wants to select a new channel, the viewer presses the appropriate command on his or her remote control. The STB takes this command and relays it to the digital subscriber line access multiplexer (DSLAM). As soon as the DSLAM receives the command, it locates the new content and begins sending it to the viewer. This is a relatively simple process for broadcast channels, where the DSLAM is already receiving the content. The switch inside the DSLAM is reconfigured to stop sending one video channel to the viewer and to start sending another, typically by way of an IGMP "Leave" command followed by a "Join" command (see Chapter 9). Although this takes a little bit of time to accomplish, it does not take noticeably more time than switching channels on a digital satellite system.

The next-higher level of interactivity, *VCR-like*, occurs when viewers are given the same set of controls they would have if they were operating their own personal video cassette recorder—that is, start, stop, pause, rewind, and fast-forward. Implementing these functions puts a much higher burden on the video delivery system, because each viewer needs to be supplied with a video stream that is unique to him or her and completely under his or her control. There are a number of ways to achieve this functionality, as we discussed in the previous section, on VOD. One thing that must be recognized is that the amount of bandwidth needed to provide VOD increases as the number of viewers increases. That is, as more subscribers are added to a DSLAM, chances are more video bandwidth will be needed to feed the DSLAM.

Content-oriented interactivity occurs when users are given the ability to respond directly to the content itself. One example of this would be responding to an advertisement by requesting more information or possibly even placing an order for a product directly through a web interface on the television (a dream of many infomercial vendors). Another example would be influencing the outcome of a video program, such as voting for the winner of a talent contest during a live broadcast and then seeing the results of the voting during the broadcast. Note that for live content, the servers used for VOD do not come into play, because the content must be distributed from the source directly to viewers without being stored on servers. Instead, a mechanism must be provided to transmit the viewers' commands or choices back to the origin of the broadcast. In the case of prerecorded content with different program branches selected by the viewer (similar to DVDs with alternate endings), the VOD server can simply treat each branch of the content as a separate piece of content that can be selected by the viewer, and the interactivity flows would terminate at the server.

The impact of these different levels of interactivity is presented in Figure 13-3, which shows the data flows that occur in an IP-video-over-DSL system under each of the preceding scenarios. For basic interactivity, the data flow starts at the user's remote control, passes through the set-top box, and then moves to the DSLAM, where it terminates. For VCR-like user control, the data starts out the same way but ends up passing through the DSLAM to video servers located further upstream. With content interaction, the viewer responses are sent even further upstream, to the content provider. It is possible that all these different data flows will need to be accommodated in a single video delivery system, because individual subscribers may choose different levels of interactivity.

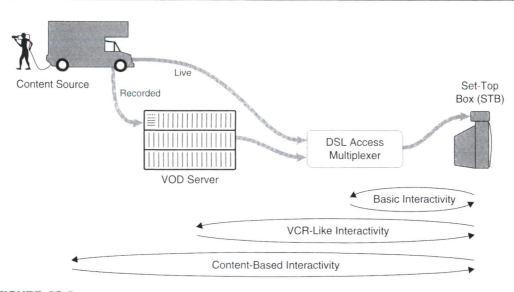

FIGURE 13-3 Interactivity Data Flows

Operations Support Systems

Profitable delivery of video services to the home requires much more than a high-reliability hardware platform. A great deal of software is also required for managing a huge array of tasks, from informing customers about the programming available on the different broadcast channels to capturing the data needed to bill subscribers for the services they have purchased. Collectively, these software systems are known as *Operations Support Systems (OSS)*, and they can take many forms. Table 13-2 lists many of the key functions provided by IPTV OSS systems.

OSS systems can be a major portion of the investment for an IPTV service provider, in terms of both time and money. Because of the wide variety of functions that can be provided, it is likely that software will need to be purchased from multiple vendors to implement the full range of functions selected by the provider. Integrating these systems can take months, and much of this work needs to be completed before large numbers of subscribers can be serviced. Furthermore, these expenses are essentially fixed costs whether the service attracts 1000 or 100,000 subscribers. As such, the costs of installing OSS systems need to be carefully considered in a service provider's business plan,

TABLE 13-2

Key OSS Functions for IPTV Systems

- An *electronic program guide* gives viewers the programming schedule for each broadcast channel and available VOD titles. This guide can be either a simple broadcast channel that scrolls through all the program choices or an interactive program guide that allows the user to navigate through listings, possibly to look at programming scheduled in the future. Many IPTV providers use outside companies (such as *TV Guide* in the United States) to supply program guide data.
- An *order entry* system is required when customers are permitted to purchase content through the IPTV system. This system needs to be able to verify that the customer's account information is valid and that the order can be filled as requested. This system needs to connect to the subscriber billing system and may also need to connect to external services for credit card validation, etc. A secure (encrypted) link is required to customer homes when personal data is being collected.
- *Online content access* (e-mail, web surfing) is provided by some IPTV systems, allowing viewers to use their television sets for functions that might otherwise require a PC.
- A *subscriber management and billing system* maintains crucial data about each subscriber, including contact and billing details, account status, and equipment identifiers. Many of the other OSS components will refer to this data to obtain information needed to authorize new services, deliver video streams, and so on. Customer service personnel will likely also be heavy users of this system because they support subscribers who move or upgrade or downgrade their services; add or remove televisions; and require repair services.

recognizing that in the early stages of deployment, these costs can exceed the costs of the system hardware for low subscriber counts. Also, the ongoing costs of maintaining the database should not be overlooked when developing a business model for an IPTV system.

IPTV DELIVERY NETWORKS

A wide variety of networks are used in delivering IPTV. There are the basic delivery mechanisms, such as DSL, passive optical networks (PONs), and traditional cable TV lines. In addition, traditional high-speed data networks connecting offices and homes can be used for applications with widely dispersed viewers. We'll take a closer look at all of these network technologies in the following sections.

Digital Subscriber Line (DSL)

Current-generation DSL technologies, such as asymmetric digital subscriber line (ADSL), provide relatively limited amounts of

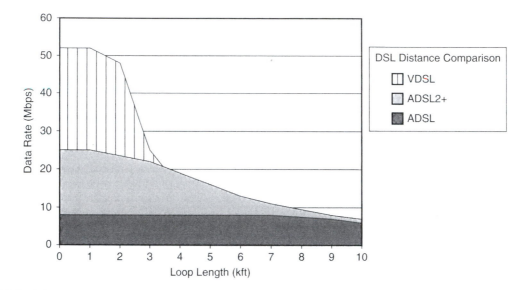

FIGURE 13-4 DSL Technology Bandwidth Comparison

bandwidth from the service provider to the consumer and even more restricted links from the consumer back to the provider. As Figure 13-4 shows, data rates of all DSL technologies decrease with increasing circuit lengths. Newer technologies, such as ADSL2 and ADSL2+, are being used for most new installations, because they offer more bandwidth in the forward path.

VDSL (very high-speed digital subscriber line) technology supports significantly more bandwidth on each subscriber line. Accordingly, more video channels can be transmitted to each VDSL subscriber, with three or four simultaneous videos possible. A few high-definition video signals could also be transmitted. One drawback to VDSL is that the range of operational distances is less than that for ADSL, so subscribers need to be closer to the service provider facilities. Also note that the speed of DSL services varies with distance, so good planning for varying data rates is essential.

H.264 technology has become critical for delivering HD IPTV services, because signal compression into the range of 4–10 Mbps is required for most DSL technologies. Good quality MPEG-2 compression usually doesn't get below 12–15 Mbps, which exceeds the bandwidth of many DSL circuits. By using bit rates near the lower end of H.264's range, it becomes possible to have more than one HD feed into each home, which could be used to support two or more HD STBs simultaneously.

Passive Optical Networks (PONs)

Although DSL-based IPTV systems represent the majority of the new circuits being installed today in North America and elsewhere, IPTV can also be implemented over PON systems. Since we talked about PON technology in Chapter 1, we won't repeat that information here.

IPTV technology can be used to distribute one or more video signals to a home via the data portion of a PON. When used in this manner, the IPTV system will look very much like the IPTV system we discussed for DSL: Individual channels will be requested by the viewer at each STB, and the service provider's IP network will deliver the requested video channels. This system merely replaces the DSL link with a PON data link.

Another alternative is a hybrid system. In this system, broadcast channels are delivered by one wavelength of light in the PON system, and the VOD and other user-specific video channels are delivered via the data transport paths. This scheme requires an STB that can accept both broadband video inputs and IPTV inputs. One advantage of this type of a hybrid system is that the IPTV equipment at the central location could be scaled back in capacity, since typically only 5 percent of viewers watch user-specific services at any given time, although this proportion might increase with greater availability of subscription VOD.

IPTV Over Cable

Traditional cable television (CATV) networks have excelled in the delivery of hundreds of channels of video content simultaneously to thousands of users. Each user can select any one of the broadcast channels available, simply by tuning a television or STB to the correct channel. These systems are easy to scale; adding new customers simply requires splitting and amplifying the signal to reach more households. In the past, interactivity has been extremely limited or not available at all, since all the content was sent in one direction only—to the viewer.

Increasingly, CATV providers have begun to look at how to provide more advanced video delivery systems and ones that allow them to offer triple-play video, voice, and data services. IP technology is a natural platform for converging these different services. Some CATV providers are considering using IPTV over a standard CATV plant.

To make this operate, it is necessary to transmit IP data packets over the cable network. To do this, special digital modulation schemes with acronyms like QAM (quadrature amplitude modulation), OFDM (orthogonal frequency-division modulation), and VSB (vestigial sideband) are used. These technologies give the CATV significant data-handling capacity—on the order of 35–40 Mbps in place of every 6-MHz analog video channel. This is quite attractive; if an average SD digital video stream operates at 2.5 Mbps (including overhead), the system can carry 15 digital video channels (for a total of 37.5 Mbps) in place of a single analog video channel. Since CATV systems typically provide in excess of 100 analog video channels, use of digital technology would permit 1500 digital video channels to be transmitted. If IPTV were being used for each of those channels, then 1500 simultaneous viewers could be supported. Since not all televisions are likely to be on simultaneously, this would be enough capacity to serve well in excess of 1000 homes, even if each home had more than one television.

Shared Data Networks

In many countries (for example, Japan, France, and Korea), high-speed data networks are already in place to serve individual subscribers. Also, many businesses have high-performance networks installed to many desktops. In this situation, it is a relatively straightforward process to overlay IPTV on an existing network that is shared with other data.

Adequate bandwidth is a key requirement for any type of video delivery system. For an IPTV system to work properly, each segment of the network must have enough capacity to handle the total bandwidth of all the simultaneous video streams passing over that segment. Multicasting (as discussed in Chapter 9) is one way to reduce the amount of bandwidth needed. In this case, the service provider's (or the corporation's) networking equipment fills the role of the DSLAM for performing the multicast "Join" and "Leave" commands required for channel changing. For VOD and VCR-like interactivity, the network must have enough bandwidth to handle the combined load of the individual streams.

Overall, it is quite feasible to implement IPTV services on a variety of different shared networks. A number of active implementations are in service today. The key to a successful IPTV deployment is ensuring that adequate capacity is available to service the peak number of simultaneous viewers, in terms of both video server capability and network capacity.

TECHNOLOGIES FOR IPTV

Various technologies are required to implement a practical IPTV system. Many are common to other video-over-IP technologies discussed elsewhere in this book; however, several are used primarily for IPTV applications. In the following sections we'll begin with a description of the systems used to prepare incoming content for IPTV distribution. We'll follow this with a deeper look at video servers. We'll conclude with a look at Multimedia Home Platform (MHP) and OpenCable Application Platform (OCAP), which are key technologies that support subscriber interactivity and the OSS functions required by service providers.

Content Processing

Content-processing systems accept real-time video signals from a wide variety of sources and shape them into a consistent format so that the customer STBs can decode the signals and display them on the viewers' televisions. This process involves several functions, as described in Table 13-3.

TABLE 13-3

Content Processor Functions

- *Compression*: For analog video sources, digital compression is performed on each video signal before it can be transmitted on an IPTV system. Items such as peak video data rate and packet length are made consistent between all of the different video sources to simplify the job of the transport and multiplexing functions.
- *Transcoding*: For video sources already in a digital format, it is sometimes necessary to convert the MPEG profile or level of the incoming stream to one that is compatible with the STBs. For HD content, it is standard procedure to change MPEG-2 sources into H.264 to achieve lower bandwidths for DSL networks.
- *Transrating*: Essentially, transrating is the process of changing the bit rate of an incoming digital video stream. For example, an SD feed at 4.5 Mbps may need to be reduced to 2.5 Mbps for use in the IPTV system.
- *Program identification*: Each video stream needs to be uniquely labeled within the IPTV system so that multiplexing devices and user STBs can locate the correct streams. Each audio or video program within each MPEG transport stream (using the PID mechanism discussed in Chapter 6) must be processed to ensure that there are no conflicting PID numbers. If there are duplicates, then one of the streams must be renumbered to a different PID, and the associated PMTs must be updated.

Content processing can be performed on either a live stream or content that is to be stored inside a video server for later playback. When content processing is done on a live stream already in a digital format, the process is called *digital turnaround*. When this process is performed on content that is to be stored on a server before it is delivered to viewers, it is called *ingest*. This process also needs to capture the rules for using the content, such as limits to viewing duration and permissions for downloading. Real-time ingest is used, for example, to take a copy of a live video signal and store it for later viewing by subscribers. Off-line ingest is used for content that is delivered in tape, disk, or file form, such as Hollywood movies.

Video-on-Demand and Video Servers

Let's look at the architecture of a typical VOD system that uses video-over-IP technology, as shown in Figure 13-5. There are four main components to a VOD system. First, the content must be prepared for storage and delivery by compressing it and (usually) encrypting it on a content-preparation station. A VOD server

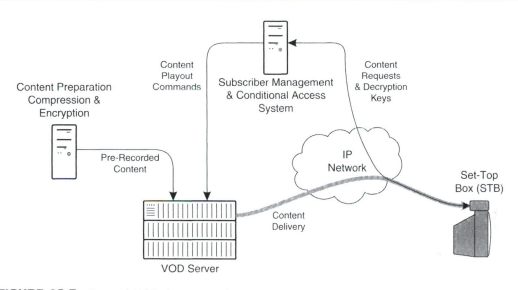

FIGURE 13-5 Typical VOD System Architecture

stores the content and creates the streams that are sent to viewers. Each viewer has an STB (or properly equipped PC) that receives the content, decrypts it, and generates a signal to feed the viewer's display. The STB also provides a means for viewers to order VOD services from the fourth and final element of the system shown: the subscriber management and conditional access system. This subsystem takes commands from viewers, sends appropriate commands to the VOD server, and delivers decryption keys to the STBs.

Video servers are essential to any VOD system, because they create the actual video streams that are sent out to each viewer. These servers can range in size from very large to fairly small, and they can be used for a variety of applications. In this section, we'll look at some of the different aspects of servers and how they are used for delivering content.

The amount of storage in a server can be large or small, and the number of streams supported can be large or small. These are not correlated; it is perfectly sensible to have a server with lots of storage and little streaming capacity if it is being used to hold video content that is only rarely viewed. Conversely, it is also sensible to have a server with relatively little storage (say, 50–100 hours of video content) but very high stream capacity if it is being used to serve first-run Hollywood movies to many viewers simultaneously.

Many varieties of video servers are available. When purchasing a server, it is important to match the capabilities of the server to the task that needs to be performed. Video servers can be broken roughly into three categories:

- Production servers are used in the video production business, such as television networks and postproduction houses. For these customers, a video server must handle a great deal of content, in a variety of formats, and rapidly deliver files containing the content to user workstations when it is needed. These servers typically do very little, if any, streaming. Instead, the focus on these devices is large capacity and good support for content searching, including tools that support the use of meta-data and that can track multiple versions of files as content moves through the production process.
- Personal and corporate servers are used in environments where a relatively few streams need to be delivered simultaneously and the total amount of content is relatively low, such as a training department of a medium-sized corporation with a few dozen titles and less than 5–10 simultaneous viewers. This class of server can often be built with off-the-shelf components on a PC chassis with specialized software.
- Service providers need specially designed servers capable of storing possibly thousands of hours of content and delivering video streams to hundreds or thousands of simultaneous viewers. The capacity of these systems is truly staggering; in order to supply 1000 simultaneous users each with a 2.5-Mbps stream, the server needs to be able to pump out 2.5 gigabits of data every second. These units typically spread content across a large number of disk drives and use multiple processors in parallel with high-speed backplanes to format streams and deliver the content.

One important constraint on a streaming video server is that end-user devices (STBs) have a precisely defined amount of buffer available. If too much data is sent (causing a buffer overflow) or too little

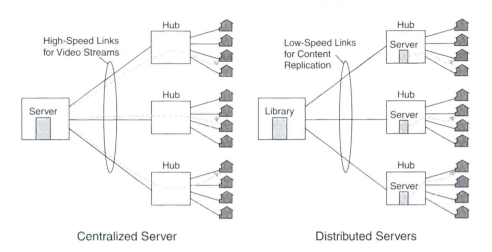

Centralized Server   Distributed Servers

FIGURE 13-6 Centralized vs. Decentralized Video Servers

(causing underflow), the video signal to the viewer will be inter-rupted. To prevent this, the video server must be carefully designed to create streams that are well behaved and won't violate the buffer constraints.

Service providers use two main philosophies for server distribution in their networks, as shown in Figure 13-6. The first is centralized, where large, high-capacity servers are installed in central locations and the streams for each viewer are delivered over high-speed com-munications links to each local service provider facility. The second is decentralized, where smaller servers are located at each facility and provide streams only to local viewers. A central library server downloads copies of content to the distributed servers whenever necessary.

On one hand, the decentralized concept makes sense because it helps to reduce the amount of bandwidth needed between loca-tions. On the other hand, the centralized concept makes sense because it reduces the number of servers that must be installed and reduces the costs of transporting and storing copies of the con-tent in each of the different locations. Overall, both centralized and decentralized systems are used in practice, depending on system architecture, capabilities, and user viewing habits that affect VOD traffic patterns.

MHP and OCAP

MHP, which stands for Multimedia Home Platform, and OCAP, which stands for OpenCable Application Platform, are both software interface standards that have been developed for STBs. The Digital Video Broadcasting (DVB) Project, based in Europe, developed MHP; and CableLabs, a joint research and development group formed by members of the CATV industry in the United States, developed OCAP. To a great extent, OCAP is based on MHP. Both are open standards, although some license fees may apply.

MHP functions as a standardized interface for "middleware." It provides a common interface between software applications and lower-level software, such as operating systems and device drivers. It does not provide user interfaces, but it does provide a platform on which user interfaces can be built. It is not an operating system; it defines a standard way that applications can access services provided by an operating system.

MHP greatly simplifies the task of application designers, by giving them a uniform platform to build on. Once an application has been designed and tested to run on MHP, it should be able to run on MHP implemented on any STB from different manufacturers. This capability helps provide a greater market for these applications than what would be available if the application was tied to the products of a single STB vendor.

MHP also simplifies the tasks of STB vendors, because it allows them to deploy applications written by third parties. This can help reduce the software development costs for a new STB and allow products to reach the market more quickly.

Table 13-4 defines some of the applications that MHP was designed to support. Table 13-5 defines some of the system resources inside an MHP device that applications can use to provide their intended functions.

Overall, MHP is designed to be a common interface for user interactivity applications and STBs, and gains in economy and efficiency should be possible if this standard is widely adopted. Perhaps the only drawback to this standard is the need for a fairly

TABLE 13-4

MHP Application Examples

- User interface for electronic program guide/interactive program guide
- Home shopping
- Access to broadcast information services—news, weather, financial information (super-teletext)
- Video games
- Applications synchronized to video content, such as sports scores, play-along games, audience voting/feedback
- Secure transactions—home banking

TABLE 13-5

Examples of Resources Available to MHP Applications

- MPEG stream control
- Text and graphics screen overlays
- Video and audio clip playback
- Program selector/tuner
- Communication protocols (e.g., TCP, UDP)
- Conditional access and encryption
- User mouse/keyboard/infrared remote control access
- Java virtual machine scripting
- Media storage and playback controls
- Internet access

powerful processor and a fair amount of memory to implement these functions in a low-cost STB. In the long run, anything like MHP or OCAP that can help drive software costs lower and provide truly open interfaces is good for service providers and, ultimately, consumers.

IPTV CASE STUDY

Kaplan Telephone is a local service provider located in south central Louisiana that has a long tradition of providing standard telephone service to a local area. Kaplan selected IPTV-over-DSL technology to offer video services to its customers, since it eliminates the need to build a second network alongside the existing twisted-pair network. DSL also helped reduce the up-front capital expense, because subscriber equipment in the home and the central office was installed only when subscribers actually purchased service. Also, because DSL can provide data services alongside traditional subscriber line voice services, Kaplan can provide a full "triple play" of consumer services.

For the digital video headend in 2004, Kaplan selected Tut Systems of Lake Oswego, Oregon,[1] who supplied the Astria® Content Processor. To understand the required functions, let's look at how the different incoming signals are processed.

- Satellite signals normally arrive in digital format, often scrambled or encrypted to prevent unauthorized reception.[2] The satellite receivers are responsible for processing the signals from the satellite dish; they can either provide streams in DVB-ASI format or convert one or more programs into baseband digital or analog video signals. Receiver processing includes any necessary descrambling or decrypting of the video signals.
- Local off-air video signals can arrive as either digital or analog signals. The demodulator is responsible for taking the broadcast video signal and converting it into either a baseband analog or digital video signal.
- In many cases, video service providers such as Kaplan are permitted to insert commercials into certain television channels at certain times. These local ad spots can come from a variety of sources: videotapes, DVDs, file transfers, etc. The spots are stored on a server, ready to play whenever they are required. The output of the server is fed into a monitoring switcher, where the commercials can be spliced into the video program streams as needed. Increasingly, digital ad splicing is being utilized that keeps both the primary stream and the ad content in the compressed domain.
- A legal requirement in the United States is the broadcast of Emergency Alert System (EAS) signals; similar requirements are present in many other countries. The EAS provides information generated by official government agencies to television

---

1. Tut Systems has since been acquired by Motorola.
2. Analog signals are still sometimes used on satellites, but they are becoming increasingly rare.

viewers regarding severe weather events and other emergency situations. Local television providers are required to broadcast the EAS signals on the television channels they are distributing. Many times, the EAS messages are text based and inserted into the bottom portion of the video screen. Suitable messages are created inside the character generator and fed into the MPEG encoders for the broadcast video channels.

Figure 13-7 shows a number of different functional blocks inside the Astria® Content Processor–based headend. On the input side, demodulators and receivers are used to convert incoming signals from their native format (broadcast television or satellite signals

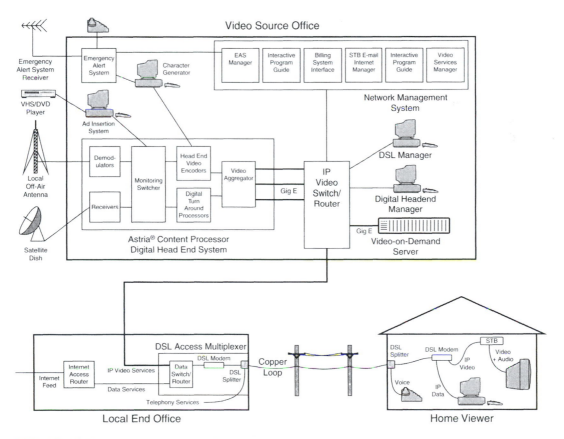

FIGURE 13-7 DSL Video System Example

with various modulation schemes) into video signals that can be processed. These signals are fed into a monitoring switcher that allows local advertisements to be switched or digitally spliced into selected video streams and provides a method for personnel to tap into video streams as needed to observe their performance. Some of the signals flowing out of the monitoring switcher are baseband video; these signals need to be digitized and compressed by the headend video encoders. Other signals that flow out of the monitoring switcher are in digital format, so these are processed to make them compatible with the DSL distribution network, by means of transrating or transcoding performed by digital turn-around processors. The final function is called *video aggregation*, in which many different video streams are multiplexed into large-capacity (gigabit Ethernet) outputs. These signals flow out to the various DSL access multiplexers around the Kaplan network by way of high-speed switches/routers and a gigabit Ethernet distribution network.

The main Operations Support System (OSS) for the Kaplan system covers a variety of functions, including the Emergency Alert System, the various video services offered to subscribers, the data interface to the subscriber billing system, the e-mail/Internet access system for subscriber set-top boxes, and the interactive program guide. A separate system is used to manage the DSL hardware and yet another to manage the Astria® Content Processor.

One point to keep in mind when reviewing the Kaplan system is the variety of different functions that must be accomplished, some of which are mandated by government regulations (such as the EAS) and others driven by economic realities (such as local ad insertion). For an IPTV system to work properly and create an operating profit for the system owner, these various functions need to be delivered efficiently and cost effectively by the system provider(s). System owners have to consider not only the costs of the individual components, but also the costs associated with integrating all the components to form a working combined network. This is in addition to the costs of purchasing the rights to content and the costs of preparing the content for distribution. Typically, the costs of acquiring and installing all of the necessary hardware and software components can be substantial; these costs need to be amortized over a number of years with a substantial number of paying subscribers before economic breakeven can be reached. Modeling these cash flows can be tricky; however, it is an essential part of IPTV system planning.

REVIEW AND CHECKLIST UPDATE

In this chapter, we covered IPTV services to the home. We began by looking at some of the market forces that are making a business out of this technology. We discussed video-on-demand (VOD) and some if its various flavors. Then we examined the functions of the Operations Support Systems (OSS) that are crucial to large-scale deployment of any kind of video to the home system. A few applications were described, and we explored some of the key technologies for IPTV, including DSL, PON, and CATV transport; content processors; video servers; and the innovative middleware technology known as MHP and OCAP. Finally, we investigated a typical IPTV installation.

Chapter 13 Checklist Update

❑ Develop a business plan prior to deploying IPTV to the home. Make sure to include capital expenditures (hardware and software), installation costs, programming costs, and ongoing maintenance and customer support costs.

❑ Determine the types of viewer interactivity that will be supported.

❑ Determine how live content will be delivered to viewers. If digital turnaround will be used, determine the format of the incoming digital signals.

❑ Consider how this might change in coming years as HD content becomes more widespread and as content owners change their requirements.

❑ If video-on-demand is to be used, consider the following issues:

    ❑ Select a method for delivering VOD services: NVOD, pay-per-view VOD, or subscription VOD. Make sure that systems are in place to support these functions if they are basic, VCR-like, or content interactive.

    ❑ For large installations, select a video server deployment strategy: centralized, distributed, or a blend of the two.

      ❑ Calculate the total number of hours of programming that will need to be stored on each server, and ensure that adequate storage capacity is purchased.

      ❑ Determine how many simultaneous streams each server must deliver, and ensure that each server purchased has enough stream processing capacity.

      ❑ Make sure an ingest system is available to get prerecorded content from a variety of sources onto the video servers.

❑ Select a supplier of electronic program guide data.

❑ For user software platforms (STBs and the systems that support them), consider using open-standard middleware, such as MHP or OCAP.

14

VIDEO FILE TRANSFER, PODCASTING, AND P2P

Video file transfer is the process of transporting video and other content as data files instead of as video streams. Podcasting is file transfer for a specific category of files—those that can be played on an iPod or similar media player. P2P is a technology that can be used for transporting all types of files, but it is most closely associated with both legal and unauthorized copies of video and audio content files. All of these technologies deserve a closer look.

File transfer is commonly used during the content production process and is similar to the process used daily by many IP network users when they send documents attached to e-mails. However, due to the extremely large size of many video content files, normal methods for file transfer (such as e-mail) won't work. In this chapter, we will discuss the specialized techniques that have been developed to transport large video files over IP networks.

OVERVIEW

Some of the largest data files sent over IP networks today are those that contain video content. This is no accident; the sheer amount of data needed to faithfully reproduce a high-quality video image is much greater than the amount of data in voice conversations or even in graphic-intensive web pages. Even when video content is highly compressed, the amount of data needed to represent an image on the viewer's display that changes 25 or 30 times each second occupies megabytes of disk space for every minute of video.

Video content files, even for routine video production, can be very large indeed.[1] A simple uncompressed standard-definition video file can occupy 2 gigabytes of disk space for every minute of footage. When high-definition video is being used, uncompressed video occupies over 11 gigabytes of storage for each minute. Data files for movie production are even larger; 40 or 50 gigabytes of data per minute of video are not unheard of, because movies are typically processed at resolutions much higher than HD television.

File sizes for consumer video viewing are also enormous. Standard-definition DVDs carrying MPEG-2 movies easily reach 7 gigabytes. 1080p HD movies encoded with H.264 that are available for downloading can easily occupy a megabyte per second, or 7.2 gigabytes for two hours. Even a 4-minute 40-second, low-resolution (320 × 240) animated podcast video consumes 24.2 megabytes.

These large file sizes pose a problem for standard IP file transfer mechanisms. One data protocol commonly used on IP networks (TCP) sends a few blocks of data and then waits for an acknowledgment before sending more data. In situations with long network delays or with very large files, the total amount of waiting time can add up quickly. This has the effect of exponentially increasing the amount of time it takes to transfer large files. For some applications on certain types of networks, transfer times can be measured in terms of hours, if not days.

---

1. Note that in this chapter we will often discuss sizes of files and data transfer rates in terms of bytes, not bits. This is deliberate because data files are always measured in units of bytes.

There are two basic choices for overcoming these problems: Change one or both devices at the ends of the network or change the network itself. One popular end-device technique involves temporarily storing (or *caching*) the data inside a special device that then sends the data file out over a network connection with limited bandwidth. A popular network-based technique involves changing the protocols normally used to transmit data files so that they will operate more efficiently over networks with long delays. Both of these techniques can be used together, and both will be described later in this chapter.

FILE TRANSFER APPLICATIONS

In addition to the well-known consumer applications, video files are used throughout the video production and distribution industry. Because of the widespread use of digital video production and editing equipment, virtually all video today spends at least part of its life as a file of one type or another. Table 14-1 lists some of the common uses of video files.

Now let's look at two of these applications in more detail.

Postproduction

For most of this book, we have been talking about delivering video in finished form: an edited product complete with a sound track, special effects, titles, and closing credits. To produce this final product, many hours typically go into scripting, filming, editing, and generating the final content. This process can be thought of in terms of a chain, where each link is one task that needs to be completed to convert the raw video content into a finished product.

For years, there was only one way to move content through the production chain: videotape transfers. After each step, a videotape was created that would be passed along to the next step. If different steps of production were done in different facilities, then videotapes had to be physically transported from one location to another, typically by use of a courier service.

TABLE 14-1

Video File Transfer Applications

- *Video capture*: When raw video from a camera or tape is transferred into a computer file that an editing or production system can manipulate, the process is called *video capture*. Capture can be done directly from digital sources, such as digital video cameras or digital tapes. When analog video sources are used, the video signal must also be digitized during the capture process.
- *Video server loading*: Video-on-demand and streaming servers need to be loaded with content before delivering it to viewers. Using IP networks to download content files to these devices is extremely popular, because it eliminates the handling of physical media (tapes, discs) and because updates can be pushed rapidly from a central server.
- *DVD authoring*: As the business of producing and selling video content on DVDs and Blu-ray discs has grown, a number of companies have gone into businesses that specialize in specific aspects of DVD production. Some companies convert film into digital formats, others compress and format the content to create the master DVDs, and still others mass-produce finished DVDs for sale. Between steps in this process, large digital data files often need to be transferred between the different companies.
- *Film and video postproduction*: As in the DVD production chain, various specialist companies have become involved in the creation of video content for broadcast and other applications. It is not uncommon for digital video content to be moved from one location to another several times during the production for a single show.
- *Advertising*: Most television advertisements today are played out from files stored on specialized servers that can be located anywhere in the video distribution system. These servers regularly need to be updated with content from a number of different sources.
- *News*: Particularly in the audio realm, digital recorders and Internet file transfer have become the norm for reports from field correspondents. This trend is also taking hold in the video realm, although the larger video file sizes are a challenge for many network connections in the field.
- *Consumer video*: Many times, delivering video files instead of streams is more practical for consumers. For example, if the video is to be viewed on a portable player or on a device not connected to the Internet, a downloaded file is the only choice. Any content that consumers buy for permanent ownership, such as a music video they purchase, is normally provided in file form. Also, consumers with low-speed connections to the Internet or those who wish to view high-quality HD content will typically have to download video files instead of viewing a live stream.

As the technology of digital production has progressed, most of the production steps moved to high-performance workstations that run specialized video production software. Due to the costs of these workstations, of the software that runs on them, and of the talented person to operate them, production fees can easily run hundreds of dollars per hour on these machines. Because of these costs, the need to move video content rapidly and cost effectively from one production step to the next has never been greater.

Fortunately, high-speed LANs operating at 100 Mbps, or 1 Gbps, can be used to transfer even the largest files in a matter of seconds or at most a few minutes when the workstations are located inside a single facility. These local networks are relatively low cost: Workstations can be equipped with gigabit Ethernet LAN interface cards for less than $100 per workstation using today's technology.

When video content files need to be transferred between facilities, different economic trade-offs come into play. Because of the costs involved, networks between facilities are commonly shared for multiple applications, including voice traffic, routine data traffic (e-mail, etc.), and video file transfer. This can mean that all of the bandwidth on the link is not available for video file transfer. Also, the bandwidth on these links is usually much less than the bandwidth available on a LAN. Hence, for successful file transport throughout the content production chain, suitable technologies need to be employed.

Advertising

Advertising is a major source of funding for many different types of programming, from sports to news to entertainment. Advertisers can choose to have individual 30- or 60-second advertising *spots* broadcast on specific programs on specific channels at specific times to specific audiences. Spots can be aired nationwide or to very local viewing audiences, including targeted neighborhoods in a city.

File transfer can play a major role in both the creation and delivery of advertising spots. During the creation process, approval copies of spots can be delivered to agency clients in order to cut down or eliminate the need to send videotapes out for review.

Finished ads must be delivered to the video file servers that are used to play advertising spots during a broadcast. These servers can be located at a television network's main facility for ads that will play to all of the network's viewers, or servers can be located at different broadcast stations or cable television headends to play ads that will be seen only in a specific region. File transfer over an IP network is often used to deliver the appropriate spots to each of these servers in advance of the time they will be broadcast. Sometimes, the transfer is done in parallel, where each file is delivered to many servers simultaneously using a multicast network (such as a satellite). Other times, the transfer is done individually for each server, using the technologies we will be discussing in the following section.

FILE TRANSFER TECHNOLOGY

First, a word of caution about file transfer: Not all video files are interchangeable. In fact, many suppliers of editing workstations and software have developed their own proprietary file formats. This makes file transfers between dissimilar machines difficult at best. A variety of converters (sometimes called *file filters*) are available. An industry group has also produced Media eXchange Format (MXF) standards that define a common file format to be used in transfers from one machine to another.

A popular application for transferring files is the File Transfer Protocol (FTP). FTP usually uses the TCP protocol for actual data transport; we will discuss TCP in more detail later in this section. One drawback to FTP is its lack of security: Passwords and file contents are not encrypted. Several new standards (several of which are confusingly called SFTP) and a flock of vendors have introduced products to address the shortcomings of FTP.

File Caching

File caching operates by providing a local storage location that can be used to store (i.e., *cache*, pronounced "cash") files temporarily before they are sent out over the network. The primary benefit of a cache is freeing up the workstations in a location, allowing them to perform other tasks while a lengthy file transfer takes place over a wide area network. Some caching devices also perform file compression and other tasks before sending files.

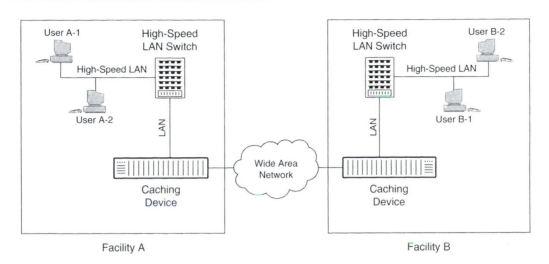

FIGURE 14-1 File Caching for Wide-Area File Transfer

Figure 14-1 shows a basic caching system in operation. In this example, User A-1 needs to send a file to User B-1 over the wide area network. First the file is copied from User A-1's workstation over the high-speed LAN to the cache device in Facility A. Then the cache device A sends the file to cache device B, with the transfer speed limited by the bandwidth available in the WAN between A and B. After the WAN transfer into B is complete, the file can be sent from cache device B to User B-1's workstation over the high-speed LAN inside Facility B.

Note that most WAN technologies are bidirectional, so it is perfectly logical for file transfers to take place in the opposite direction at the same time, say, from User B-2 to User A-2.

Consider the system and file management transactions that need to take place during this transfer. First device A-1 must check that there is enough storage available for the entire file inside cache A. Second, User A-1 needs to provide cache A with one or more ultimate destinations of the file so that it can be forwarded properly over the WAN. Third, cache B needs to have a mechanism to inform User B-1 that a file has arrived so that it can be transferred to the user's workstation. Finally, if WAN encryption is used, the keys must be distributed to both the sending and the receiving caches.

Issues with TCP

TCP uses *handshaking* to allow the two ends of a data link to communicate the success or failure of packet transfers. Handshaking means that the sender expects the receiver to acknowledge the receipt of data periodically. The sender uses these responses to gauge how quickly to send more data. A good analogy of this is when one person gives another person some specific information during a telephone conversation, such as a credit card number. Typically, one person will begin by saying the first three or four digits of the number and then pausing until the listener makes a suitable response such as "Mm-hmm." After hearing this response, the speaker says the next part of the number, pausing for another acknowledgment, and continuing this process until the entire number is communicated. TCP handshaking is very similar to this process.

In TCP, each byte of data is assigned a sequence number as it gets sent. In each transmitted packet, the sequence number of the first byte of data contained in that packet is included in the packet header. This supports several very useful functions of TCP:

- The receiver can sort out any packets of data that have been delivered in the wrong order by looking at the sequence numbers.
- The receiver can detect whether any packets are missing by looking for gaps in the packet sequence numbers.
- The receiver can indicate to the sender which data bytes have been received and the sequence number of the next data byte the receiver is ready to receive.

To accomplish this handshaking, each packet of data sent by the receiver back to the sender contains an acknowledgment sequence number. This number represents the sequence number of the next byte of data the receiver is ready to accept.

In the exchange shown in Figure 14-2, the sender begins by sending 1000 bytes of data, with a sequence number 1, to indicate that the first byte of data is contained in this packet. (In reality, the sequence number of the first byte is a pseudo-random number.) The receiver processes this data and replies to the sender with an acknowledgment that it is now ready for byte 1001. When the sender gets the

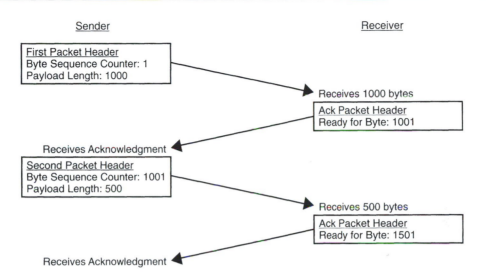

FIGURE 14-2   Acknowledgment Handshaking in TCP

acknowledgment, it sends the next packet of data using a sequence number of 1001. When the receiver gets the second packet, it sends an acknowledgment stating it is now ready to receive sequence number 1501, and the process continues.

In reality, the sender is allowed to send several packets of data in a row without receiving an acknowledgment, but the total amount of data sent can't exceed a limit set by the receiver when the TCP connection is established. If, for example, this limit (called the *acknowledgment window*) were set to 8000 bytes, the sender could transmit up to 8 packets that each contained 1000 bytes before it had to wait for an acknowledgment from the receiver.

Acknowledgment Delay

When there is a long delay between a sender and a receiver, it can have a big impact on the speed of data transfer. For example, consider a network round-trip delay of 200 milliseconds. Using an 8000-byte acknowledgment window, the sender can transmit only 8000 bytes of data at a time before having to wait for the first acknowledgment. Then the sender could transmit another 8000 bytes of data and wait another 200 milliseconds. In all, this process could be repeated up to five times in 1 second, allowing five batches of data to be sent, for a total throughput of 40,000 bytes per second. Contrast this with the situation if the round-trip delay were only 10 milliseconds; in this case 100 round trips per second would be possible, increasing the total throughput to 800 Kbytes/sec, an improvement by a factor of 20.

TCP performance also suffers as packet-loss rates increase. Throwing additional bandwidth at the problem has little or no impact on the overall throughput.

Most implementations of TCP use a technique called *additive increase/multiplicative decrease*, or AIMD. This technique controls the rate at which packets are sent. In essence, each time a group of packets is delivered successfully, the transmission rate is increased by a fixed step (additive increase). In contrast, each time a group of packets is not delivered successfully, the packet sending rate is decreased by a multiple, often by a factor of 2 (i.e., cut in half). For the small flows over low-speed data connections that were present when TCP was designed (i.e., text e-mails over 1200-baud dial-up circuits), these behaviors were reasonable and prudent. However, when trying to fill a 100-Mbps pipe with data, it can take awhile for the data rate to get up to the maximum, particularly on a circuit with a long RTT. Moreover, as soon as the maximum rate is reached and some packets are lost due to a buffer overflow, the transmit rate drops by half, and then the slow buildup begins once again. This process tends to make the overall data transmission rate very uneven and lowers overall bandwidth utilization.

Another issue with current TCP implementations is the fact that the AIMD algorithm constantly pushes network loads into an overflow condition. This occurs because the only feedback the sender gets from the receiver is whether or not packets are lost along the way. If packets aren't lost, then the assumption is that the sending rate can be increased; if packets are lost, then the sending rate needs to be decreased. In this situation, senders are constantly ramping up data rates to the point when buffer overflow occurs.

These issues can have a big impact on the transport of large media files. Experiments have shown that the total throughput of a link has little or nothing to do with the total speed of the link and everything to do with the performance of FTP. For example, information proved by Aspera shows a Los Angeles–to–New York cross-country link with 90 msec of RTT and a packet loss ratio of 1 percent operating at a maximum throughput of 1.4 Mbps, regardless of the actual bandwidth capacity of the link. If a user wanted to send a 1-gigabyte file over this link, it would take 1 hour and 42 minutes, regardless of whether there was a 10-Mbps or a gigabit circuit.[2]

A variety of solutions have been built to solve the problems with TCP for large video files. Vendors are able to supply software to modify the way that TCP works in end devices. Hardware solutions also exist, some of which don't require any changes to the end devices. These solutions (sometimes called *WAN accelerators*) are definitely worth investigating for any media company that needs to send video files over a WAN.

Jumbo Frames

One way to make file transfer more efficient is to use jumbo frames, which are essentially large packets. Standard Ethernet frames (packets) are limited to 1500 bytes in length; jumbo frames expand that limit to 9000+ bytes. This improves file transfer efficiency in two ways:

- Large packets mean a higher percentage of each packet is data, since the amount of header data is fixed, regardless of the packet length.
- In protocols like TCP, the number of acknowledgments that need to be sent is reduced. This allows the acknowledgment window in the transmitter to be expanded, thereby improving end-to-end performance on networks with long round-trip delays.

Unfortunately, most networks, particularly wide area networks, do not support jumbo frames. For private or local area networks, this technology can be useful for transferring files with less IP and Ethernet overhead. Some high-end video-editing systems routinely use jumbo frames for content transport.

---

2.   "Alternatives to TCP." TV Technology, p. 28, January 9, 2008.

PODCASTING

Podcasting is a form of video file transfer in which a content file is stored permanently on the viewer's device (for example, an Apple iPod, the device from which podcasting got its name), where it can be played back at any time. XML tools are also available for syndicating podcasts, which allows automatic downloading of new content files as they are created. Most podcasts are audio only, but an increasing number are being distributed in video form.

Podcast files are distributed via the same process used in normal web surfing: HTTP and TCP. Once they are delivered, these files can be played on a PC or a portable device, copied to other media (such as recordable CDs or flash drives), and transferred to other devices. Occasionally, DRM technology (such as Apple's Fair Play) is used to control the redistribution of podcasts, but this is not a common practice.

One special feature of podcasts is the use of RSS (Really Simple Syndication) for distributing content. This is an XML tool that identifies specific files or portions of web pages for attention by other programs called *aggregators* or *podcast receivers*. These programs run periodically on a user's PC to visit a list of websites and automatically download content for that user. Apple's iTunes is one popular program for colleting podcasts, and a number of other software packages are available on the web. These programs normally run in the background on a PC, and they pay periodic visits to websites to which the user has subscribed. The podcast collection process has also been automated with some of the newer web browsers that are on the market.

Figure 14-3 shows the typical content flow for a podcast file. The first three steps are similar to the ones used for preparing and publishing video content for the web. If an audio file is being prepared, then MP3 files are commonly used or MPEG-4 AAC. For video, H.264 is commonly used, with a 320 × 240 image size if the video is to be played back on an iPod. The fourth step is where the content owner's web page is modified to list the new content as being available via RSS. The fifth step occurs when the user decides to subscribe to the RSS feed of a particular website; this normally happens before the new content is posted so that when the podcast receiver runs on each user's PC it will find the new content and download it, as

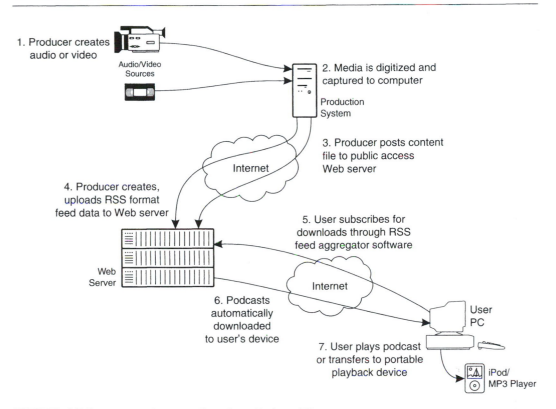

1. Producer creates audio or video

Audio/Video Sources

2. Media is digitized and captured to computer

Production System

3. Producer posts content file to public access Web server

Internet

4. Producer creates, uploads RSS format feed data to Web server

5. User subscribes for downloads through RSS feed aggregator software

Web Server

Internet

6. Podcasts automatically downloaded to user's device

User PC

7. User plays podcast or transfers to portable playback device

iPod/ MP3 Player

FIGURE 14-3 Typical Content Flow for a Podcast File

shown in the sixth step. In the seventh step, the user can decide to play the podcast on her or his own PC, or the user can download the content to a portable player for later listening or viewing.

P2P FILE SHARING

Peer-to-peer (P2P) file sharing is an exciting technology for delivering big content files to users distributed around a network. In contrast to traditional file servers, where large amounts of bandwidth are consumed to send out files from a central location, each P2P client (i.e., a user's PC with client software running) obtains files from other clients who already have copies of the files. This essentially eliminates the need for central file servers, all that is required is a way for clients to locate other clients who have the files they need and a method to download those files from the other clients.

Unfortunately, in the world of professional media, P2P has less than a perfect reputation. This is due to some of the applications that have been operated over P2P networks, including the original Napster, eDonkey, and Grokster, to name a few. Although these technologies had legitimate applications, many users employed these networks for sharing unauthorized copies of copyrighted material, particularly music ripped from CDs. As a result of some major court cases earlier this decade, the operators of these networks were found to be liable for damages, and all of the aforementioned networks have been shut down by lawsuits.

Recently, however, the technology has received somewhat of a reprieve, due to legitimate applications powered by applications such as BitTorrent. This particular technology has even been embraced by many of the large Hollywood studios for distributing their online video content. P2P's bad reputation is truly unfortunate, because the technology can be a highly efficient delivery system for large media files.

How P2P Works

The concept of P2P is quite simple, as shown in Figure 14-4. On the left side of the illustration, a traditional client-server architecture is

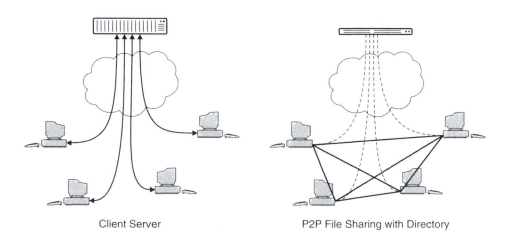

Client Server　　　　　　　　　　P2P File Sharing with Directory

FIGURE 14-4 Client Server versus P2P Network.

shown. In this setup, each client must contact the server for any and all of the files it requires, operating just like a standard PC browser connecting to a web server. For simple web pages stored in small files this is not a problem, since the chances are low that all of the clients will request a file at the same time. However, when clients request large media files that may each require multiple minutes to download, the chances of contention for the server resources are greatly increased. P2P was designed to address this problem.

On the right side of Figure 14-4, a P2P network is shown, with clients able to obtain the files they require from any other client that already has a copy of the file. This essentially eliminates the bottleneck of the server, since clients have a choice of where to obtain their files. If one source is busy or off-line, another source can be chosen. Also, the process for downloading the files in P2P can employ the same array of protocols used by client-server systems.

Finding Files

One of the big problems for any P2P network is enabling clients to locate the content they need. Since files can be located on any other client in the network, an efficient method of finding them is required for the system to perform well.

First-generation P2P networks, such as Napster, used a centralized file registry, which contained a set of servers with information about the locations of files on all of the clients that were actively online. When a client wanted to download a particular file, it would contact the central server, which would then give out a list of other clients that already had the file. The requesting client would select one of the listed clients and then attempt to make contact and download the file from that client. This scheme worked fairly well but had some drawbacks. First, a receiving client needed to maintain contact with the sending client for whatever time was required to download the file; if contact was broken, then the process would have to be repeated, possibly with another sending client. Second, the central server was a single point of vulnerability for the network; when legal challenges finally forced Napster's central server to be shut down, the network ceased to function.

Second-generation P2P networks have made a jump forward by eliminating the central server. Instead, each client is required to know the IP address of at least one other client. Whenever a user decides to look for a file, a request is issued from that user's client to any or all of the other clients it knows about. If one of those clients has the desired file, then the requesting client can download the file directly from that client. If not, then the clients forward the requests to other clients with which they are in contact, and the request propagates through the network. As soon as a source is found for the content, the requesting client can then begin a download. If multiple sources of the file are located, then the requesting client can choose one of the sources. The big benefit of eliminating the central server is the removal of a single point of vulnerability for the P2P system.

BitTorrent takes a different approach: The content files are broken up into smaller pieces before they are distributed. To find content, a user navigates with a standard web browser to find a website that describes a desired piece of content, which is represented by a "torrent" file. The user downloads this file, which is not the content; rather, it is meta-data about the pieces that make up the content file. The user's BitTorrent application then sends the ".torrent" file to a specified *tracker*, which is a form of server that tracks all of the clients that have received pieces of the file. The tracker responds to the requesting client with a list that gives a location for each piece of the file that is needed to make up the whole content file. The client is then able to download all of the content pieces from the listed locations, assemble them, and play the content for the user. These tracker systems could be seen as a single point of failure, but for content owners they provide a benefit: They keep track of which clients have which files.

ISP Headaches

All P2P networks can drive significant loads on Internet service provider (ISP) networks, because files that are transferred to a user's client have to come from somewhere. In other words, whenever a device is receiving data, another device on the network has to be sending that same data. (This wouldn't be true if the Internet were multicast enabled, but sadly it isn't.) Unfortunately for ISPs, both DSL and cable modem technologies are asymmetrical, with more bandwidth in the forward direction (to users) than in the reverse path (from users). Whenever a client is sourcing data, the reverse path from that client can be filled with traffic.

BitTorrent can also create significant bandwidth spikes on forward paths that connect to clients, because multiple clients can send data simultaneously to a single client. This helps speed downloads for that client and helps to distribute popular files rapidly throughout the network. Of course, when this happens, each source client's return path becomes saturated, and the forward path to the receiving client can also become swamped with data.

Overall, the reasons why content providers and users like P2P are pretty clear: faster downloads and lower bandwidth charges for the content providers' servers. It's also pretty clear why P2P is a headache for ISP's: heavy loads on the low bandwidth side of their user connections and traffic spikes in the forward path. Engineering a network to serve both standard client-server users as well as P2P users is a substantial engineering challenge indeed.

REVIEW AND CHECKLIST UPDATE

In this chapter, we covered IP file transfer technology, with a particular focus on the large files that are common in video applications. We began by looking at why video applications tend to generate large data files. We discussed applications for large file transfers, with a focus on postproduction and advertising as places where large file transfers occur frequently. We then discussed caching, which uses intermediate devices (called *caches*) to store video content temporarily while it is being sent over a long-distance IP network. We followed that with a discussion of some of the issues that occur when using TCP for file transfer. We concluded the chapter with a discussion of podcasting and P2P file sharing, which are ways to deliver large content files to consumers.

Chapter 14 Checklist Update

❏ If file transfer is to be used, determine the size range of the files, and estimate how often they need to be transferred.

❏ Make sure that the file formats are compatible between the source and destination machines, particularly if they use different editing software.

❏ Consider using caching when large files need to be sent over networks that have slow data transfer rates or long end-to-end delays.

❏ Consider using some form of WAN acceleration technique to improve the performance of standard TCP for large data files as long as the network has a reasonably low error rate.

❏ Consider using low-resolution video (with less data per video frame) in place of large video files whenever possible.

❏ Strongly consider using a secure file transfer protocol in place of standard FTP.

❏ If the application calls for delivering large content files to consumers, consider using RSS/podcasting and peer-to-peer distribution techniques.

15

INTERNET VIDEO

Internet video is a relatively new phenomenon in the world of video delivery. Just a few years ago, people who wanted to send video over an IP network had to build their own infrastructure, including video encoders, delivery systems, client playback hardware/software, and a management system to connect viewers with the content they desire. Plus, due to performance constraints, most delivery had to be done over private networks. Now, all or most of that groundwork has been done by a variety of online services and off-line utilities, so the costs of entering this market have dropped dramatically. In addition, millions of viewers have upgraded to broadband Internet connections and have become accustomed to searching for videos and playing them through web-browser plug-ins already downloaded and installed on their client devices.

YouTube is by far the most viewed site on the Internet for video content. While there is a significant amount of junk, there is also a surprising amount of high-quality content produced by talented individuals. In addition, there is an increasing amount of professionally produced content supported by paid sponsors. Some of these latter videos are hosted on YouTube but embedded in corporate web pages for viewing.

Many users will have encountered video streaming on sites other than YouTube while surfing the web, particularly if they sought out video content. Popular video sites include CNN.com for news stories; sonypictures.com, warnerbros.com, and Disney.com for trailers of upcoming movies; and mtv.com and music.yahoo.com for music videos. In addition, a number of sites offer continuous channels of television-quality programming over the Internet, including researchchannel.com (a lovely 1200-kbps signal) and Bloomberg television (at www.bloomberg.com).

In this chapter, we begin with a discussion of the key attributes of Internet video, including the basic system architecture. We'll then go into some of the unique applications of Internet video. This is followed by an overview of a typical system architecture and different platforms that can be used for Internet video services. We'll wrap up the chapter with a discussion about some specific technologies, including client software and embedding videos that are hosted by other websites.

KEY ATTRIBUTES OF INTERNET VIDEO

Viewers' experiences and expectations for Internet video are very different from those for most other forms of video entertainment, such as IPTV and broadcast television. Most viewers have much lower expectations for Internet video, particularly if they have ever tried to watch video over a dial-up connection. People seem willing to tolerate things they would never tolerate with broadcast television, such as seconds (or even tens of seconds) of blank screens before a video starts to play, low resolutions on many websites, issues with video and audio synchronization, and other technical drawbacks. Of course, technology marches on, and the Internet video viewer experience continues to improve.

Figure 15-1 shows a very simplified view of an Internet video network. This diagram is broken into two sections, labeled *production*

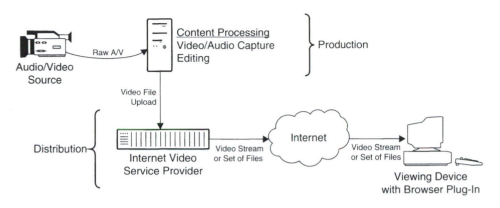

FIGURE 15-1 Typical Internet Video Network

and *distribution*. In production, the video content is captured from a source, digitized, edited, labeled, and bundled into a file that is placed on a server where it can be accessed. In distribution, a person uses an Internet-connected PC to search for content, connect to the server, acquire rights to view the content, and then either download a video file or request a video stream of the content for viewing on their PC using specialized multimedia viewing software.

A person using a PC or other device initiates each viewing session. First, the user must identify where the content is located on the Internet. For example, a user might have received an e-mail from a friend with a link to a website containing the video. When the user clicks on the link, the browser on the PC connects to the appropriate web server. Typically, the web server then displays a screen that gives some information about the video (such as a description and the clip's duration). The user then may be asked to click on a link embedded in that page, which begins the video playing process. One important step that happens at this time is an exchange of information between the server and the browser software on the PC that tells the browser to run a plug-in application called a *media player*. The media player is fed data that the browser has retrieved from the web, decodes the video, and converts it into an image that can be displayed. If the proper media player software isn't installed on the PC, the user is normally prompted to install it by downloading the software from a suitable source. Then, as the video file is delivered, the user can watch the content.

We first defined the key attributes of Internet video in Chapter 1: discrete content elements that are selected by users from millions of choices that are delivered via the Internet in a wide variety of formats for playback using PCs or other devices. This is in contrast to IPTV, which provides hundreds of continuous streams of professionally produced TV channels that are delivered over dedicated networks to televisions by means of a set-top box. Internet video should also not be confused with podcasting, where video content files are delivered to portable devices for later playback and user storage. Both IPTV and podcasting are covered in other chapters in this book. Let's discuss the attributes of Internet video in more detail.

Discrete Content Elements

Instead of continuous channels of highly produced programming, most Internet video content is available in the form of clips for viewers to watch at a convenient time. Many of the video files available for viewing or downloading are relatively short, five minutes or less. (YouTube imposes a limit of 10 minutes on most of the video clips that it hosts.) Certainly, longer-duration files are available, but they tend to be available on advertiser-supported or viewer-paid sites.

Of course, not all Internet video involves discrete content elements; some real-time streaming broadcasts are available. For example, NASA TV offers some live video content each day from the International Space Station as well as live coverage of major events such as shuttle launches and space walks. In between, educational, news, and other programming are provided. For-profit real-time Internet video channels are also becoming a reality, as the number of viewers with high-bandwidth Internet connections reaches a level that is attractive for subscription or advertising-based services.

Millions of Content Offerings

Any quick search of some of the more popular video websites will show that there are literally millions of different video files available for viewing, with thousands more being added each day. Locating a specific piece of content for viewing can be a challenge with Internet video. Many viewers find content by following links on web pages or in e-mails that direct them to video content sites. Others use the listings of popular titles on these websites. Still other viewers find videos to watch using general-purpose search engines (such as Google) or site-specific search engines. Unfortunately, there is no master program guide for the Internet—there's simply too much new content being added each day for this to be practical.

Multiple Content Formats

A wide variety of formats can be used for video files, and virtually all of them have found their way onto the Internet. There are many choices, including various camera formats (such as DV), MPEG family (1, 2, or 4), JPEG (basic or 2000), player-specific formats (Windows Media, QuickTime, Real Networks, etc.), and a variety of computer file formats (such as AVI). Consumers who view a significant amount of Internet video content often end up with a variety of different video players loaded onto their computers in order to handle the various video file formats.

For content providers, this variety can present a dilemma. If the provider chooses to support only a single video format, then any viewer who wishes to watch the content must already have the appropriate player software installed or find a way to get the proper player (most of which are distributed for free). If, on the other hand, the provider chooses to support multiple formats, then they assume the burden of producing and managing multiple versions of their content.

In addition to the choice of video compression technology, content providers must decide on the screen resolutions they will support. Low resolutions offer small file sizes that are easier to download over low-bandwidth network connections but also create small images for viewing. Higher resolutions offer increased picture quality but can require a long time to download or a high-bandwidth connection for live streaming. Of course, the choices may be limited, since some devices (such as Apple's iPod) and some video-hosting websites (such as YouTube) only support specific image resolutions.

Delivered Over the Public Internet

One big strength of Internet video is that it can be delivered to any viewer with a connection to the Internet. Of course, high-bandwidth connections are easier to use and deliver quicker results, but even consumers with low-speed dial-up connections can download video files if they are patient enough.

Because video sites can be accessed from around the globe, the potential audience for any video can be very large, particularly if a good mechanism is in place to inform consumers about available content.

Use of the public Internet also means that content providers don't need to build network facilities to their viewers, resulting in a significant cost savings. Unfortunately, this means that the network must be shared with a host of other applications that consume bandwidth. Also, there is no means for video content to be given higher priority than other types of traffic, which can dramatically increase the difficulty of delivering high-quality, high-bandwidth content in real time to viewers, as is commonly done on IPTV systems.

Viewed on Consumer PCs

A reasonably powerful consumer desktop or laptop PC is capable of running the player software required to decompress and display most compressed video formats. Performance can sometimes be helped through the use of graphics accelerator cards or additional memory that is added to the system. In some cases, viewers will watch the content on the display screen of the PC itself; in other cases, the video will be displayed on a television set connected to a video output port of the PC.

Other consumer video playback devices have begun to enter the market for Internet video content. One of the most popular portable video viewers is the Apple Video iPod, which features a screen resolution of 320 × 240 pixels. Most of these portable devices have a limited range of video file types they will support, so it is essential for consumers to select only those content files that are compatible with their device's capabilities. Some appliances have also appeared on the market that can receive video content directly from an Internet connection and display it on a television.

INTERNET VIDEO APPLICATIONS

Internet video can be used for essentially all the same applications as other video-delivery systems, including entertainment, advertising, videoconferencing, and training and education. However, there are some unique applications for Internet video that bear discussing.

Narrowcasting

In narrowcasting, IP video signals are sent over an established data network to reach an audience for programming that might not appeal to a large audience. For example, for the past five years the PGA Tour has broadcast live Internet video coverage of every player on a single hole during the first two days of a golf tournament (the island 17th green of the Tournament Players Club at Sawgrass course used for The Player's Championship tournament, for those who must know). Also available are major league baseball games, television feeds from a number of different countries, and a great deal of prerecorded content. A surprising amount of content is available by narrowcast; consumers need only go to the homepages of any of the major media player companies to see a smattering of what is available.

Narrowcast video streams are normally displayed only on a user's PC, but the same signal can be processed for display on a normal television as well, using a PC equipped with a video output card or a stand-alone adapter. Narrowcasting content is provided free of charge (supported by advertising), on a pay-per-view basis, or on a subscription basis (such as RealNetworks' SuperPass).

A typical narrowcasting system is set up using a centralized server for video content. Viewers obtain the video by connecting to the server through the Internet or other IP communications network. The streams can be served using a streaming protocol such as RTP or a download-and-play protocol such as HTTP. Because the Internet is not multicast enabled, the server needs to create a stream for each user. For unexpectedly popular live services, viewers can experience choppy or even frozen video if the servers don't have enough capacity to meet the surge in demand. To prevent these problems, an admission control method is often used to deny service to newcomers once system capacity has been reached.

Movie Previews

Video over the Internet really got a jump start in the late 1990s with the availability of Hollywood movie previews on websites. No longer constrained to showing their wares on expensive television commercials or as "coming attractions" in theaters, movie studios began to reach out to the online community. At first, much of this content was set up for download and play, because very few home users had access to broadband connections suitable for high-quality streaming. One of the classics was the *Star Wars Episode 1* trailer at a (then) hefty 10.4 megabytes; it was released in March 1999 and downloaded 3.5 million times in its first five days of availability, according to a press release at the time.[1] Many of the downloads would have taken upwards of half an hour for people who, like the author at the time, had dial-up service. (A good source of movie information and links to trailers can be found at www.imdb.com, the Internet Movie Database.)

By the end of 2007, over 80 percent of the active Internet users in the United States employed a broadband service (cable modem, DSL, wireless, or similar). As a result, more and more content is available in streaming form. Today, a user can log onto a number of different websites and look at movie trailers from essentially all new and forthcoming Hollywood releases.

---

1.   From a press release that was previously available in April 2004 at http://www.starwars.com/ episode-i/news/1999/03/news19990316b.html.

Internet Radio and TV

A number of free and subscription services have appeared on the Internet to provide both audio and video content. There are literally thousands of Internet radio stations, due in part to the relatively low cost of equipment and the low bandwidth required. Internet television stations are much less common, but they are becoming more feasible as the number of users with broadband connections increases.

Video- and audio-streaming sites have been developed for a number of purposes, including corporate branding (free sites), advertising supported (also free), and subscription (monthly or other periodic payment system). A huge variety of content is available, including newscasts, music, adult programming, and entertainment. Because this material is organized similar to a traditional radio or television broadcast, users are restricted to viewing the content in the order in which it is presented. It is not a content-on-demand service, where each user can watch any content he or she chooses in any order.

Much of this content is prerecorded, so download-and-play technology is perfectly adequate. However, this can be somewhat disruptive to the flow of the broadcast, because each file must be downloaded before play can begin. (This technology is much more disruptive for video files than for audio files, simply because video files are much larger and take much longer to download.) Progressive download greatly alleviates this problem, because playback of each new file of content can begin as soon as the first segment of it is downloaded to the PC.

Live Content

For live content, particularly for any type of interactive Internet video, true streaming is the only practical choice. When this is implemented, the video signal goes directly from the source into a real-time video encoder, and then output is immediately wrapped in IP packets and transmitted out to the network. Adequate bandwidth needs to be available along the entire path from the source to the viewer for the entire stream, including video, audio, and any control data. At the viewer's location, the client device receives the incoming stream, decodes it in real time (often by use of a browser plug-in), and delivers the signal directly to the viewing device.

Webcams, which are now embedded in many laptops, are popular sources for live content, particularly in two-way connections. Similar in functionality to video conferences, these applications use different technologies to achieve the same goal: live two-way communication with combined video and audio signals. As long as the delay is short enough, almost any Internet video architecture can be used to support webcams, including P2P networks such as Skype, which has built-in support for several types of video camera. In many applications, the bandwidth of webcam video is kept low by using low frame rates and low video resolutions. This also helps limit the amount of processing power needed for the compression and decompression calculations and reduces the amount of internal device bandwidth occupied by the raw and compressed video signals. These considerations are not trivial, because any PC involved in a two-way webcam call must simultaneously encode an outgoing audio/video signal and decode an incoming audio/video signal, which can create a significant processing load.

Another popular application for live Internet video is live viewing of traffic and weather conditions at various locations around a metropolis. These are typically configured to support a number of simultaneous viewers, possibly through the use of a content-delivery network (CDN, described later in this chapter) if large numbers of viewers are to be supported simultaneously. Enough processing power is needed to generate a unique IP stream for each viewer, with some mechanism required to handle overload conditions, which may occur, for example, during periods of severe weather.

Placeshifting

Many readers may be familiar with the concept of timeshifting, where viewers record off-air video programs for playback at a more convenient time, usually by means of a PVR. *Placeshifting* is a related concept where the viewer is in a location outside the home but still able to watch video programming available at home. This is accomplished through the use of a small Internet streaming server located at the home that is connected to the viewer's normal video equipment. The user can remotely control this server by means of their PC that is also used to display the content. In addition, the user can control the home video equipment by way of software controls on the PC that are converted into infrared remote commands in the home installation. Sling Media is a pioneer in this market space.

One of the big benefits of this technology is enabling users to watch subscription TV programming that they have available in their home but not in their current location. Local news and sports programming might also be of interest. In addition, with the right connections and software, the remote user could view programming stored on their home PVR or other video content storage device. Of course, there are downsides. This technology requires use of the valuable return path bandwidth from the home to the viewer's ISP, which typically has limited bandwidth. In addition, any devices such as CATV or DTH STBs that are being used and controlled by the remote viewer are not available for viewers in the home to use, unless they are watching the same programming. Overall, placeshifting is an interesting concept, which may become popular with some classes of viewers.

SYSTEM ARCHITECTURE

The basic architecture for an Internet video system is essentially identical to the ones used for private video streaming or any web-based service. A server loaded with content is able to deliver files to client devices upon request. These client devices take the incoming media content files and decode them using a software application for presentation to the user via a connected display.

There are some differences, of course. An Internet video server has a fixed public IP address that is made visible to the World Wide Web and is accessible to any connected user. Content-delivery networks (CDNs) can be used to assist in the delivery of files, particularly for popular websites with large amounts of traffic that could easily overwhelm even a high-capacity web server. Instead of a program guide that many private video systems provide, users can browse for content by going to a suitable search engine or simply click on links embedded

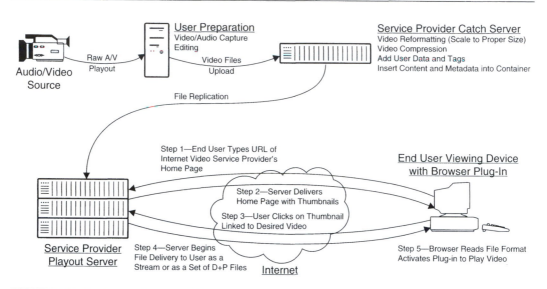

FIGURE 15-2   Detailed View of Internet Video Network

in information sources they trust. Web browsers with video decoding plug-ins are used in place of stand-alone viewing software. Figure 15-2 shows a more complex view of an Internet video system.

Many video delivery services today use progressive download and play for one big reason: the ability to transit firewalls. Many firewalls block all or most RTP/UDP packets to prevent rogue users from inserting packets containing viruses or other malicious code into legitimate content streams. (TCP streams are much more immune to these types of attacks because of the packet sequence numbers used to ensure that all packets are delivered properly.) The files used in progressive D+P applications are essentially identical to any other file that can be delivered by HTTP, and in fact these files can be served by any standard web server software (such as Apache).

The key to smooth playback of the video signal is to ensure that each video file is delivered before it is needed. To make this easier, many players establish a buffer with enough storage to hold, say, 15 or 30 seconds' worth of video before playback begins. Then, during playback, the player continues to download more content files in sequence, normally trying to maintain a constant buffer of content that is ready to play. In the event that delays occur in the download, the buffer may shrink; but as long as it doesn't become empty, video playback will continue smoothly. If the buffer does become empty, then the video display will typically freeze until more content can be downloaded and the buffer becomes at least partially filled. This happens noticeably more often on HD content than on SD content because of the larger amounts of data that must be streamed for HD.

For those delivery services that do not use progressive D+P, video streaming is another popular choice for distributing video content. This technology is required for live events and can also be used for applications that need extremely fast start-up or large amounts of user playback control. One big advantage of true streaming is that a video file is never stored on the user's device—it simply occupies some memory for buffering during playout. Of course, if the connection between the server and the viewer is interrupted, even momentarily, the video signal will be corrupted, unless a large enough buffer is used.

DELIVERY PLATFORMS AND SERVICES

A number of delivery platforms are available for use in Internet video applications. They can be broken down into three rough categories: free services, free services with in-stream advertisements, and user-paid services. *Free* services are ones that a viewer does not need to pay for but may include advertising that is not part of the actual video stream. *In-stream advertisement* services are ones that use video advertising inserted into the content, either before, during, or after the video the user actually wants to watch. *Paid* services are ones that the user pays for, either on a per-item basis or on a subscription basis. Of course, since there are many areas of overlap, some additional explanation of the types of advertising will be useful.

Types of Advertising

Many different ways can be used to communicate an advertiser's message to a viewer. These range from fairly noninvasive to quite invasive and can be combined on the same video at different points in the content file. Figure 15-3 shows the types of ads as they would appear in a media player display.

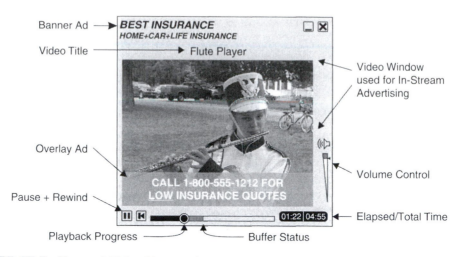

FIGURE 15-3   Types of Video Player Advertising

- *Website or banner ads*, which may be text or graphics that appear adjacent to the video display window. These may be static or animated and may or may not bear any relation to the content being played. Typically these ads include a hotlink that will cause another browser window to open up if the viewer clicks on them.
- *Animated overlays* are graphics that appear in the video window while the user's selected video is playing, but they do not interrupt the flow of the main window or the audio track. In many implementations, overlays appear a short while after the video has started playing, last 10 seconds or so, and then disappear if the user does not click on them. (Sometimes the video display window will show a button or a tab to reactivate the overlay after it disappears.) In most implementations, the overlays occupy only a portion of the video window (perhaps the lower 20 percent) and may or may not be translucent to show the video behind. If the user does click on the overlay, then either another browser window can be opened or the current video can pause to allow the advertiser's content to be displayed.
- *In-stream advertising* consists of video content that completely replaces the viewer's selected content for a short duration. This user experience is exactly the same as with traditional television advertising, where the flow of the program is interrupted and replaced with completely different audio and video. When the

ad has completed playing, the user's content will resume automatically. These ads can be placed before the viewer's content (called *preroll*), in the middle of the content (*mid-roll*), or after the viewer's content has played (*postroll*). These three different delivery scenarios bring obvious differences in viewer experience, so content suppliers need to choose their model carefully.

Free Services

Internet video delivery services are considered free when there is no direct payment by the user to access the video and they are also free of embedded advertising. This does not mean there is no advertising on the site; it simply means that the advertising is either in the form of website or banner ads. These ads are often placed selectively; advertisers generally do not want their ads to appear on a random collection of videos that may contain content of questionable origin or quality.

YouTube is the prime example of a free service. It provides an enormous library of user-generated content, some of which is in violation of content owners' rights. In addition, a significant amount of content is provided by professional sources, such as movie studios, music labels, and other companies trying to target a specific demographic for their products. There is even a surprising number of actual television commercials on the site, although these tend more toward humor. Profit for providers can come from programs such as YouTube's partner program, where the revenues generated by advertising that appears alongside videos during playback are shared with the providers.

Advertising-Supported Websites

Advertising-supported websites typically make use of in-stream advertising, often in the preroll format (advertising plays before the requested content plays). These sites offer primarily licensed content that is professionally produced for entertainment purposes, such as episodes or excerpts of television shows, movies, animated shorts, and any other content of known quality to both the website provider and viewers. This level of trust is essential, because viewers would quickly tire of a website that did not provide good quality content after they have been forced to view a 15- to 30-second commercial.

Hulu is a good example of a website that provides a wide range of licensed video content coupled with mid-roll, in-stream advertising. In the playback timeline on the video player each of the ads is indicated by a small dot, enabling the viewer to see when the next ad will occur. A very nice feature of Hulu requires a viewer to watch a commercial only once; if the viewer rewinds after watching an ad, then the ad will not play a second time to that viewer in that session.

Paid Services

Paid services are almost entirely licensed and provide the most valuable forms of content, including live sports and adult programming. Essentially all the content on these sites is licensed from a provider; even supposed "amateur" adult video performers get paid for their appearances on these sites.

One example of a paid video site is MLB.com, which is owned by major league baseball in the United States. During the baseball season, sports fans can subscribe to the site, allowing them access to live video coverage of all of the televised baseball games not in their home city (so fans will still have incentive to attend games in person).

Content-Delivery Networks

CDNs such as Akamai and Limelight provide a range of valuable services to Internet video content providers. One of the basic functions is to deliver large media files to a user who has requested a web page from a content provider. Another function is to host reflecting servers that can be used to simulate multicast streaming over the Internet.

Figure 15-4 shows a basic transaction for a simple web page request that is supported by a CDN. In this example, the user has requested a web page that contains large files (such as a graphic or a video) from a website hosted by Taggart Transcontinental. This website

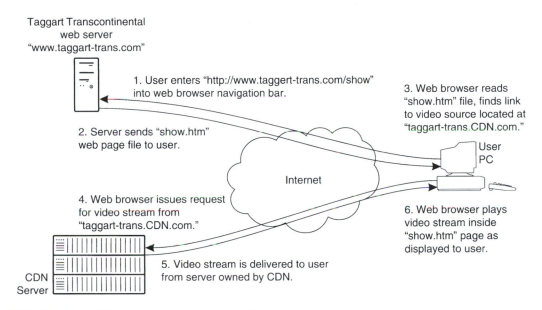

Taggart Transcontinental
web server
"www.taggart-trans.com"

1. User enters "http://www.taggert-trans.com/show"
into web browser navigation bar.

3. Web browser reads
"show.htm" file, finds link
to video source located at
"taggart-trans.CDN.com."

2. Server sends "show.htm"
web page file to user.

Internet

User
PC

4. Web browser issues request
for video stream from
"taggart-trans.CDN.com."

6. Web browser plays
video stream inside
"show.htm" page as
displayed to user.

CDN
Server

5. Video stream is delivered to user
from server owned by CDN.

FIGURE 15-4 Typical Internet Content-Delivery Network Application

responds by sending a simple HTML file that contains the code for
the overall shape and basic working of the web page, along with a
series of links to the large media files. Since these files are not hosted
by Taggart but, instead, by the CDN, the URLs in the HTML file
point to addresses that belong to the CDN. The CDN then proceeds
to deliver the files to the user's browser, where the content can be
displayed. Live stream reflecting works in a similar manner: Browsers are redirected to obtain a live stream from a CDN server by
means of a link embedded in an HTML file that is downloaded from
the website advertising the stream.

CLIENT SOFTWARE

Since all Internet video is delivered in a compressed format, the
viewer needs to have the correct software installed on an Internet-
connected PC. Suitable software exists for a wide range of platforms
and operating systems.

Viewers may or may not have their choice of media player software
to use, particularly if DRM is employed. Most DRM systems are

closed; that is, content files that have been encoded with DRM will only play back on a specific brand of media player, and sometimes the player needs to be a specific version.

Browser Plug-ins

Some standard web browsers come equipped with little or no ability to display video files, and through the use of media player plug-ins, users can view a wide variety of content. Plug-ins (also known as *Browser Helper Objects* in Microsoft's Internet Explorer) contain software that is triggered by the browser when needed to display certain types of content, such as an Adobe Flash file. They can also be used to perform functions such as deciphering encrypted content and adding functions to a browser such as a toolbar.

One big advantage of plug-ins is that they can add significant functionality to a browser without requiring modifications to the browser as a whole. In particular, as video-streaming formats are updated or as encryption schemes are enhanced, changes can be implemented simply by updating a plug-in, not modifying the entire browser.

Many plug-ins have advanced capabilities beyond video decoding. They can present an entire customized user interface for playback, complete with advertisements, playback controls, etc. They can also restrict what a user can do, such as forcing a banner ad to be visible while the media playback is happening.

Stand-Alone Media Players

Many video decoders are available in the form of stand-alone media players, such as the QuickTime player. These stand-alone programs work like any other application on a PC; they do not depend on a web browser for operation. These players have a number of built-in capabilities, including the ability to play files stored on the local disk of the PC (often including DVD drives), the ability to locate and play files on the Internet, and the ability to play live streams from a number of sites. In addition, these players can launch other programs, such as web browsers, to display other nonmedia content when the user navigates to normal web pages. The most common stand-alone players also offer users the ability to purchase and download content directly from the Internet, without having to go through a separate web browser interface.

From a content provider standpoint, the differences between plug-in and stand-alone media players are subtle. Plug-ins are more automatic for users; because plug-ins are loaded when the browser loads, they are ready to play as soon as the content arrives. Stand-alone players give viewers more control over how their media players appear, through the use of "skins" that change the borders around the viewing screen and the user controls. Stand-alone players also typically give the user more ability to control the size and location of the playout window, and they are easy to separate from a web page.

Content Preparation

Preparing content for Internet video distribution is a straightforward process. First, the video needs to be recorded and captured into a computer file. Editing can then take place, using any of a number of commercially available programs. Some basic editing packages are provided free with operating systems or cameras; others with advanced capabilities can be purchased from a number of suppliers. This is also the stage where sound, music, and effects should be added and any titles or credits should be prepared. This stage is done when the video is completely ready for viewing with all desired content included, because there is no practical way to add additional content in the subsequent steps.

The next step is to compress the video content. This step is required from a purely practical standpoint—uncompressed video files can be extremely large and would take a long time to upload to a website. In addition, most Internet video hosting sites have a limited number of video file formats they will support, and they may also have a limit on the size of the files that can be uploaded. For all these reasons, it makes sense to do a first-pass compression during the editing process.

Many Internet video-hosting sites will take uploaded videos and compress them into a standard format. This allows all of the (potentially millions of) content items to be stored and processed in a consistent manner on the site and for a uniform video player window to be used by all of the content. Depending on the site, more than one version of the compression can be done on uploaded content to provide low-bandwidth, low-resolution videos to users with low-speed Internet connections and high-resolution (even HD) videos to other users.

Some video producers have reported better video quality when video signals are compressed to exactly the target format before uploading. By selecting the correct file format, compression codec, resolution, aspect ratio, and frame rate, a user can match closely if not perfectly the desired format of the website.

A number of free and paid tools are available for performing editing and compression. As a rule, the free tools offer fewer editing features, generally saving more advanced scene transitions such as fades and wipes for paid versions. Also, the free tools offer a smaller selection of encoding formats and rates for both audio and video, and they don't offer the automation capabilities of the paid tools. However, the free tools do an adequate job for most content, and because they are free it is likely that a content developer will have access to a wide variety of them on an authoring system.

Inserting Video into Websites and Blogs

With the website development tools available today, it is possible to include many different types of content in web pages, such as photographs, illustrations, sound clips, animated buttons, and video content. From the viewpoint of a web browser, this multimedia content simply looks like any other content on the website—a series of files that need to be downloaded and displayed to the user. With the proper tools, HTML or XML code can be written to format the web pages, and any media files encountered by browsers are handed to plug-ins for user playback. So, in a basic sense, all that is needed to embed video in a website is a suitable website authoring tool.

When a single web server hosts all the different multimedia elements for a website, bandwidth charges will accrue whenever a visitor views the content. To help mitigate these charges, it is possible to upload content to a video-hosting website such as YouTube and still have it appear to be part of the website. When this process works, the website owner is responsible for the bandwidth charges of the materials hosted on the main server, but the video-hosting website is responsible for the bandwidth needed to deliver the hosted content to the viewer. This process, called *embedding*, is supported by some video-hosting websites. Note that embedding may also be preferred to hotlinking because it helps to prevent visitors from leaving the original website and never returning. There is typically no charge for this, but the hosting site may insert their corporate logo into the video player window. Table 15-1 lists some of the activities supported by video-hosting websites for use by independent website developers.

TABLE 15-1

Activities Supported by Video-Hosting Websites

- *Video uploading*: The process required to upload videos into a site like YouTube can be daunting for many web users. Using APIs (application programming interfaces) supplied by video-hosting websites, it becomes possible for an independent website developer to allow his or her visitors to upload videos to the hosting site without having to navigate to the hosting site's homepage, log in, and upload the video, greatly simplifying the process. This tool also allows the independent website to add tags to any videos that are uploaded to allow later searching based on these tags.
- *Displaying a list of videos*: Some website developers might wish to provide visitors with a list of different content options to view without leaving the current page. This capability can allow a website to provide a sort of program guide to visitors.
- *Controlling an embedded playback window*: Managing the look and feel of a website is important to many developers, so video-hosting websites have responded by allowing independent developers to design their own user interfaces for the playback window. Using APIs for JavaScript and Flash Player, the website developer can change how the video window borders appear on the screen, start videos at specific times, and synchronize other events on the webpage, to name a few tools.
- *Add or remove playback controls*: The user controls can also be extensively modified, to provide, for example, an oversize audio mute control for videos that may have dynamic audio performances.
- *Automatic blog posting*: For bloggers who wish to embed video content into their blogs, the process of doing so can be automated through the use of tools on some video-hosting websites. With these tools, the blogger can simply log in, select the video(s) to be posted, and then proceed to add any comments or other material he or she wants.

Finding Content

There are a number of ways to locate content on the Internet. Normal search engines (such as Ask.com) often lead to web pages that have video content, based either on the titles that users have given the videos or on tags that have been associated with the videos by their owner. Specialized search engines are also available, such as video. google.com, which will search only for video content on a wide variety of web pages, including many not hosted by Google or YouTube. Searching on websites specifically devoted to video content (such as YouTube) can be done either with keywords, as with a normal web search, or through the use of tags. Users who upload videos can apply tags in the form of keywords to their content to make it easier for viewers to locate using text-based search engines. Some video-hosting sites support hidden tags for website developers, allowing them to identify videos that may have been uploaded through their site to simplify later cataloging.

REVIEW AND CHECKLIST UPDATE

In this chapter, we first discussed the key attributes of Internet video and the basic system architecture. We next covered some of the unique applications of Internet video. This was followed by an overview of a typical system architecture and different platforms that can be used for Internet video services. We concluded with a discussion of some specific technologies, including client software and embedding videos that are hosted by other websites.

Chapter 15 Checklist Update

❑ Determine if video content is to be hosted on a private website or on a video-hosting website.
  ❑ If on a private server, make sure there is adequate storage and bandwidth to deliver the video streams to all visitors. Also determine which delivery method and which compression method will be available to the desired audience.

❏ If on a video-hosting site, make sure that the video is properly formatted for the selected site and that the proper website coding has been done to be compatible with the host's APIs.

❏ If advertising is to be used, select the appropriate type:
   ❏ Website or banner ads are suitable for almost any type of content.
   ❏ Overlay ads for content that is to be closely associated with the content provider.
   ❏ Preroll, mid-roll, or postroll ads for high-quality content where users will accept the interruptions.

❏ Consider using a CDN if large surges in audience are expected to occur or if the traffic levels do not warrant the costs of setting up a private server.

❏ If video content is to be inserted into a web page, consider using video websites such as YouTube to host the video, thereby reducing the costs of delivering the video files to website visitors.

16

NETWORK ADMINISTRATION

Network administration is a catch-all term that refers to the procedures and technologies used to monitor and control a network. It covers a variety of tasks, including installing and configuring devices or services, monitoring network activity, detecting and repairing network congestion or failures, and managing the financial aspects of the network. These tasks can be performed either manually by trained staff or with the assistance of automated systems. Having a clearly defined network management strategy is essential for any video transport network.

Network management can range from complex to simple. In some cases (particularly for larger systems), network management is performed by a dedicated team of technicians supported by specialized hardware and software systems. In other cases (more commonly in smaller systems), network management tasks are performed on an ad hoc basis by people with a variety of job titles. Also, different types of systems monitor different aspects of a network; some focus on hardware, some on the IP layer, and some on the applications software. No matter what, end users of a video network need to know what to do (or who to call) in the event of a network problem.

In this chapter, we will start by discussing the major network administration functions that need to be accomplished, whether done manually or supported by an automatic network management system. We will then explore several technologies that can be used for managing IP-based networks, including web-browser-based device management and the Simple Network Management Protocol (SNMP). We will also review an excellent example of an off-the-shelf application layer system for managing distance learning networks. We will conclude with the final update to the checklist we have been creating throughout this book.

MANAGEMENT TASKS

Video networks can present a challenge for network managers, particularly if video is being newly introduced into an existing data network. Not only are the bandwidths for video much larger than for most data flows, but the impact of a momentary network glitch on a video signal can also be much more immediate than on a routine data transmission. Of course, a number of networks carry time-critical data, but an unexpected delay of a few milliseconds in these networks generally doesn't cause the user application to fail. Contrast this with a video network, where even a short interruption of the video stream can cause video displays to go dark, or one lost IP packet can cause visible artifacts on the display. One compensating factor is that many video networks are used intermittently, particularly for contribution networks. Any downtimes are ideal for performing network maintenance.

The following sections describe some of the major tasks that need to be performed on an operational network. The tasks are grouped together here for ease of discussion. This is not meant to imply that separate systems are used for each function; quite the contrary—many automated systems include a wide selection of the tasks described in this chapter.

Installation

Video network installation can range from simple connection of a video device to an existing network to the construction of a complete

TABLE 16-1

Typical System Installation Tasks

- *Address allocation*: Typically, video sources are given fixed IP addresses so that the viewing devices can locate them. End-user viewing devices are often given temporary addresses using the DHCP process. Global IP addresses can be assigned to each network element, or the IP addresses can be restricted in scope to a single network segment.
- *Video source installation*: This is normally performed early in the installation process so that client devices can be tested with actual video when they are installed. Low bandwidths are typically needed for multicast sources; unicast sources need enough bandwidth to send one copy of the video stream to each supported simultaneous viewer.
- *Software client installation*: Most commercial software media players (such as QuickTime) come with self-installing packages, and most recent-vintage PCs have enough performance to handle common video players.
- *Hardware client installation*: When IPTV STBs or other client hardware devices are being installed, many service providers elect to send a technician to the customer's premises. This allows a full network test to be performed and helps verify that any required decryption technology is installed properly and associated with the correct user (who will be responsible for any purchases made).
- *Configuring for multicasting*: If multicasting is to be used, part of the installation process must be to verify that all of the networking equipment is capable of processing multicast streams. This may require software or possibly even hardware upgrades in network devices such as routers.
- *Network management infrastructure configuration*: One big advantage of IP-based video networks is that the same physical network can be used to send and receive network management commands and transport video, as long as two-way capability is provided. Typically, the network management software inside each user device will communicate via a separate UDP or TCP port from the ones being used by the video content.
- *Managing device removal or relocation*: Whenever devices are removed or relocated, it is essential to update the system configuration to ensure that any error reports are tied to the proper physical equipment location.

residential video delivery network. In spite of these differences in scope and scale, many of the core tasks are common to all video network installations; these are listed in Table 16-1.

Performance Monitoring

Performance monitoring is the process of observing the behavior of a network to determine if it is operating properly. All sorts of behavior can be monitored, from counting the errors on a data link to tracking the number of simultaneous viewers for a piece of content. If the performance drops below a predetermined threshold, alarms are generated to serve as early predictors of network failures, particularly for systems such as an IP network that tend to degrade before failing completely.

Normally, monitoring is a shared responsibility, where the individual devices gather statistical data about their own operations, and a central management system compiles this data periodically for analysis. In some systems, the data is stored locally in each device and used only when a system technician decides to retrieve it. In others, a central processor continuously analyzes incoming data and notifies technicians when equipment error counts have exceeded a specified threshold. Table 16-2 lists some of the types of data gathered and analyzed by performance-monitoring systems.

Performance monitoring works to prevent network failures because some devices exhibit degraded performance before they fail completely.

TABLE 16-2

Typical Performance-Monitoring Data

- *Bit errors*: Many types of networks include a checksum or parity byte that will indicate whether any of the bits in a stream or a packet have become corrupted. Error counts can be accumulated in a variety of ways, such as a running total of errors during specific time periods.
- *Optical signal levels*: Many signal receivers have the ability to measure the incoming optical signal levels.
- *Lost packets*: In the event of congestion, some network devices will discard packets that cannot be sent in a reasonable amount of time. By monitoring the quantities of lost packets at various locations in a network, system operators can determine if more network capacity needs to be added, if alternate routes need to be placed into service, or if existing links need maintenance action.
- *User statistics*: All kinds of data can be gathered about users, from a simple head count to an analysis of usage patterns and favorite content sources. Usage statistics can be analyzed to determine whether users are having problems with unexpected disconnections, which can be an early warning signal for network problems.
- *User logon behavior*: This can indicate that users are having problems getting access to the system or that user credentials have been misappropriated, such as when the same user is logged on to the system in several different locations at the same time.
- *Security system monitoring*: By gathering data about the performance of security systems, operators may be able to determine if firewalls are working properly or if network attacks are coming from inside or outside an organization, and it may provide early warning if a virus outbreak is occurring so that preventative measures can be taken. This information can also be used after a security breach to determine how to prevent future security problems.

For example, in an optical network, the output power of a laser will normally drop before it fails completely, so monitoring can alert technicians to replace a failing device before it causes a major network outage. Similarly, a router might detect that an incoming stream has an increasing error rate, which could indicate that the source of the signal has a problem or that the data connection is degrading.

There are limits to the effectiveness of performance monitoring. For instance, a trade-off has to be made concerning the frequency of device polling: Poll too often and the system will be kept busy transmitting and processing the poll requests and burdened with data to be analyzed; poll too infrequently and transient errors can be overlooked. Also, as network complexity grows, the difficulty of analyzing the data provided by the network increases exponentially, so the amount gathered should be limited to the amount that can be analyzed.

Fault Detection and Management

Network problems can be detected in several different ways. A performance management system can detect them by finding trends. An administrator using a management tool can discover them. Or an end user can call in a trouble report. No matter which method of detection is involved, the fault management system plays an essential role in collecting the fault data and organizing it into a logical pattern. Network fault records can also be stored, in case they are needed for analyzing future trouble reports or to help identify long-term network performance trends.

Once problems are detected, fault management is used to mitigate the impact of the problems and to manage the network repair process. The main tasks that need to be performed by a fault management system are fault tracking, failure diagnosis, and fault workaround.

As failure data is collected, it needs to be analyzed. This process, called *root cause analysis*, attempts to figure out the specific failure that could have caused the reported problems to occur. For example, consider some typical failures that might occur on a computer network. If only one user's PC is having trouble, it is logical to assume that the root cause of the problem has to do with that PC or its connection to the network. If a group of PCs that are all connected to the same Ethernet switch are experiencing problems, then it makes more sense to examine that switch for problems before checking into other possible failures.

One simple method for doing root cause analysis is to present a list of system failures to a network technician, who then analyzes where the failure may have occurred. This analysis may involve looking at the operating data for various devices, using test equipment, or simply replacing devices until the problem goes away.

A second method for root cause analysis involves the use of software systems to analyze the reported failures and come up with a potential diagnosis. This requires the software system to have a detailed understanding of all the devices in the network and how they are interconnected. With this information, sophisticated algorithms can sometimes determine the root cause of a set of network problems. However, in reality, these systems can be enormously complex and costly to maintain. So, for most networks, humans are involved in the diagnosis process.

Sometimes, it might be possible to reconfigure the network to work around a failure. For instance, many SONET links have a main and a backup path. In the event of a failure on the main path, the backup is designed to take over operation within 50 milliseconds. In other cases, it may be possible for IP routers to send data along another route in place of one that has failed. These techniques are a powerful tool for improving network reliability.

Repair Dispatch and Verification

Once a problem has been diagnosed, repairs are usually required. When repair technicians are dispatched, it is important to make sure they have the proper training and the correct tools to complete the diagnosis and fix the problem. If at all possible, it is also good to make sure that the technicians have replacement units for any modules or systems that might have failed.

Once a repair has been completed, it is critical to make sure the repair has corrected the problem. Ideally, this needs to take place before the repair technician has left the work site, in order to avoid a second repair dispatch to correct a single problem. This normally involves sending a test signal and verifying correct operation.

Repair activities should also be scheduled to avoid interrupting live video feeds whenever possible. Technicians need to avoid causing an automated protection switch that could cause an interruption to an important broadcast signal.

Accounting Issues

Many of the most useful video communication systems support users from different companies or organizations, so dividing up the costs or revenues that result from network activities can be a major responsibility for the network manager. In general, a network management system does not actually produce bills or modify a company's accounts; instead, usage data is simply gathered by the network management system and reported to accounting systems.

A common accounting issue is tracking the amount of network usage from each user site, to allow a larger portion of the costs to be assigned to the more frequent system users. This can simply be a tally of the number of minutes of usage. More complicated schemes can be used when the system costs vary by site, such as when some users require more bandwidth or long-distance network connections. Overall, it is important to balance the costs of gathering this data against the benefits of performing this accounting.

CASE STUDY: ST. CLAIR COUNTY SCHOOLS

Let's look at one successful installation of a network management solution that operates at the application level. St. Clair County is located in the far eastern portion of Michigan and makes up part of the border between the United States and Canada. The St. Clair County Regional Educational Service Agency (SCCRESA) serves a population of approximately 28,000 students, ranging from kindergarten (age 5) through high school (age 18). District network facilities are also used for higher education (by the St. Clair County Community College) and adult education.

SCCRESA first used interactive video distance learning in the late 1990s. The system has grown over time, reaching a total of 62 end-points in early 2005: 15 units using MPEG-2 over IP technology operating at 5 Mbps and 47 units using H.323 technology operating between 384 and 1024 kbps. Connections are made over a private broadband IP network using RTP/UDP and multicasting technology. Typically, the conferences are configured to be 1×3, consisting of one main classroom where the instructor is located and three remote classrooms. System usage has grown over time; in the last period measured, 14,000 conferences each lasting 1–3 hours were logged.

One interesting feature of this system is the gateway, which functions to make connections between classrooms that use incompatible technologies (H.323 and MPEG-2). Inside the gateway shown in Figure 16-1, three MPEG-2-over-IP encoder/decoders are connected to three H.323 encoders/decoders by means of baseband audio and video circuits. Without this gateway, classrooms equipped with one technology could not communicate with classrooms employing the other technology, even though both systems share the same IP network infrastructure.

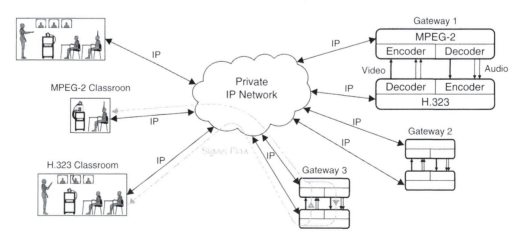

FIGURE 16-1   MPEG-2 to H.323 Gateway

System resources must be managed to prevent conflicts. For example, each classroom can participate in only one conference at a time. Similarly, the gateway is limited to supporting three different conferences at a time. The network links to each school must also be managed to ensure that each link's capacity is not exceeded by too many simultaneous conferences.

Three professional staff manage this network using a sophisticated network administration software package supplied by Renovo Software of Edina, Minnesota (www.renovosoftware.com). The management console operates on a single web server platform and consists of an Oracle database with three main tools:

- Administration tool
- Scheduling tool
- Automation tool

The administration tool is used to enter and control the basic data required by the management system. The video network layout is defined using this tool, including descriptions of each video encoder/ decoder location and data about each authorized user that is allowed to set up and reserve conferences at each location. Capacity limits are also required for each network link that connects between sites, allowing the administration system to ensure that network capacities are not exceeded when multiple simultaneous conferences occur. The administration tool also manages common data used by the conference scheduler, such as information about the school calendar.

The scheduling tool is accessed by authorized users, such as instructors and school administrators, to set up and schedule conferences. It is implemented as a web server, with the flexibility to give customized interfaces to different classes of users. Immediate feedback is provided so that users can find out if the conference they are trying to schedule is allowed or is denied due to a resource conflict (such as a classroom already reserved by another user or too many conferences on one network link). The scheduling tool also includes a notification module that can be used to send out reminders (in the form of e-mail or faxes) to conference participants or to technicians who may need to reconfigure a classroom for a particular conference.

The automation tool is responsible for implementing all of the scheduled network connections on a timely basis. Each time a conference is started, the appropriate information needs to be loaded into each conference device. For example, IP destination addresses need to be given to each end device for formatting unicast packet streams. Other tasks include configuring the in-room equipment for each conference and connecting to the MPEG-2/H.323 gateway if necessary. The automation tool is typically configured to set up each conference five minutes before the scheduled start time, leaving a short time window for fault correction (if, for example, one of the required devices has been unintentionally powered down).

This software is a classic example of application-focused network management. It focuses on all of the tasks required to manage an application successfully (videoconferencing in this example), without having to manage all of the underlying networking hardware (IP routers and optical transmission equipment) that makes up the physical layer of the network, which is maintained by the companies that provide telecom services to SCCRESA.

TECHNOLOGIES FOR NETWORK ADMINISTRATION

Various technologies are used in managing modern data and video networks. We'll look at two of the most popular ones in this section: web browser–based and SNMP-based systems. These two technologies provide some similar functions, but they differ greatly in terms of the amount of effort required to install them and the functionality they provide a network manager. After discussing each technology, we'll summarize the differences between the two.

Web Browser Device Management

Web browser device management allows a networking device to be managed from another location through the use of a standard web browser. Information about the device is displayed in the browser window, and modifications to the device's operation or configuration can be made via standard user interfaces. Networking devices with this capability are available from a number of manufacturers, although it is up to each manufacturer to determine if and how they implement this function. Let's examine this technology in a little more detail.

Most modern networking devices contain a processor that is capable of a variety of tasks, such as controlling the operation of the device and communicating with the outside world. This communication can take many forms. It can be as simple as turning on a light on the front panel of the device or as complicated as an automatic alarm management and reporting system. Many devices that use IP interfaces for their standard operation are beginning to include a web server function. This built-in server allows remote web users to communicate with the device processor for a number of functions. (Note that in this context, the term *server* is not meant to imply that the device has a hard disk drive.) One of the most popular functions implemented in the web server is device management. Figure 16-2 shows how the different functions work together.

In Figure 16-2, the device on the right is a network element, such as an MPEG video encoder with an IP network connection or an IP switch with a management IP port or any number of other devices. Software inside the device implements a web server function that is monitoring port 80 in the incoming side of the IP interface and processing Hypertext Transfer Protocol (HTTP) requests as they come in. These requests can come from a number of different users with different levels of access permission. In response to these requests, the server will supply web pages that have been custom designed to allow the user to view important information about the device.

In the example given in Figure 16-2, three access classes are provided: network manager, maintenance technician, and authorized user. The

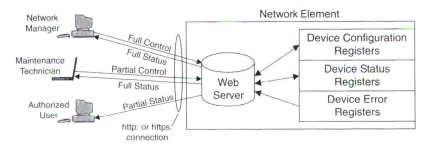

FIGURE 16-2 Web-Based Device Management Architecture

network manager has full access to observe all aspects of the network element and is able to modify any portion of the device's configuration. The maintenance technician can observe all of the status and configuration of the device but can modify only portions of the configuration. The authorized user may be given limited permission to observe the status of the device and may not be allowed to make configuration changes. Different access classes are quite common for network devices and are commonly implemented in the web server software through the use of account names and passwords transmitted over secure (HTTPS) connections.

The device's web pages typically have a fixed layout but can have rapidly changing status information contained in them. This information can be a complete display of all of the operating parameters of the device, or it can be limited to a subset. Many times, configuration data is also accessible, including such data as network addresses, active or inactive device features, optional cards that are present or absent, and a list of user names and passwords of those people who are allowed to access the device.

For example, think of the configuration options for a simple MPEG video compression device. Most likely, a web server in this device would allow control of the operating bit rate for the MPEG stream, the compression GOP, the number of active audio channels, plus a variety of other configuration data. All this information can be collected by the web server inside the device and served up to the user. In many instances, the user is given the ability to enter new data via his or her browser; this information gets communicated to the device, which then modifies its configuration. When the web page is refreshed to the user's browser, the new configuration data should appear.

Web browser–based management is very useful for managing a network that consists of a widely dispersed collection of devices, particularly when a shared network is involved. For example, consider a video-based training system that is implemented on a corporate data network. Staff in the training department would be a logical choice for controlling the video devices, such as video encoders, video servers, and any other classroom-based devices. However, the network connecting the training locations might be controlled by another department, particularly if other applications and users are on the network.

The relatively simple method of supplying the training manager with a web browser and connectivity to each video device might be the perfect network management solution for this type of application.

SNMP

Simple Network Management Protocol (SNMP) is a powerful method for monitoring and controlling devices on both IP and non-IP networks. It is a well-specified, structured approach to defining all of the key management parameters of a device. SNMP was originally developed in 1988 for devices on an IP network but has since been adapted to a wide variety of devices and protocols. Various commercial tools are available for building SNMP systems.

At the most basic level, SNMP is a communication protocol that defines how system performance and operational data can be gathered from devices and how commands can be sent to these devices. Figure 16-3 shows the layout of a basic system. Table 16-3 describes the key components of this system.

One of the biggest benefits of an SNMP system is that the data-collection and display functions can be automated using a variety

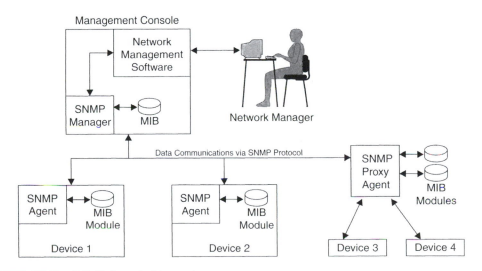

FIGURE 16-3   SNMP Sample Network

TABLE 16-3

SNMP Sample Network Description

- The *network manager* is a person responsible for the proper operation of a network, be it video or other.
- This person is equipped with a *management console*, which is responsible for gathering information about the network, displaying it, and handling any commands the network manager issues.
- *Network management software* runs on the management console to perform key tasks, including displaying network status, logging alarms, and sending commands to network devices. This software uses the SNMP manager to gather information from the various devices in the network.
- The *SNMP manager* is responsible for management communications with the managed devices and keeps a local record of the current status of the network in a master database called the *management information base (MIB)*.[1]
- *SNMP* is used to communicate with the various devices that make up the network, several of which are shown in Figure 16-3.
- Devices 1 and 2 are both managed directly, because they are equipped with an *SNMP agent* and a local module of the MIB database. The SNMP agent is responsible for gathering and storing local device status in the MIB module and for responding to commands and requests for MIB data from the SNMP manager. The SNMP agent is also able to generate special requests (called *traps*) to the SNMP manager in the event of special events, such as a system reboot that requires immediate attention.
- Devices 3 and 4 do not have built-in SNMP capability, so a specialized device called a *proxy agent* manages them. The proxy agent contains the SNMP agent software and a local MIB module that compiles data from the attached devices. The proxy agent must gather data from each device using whatever means are possible, such as a serial port on the device, contact closure monitoring, or other methods.

---

[1]Technically, a MIB is simply a format for a database and not a database itself. However, for the sake of brevity, we will refer to the database that is formatted according to the MIB format as a MIB.

of off-the-shelf and custom-built tools. The key data from each device can be periodically gathered and shown to a user for analysis and possible action. For example, SNMP is often used to collect network performance data, such as counts of lost packets, and to display it to a network manager. In the event that congestion on a link exceeded a limit, the links might change color on the management console display and possibly start to blink. This would signal the network manager to investigate the cause of the congestion and possibly take some corrective action, such as dispatching a repair technician or reconfiguring the network to send packets via a different route.

SNMP is implemented in a huge variety of network equipment, including devices used for data networking and those used for video applications. Since each device may have different functions, the types of management data will vary. SNMP represents all this different data in a systematic way—through the use of a *management information base*, or MIB. Each SNMP device manufacturer will develop and publish a MIB for each product. Technically, the MIB in each unit is just a portion of the global MIB that exists for the Internet; but in practical terms, functions can be added to a device's private MIB as long as the resulting data is compliant with the standard formats and is well described to the user. A MIB can contain a wide variety of information, such as the name of a particular device, the number of seconds a device has been active, and the number of bad packets the device has received since the last time the bad packet counter was reset, and so on. Each device's manufacturer should be able to supply a document describing the exact configuration of the data in its MIB.

The key to a well-functioning SNMP system is having a reliable bidirectional network to transport commands, responses, and traps to every device from the SNMP manager software. Consideration should be given to providing a means of communication with devices in the event of a network failure. Alternative network routes and even dial-up communication links have been used successfully in many cases.

Before an SNMP system can operate, the SNMP manager software must be set up to handle all of the different types of equipment that need to be monitored. Configuring SNMP manager software is greatly eased through the use of standards. Each MIB module must be described using a highly structured specification language called ASN.1 (which stands for Abstract Syntax Notation One). In many cases, these descriptions can be parsed automatically by the SNMP manager software so that the data contained in the MIB can be understood and labeled on the management console display.

Comparison of Web Browsing and SNMP

The technologies of web browsing and SNMP can be viewed as both substitutes and complements. They can substitute for each other because they have overlapping capabilities. They complement each other because one is better for overall management of a complicated network (SNMP), whereas the other is better for hands-on troubleshooting of network components (web browsing).

As a general rule, a web browsing system is a low-cost solution for uncomplicated networks with relatively few network elements. Each device acts on its own, without a central management system to process data from a variety of sources. This system relies on the (human) network manager to identify, analyze, and diagnose system problems. No specialized hardware or software is required to operate this network management system; a simple PC with a standard browser will normally suffice.

SNMP systems are more suited for large, complex networks, with multiple vendors' equipment and where adequate funding is available to perform the necessary system integration. Because they can gather information from a variety of different devices, these systems can be made aware of the connections between the devices they are monitoring. This, in turn, makes it possible to analyze individual error reports and determine the source of certain types of errors, although not all network management software provides this capability.

Some network management designs use both web browser and SNMP technologies—SNMP for routine scanning and monitoring of a variety of different devices, and a web browser to perform detailed troubleshooting once a fault has been detected. It is also not unusual for different types of equipment to use different monitoring schemes. Physical layer parameters may be easier to manage with SNMP, whereas application layer software may be simpler to monitor with web browsers.

Table 16-4 shows a comparison of web browsing and SNMP for several aspects of network management installation and usage.

REVIEW AND CHECKLIST UPDATE

In this chapter, we discussed the process of network administration, which grows in importance as the size of the video network

TABLE 16-4

Web Browsing vs. SNMP Network Management

	Web Browsing Network Management	SNMP Network Management
Device configuration	Simple. Browser can be used before or after devices have been installed.	Complex. Configuration settings must be transmitted to a device using SNMP "SET" commands for each setting. This process is often automated.
System installation	Moderate. May be required if devices are to be accessed from a central location. Otherwise, little setup is needed.	Complex. Each device type must have its MIB processed by the network management software so alarms and status information for that device type can be recognized.
Management console	Standard PC; adequate to operate browser software and communicate with devices.	Standard PC, with capacity to run network management software and communicate regularly with each device.
Network management software	None required. Standard browser software is used to check status of each device.	Required. Off-the-shelf or custom solutions can be used.
Management network bandwidth	High. Must have enough bandwidth to support web pages as they are served from each managed device and to prevent excessive delay.	Low. Just enough to send and receive SNMP packets (which are fairly small) periodically to each device.
Support for nonintelligent devices	Limited to nonexistent. A remote system could be installed to monitor these devices, but this could be hard to configure and manage.	Good with SNMP proxy agent.
Multivendor compatibility	Low; no widely accepted standards exist for network management server page layout or content.	Moderate to high; major parts of many MIBs are standardized; however, vendor-specific portions of a MIB can vary widely.
Event monitoring	Low to none; continuous display of device web status pages is possible, although it is rarely done.	High; most devices can be set to report automatically certain conditions, without waiting for a central system to poll.
Event logging	Poor. Events are sometimes logged in individual devices, but data is hard to gather and analyze.	Good. Most network management software will log major events for trend analysis.
Root cause analysis	Not possible. When each device is managed separately, it is impossible to compare alarms automatically from different devices to find root causes.	Possible, once appropriate software has been installed and the network configuration has been entered.

increases and as its proper operation becomes more essential to the user. We began our discussion with an analysis of the different network management tasks that need to be accomplished. They included installation, performance monitoring, fault management, repair dispatch/validation, and accounting issues. We discussed how these tasks can be performed using completely manual systems (i.e., paper, pencil, and telephone) or can be supported with automated systems. We then moved on to a discussion of two popular network management technologies. The first uses a web server in every managed device to provide information to the network manager who employs web browsing to monitor the health of the video system. The second uses specialized software in each device and a central management system that communicates using the SNMP protocol. We followed this discussion with a comparison of these two management technologies.

Chapter 16 Checklist Update

- ❑ Develop policies and procedures for handling routine system management tasks, including the following items:
  - ❑ System installation, for video sources and destinations
  - ❑ New user setup, including software/hardware setup and user account information
  - ❑ Equipment moves, changes, and reinstallations
  - ❑ Performance monitoring and trouble reporting
  - ❑ System restoration and repair verification
  - ❑ Equipment tracking for units that have been removed from the system for vendor repair
  - ❑ Usage tracking as needed for accounting purposes
- ❑ Determine which management functions will be performed manually and which will be supported by automatic systems.
- ❑ If automated systems are to be used, survey the management capabilities of the equipment that will be deployed in the video system. Typically, some devices will support web browsing, others will support SNMP, and many newer devices will support both.
- ❑ For simple systems, such as those where only video devices are the responsibility of the video network manager, consider using web browsing device management.

❑ For complex systems, where multiple video and nonvideo devices need to be managed, consider using an SNMP-based management system.

❑ When purchasing new equipment, examine what types of network management tools are available from equipment vendors. Determine if there is a benefit in terms of network management of buying most or all equipment from a single vendor.

❑ Make sure that all elements of a network system have the flexibility to accommodate the needs of video transport, including high bandwidth, low latencies, accurate bandwidth allocation, and the ability to support video-oriented applications layer management.

APPENDIX A

DIFFIE–HELLMAN KEY EXCHANGE

In 1976, Whitfield Diffie and Martin Hellman published a paper[1] that first described one of the key underlying technologies for exchanging cryptographic keys between two parties that wish to communicate. This process, which has come to be known as the Diffie–Hellman key exchange, is now in common use throughout the Internet, particularly since the key U.S. patents covering this technology expired in 1997. Since this is such an important technology, let's look at how it works.

Let's say two users, whom we'll call Bonnie and Clyde, are trying to exchange a secret message. In order to do this, they need to agree on a common key that will be used to encrypt messages by the sender and decrypt messages for the receiver. Both Bonnie and Clyde need to have the same key, but this shared secret must be kept private

---

1. W. Diffie and M. E. Hellman, "New Directions in Cryptography," *IEEE Transactions on Information Theory*, vol. 22, no. 6 (1976): 644–654.

between them so that nobody else can intercept and decipher their messages.

Before they begin, Bonnie and Clyde need to agree on two numbers: a prime number (p), and a second, smaller number called a generator (g).[2] For this example, let's say they choose $p = 19$ and $g = 2$.

The first thing Bonnie does is choose her private key (a). Let's say she picks the number 7. Bonnie keeps this number secret but calculates her public number (x) by doing the following calculation: $x = g^a$ modulo p, or $x = 2^7$ mod 19. This gives her a public number $x = 14$, which she makes available to anyone who wants to communicate with her, such as Clyde.[3]

Meanwhile, Clyde picks his own private key (b). Let's say he picks the number 8. Clyde keeps this number secret but calculates his public number (y) by doing the following calculation: $y = g^b$ modulo p, or $y = 2^8$ mod 19. This gives him a public number of 9, which he also makes public for Bonnie to see.

When Bonnie looks up Clyde's public number (y), she needs to perform a calculation. She already knows (g) and (p) because of the common agreement, and she knows (a) because it is her private secret. She needs to calculate the key (k), which is a shared secret between her and Clyde. To get the key, Bonnie does the following calculation: $k = y^a$ modulo p, or $k = 9^7$ mod 19 = 4. Bonnie will use this value ($k = 4$) both to encrypt messages she sends to Clyde and to decrypt messages she receives from Clyde.

Similarly, when Clyde gets Bonnie's public number (x), he needs to perform a calculation. He already knows (g) and (p) because of his agreement with Bonnie, and he knows (b) because it is his private secret. He needs to calculate the key (k), which is a shared secret

2. The number g needs to be a primitive root of p, such that when x goes from 1 to $p - 1$, then g raised to the x power (modulo p) goes through all the numbers 1, 2, 3, ... ($p - 1$) in some order.
3. The modulo function returns the remainder of the result of dividing the first argument of the function by the second, i.e., n modulo m gives a value of the remainder when n is divided by m. For example, 27 mod 4 is equal to 3 (3 is the remainder when 27 is divided by 4).

between him and Bonnie. To get the key, Clyde does the following calculation: $k = x^b$ modulo p, or $k = 14^8 \bmod 19 = 4$.

Now that both Bonnie and Clyde have a shared secret key ($k = 4$) that is a secret between only the two of them, they can use this value to encrypt all the communications between them. Note that at no time did either Bonnie or Clyde have to tell the other party her or his private key (a or b), and they did not need to send the shared secret key (k) to each other; each one was able to calculate the key on her or his own.

In practice, of course, much larger numbers are used. For example, one system for securing domain name servers uses a 768-bit prime number for (p). The generator number (g) can be quite small (2 is a popular choice). With these values, and if Bonnie and Clyde also pick large numbers for their secret values (a) and (b), then it will be virtually impossible for a third party to figure out the common key (k), due to the amount of computing power that would be required by an attacker who knows only (p), (g), (x), and (y). It is interesting to note that it is also extremely difficult for either Bonnie or Clyde to determine each other's secret value (a or b).

APPENDIX B

IP VIDEO USER CHECKLIST

Chapter 1 Checklist Update

- ❑ *Source of Content:* Who will be supplying the content? Who owns the content? Are there any restrictions on use of the content? Can only certain users view the content? Will the content need to be protected against copying?
- ❑ *Type of Content:* What types of scenes are included in the content? How much detail is there? How much motion is present? Does the detail level of the content need to be preserved for the viewer?
- ❑ *Content Technical Requirements:* Does the content come from film, videotape, or a live camera? Is there a synchronized audio track? Is there more than one audio track (second language, commentary)? Is there any data that must be included with the content, such as closed captioning, V-chip data, or program descriptions? Are there any limits mandated by the content owner on the amount or type of compression that can be used?
- ❑ *System Funding:* How will the content be paid for? How will the network usage be paid for? Will payments be required from each viewer? Will advertising be used?

❑ *Viewer Profile:* How many users will be viewing the content? Where will they be located? What equipment will they use to view the content?

❑ *Network Capabilities:* What bit rates will the network support? Will the network support multicasting? What security features does the network offer? Who owns the network?

❑ *Performance Requirements:* How much delay will be acceptable in this application? What video and audio quality levels will users accept? Will all users get the content at the same time? Will users be allowed to pause, rewind, and fast-forward the content? What is the financial impact of a service interruption?

Chapter 2 Checklist Update

❑ If the application is entertainment television, determine if the network will be used primarily for contribution, distribution, or delivery.

❑ If the network will be used for contribution, consider using lightly compressed or uncompressed video signals for feeds where lots of postproduction work will be done.

❑ If the network is to be used for distribution, make sure that all categories of delivery providers can be reached as required by the application. Also, make sure that the network is reliable enough to handle this class of traffic.

❑ If the network is to be used for delivery, determine the number of subscribers that will be served simultaneously. Make sure that the chosen delivery system can scale up to this number. Also, consider the costs that will be incurred to equip each new viewer.

❑ For interactive video, make sure that the video quality is high enough to suit the application and that the delay is low. Generally, lower delay is more important than video quality, except for applications that require high image fidelity (e.g., telemedicine).

❑ For narrowcasting, determine if live feeds will be required, or if content can be stored and then streamed. If live feeds are required, then real-time video compression equipment will also be needed.

❏ For live narrowcasting, determine how many viewers will be served simultaneously, and select a mechanism to create an adequate number of streams for all the viewers.

❏ When creating a business plan for a video delivery system, make sure that all the key factors are analyzed. Pay close attention to costs for obtaining necessary permits and the costs of providing content security.

❏ Make sure that content/programming costs are included in any video delivery system business case.

Chapter 3 Checklist Update

❏ Determine the type of video signal that will be used: NTSC, PAL, or SECAM; composite, S-video, component, SDI, or HD.

❏ Determine the audio signal type: analog, digital stereo, digital multichannel.

❏ Make sure that video and audio sources and destinations are configured for the correct signal types and that appropriate cables are used.

❏ If 270-Mbps SDI signals are used, check to see if the signals are 625/50 (PAL) or 525/60 (NTSC), since they are not compatible, even at the SDI level.

❏ If 1,485 Mbps HD-SDI signals are used, determine which of the four popular formats will be used:
   ❏ 720p with 50 frames per second
   ❏ 720p with 59.94 frames per second
   ❏ 1080i with 25 frames per second
   ❏ 1080i with 29.97 frames per second
   Note that these are not interchangeable

❏ If SDI or HD-SDI signals are used, determine whether audio signals will be embedded.

❏ Find out about any required or optional services that are being carried in the VBI, particularly closed captioning, V-chip, or other government mandates.

❏ If compression equipment is to be used, make sure that any required VBI signals are processed.

❏ Make sure that any video or audio switches include enough conductors to handle all the required signals, such as multiple channels of audio.

Chapter 4 Checklist Update

❑ Decide if compression will be used on video and/or audio content. If compression isn't going to be used, will all the networks that will be used have adequate bandwidth to handle the digital video content?

❑ Examine the devices that will be responsible for transmitting and receiving the video/audio content. Will they have adequate performance to encode and/or decode the video in addition to other required tasks?

❑ If desktop PCs will be used, will hardware encoders or decoders need to be added, or will software encoders and decoders be adequate?

❑ If stand-alone hardware devices are to be used (such as set-top boxes), how will the users select programming and control other functions?

❑ Make sure that both content sources and destinations are equipped with compatible technology. Even when the chosen technology is based on the same standards, it is important to make sure that each supplier has implemented a compatible set of features. Be particularly careful to check the supported profiles and levels of MPEG-2 and MPEG-4.

❑ For MPEG systems, a fair amount of configuration of the units may be required. Make sure both encoder and decoder are configured to identical values for all parameters. Users must select a GOP length and pattern, a target video and audio bandwidth, a video resolution, a network interface bit rate, audio format, etc.

❑ Make sure to evaluate compression systems in all critical areas, including:
    ❑ video quality
    ❑ audio quality
    ❑ system delay and audio/video (lip) synchronization
    ❑ compression efficiency

❑ Make sure to use high-quality source material, displays, and speakers for evaluations. Make sure to use multiple people to evaluate the systems and score the results; different individuals will have different perceptions of compression artifacts.

❑ Make sure that the encoder and decoder correctly handle any required data contained in the VBI, such as closed captioning.

❏ Ensure that equipment and software vendors have paid the appropriate licensing fees for any technology products that are being purchased and that the proper fees are paid to all content rights holders.

❏ For applications in which viewers will be charged for video and audio content, determine whether royalties need to be paid on a per-stream or per-user basis due to the license terms for the compression technologies used, such as MPEG-4.

❏ If new networks are to be constructed, make sure that they can handle the full number of streams with each one operating at the maximum allowed bit rate.

Chapter 5 Checklist Update

❏ What is the IP addressing scheme—private network or Internet compliant?

❏ For video sources, will NAT be used? If so, how will clients link to source?

❏ For video sources, DHCP may not be suitable.

❏ Will the Ethernet network have shared segments, or will each device have a dedicated switch port? Dedicated ports are preferred for high-bandwidth video.

❏ Will the Ethernet connections be half-duplex or full-duplex? Full duplex is better for video, if available.

❏ Ensure that the network bandwidth is greater than the combined video/audio data rate and that there is enough bandwidth for other devices using the same network.

❏ Will wireless Ethernet links be used? If so, will the video application be able to tolerate sudden bit rate changes?

Chapter 6 Checklist Update

❏ Determine if long or short packets are going to be used for video transport, keeping in mind the pros and cons of each approach.

❏ Make sure that the selected packet length will not be so long as to cause fragmentation over the data networks that will be used.

❑ When choosing a stream format, keep in mind that transport streams have several functions specifically designed to operate in difficult environments, such as RS error correction, and a robust mechanism for handling the required clocks.

❑ Elementary streams should not, as a general rule, be used for video transport.

❑ If multiplexed DVB-ASI signals with multiple transport streams are used, make sure that the receivers are configured to process the correct stream, based on the PAT, PMT, and PID values.

❑ If non-MPEG streams are to be used, make sure that a mechanism exists to identify which audio and video content belongs to a given program and that there is a way to synchronize the streams after they have been transported across a network.

❑ Use Reed-Solomon forward error correction and packet interleaving to make video streams less sensitive to transmission errors. When doing so, keep in mind the extra bandwidth required for the RS data, and be careful not to allow packets to become so large that they cause fragmentation.

❑ If possible, choose RTP instead of TCP or plain UDP. TCP has some built-in behaviors that are great for data transfer but are not well suited for real-time video transport. UDP alone lacks some of the nice features of RTP for real-time streams. RTP with UDP is well suited for video transport, provided the network devices support RTP.

❑ Keep in mind that RTP streams, which ride inside UDP packets, may be blocked by some firewalls. This should not be a problem for users with private networks (either physical or VPNs), but it may be an issue if the streams are to be sent over the Internet.

Chapter 7 Checklist Update

❑ Verify that the wide-area network capacity and technology are suitable for the video traffic that is to be transported.

❑ Configure the video endpoint devices to handle impairments to the video stream. Consider the impact of packet loss, packet reordering, and jitter.

❑ Calculate the total bandwidth needed for the video signals, including any associated audio signals, ancillary data, MPEG overhead, and IP and Ethernet encapsulation overhead. Make sure the network can handle the expected peak bit rate.

❑ Make sure network delay is suitable for the application. For interactive video, delay in each direction should be below 150 msec and normally must be below 400 msec. For one-way applications, delay is usually not a significant factor.

❑ Consider using multiplexing to reduce the cost of bandwidth when multiple video signals are being transported.

❑ Ensure that network firewalls are configured correctly. In particular, make sure the necessary TCP or UDP ports are not blocked. Also, check whether UDP traffic is allowed to flow when RTP-over-UDP streams will be used.

❑ Decide whether the public Internet will be used. If so, ensure that video sources and destinations are configured to handle lost packets and large delay variation.

❑ If private networks will be used, determine whether different classes of service will be employed for video. Create policies for video QoS; make sure adequate bandwidth is available for nonvideo communications.

❑ Examine carrier SLAs. Will networks provide a suitable level of service for video?

Chapter 8 Checklist Update

❑ Determine the number of users who will want to view the content, and determine the maximum number of simultaneous viewers permitted.

❑ Determine if public, private, or virtual private networks will be used (or some combination thereof). If video content is going to be delivered to the general public, then ensure that there is a mechanism for users to get the necessary player software and load it onto their personal computers.

❑ Select a video streaming format—download and play, progressive download, or true streaming—based on the application and the capabilities of the viewer devices.

❑ For live content, true streaming is used.

❑ Determine the requirements for a content preparation system. Will this system be used frequently or occasionally? All three major streaming-format vendors offer free or very low-cost software encoders for their own format, but paid versions offer better performance and may be easier to use.

❏ Capacity requirements can vary greatly for streaming servers, depending on the amount of content, the number of simultaneous viewers, and the speed of each created stream.

❏ Evaluate and select authoring tools to create the necessary compressed data files.

❏ Select a wrapper format that will be compatible with the chosen viewer(s); ensure that any desired ancillary data (such as album cover art) is supported and prepared for each file.

❏ If third-party content is to be used, ensure that reliable copy protection/encryption software is available for file creation, storage, and playback.

Chapter 9 Checklist Update

❏ Determine whether multicasting is possible. Are all viewers going to be satisfied with receiving the same video/audio at the same time?

❏ If a private network is used, will it be technically possible to enable multicasting on all of the network routers? If so, the network should be reviewed to ensure that router performance will be adequate at each of the major nodes.

❏ If true multicasting isn't possible, it can be simulated using a unicast network or a CDN (see Chapter 15).

❏ Make sure that the viewer devices are capable of receiving and processing SAP packets and that they support IGMP Version 2 or 3.

❏ For networks that won't allow multicasting, determine the maximum number of simultaneous users that will be connected at one time. Then determine if more than one server will be required to create all of the required streams.

Chapter 10 Checklist Update

❑ Ensure that each videoconference location is properly equipped with cameras, microphones, and echo cancellers.

❑ Multipoint conferencing (with more than two parties involved in the conference) can be implemented in two different ways: switched video and continuous presence.

    ❑ Consider using switched video for applications with limited network bandwidth and where a central video switch (MCU) can be installed.

    ❑ Consider using continuous presence for high-bandwidth networks and for applications where users (such as schoolchildren) may be distracted by video switching.

❑ If multicasting is to be used for continuous-presence conferencing, make sure that all segments of the network are capable of supporting multicasts.

❑ Consider using H.323-based videoconferencing systems, which currently have a very large installed base of compatible systems, if videoconferences will frequently be held with parties that are outside the user's network.

❑ Before purchasing new systems, determine whether the supplier has the ability to support H.264.

❑ Many remote meeting needs can be handled with audio and data conferencing alone.

❑ If T.120 data conferencing is to be used, make sure that appropriate security measures and restrictions are put in place.

Chapter 11 Checklist Update

❑ Make sure that all video and audio content that is to be transmitted on a network is licensed for use on that network. Failure to do so can expose network owners and users to potential claims for royalties, lawsuits, and loss of access to content in the future.

❑ Consider using copy prevention circuits within video playback devices such as videotape players, DVD players, and STBs to make recording of the video content impractical or of exceedingly poor quality.

❑ When authorized to use prerecorded content from videotapes or DVDs, make sure that copy protection schemes won't interfere with the video capture or encoding process.

❑ Encryption or scrambling is normally required when transmitting valuable content over public or private networks with multiple users.

❑ Consider using automated key distribution. The biggest challenge for encryption and scrambling systems is ensuring that the proper keys are distributed to users whenever they have acquired the rights to view a piece of content.

❑ Smart-card systems, with card readers at each viewer location, are a popular means for securely distributing descrambling or decryption keys to viewers, particularly for IPTV systems that use STBs. USB-based smart-card readers are also available for personal computers.

Chapter 12 Checklist Update

❑ Transport security is an inherent trait of private networking technology.

❑ ATM, Frame Relay, leased line, and IP services can be obtained from most public network providers (telephone companies). Local and long-distance segments may need to be purchased from different suppliers, which may require user coordination.

❑ Optical networks are typically built to customer specifications and may require the end user to purchase and maintain the necessary optical equipment. Obtaining fiber and associated rights-of-way can be expensive and difficult.

❑ Many carriers are phasing out Frame Relay and ATM services in favor of direct IP transport, so these technologies should be avoided for new applications.

❑ Virtual private networks have to be configured properly to protect video content. A secure encryption scheme such as IPSec needs to be implemented to prevent content from being copied by others sharing the same network.

❑ Private networking technology does not prevent authorized viewers from making unauthorized copies of content (such as copying video that streamed over a private network). To prevent this, some form of copy protection is needed, as discussed in Chapter 11.

Chapter 13 Checklist Update

❏ Develop a business plan prior to deploying IPTV to the home. Make sure to include capital expenditures (hardware and software), installation costs, programming costs, and ongoing maintenance and customer support costs.

❏ Determine the types of viewer interactivity that will be supported.

❏ Determine how live content will be delivered to viewers. If digital turnaround will be used, determine the format of the incoming digital signals.

❏ Consider how this might change in coming years as HD content becomes more widespread and as content owners change their requirements.

❏ If video-on-demand is to be used, consider the following issues:

    ❏ Select a method for delivering VOD services: NVOD, pay-per-view VOD, or subscription VOD. Make sure that systems are in place to support these functions if they are basic, VCR-like, or content interactive.

    ❏ For large installations, select a video server deployment strategy: centralized, distributed, or a blend of the two.

    ❏ Calculate the total number of hours of programming that will need to be stored on each server, and ensure that adequate storage capacity is purchased.

    ❏ Determine how many simultaneous streams each server must deliver, and ensure that each server purchased has enough stream processing capacity.

    ❏ Make sure an ingest system is available to get prerecorded content from a variety of sources onto the video servers.

❏ Select a supplier of electronic program guide data.

❏ For user software platforms (STBs and the systems that support them), consider using open-standard middleware, such as MHP or OCAP.

Chapter 14 Checklist Update

❏ If file transfer is to be used, determine the size range of the files, and estimate how often they need to be transferred.

❑ Make sure that the file formats are compatible between the source and destination machines, particularly if they use different editing software.

❑ Consider using caching when large files need to be sent over networks that have slow data transfer rates or long end-to-end delays.

❑ Consider using some form of WAN acceleration technique to improve the performance of standard TCP for large data files as long as the network has a reasonably low error rate.

❑ Consider using low-resolution video (with less data per video frame) in place of large video files whenever possible.

❑ Strongly consider using a secure file transfer protocol in place of standard FTP.

❑ If the application calls for delivering large content files to consumers, consider using RSS/podcasting and peer-to-peer distribution techniques.

Chapter 15 Checklist Update

❑ Determine if video content is to be hosted on a private website or on a video-hosting website.

 ❑ If on a private server, make sure there is adequate storage and bandwidth to deliver the video streams to all visitors. Also determine which delivery method and which compression method will be available to the desired audience.

 ❑ If on a video-hosting site, make sure that the video is properly formatted for the selected site and that the proper website coding has been done to be compatible with the host's APIs.

❑ If advertising is to be used, select the appropriate type:

 ❑ Website or banner ads are suitable for almost any type of content.

 ❑ Overlay ads for content that is to be closely associated with the content provider.

 ❑ Preroll, mid-roll, or postroll ads for high-quality content where users will accept the interruptions.

❑ Consider using a CDN if large surges in audience are expected to occur or if the traffic levels do not warrant the costs of setting up a private server.
❑ If video content is to be inserted into a web page, consider using video websites such as YouTube to host the video, thereby reducing the costs of delivering the video files to website visitors.

Chapter 16 Checklist Update

❑ Develop policies and procedures for handling routine system management tasks, including the following items:
  ❑ System installation, for video sources and destinations
  ❑ New user setup, including software/hardware setup and user account information
  ❑ Equipment moves, changes, and reinstallations
  ❑ Performance monitoring and trouble reporting
  ❑ System restoration and repair verification
  ❑ Equipment tracking for units that have been removed from the system for vendor repair
  ❑ Usage tracking as needed for accounting purposes
❑ Determine which management functions will be performed manually and which will be supported by automatic systems.
❑ If automated systems are to be used, survey the management capabilities of the equipment that will be deployed in the video system. Typically, some devices will support web browsing, others will support SNMP, and many newer devices will support both.
❑ For simple systems, such as those where only video devices are the responsibility of the video network manager, consider using web browsing device management.
❑ For complex systems, where multiple video and nonvideo devices need to be managed, consider using an SNMP-based management system.
❑ When purchasing new equipment, examine what types of network management tools are available from equipment vendors. Determine if there is a benefit in terms of network management of buying most or all equipment from a single vendor.

❏ Make sure that all elements of a network system have the flexibility to accommodate the needs of video transport, including high bandwidth, low latencies, accurate bandwidth allocation, and the ability to support video-oriented applications layer management.

GLOSSARY

1080i (1080 line interlaced)—High-definition (HD) video format with 1080 active horizontal lines using the interlaced scanning system. Typically implemented with 1920 active pixels per line.

24P (24-frames-per-second, progressively scanned video)—Video capture and recording format commonly used for theatrical movie production because the frame rate (24 frames per second) matches the frame rate of cinema production equipment and film projectors.

3:2 Pulldown—Process for converting 24-frames-per-second material (e.g., cinema films) into 30-frames-per-second material (e.g., NTSC television). Process involves converting movie frames into an alternating pattern of 3 video fields and 2 video fields, hence the name.

4 CIF—Video image with an image area that is four times larger than CIF resolution, or 704 × 576 pixels.

5.1 Surround Sound—Audio signal format consisting of 5 channels of audio (left, center, right, left surround, right surround) plus a sixth low-bandwidth, low-frequency effects channel.

720p (720-line progressive scanning)—High-definition (HD) video format with 720 active horizontal lines using the progressive scanning system. Typically implemented with 1280 active pixels per line.

AAC (Advanced Audio Coding)—High-performance audio encoding format first developed for MPEG-2 and further enhanced for MPEG-4. Produces high-quality sound at reduced bit rates, plus offers efficient support for 5.1 surround sound. Also handles audio content that has a high sampling rate (96 KHz).

AAF (Advanced Authoring Format)—Industry standards that describe formats to be used for the exchange of video, audio, and related content between creators as well as standards for the meta-data that describes the content for human and machine reading.

AC-3—A perceptual audio compression system that is often used to provide "5.1" channels of audio (called left, right, center, left surround, right surround, and a low frequency sound effects channel ".1"). This audio format is commonly used on DVDs. Dolby AC-3 audio coding is also commonly known as Dolby Digital®.

ADSL (Asymmetric Digital Subscriber Line)—Technology that allows a standard telephone line to carry high-speed data in addition to normal voice telephony. Operates by using very high frequencies to carry data; requires DSL modem devices to be installed at customer premises and in provider facilities. Technology is termed *asymmetric* because the data rate from the service provider to the end user is higher than the data rate from the user back to the provider.

AIMD (Additive Increase/Multiplicative Decrease)—Techniques used widely in TCP implementations for rate control and congestion avoidance in a sending device. Systems using AIMD will exhibit a slowly increasing transmit bit rate until network saturation occurs, at which point the rate will fall dramatically before increasing again.

Alpha Channel—Portion of a 32-bit color signal often used to indicate the level of transparency of each pixel in an image.

ASP (Advanced Simple Profile)—Enhanced functionality version of MPEG-4 Simple Profile. Adds capability to do bidirectional (B) frames and ¼-pixel motion estimation and to handle interlaced video signals.

Aspect Ratio—Relationship between the horizontal width and vertical height of an image. For example, an image with a 16:9 aspect ratio has a width of 16 units and a height of 9 units.

ATM (Asynchronous Transfer Mode)—Digital multiplexing and networking standard that transports information in uniform-size packets called *cells*. Each cell contains 48 bytes of user data and a 5-byte header. Popularized in the 1990s for video and data transport.

ATSC (Advanced Television Systems Committee)—Industry consortium originally formed in 1982 to coordinate television standards across different media.

ATSC was instrumental in developing standards for digital and high-definition television broadcasts in the United States. Current standards cover many areas of digital broadcasting, including compression profiles, RF modulation techniques, and other areas needed to ensure compatibility between broadcaster and viewer equipment.

AVC (Advanced Video Coding)—Video compression system standardized in 2003 that provides significant improvement in coding efficiency over earlier algorithms. Also known as H.264 and MPEG-4 Part 10.

AVI (Audio Video Interleave)—File format developed by Microsoft for video and audio data. Supports a wide variety of video compression algorithms and can be converted to or from a variety of other video formats, including MPEG.

Blowfish—Public domain encryption algorithm used in a variety of applications as an alternative to DES encryption. Offers key lengths from 32 to 448 bits.

Blu-ray™ disc—High-capacity optical storage disc used frequently for HD video content. Can hold up to 50 gigabytes of data.

BNC—A type of connector normally used for terminating and connecting coaxial cables. Very common in video applications.

Broadband—Term used to describe signals or systems that cover a wide range of frequencies, usually more than several hundred megahertz of signal bandwidth.

CA (Conditional Access)—Policies for controlling the access to video, audio, or other data files. User access, such as viewing or recording of video files, can be limited to specific categories of viewers that meet specific conditions, such as only those viewers who subscribe to a premium movie service.

Cache—Temporary storage location, used to place data for short-term storage. Commonly employed in conjunction with disk drives and microprocessors to speed up data transfer by allowing larger blocks of data to be transferred in each read or write operation. Can also be used to simplify the connection between high-speed devices and low-speed networks.

Caching—Process of placing data into a cache, or temporary storage location.

Capture—Process of converting raw audio and video content into files that can be manipulated by computer-based editing, production, and streaming systems.

CAS (Conditional Access System)—Hardware and/or software system that enforces conditional access policies. Typically includes mechanism for scrambling or encrypting content prior to transmission, a mechanism to permit authorized user devices to descramble or decrypt content at the user's location, and a mechanism to distribute securely the required descrambling or decryption keys to authorized users.

CAT5 (Category 5 Unshielded Twisted-Pair Cable)—Type of data communication cable certified for use in 10BaseT and 100BaseT (Ethernet) network connections.

CAT6 (Category 6 Unshielded Twisted-Pair Cable)—Type of data communication cable certified for use in 1000BaseT (gigabit Ethernet) network connections.

CATV (Cable Television or Community Antenna Television)—System that distributes video programming to subscribers through the use of broadband fiber and coaxial cables. Modern systems offer several hundred channels of broadcast and on-demand video programming as well as data and voice services.

CDN (Content Delivery Network)—Network of distributed servers used to deliver content such as web pages and video/audio files to users in multiple geographic areas.

Checksum—Method for detecting bit errors on digital signals. In simplest form, a data sender adds up the values of all the bytes in a block of data (such as a packet header) and calculates the total. This total is sent along with the data and called the checksum. At the receiving end of the data, the same addition operation is performed on the data block, generating a received checksum. The received checksum is then compared with the checksum that was sent with the original data. If the two checksum values don't match, then at least one bit of the data block has changed value, and the data block will be designated as corrupted. Note that in most cases, a more complicated mathematical process is used instead of addition so as to make the checksum more robust.

Chroma—Portion of an analog video signal that carries the color-difference signals. When a chroma signal is processed by a television display along with the luma signal, a full color image (with red, green, and blue pixels) can be created.

CIF (Common Intermediate Format)—Specialized video format used for videoconferencing. Picture is progressively scanned, contains 352 × 288 pixels, and uses a frame rate of 29.97 frames per second.

Closed Captioning—Process that adds text captions to video images that can be displayed on suitably equipped televisions. These captions are called *closed* because they are not visible on-screen unless the viewer chooses to display them. In many cases these captions will include descriptions of sound effects in addition to a text rendition of any spoken dialog.

CO (Central Office)—Facility used by a telephone company or other service provider to deliver signals to subscribers. A telephone CO will contain equipment for processing user telephone calls and may contain data or video transport and processing equipment.

Coaxial—Cable or connector that contains two conductors, one in the center of the cable and another that completely surrounds it, separated by an insulating layer. Coaxial cables are frequently used for video applications, because of their superior performance with both analog and digital video signals.

Codec—Short for "Encoder and Decoder"; often used to describe video or audio compression equiptment.

Component—Analog video signal in which different portions of the video signal are carried on separate conductors. One example is RGB video, in which each of the three video image signals (red, green, and blue) is carried on a separate conductor.

Composite—Video signal in which all of the video information is combined into a single signal path, such as a coaxial cable. Contrast with *Component* and *S-Video*.

Container Format—File format specification for media files; allows media player software to locate key data values and identifiers in both streamed and file-based content.

COP3 (Code of Practice 3)—Original name for a set of standards developed by the Pro-MPEG Forum that became the basis for SMPTE 2022M. Provides standard method for IP encapsulation and FEC for constant-bit-rate DVB/ASI compressed video signals.

CSS (Content Scramble System)—Method used to scramble the content of DVDs and thereby prevent them from being duplicated or played on unauthorized playback devices.

CSU/DSU (Channel Service Unit/Data Service Unit)—Equipment located on a customer's premises that denotes the boundary between the carrier's network and the customer's network, used primarily for data circuits.

DCT (Discrete Cosine Transform)—Mathematical technique in MPEG and other compression systems. Used to reduce the amount of data required to represent a block of pixels while still allowing reconstruction of an image that is pleasing to viewers.

DeCSS—Software program designed to defeat the scrambling system (CSS) used on commercial DVDs.

DES (Data Encryption Standard)—U.S. government–approved method for encrypting data.

DHCP (Dynamic Host Configuration Protocol)—Method for assigning an IP address to a device when it first joins a network. Allows scarce IP addresses to be reused and simplifies network administration, particularly for users with mobile laptop computers.

Distance Education—Method for providing courses and other teaching services to students who are located at a different location from an instructor. Typically implemented using live videoconferencing to allow for teach/pupil interaction.

Dolby Digital®—High-quality digital audio format. See *AC-3*.

DRM (Digital Rights Management)—A generic term to describe various mechanisms for controlling users' access to digital content. This can involve a variety of functions, including encryption, scrambling, and copy protection, which are commonly applied to copyrighted or other proprietary works.

DS1 (Digital Signal Level 1)—Standard North American signal for telephony networks; operates at a speed of 1.544 million bits per second.

DS3 (Digital Signal Level 3)—Standard North American signal for telephony networks; operates at a speed of 44.736 million bits per second.

DSL (Digital Subscriber Line)—Popular mechanism for providing high-speed data connections to users over existing telephone wiring. Several different generations of technology have come to market, with varying combinations of speed and useful distance.

DTH (Direct-to-Home)—Satellite television broadcasting system in which programming is transmitted directly to antennas mounted on subscribers' premises.

DTV (Digital Television)—System for broadcasting video using compressed digital signals. Can be either standard-definition or high-definition video images. Employs analog 6-MHz television channel that has been converted into a digital transmission channel capable of carrying 19 Mbps of compressed HD or SD content.

DVB (Digital Video Broadcasting)—Organization formed in Europe to create standards for broadcasting digital television signals. Includes a variety of distribution methods (see immediately following entries) and formats that can be used in the content-creation process.

DVB-C—Digital Video Broadcasting standards for cable television applications.

DVB-S—Digital Video Broadcasting standards for satellite television applications.

DVB-T—Digital Video Broadcasting standards for terrestrial (land-based antenna) broadcast television applications.

DVB/ASI (Digital Video Broadcasting Asynchronous Serial Interface)—270-Mbps digital signal used to carry one or more compressed video, audio, or data signals contained in MPEG Transport Stream packets.

DVD (Digital Versatile Disc)—High-density, removable storage medium commonly used for recording high-quality digital video and audio signals. Widely used for movie and other video content sales/rentals to consumers.

DVI (Digital Visual Interface)—Connector used to carry digital video signals between signal sources (PCs, DVD players, set-top boxes) and displays of various types. Supports HDCP content security system.

EAS (Emergency Alert System)—Government-mandated system for broadcasters in the United States that is used for transmitting emergency alerts to the public in the event of a natural or man-made disaster or other emergency.

Echo Canceller—Device used to prevent the outputs from speakers in a videoconferencing room from being picked up by a microphone and retransmitted to other sites participating in the conference.

Encapsulation—Process of converting data from a source format into a series of packets or frames that can be transported over a packet network, such as IP or Ethernet.

Encryption—Technique used to make data unreadable to parties other than the sender and intended recipients. Normally accomplished through the use of a mathematical operation performed on raw data in conjunction with a key known only to the sender and the recipients.

ES (Elementary Stream)—Term used in MPEG systems to describe the raw compressed data stream generated by a video or an audio encoder. These streams are converted into other forms for recording (see *Program Stream*) or transport (see *Transport Stream*).

Extranet—Network configuration using VPN, pseudowire, or other secure communications protocol over an IP network to give a remote user access to a private network.

Feeder Plant—Portion of a telephone network that transports signals between local central offices and remote terminals. Remote terminals are in turn connected by means of local loops to individual houses over twisted-pair copper or other technology.

Firewall—Device used at junction point between two networks to ensure that certain types of data on one network do not get transmitted to the other network. Commonly used when connecting private LANs to the Internet to protect the local users from harmful data or unwanted probes.

Flash—Adobe technology for animating, displaying video, and providing interactivity on web pages. Supports a variety of container formats, including .swf and .flv, used in many web applications.

Frame—In Ethernet, the fundamental unit of data transmission over a Layer 2 (Ethernet) network. Consists of a fixed, 26-byte header and a variable-length data field.

FTTH (Fiber to the Home)—System for distributing high-speed data and video services directly to customer premises using optical fiber for the entire link. Also known as *fiber to the premises (FTTP)*. Contrast with DSL and HFC networks, both of which typically employ fiber in portions of the network but use electrical cables for connection to customers.

Full D1—Digital format with the full resolution of an SD video signal. For 525-line (NTSC) systems, full D1 is at least 720×480 pixels; for 625-line (PAL/SECAM) systems Full D1 is at least 720×576 pixels. This format is commonly used in high-quality video production.

G.983—Broadband passive optical network point-to-multipoint data transport specification that handles multiple users with one wavelength in each direction (upstream and downstream) and employs a time-division multiple access system for bandwidth sharing.

Gbps (gigabits per second)—Data transmission speed of 1 billion bits per second.

GigE (gigabit Ethernet)—LAN data transmission standard operating at 1 Gbps, standardized in IEEE 802.3.

H.264—Advance compression technique for natural images used in entertainment and videoconferencing applications. Offers approximately twice the level of compression performance (half the bandwidth) of MPEG-2 compression systems.

Half D1—Digital video format with half the horizontal resolution of a D1 signal (actually, slightly less than half). For 525-line (NTSC) systems, Half D1 is 352 × 480 pixels; for 625-line (PAL/SECAM) systems, half D1 is 352 × 576 pixels. This format is commonly used in MPEG compression applications.

Hard Real Time—Video transport application in which the video destination is synchronized to the video source and the end-to-end delay has to be kept to a minimum. Failure of the video signal to arrive on time could lead to failure of the application, such as a videoconference.

HD (High Definition)—Video image with resolution greater than standard definition. Typical formats include 720-line progressively scanned images, 1080-line interlaced images, and other formats. Most HD signals have an aspect ratio of 16:9.

HD-SDI (High-Definition Serial Digital Interface)—Serial digital transmission interface for uncompressed high-definition video signals, operates at a bit rate of 1.485 Gbps or 1.485/1.001 Gbps. Used to link cameras and other production equipment for HD signals by means of a single coaxial cable. Standardized in SMPTE-292M.

HDCP (High-bandwidth Digital Content Protection)—Digital content-protection system to prevent unauthorized recordings or other uses of protected content. Requires handshaking and encryption between all signal sources and destinations. Available on both DVI and HDMI connector systems.

HDMI™ (High-Definition Multimedia Interface)—Video/audio connector specification used to connect high-performance sources and displays. Supports HDCP security.

HDTV (High-Definition Television)—Broadcast version of HD signal, typically compressed to 18 Mbps or lower to fit into a single DTV broadcast channel.

Headend—In a CATV system, the source of video and other programming that is distributed to numerous subscribers.

HFC (Hybrid Fiber Coax)—Architecture commonly found in CATV distribution systems, in which fiber-optic cable is used for long-distance connections from the headend into local areas and coaxial cables are used to distribute the signals into subscriber premises.

HTTP (Hypertext Transfer Protocol)—The primary protocol used on the World Wide Web to provide communications between clients and servers. Much of the information transported by HTTP consists of web pages and related data. Note that HTTP is stateless, meaning that each transaction is self-contained and that there is no built-in mechanism to connect a server to a particular client. To get around this limitation, many servers issue *cookies* to clients to allow the server to keep track of the status of different clients.

Hub—Data communications device used in twisted-pair Ethernet networks to connect multiple circuits within the same collision domain.

Hz (Hertz)—Measurement unit representing the frequency of an electronic signal; 1 Hz corresponds to a frequency of 1 cycle per second. Commonly used for describing items such as stations on an FM radio dial (107.9 MHz is equivalent to a radio frequency of 107,900,000 cycles per second).

IEEE (Institute of Electrical and Electronics Engineers)—Professional organization and standards-setting body. Responsible for a number of data networking standards, including the 802 series that define Ethernet and other popular networks for IP data transport. For more information, go to www.ieee.org.

IETF (Internet Engineering Task Force)—Group of engineers that develop solutions and specifications needed to provide a common framework for the operation of the Internet. The IETF is responsible for creating the technical content of the RFCs that make up the standards that govern the operation of the Internet.

Impulse PPV—Method used by consumers to order video-on-demand (VOD) services that are offered on a pay-per-view (PPV) basis. With Impulse PPV, subscribers can simply use their remote control to order VOD content, with the charges normally being deducted from a prearranged account.

Interlaced—Horizontal video scanning system that separates each video frame into two video fields, each of which is imaged at a distinct time. The contents of field 1 make up the odd-numbered lines (1, 3, 5, . . .) and those of field 2 make up the even-numbered lines (2, 4, 6, . . .) of the displayed video image. Interlaced scanning is used in both PAL and NTSC standard-definition broadcast video signals. Contrast with *Progressive*.

Internet Video—System for delivery of video over IP networks that is characterized by:
- Discrete content elements, ranging from clips lasting a handful of seconds to full-length movies
- Millions of content offerings
- Widely varying content formats, including dozens of different types of video compression, rights management technologies, and image resolutions
- Delivered over the public Internet
- Viewed on PCs via software, on portable video players, or on televisions by means of network adapters

Inverse TeleCine—Process for converting 30-fps (or 29.97-fps) video movie content into 24-fps (or 23.976-fps) video content. This is normally done prior to displaying or editing the content on a progressive scan display or workstation. Note that this process is sensible only for content that was originally in 24-fps movie format and was subsequently converted into 30/29.97-fps video using the 3:2 pulldown process (see earlier listing).

IP (Internet Protocol)—Standard set of rules for formatting and transporting data across the Internet and other networks that use packetized datagrams for communication. These rules include a standard format for headers that appear on each packet and a mechanism for addressing packets so that they can be sent from a source to a destination. The standard that we call IP today was defined in RFC 791 in September 1981 for the Defense Advanced Research Projects Agency of the U.S. government; it is now part of the set of standards maintained by the IETF.

IPSec (Secure IP)—Set of secure IP transport protocols, typically implemented using public key cryptography.

IPTV (Internet Protocol Television)—System for delivery of video over IP networks that is characterized by:
- Continuous streams of professionally produced content (such as a TV network feed)
- Hundreds of 24 × 7 channels
- Uniform content format (all channels typically share one compression method and use roughly the same bit rate)
- Delivered over a private network, such as a telco digital subscriber line (DSL)
- Viewed on consumer televisions by way of a set-top box

IRD (Integrated Receiver/Decoder)—Device used in satellite television systems to receive an incoming signal and decode it for display on a consumer television set. Often includes circuits necessary to descramble protected content and to convert digital satellite signals into analog or digital video signals compatible with a consumer television set.

ISO (International Organization for Standardization)—International body made up of member organizations from around the world that defines and establishes international standards in a wide variety of areas.

ISO/IEC—The International Organization for Standardization and the International Electrotechnical Commission have a joint committee that is responsible for developing standards on information and communications technology. Many of the MPEG standards have been approved by this committee and so carry the designation ISO/IEC before their number.

ISP (Internet Service Provider)—Company or group that provides network access to the public Internet for businesses and individuals, generally on a fee-for-service basis.

ITS (Intelligent Transportation System)—Program sponsored by the U.S. Department of Transportation that supports the addition of information technology to the country's roads and public transport systems. Video networking technology has a number of applications in ITS, including traffic monitoring, vehicle identification, and automated toll collection.

kbps (kilobits per second)—Data transmission rate equal to 1000 bits per second.

kbyte (kilobyte)—1024 bytes of data.

Key (Encryption Key)—Secret digital value that is manipulated along with user data by an encryption algorithm to produce an encoded message. If only the sender and the receiver possess the key to an encoded message, then other parties will not be able to understand the message, provided the encryption algorithm has not been compromised.

kft (kilofoot)—1000 feet (measure of distance). Commonly employed to measure the length of copper telephone loops used by telephone companies in the United States.

JPEG (Joint Photographic Experts Group)—Standards development organization responsible for developing a number of still-image compression formats. These have been applied in number video applications, where they are called *Motion JPEG*. One of the most recent developments in this area is *Motion JPEG2000*, a wavelet-based, intraframe-only compression system for contribution video applications and digital cinema applications.

L2TP (Layer 2 Tunneling Protocol)—Method for encapsulating and transporting Layer 2 packets (such as Ethernet frames) over an IP network. Often used to implement Layer 2 VPNs.

LAN (Local Area Network)—Data communications network that covers a local area, such as a house, a business office, or a small building. Most LAN technologies are limited to transmission distances on the order of hundreds of meters.

LCD (Liquid Crystal Display)—Video display that uses specialized chemicals (liquid crystals) that can be made to be transparent or opaque under the control of an electric field. LCD displays differ from CRTs in that they are purely digital; each pixel in an LCD is individually controlled by the display processor.

Lip-sync—Property of video and audio signals in which both are aligned in time so that on-screen images of lip motions match the voice sounds. When lip-sync is absent, video programming can be annoying to watch.

LNB (Low-noise block converter)—Key component of many satellite dish receivers, converts a block of high-frequency signals collected by a satellite dish into an intermediate frequency that can be processed by a satellite receiver.

Loudspeaker—Device used to convert electrical audio signals into sounds that can be perceived by the human ear.

Luma—The part of an analog video signal that carries the brightness portion of the video image. When used by itself, a luma signal can be converted into a monochrome (black-and-white) video image. When a luma signal is processed by a television display in conjunction with a chroma signal, a full-color image (with red, green, and blue pixels) can be created.

Macroblock—Fundamental working unit of the MPEG compression system that contains a 16 × 16-pixel portion of one frame or field of a video sequence. The term *macroblocking* is often used to describe a deteriorated MPEG image in which portions of the image have been replaced with single color blocks that occupy a 16 × 16-pixel portion of the displayed image; this is normally caused by missing or corrupt data in a compressed video stream that is being processed by an MPEG decoder.

Mbps (megabits per second)—Data transmission rate equal to 1 million bits per second.

MCU (Multipoint Control Unit)—Device used to perform video and audio switching in video conference with more than two endpoints.

Meta-data—Literally, "data about data." Meta-data is used to describe the contents of digital files, with the goal of making the files easier to locate and work with. Meta-data about video content might include information such as the title of the work, the duration, and the format. Often, some meta-data is inserted into the video stream itself (in the VBI, for example) to allow automatic identification of the content of the video. An analogy for meta-data would be a label on the outside of a videotape cassette, which allows a person to find a specific piece of material without needing to view the actual content of each tape.

MHE (Master Headend)—In a CATV system, an MHE is commonly used to receive signals from various sources and distribute them to headends located within an MSO's territory. It is not uncommon for one MHE to provide service to several hundred thousand subscribers.

MHP (Multimedia Home Platform)—Middleware standard developed by DVB that defines the interfaces between operating system software and user applications on set-top boxes. Used to simplify the tasks of applications software developers and STB designers and to provide a common platform for development and deployment.

MIB (Management Information Base)—Data structure defined in SNMP that contains the management information available from a particular networking device and that also specifies the device functions that can be controlled by a management system.

Middleware—Software used in many IPTV, CATV, and other systems to provide an interface between applications for STB users and the low-level hardware and operating system of a particular STB. Also used to provide services such as user authentication and electronic program guides.

Motion Estimation—A key part of the compression process used in MPEG. Successive frames of video are analyzed and compared to determine if any portions of the image have moved. If so, the MPEG decoder can be instructed simply to move one or more macroblocks (of pixels) from one location in the image to another location in the following frame.

Motion Vector—This describes the motion of a macroblock from one position to another between two successive frames of a video image, including both the direction and the magnitude of the motion.

MP@ML (Main Profile at Main Level)—Common format for MPEG video compression, used for standard-definition video images with interlacing (normal television broadcast signal). Color space is 4:2:0.

MPEG (Moving Pictures Experts Group)—A committee first formed in 1988 to develop international standards for video and encoding for digital storage. Numerous standards have been produced by this group and given international approval by ISO/IEC. Today, the MPEG acronym is used to describe a wide range of different compression formats.

MP3 (MPEG Layer 3)—Audio compression format popular for use in portable music players.

MSO (Multiple System Operator)—In CATV terminology, an MSO is a company that owns multiple cable television distribution systems. They can be in adjacent territories or spread out in different provinces or countries.

Multicast—Data transmission from a single source to multiple, simultaneous destinations. Contrast with *Unicast*.

Musicam—Another name for MPEG Layer 2 audio. This is used in DAB (Digital Audio Broadcasting) and DVB (Digital Video Broadcasting) systems in Europe.

MXF (Media eXchange Format)—Set of standards that have been developed to simplify the exchange of files containing video and audio content between different manufacturers of editing systems and software. SMPTE standard 377M specifies the overall file format defined by MXF, and many other documents describe the data/meta-data covered by this format.

$n + 1$—System for deploying redundant equipment for protection against failures, where "1" standby unit is provided for every "n" active units.

NTSC (National Television System Committee)—Committee that in the early 1950s selected the color television broadcast standard for the United States. NTSC is often used as an abbreviation for the 525-line, 29.97-frames-per-second, interlaced SD video standard used in North America, Japan, and a number of other countries.

NVOD (Near Video-on-Demand)—Video delivery system that simulates some of the attributes of a video-on-demand system without the individual video stream control capabilities. One common form of NVOD is sometimes called *staggercasting*, in which multiple copies of a program are played starting at five-minute intervals, thereby limiting any individual viewer to no more than a five-minute wait before his or her program begins to play.

OCAP (OpenCable Application Platform)—Middleware interface standard developed by CableLabs to permit portability of software applications and STBs for cable operators in the United States. Based in part on MHP standards.

P2P (Peer-to-Peer)—File distribution system that relies on computers to act as "peers" instead of clients and servers; each device can act simultaneously as both a receiver of files and a sender of files.

PAL (Phase Alternating Line)—Color video signal commonly used in Europe, where the individual lines alternate in phase from one line to the next. Also used as shorthand for the 625-line, 25-frames-per-second interlaced SD video standard used extensively in Europe and other countries around the world.

PAT (Program Association Table)—Data structure used in an MPEG transport stream to list all of the different programs it contains. This is carried in PID 0 of every transport stream. Each entry in the PAT is a pointer to a PMT for a single program.

Parity—Method for detecting bit errors on digital signals. In simplest form, one parity bit is added to each byte (8 bits) of user data. For odd parity, the extra bit is set to a "1" or a "0" so as to make the binary sum of all nine bits equal to "1." For even parity, the sum is made equal to "0." If any one of the nine bits is changed, the sum will no longer be odd or even, and the byte will be marked as corrupted.

PC (Personal Computer)—Generic term used to describe desktop and portable computers, generally those based on Intel/AMD processors and running an operating system supplied by Microsoft. Can also be used to describe Macintosh- and Linux-based computers in some contexts.

PES (Packetized Elementary Stream)—Term used in MPEG to describe an elementary stream that has been divided into packets prior to further processing. PES packets can be hundreds of kilobytes long, so they typically need further processing into transport stream packets before they are sent over an IP network.

PID (Packet Identifier)—Method used to identify each of the different video and audio content streams contained in an MPEG transport stream. Each packet contained in a transport stream can have data from only one elementary stream, such as a video or an audio ES, and each packet has a single PID. A demultiplexer can easily locate the streams it desires by sorting the incoming packets by their PID.

PMT (Program Map Table)—Data structure used in MPEG to list all of the PIDs that make up a program. A typical PMT will have one PID for a video stream, another PID for an audio stream, and possibly other PIDs if different languages or data streams (such as closed captioning) are part of the program.

PPTP (Point-to-Point Tunneling Protocol)—Early method used to establish VPNs over an IP network. Newer implementations tend to favor L2TP.

PPV (Pay-per-View)—Method for charging viewers for the right to watch or listen to a specific piece of content for a specific time. Rights may be limited to a single showing of the content or may expire after a designated period of time (such as 24 hours).

Progressive—Horizontal video scanning system that displays each horizontal line of video in numerical order from the top to the bottom of the video display (1, 2, 3, 4, 5, ...). Commonly used in computer displays and some forms of HD video.

PS (Program Stream)—An MPEG stream that contains one or more packetized elementary streams that have a common clock source. These streams can be different types (such as video and audio) and they can be played in synchronization. Program streams are not well suited for transport, but they do work well for recording purposes and disk storage, including DVDs.

Pseudowire—Concept of establishing a low-level connection that behaves like a CAT5 (or other) cable connecting two networks but implemented by means of an IP network.

PVC (Permanent Virtual Circuit)—In ATM, a circuit that is established by system configuration and remains available at all times. Note that a PVC does not require a fixed amount of bandwidth; it is very common for a PVC to occupy little or no network bandwidth if no data is currently flowing.

PVR (Personal Video Recorder)—Device that allows the recording and playback of content under the control of an end user; normally based on video compression and hard disk technology. TiVo was a pioneer in the development and sales of these devices, which can now be found from a number of manufacturers and in a variety of form factors.

QCIF (Quarter CIF)—Video image that is 176 × 144 pixels, equivalent to one-quarter of the CIF video image size.

QSIF (Quarter SIF)—Video image with resolution that is approximately one-quarter that of SIF, or 176 × 112 for 59.94-Hz video systems and 176 × 144 for 50-Hz video systems.

Quad-Split Converter—Device that takes four video pictures and combines them into one by reducing each input to occupy one-quarter of the output video image. Can sometimes be found in videoconferencing applications where multiple images are present.

Quantization—Process of taking a continuously varying signal, such as a sound wave, and converting it into a numerical representation suitable for digital processing. Quantization can be uniform, in which each step in the digital scale is the same size, or it can be nonuniform, in which the size of the steps varies according to the magnitude of the input signal.

Quantization Error—Difference between the actual value of an input signal and the value assigned to represent it during the quantization process. Errors show up as distortions to a signal when it is converted back from a digital to an analog representation; large errors can introduce significant noise or other distortions to the converted signal.

Replicate—Process of making a near-exact copy of a packet stream to allow one source to be fed to two or more destinations. Resulting streams may differ slightly in terms of the header data used to distinguish the resulting packet streams.

Return Path—Communications channel flowing in the opposite direction to the principal flow of information. Term popularized in cable television applications, in which many networks were originally constructed to operate in one direction only (from cable TV provider to subscriber homes). A return path is required for two-way applications such as data or voice communication.

RF (Radio Frequency)—High-frequency electrical signals that are capable of radiating from or being received by an antenna. A huge variety of devices use RF signals, including AM/FM radios, televisions, cellular phones, satellite receivers, and all modern computing devices.

RFC (Request for Comments)—Name given to documents that define the standards and protocols that govern the operation of the Internet. Documents produced by the IETF become RFCs once they have been approved by the Internet Engineering Steering Group, which is an arm of the Internet Society.

RJ-45—Standard connector for 10BaseT and subsequent data communication standards that are commonly used for Ethernet communication. The RJ-45 connector is a small plastic plug with up to eight wires and a plastic retaining clip. "RJ" stands for "Registered Jack."

Round-Trip Delay—Measurement of the amount of time a video image takes to complete the journey from the input at one end of a network to the far end and then back to the near end and then being displayed. Many things can affect delay, including the processing time of compression equipment and the distance the signals must travel.

Router—(1) In IP networks, a device that is responsible for processing the headers on IP packets and forwarding them on toward their ultimate destination. (2) In video networks, a device that provides switching of connections between video sources and their destinations.

Routing Switch—(1) In IP networks, a Layer 2 Ethernet switch that provides some processing of IP packet headers, although generally not with as much flexibility and functionality as a true router (see *Router*). Typically, this processing is hardware-based, so the routing switch can operate at high speeds. (2) In video networks, a router (see *Router*).

RS-232—Standard for low-speed, serial data transmission over short distances. Commonly used for low-cost data connections to PCs or other intelligent devices; rarely implemented at speeds exceeding 56 kbps.

RS-530—Standard for data transport, sometimes used in digital audio applications.

RTCP (Real-Time Control Protocol)—Data transport control protocol that works in conjunction with RTP for transporting real-time media streams. Includes functions to support synchronization between different media types (e.g., audio and video) and to provide information to streaming applications about network quality, number of viewers, identity of viewers, etc.

RTP (Real-Time Protocol or Real-Time Transport Protocol)—Data transport protocol that is specifically designed for transporting real-time signals such as streaming video and audio. RTP is often used in conjunction with UDP and provides important functions such as packet sequence numbering and packet time stamping. RTP is used in conjunction with RTCP.

RTSP (Real-Time Streaming Protocol)—Protocol used to set up and control real-time streams. Commonly used to create links on websites that point to streaming media files.

RTT (Round-Trip-Time)—Amount of time required for a packet to circulate completely through a data circuit, from source to destination and back to source; often measured in milliseconds.

RU (Rack Unit)—Standardized measurement for the height of electrical devices to be mounted in an equipment rack or cabinet; 1 RU is 44.45 mm, or 1.75 inches.

SAP (Secondary Audio Program)—Audio channels added to broadcasts in the United States to support alternative languages. Now more commonly used for video description.

SAP (Session Announcement Protocol)—Broadcast IP packets used to send out information about each of the multicast streams available on a network along with information that user devices need to connect to a multicast.

SD (Standard Definition)—Video image with a resolution defined in standards popularized in the 1950s and widely used for television around the world. For 60-Hz NTSC systems, the video image is composed of 525 interlaced horizontal lines, of which 485 represent the actual image. For 50-Hz PAL systems, the video image is composed of 625 interlaced horizontal lines, of which 576 represent the actual image. Both of these standards use a 4:3 aspect ratio.

SDI (Serial Digital Interface)—High-speed, uncompressed digital video signal. Can be either 270 Mbps for standard-definition signals or 1.485 Mbps for high-definition signals. Usually, if *SDI* is used alone, it implies an SD signal; HD is normally written *HD-SDI*.

SIF (Standard Interchange Format)—A video signal with roughly one-quarter the resolution of SD that is commonly used in compression applications in which data rates are extremely limited, so reduced image resolution helps reduce the amount of data needed. For 59.94-Hz systems (NTSC), SIF resolution is 352×240; and for 50-Hz systems (PAL), SIF resolution is 352×288.

SIP (Session Initiation Protocol)—A signaling protocol used to set up multimedia sessions. Often employed for voice-over-IP applications, and growing in use for videoconferencing-over-IP connections. SIP does not provide transport; that is the function of RTP and other transport protocols.

SLA (Service-Level Agreement)—A contractual agreement between a carrier and a customer that specifies the level of network performance the carrier will deliver to the customer. This often includes a set of network performance guarantees (minimum availability, maximum error rate, etc.) and a set of remedies (such as billing credits) if these minimums are not met.

Smart Card—Small plastic card or chip that contains a microprocessor and memory. Often used for storing and transporting decryption and authorization codes for devices such as set-top boxes and mobile phones.

SMPTE (Society of Motion Picture and Television Engineers)—United States–based organization that, among other things, develops standards for movie and video technology. For more information, please visit www.smpte.org

SNMP (Simple Network Management Protocol)—Communication standard for monitoring and controlling the operation of a wide variety of networking equipment, including end-user devices, routers, switches, and fiber-optic transmission equipment, among many other network components. Devices that offer SNMP functionality will have a well-defined MIB.

Soft Real Time—Video transport application in which the video signals are transported in the same amount of time as it takes to display them. Video signals may be live or prerecorded for soft real time, and significant end-to-end delays are acceptable.

SP (Simple Profile)—MPEG compression performance profile, which requires less processing than other, more elaborate profiles. Does not allow the use of B frames, and is defined for use only at the main level of resolution. SP is useful for low-delay applications and for applications in which encoder and decoder implementations need to operate with minimal processing power.

STB (Set-Top Box)—Device used in conjunction with video delivery systems that performs a variety of tasks, including signal processing, demodulation, decryption, and digital-to-analog conversion. STBs are normally required for DSL and DTH satellite television systems and are frequently required on CATV systems.

STL (Studio-to-Transmitter Link)—Signal transmission network used to deliver video and audio (and possibly other) signals from a broadcaster's production facility to a broadcast transmitter site. In most applications, high quality and high reliability are key STL requirements.

Streaming—Method for delivering video or other content over a network in a continuous flow at a rate that matches the speed at which data is consumed by the display device.

Subtitles—Text that is added to motion picture and television content for many purposes, including content display in another language. When content is subtitled, the text becomes part of the video image and is displayed to all viewers. Contrast this with closed captioning in the United States, which can be displayed or hidden upon viewer command.

Supertrunk—High-performance link commonly used in CATV applications to transmit multichannel signals from one headend to another. These signals can be either analog or digital, depending on the distances and the application.

SVC (Switched Virtual Circuit)—Type of ATM connection that is established just prior to data transmission and then disconnected after it is no longer needed.

S-video—Analog video signal in which the chroma and luma signals are carried over separate signal paths. This can improve video quality as compared to a composite signal by eliminating the need to separate the chroma and luma signals in the television display.

Switch—In Ethernet networks, a device that provides multiple ports that each have a separate logical and physical network interface. This feature eliminates the possibility of packet collisions between devices on separate ports of the switch, thereby improving overall system performance.

T1—Basic building block for the digital telephone system in North America. Overall bit rate is 1.544 Mbps, with a usable payload (after framing is removed) of 1.536 Mbps.

TCP (Transmission Control Protocol)—Reliable data transfer protocol used in IP networks that offers connection-oriented data transport along with automatic data transfer rate control and retransmission of corrupted packets. One of the most widely used data transport protocols, TCP is found throughout the public Internet. However, for live or streaming media signals, RTP over UDP is often a better choice.

Telepresence—Real-time, high-performance videoconferencing system intended to give users the impression that they are in the same room as other conferees. Often implemented using HD video and high-resolution monitors able to generate life-size images.

Teletext—Method devised to support the broadcast of textual information inside the VBI of a video signal for display on specially equipped televisions. Lost popularity as other technologies grew to provide similar function, such as the World Wide Web.

Trick Modes—Nonstandard video display modes, such as fast-forward, reverse, and fast- or slow-motion playback.

Triple DES—Data encryption algorithm that applies the DES encryption algorithm three times to each packet, generally with three different encryption keys.

TS (Transport Stream)—Standard method used in MPEG for converting PES streams into a stream of packets that can easily be transported over links such as an IP network or a satellite link or over a digital television broadcast to a home. Each TS packet is a fixed 188 bytes long, although FEC data can be added, bringing the TS packet size up to 204 or 208 bytes. Note that MPEG IP packets generally contain multiple transport stream packets.

Tunneling—Process of sending a data stream through a network that is not normally designed to handle that type of stream. A classic example is sending private network data securely over the public Internet without any exposure of the data to anyone other than the intended recipient.

TV1—Name for standard-definition, analog video transport service provided by many local telephone networks in the United States. Typically offers 4–5 MHz of video bandwidth and up to four channels of audio.

Unicast—Data transmission from a single source to a single destination. Contrast with *Multicast*.

UDP (User Datagram Protocol)—Data transfer protocol used on IP networks that offers connectionless, stateless data transport. It is often involved in video transport applications (along with RTP) because it offers low overhead and does not provide automatic rate reductions and packet retransmissions (supplied by TCP), which can interfere with video transport.

URL (Uniform Resource Locator)—On the World Wide Web, a method for naming websites that is simpler for humans to read than an IP address.

UTP (Unshielded Twisted Pair)—Form of electrical cable used to transmit data signals, including a variety of forms of Ethernet.

VBI (Vertical Blanking Interval)—Portion of a normal video signal located between successive fields or frames that carries no image information (i.e., it is blank). In traditional CRT-based displays, this time interval was required to allow the electron gun to reposition from the bottom of the display to the top. Although some modern forms of display do not require this blanking time, the VBI is part of universal video standards. Ancillary data, such as audio signals, time codes, and test signals, is often inserted into the VBI portions of video signals.

VC-1—Video compression technique standardized by SMPTE as 421M. Formerly known as Windows Media 9.

VCR (Videocassette Recorder)—Videotape recording and playback device that became popular with consumers in the 1980s. The most popular tape format for consumers is VHS; a large number of professional tape formats are also widely used.

VDSL (Very high-speed Digital Subscriber Line)—Digital subscriber line technology capable of delivering a large amount of data every second, typically defined as above 210 Mbps. Speeds in this range are generally required in order to deliver multiple simultaneous video streams to multiple television sets over a single DSL circuit.

VOD (Video-on-Demand)—Process for delivering video programming to viewers on demand, i.e., when they want it. Commonly includes the ability to skip ahead (fast-forward) or rewind the video signal under user control. Contrast with *NVOD*.

VPN (Virtual Private Network)—Network owned and operated by a private individual that may span several locations, where the interconnections are implemented over a public or carrier network, using technology such as MPLS or IP. Encryption is often employed to prevent other parties from accessing data sent over the VPN.

WAN (Wide Area Network)—Network that connects two or more network segments across a significant geographic distance—between buildings, across a city, or around the world.

Webcam—Camera usually attached to a PC to provide video signals for transmission over the web. Typically, frame rates, resolution, and video quality are well below broadcast quality. Webcams are increasingly being built into laptops and are suitable for use in videoconferencing applications.

Web TV—Usually, a synonym for *Internet video*. Also used to describe continuous channels of television programming delivered via the Internet.

WM9 (Windows Media Nine)—High-performance video compression system created by Microsoft that has been submitted to SMPTE for standardization. Renamed "VC1" for the purpose of creating standards.

Wrapper—Colloquial name for *Container Format*.

xDSL (Digital Subscriber Line)—In this acronym "x" represents any one of a selection of words, including "A" for "Asymmetric" DSL and "H" for "High-Speed" DSL, among others. xDSL is a generic term intended to mean "any form of DSL."

Y/C—Baseband analog video format used in S-video connectors. Here, Y stands for luma (luminance) and C stands for chroma (chrominance).

INDEX

Page references followed by "f" denote figures; those followed by "t" denote tables

3:2 pulldown, 76–77, 77f
4:2:0, 97–98
4:2:2, 97–98, 109
5.1 (surround sound), 81, 116, 119, 130
720p, 65
1080i, 65

A

AAC, 118–120, 374
ABR. *See* Available bit rate
AC-3 compressed audio format, 80
Acknowledgment delay, 371–373
Acknowledgment Identifier, 172
Acknowledgment window, 371
Ad skipping, 341
Ad timeliness, 341
Additive increase/multiplicative decrease. *See* AIMD
Addresses/addressing
  allocation of, 407t
  Ethernet, 147–148
  IP, 138, 141–142, 229
  media access control, 147

ADSL, 16t, 184, 347–348
Advanced audio coding, 118–120
Advanced video codec, 114–116
Advertising
  description of, 35–36, 366t
  file transfer applications, 367–368
  in-stream, 393–395
  Internet video, 393–395
  websites, 394–396
AES/EBU digital audio format. *See* Audio Engineering Society/European Broadcasting Union digital audio format
Aggregators, 374
AIMD, 372

Printed in the USA/Agawam, MA
July 29, 2013